A South
You Never
Ate

A South You Never Ate

SAVORING FLAVORS AND
STORIES FROM THE EASTERN
SHORE OF VIRGINIA

Bernard L. Herman

THE UNIVERSITY OF NORTH CAROLINA PRESS

Chapel Hill

*This book was published with support from the
Chair's Discretionary Fund to Support Southern
Studies at the University of North Carolina and
the assistance of the H. Eugene and Lillian Youngs
Lehman Fund of the University of North Carolina
Press. A complete list of books published in the
Lehman Series appears at the end of the book.*

© 2019 Bernard L. Herman

Manufactured in the United States of America
Set in Chaparral and TheSans by Tseng Information Systems, Inc.

The University of North Carolina Press has been a member of the
Green Press Initiative since 2003.

Cover illustrations: Front cover (top and bottom) and back cover
photographs by Bernie Herman; aerial photograph of Nassawadox Creek
© Gordon Campbell / At Altitude Gallery

Library of Congress Cataloging-in-Publication Data
Names: Herman, Bernard L., 1951– author.
Title: A South you never ate : savoring flavors and stories from the
eastern shore of Virginia / Bernard L. Herman.
Description: Chapel Hill : The University of North Carolina Press, [2019] |
Includes bibliographical references and index.
Identifiers: LCCN 2019019166 | ISBN 9781469653471 (cloth : alk. paper) |
ISBN 9781469669359 (pbk. : alk. paper) | ISBN 9781469653488 (ebook)
Subjects: LCSH: Eastern Shore (Md. and Va.)—History. | Eastern Shore (Md.
and Va.)—Social life and customs. | Cooking—Eastern Shore (Md. and Va.)
Classification: LCC F232.E2 H47 2019 | DDC 975.2/1—dc23
LC record available at https://lccn.loc.gov/2019019166

For Rebecca

Contents

CHEFS' RECIPES FOR HOME

A South You Never Ate

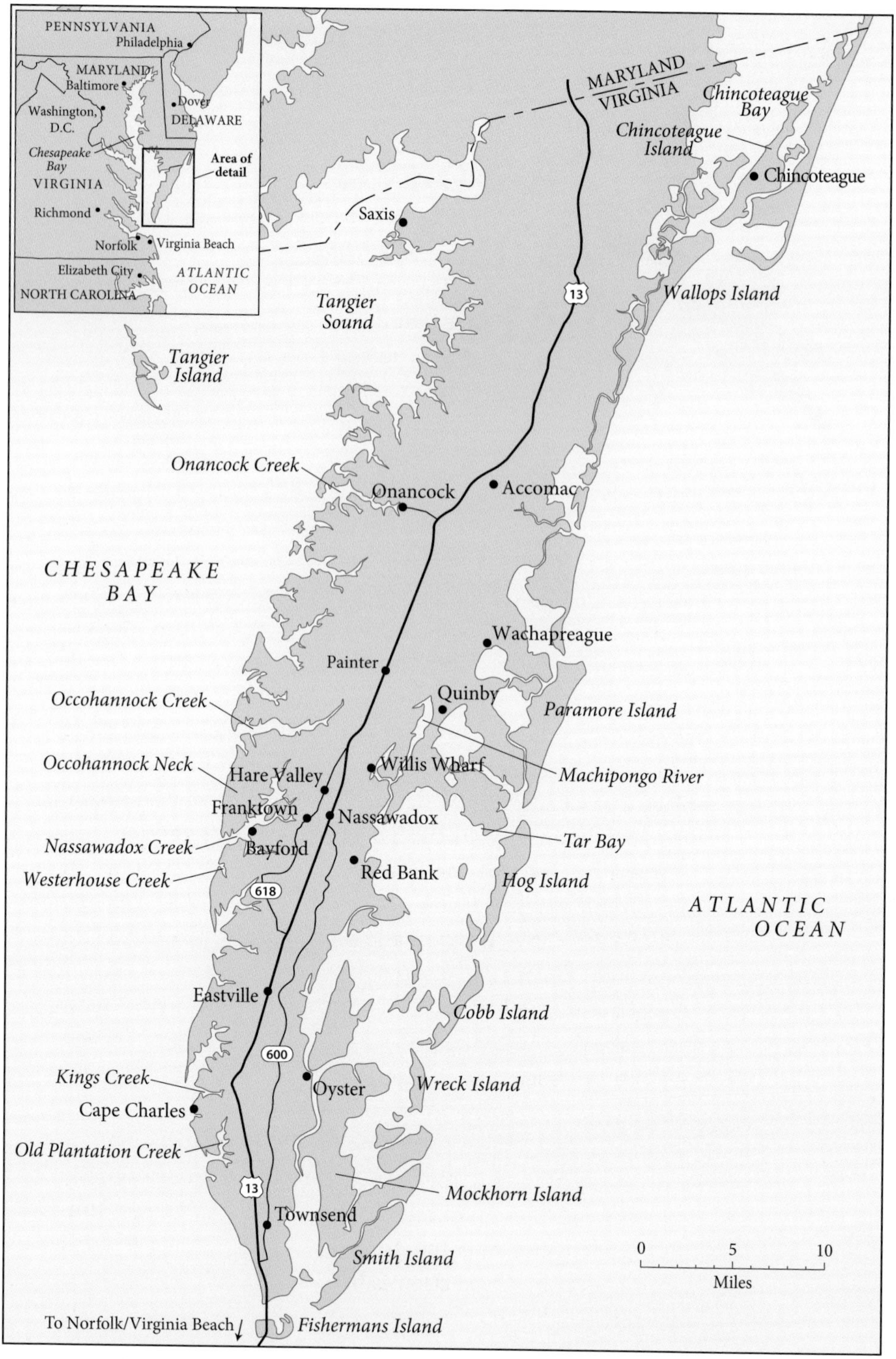
PENNSYLVANIA
Philadelphia
MARYLAND
Baltimore
Washington, D.C.
Dover
DELAWARE
Chesapeake Bay
VIRGINIA
Area of detail
Richmond
Norfolk
Virginia Beach
Elizabeth City
ATLANTIC OCEAN
NORTH CAROLINA
MARYLAND
VIRGINIA
Chincoteague Bay
Chincoteague Island
Chincoteague
Saxis
13
Tangier Sound
Wallops Island
Tangier Island
Onancock Creek
Onancock
Accomac
CHESAPEAKE BAY
Wachapreague
Painter
Quinby
Occohannock Creek
Paramore Island
Occohannock Neck
Hare Valley
Willis Wharf
Machipongo River
Franktown
Nassawadox
Nassawadox Creek
Bayford
Tar Bay
Westerhouse Creek
Red Bank
Hog Island
618
ATLANTIC OCEAN
Eastville
Cobb Island
600
Kings Creek
Oyster
Wreck Island
Cape Charles
Old Plantation Creek
13
Mockhorn Island
Townsend
0
5
10
Miles
Smith Island
To Norfolk/Virginia Beach
Fishermans Island

Virginia's Eastern Shore

Introduction On Place and Plate

This is a book about the taste of place and the styles and stories of cooking that define it. It is a book about how people talk about their lives and their histories through the stories that flow from field, marsh, kitchen, and table. This is a book about tradition—the human process of making sense and discovering invention through experience, lived, remembered, imagined. This book contains recipes, recollections, instructions, and insights about a universe of food. It taps into local histories, natural histories, material histories, and oral histories. It is about discovery through the worlds we eat and absorb into our bodies and memories. Most of all it is a book about the stories people tell about what they eat and why it holds meaning—not just for them but for all those folks who sit at their table—and at other tables in other places near and far. It is a book about how the taste of place expresses a love of place. This book originates in a particular place, but it resonates with foodways far beyond its borders. The place in question is the Eastern Shore of Virginia.

Asked to describe the Eastern Shore of Virginia, I begin, "It's a place where the sun rises and sets over water with the Chesapeake Bay to the west and the Atlantic on the east." "It's a place," I continue, "where the rest of Virginia hovers just out of sight over the horizon." The Eastern Shore extends south from Maryland's Eastern Shore—and the two should never, ever be confused, but it happens all the time. Two counties compose the Eastern Shore of Virginia: Accomack to the north and smaller Northampton to the south. Although the Eastern Shore may be bound to the Virginia mainland only by the thinnest ligature of steel and concrete bridges and tunnels, it identifies with the American South. Locally, a much more important distinction is between Seaside and Bayside and the people who associate with either side of the divide conveniently delineated by Route 13, the primary north-south thoroughfare that bisects the peninsula. Although the

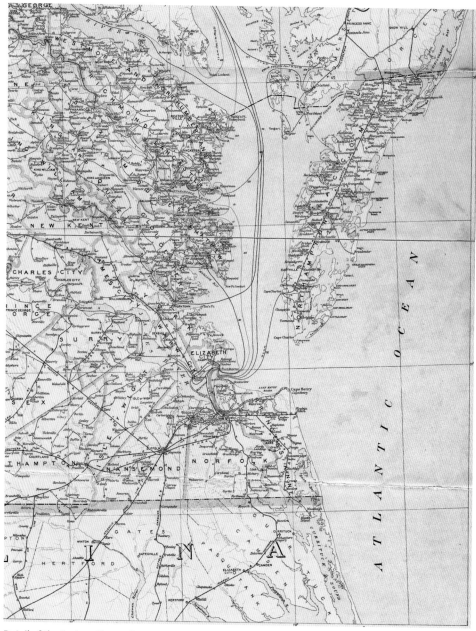

Detail of the Eastern Shore of Virginia with the Atlantic Ocean and Chesapeake Bay, from A. Von Haake, *Post Route Map of the States of Virginia and West Virginia Showing Post Offices with the Intermediate Distances on Mail Routes in Operation on the 1st of December, 1903* (1903). Norman B. Leventhal Map Collection, Boston Public Library.

Eastern Shore of Virginia may be no more than three miles from tide to tide in its lower reaches, the Seaside-Bayside division is reflected in everything from family histories and foodways to the size and ferocity of greenhead flies and mosquitoes. I tend to think of the Eastern Shore of Virginia as an island in a far-flung southern archipelago.

The soils are sandy, and the countryside is intercut with a multitude of tidal creeks and branches. Pine, holly, hickory, white and red oak, and bay populate the shorelines and woodlands. Although the principal crops cultivated since the 1980s reflect an iteration of monoculture based on a rotation of soybeans, field corn, winter wheat, cotton, and forced-irrigation tomatoes, stalwart small-scale growers and home gardeners persevere with sweet potatoes, strawberries, melons, greens, and garden tomatoes. Accomack County has embraced the modern poultry industry with a fervor akin to idolatry. Northampton County cleaves to righteous ways with an eye to protecting its fragile watershed and estuaries. The farming generation before the advent of monoculture cultivated potatoes, sweet potatoes, tomatoes, cucumbers, peppers, cabbage, strawberries, and much more. Canneries processed some of the produce; the bulk was shipped to northern cities, predominantly Philadelphia and New York, or across the bay to Baltimore and Norfolk. Basket and crate factories supplied packinghouses with containers for shipping fresh produce.

Before the arrival of the railroad in the 1880s and its successor, truck farming, in the twentieth century, local growers produced a varied array of crops that included corn, rye, oats, and, most important, extensive kitchen gardens. The earliest written county records, begun in 1632 (the oldest continuous court records in the United States), describe the cultivation of tobacco, corn, watermelons, and pumpkins along with orchards of apple, pear, plum, cherry, and fig. Those early records also preserve a culture where conversations and storytelling stood at the heart of everyday life. People—over thousands of years in an overlapping succession of Indians, Europeans, Africans, and Latin Americans—have worked and fished the vast Seaside wetlands stretching to the offshore Atlantic barrier islands and the Bayside's labyrinthine saltwater creeks and inlets. Those generations witnessed shifts in agriculture from tobacco to corn and oats to fruit and vegetables to soybeans, field corn, cotton, and winter wheat. The coming of the railroad in the Victorian era brought prosperity with high-speed links to northern industrial markets. The Great Depression marked the beginning of a long arc of agricultural change and population decline.

The grit of sandy soils, the wide skies over Atlantic marshes, the ebb and flow of Bayside creeks, the black slash of native pine looming over stands of holly, hickory, oak, and bramble seem timeless, but the impression of a timeless landscape is illusory. Place is an artifact, and it changes even as it endures. Entire towns have disappeared within living memory and new settlements popped up elsewhere. Corn, wheat, soybeans, and drip-irrigated tomatoes have replaced fields of cucumbers, potatoes, cabbages, and strawberries. Infrastructure evolves with crops. Packing sheds, a commonplace in the heyday of rail and highway produce shipping, stand as relics of a bygone countryside. Still, a profound sense of place and an ache of belonging flavor the foodways of Virginia's Eastern Shore and unite ingredients, recipes, and recollections in a seamless whole discovered in the celebration and consumption of everyday life.

Through all those changes, Eastern Shore women and men worked the vast wetlands and maintained family gardens. The foods they cooked morphed with the availability of new ingredients and household technologies, but the prospect of old favorites still whets local appetites. A powerful sense of place and belonging defines the Eastern Shore of Virginia. People tell stories about and around food, and the tales they share reveal "a South you never ate." Place, plate, and conversation are three strands twisted into one lifeline.

Place, plate, and conversation stand at the heart of this book. When it comes to the Eastern Shore, those three things are tightly wound and knotted. The French, always a go-to source when talking and writing about food, offer the idea of *terroir*—the taste of place—as a coming together of how we provision, how we cook, how we eat, and how we talk about it. Terroir defines the particular attributes of place embodied in cuisine—the style of cooking associated with place—and narrated through words, actions, and objects. Place, simply framed as a geography and locale, fails to translate the deeper associations that terroir projects about people and the worlds they cook and eat. In the moment of its most literal consumption, we ingest and digest terroir, imbuing ourselves with the tastes of identity and memory—a combination glibly encapsulated as authenticity. The body literally absorbs the substance of terroir and translates it into narratives of place and experience. It captures a consciousness of association and belonging. We eat, therefore we are. Terroir is experience and emotion, embodiment and immediacy, custom and invention, destiny and storytelling. It manifests itself in a constantly evolving style and synthesis of ingredients, recipes, preparations, and eating, from fancy holiday meals to workaday lunches. When people speak about terroir, they speak about themselves. It is in that spirit that the following thoughts on terroir privilege the personal recollections of the voices of the Eastern Shore of Virginia.

The underlying principles that gave shape and substance to the foodways of Virginia's Eastern Shore came together in the first half of the

H. M. Arnold and Theodore Peed, Bayford, Virginia.

1600s. In that half century, people came together from around the Atlantic World. Indigenous peoples were joined by newcomers from the British Isles and across Europe and West Africa. They introduced one another to new worlds of ingredients, preparations, and flavors. Europeans learned about hominy and pumpkins. Indians encountered cheese and pork. Africans introduced puffy fritters. Subsequent generations added new cultivars: sweet potatoes from the Caribbean, strawberries perfected in northwestern France, and figs from the Levant. Novel ingredients like baking powder facilitated new dishes. Freezing superseded home canning, which eclipsed salting and drying. High-speed transportation networks and scientific agriculture opened new markets for everything from tomatoes to oysters. Canneries and all their supporting industries prospered—and in time failed. Field labor evolved through slavery, tenancy, daywork, and migrant crews. Indigenous populations declined through the 1700s even as the numbers of Latino and Latina residents accelerated into the twenty-first century. The story is not unique to the Eastern Shore but is interwoven with much larger national narratives about people in constant motion and what they grow, cook, and eat in an unending exchange of ideas about food in every possible dimension of everyday life.

Terroir maps a point where nostalgia—longing for an imagined past— and desire—longing for an imagined future—combine. Terroir is about culture and conversation revealed through food—and about how the cultural resonance of food is rendered through language. Narratives surround ingredients, preparations, and events. These are powerful memories that, shared through anecdote and recollection, evoke the sense and sensation of connection and excitement and enable us to consume vicariously the flavors and pleasures of place. They also include the possibility of the unpalatable, the sour, and the bitter.

Terroir not only entails the distinct flavors of place but also evokes how place "flavors" people, speech, foodways, and the multitude of objects that constitute the local. Terroir is as much about where and how stories are told as it is about the stories themselves. The recollections shared by Andrew Bunce leaning over the counter of Sand Dollar Seafood and talking over the clamor of cooks as they rustled up clam fritters in the kitchen, by H. M. Arnold sitting in the late afternoon shade cast by the old Bayford oyster house reprising great hunts in the Seaside marshes, by Violet Trower recollecting meals for hard times while stirring a pot of fig preserves bubbling on the stove in Ellen Rue's kitchen, and by Tim and Dorothy Bailey assembling drum sandwiches for the Juneteenth celebration at the county airfield near Weirwood all recount and embody the nuances of terroir.

When it comes to local perspectives on terroir, what matters most in the telling is that food always brings people together. Terroir, continually enacted and voiced through food, binds people through kinship, community, work, pleasure, and faith—and separates them, too. Thus, an awareness of terroir focuses on the act of tasting—tasting and experiencing food from cultivation to consummation.

The idea of cuisine goes hand in hand with terroir. At its most basic, cuisine is defined as a style of cooking closely associated with a place and its people. *Cuisine*, the French word for kitchen, carries the implication that the style of a place is created in the creative space of cooking, bracketed on one side by the use of local ingredients and on the other by how people imagine, make, and consume their meals. As an idea, cuisine unifies sourcing, preparing, and eating. Each of those actions draws on myriad skills developed over generations and in a constant state of reinvention, accident, and discovery. The clams in Eastern Shore of Virginia clam fritters invoke visions of terroir; the thousands of clam fritters, no two batches ever exactly the same, skillet-fried by Kenny Marshall over a lifetime, re-

Listening to conversations, Bayford oyster house, Bayford, Virginia.

Coming
into Bayford,
Bayford,
Virginia.

Marilyn Sharp shucking butter beans, Exmore, Virginia.

veal a mastery of cuisine. Tradition doesn't stand still. If terroir is the taste of place, then cuisine is the taste of culinary knowledge.

Several qualities convey the importance of everyday life and common-place things—food perhaps most strikingly. Intimacy, surely. Qualities of familiarity and affection, perhaps. Most of all, though, these things—and food in particular—offer an open-ended invitation for storytelling. Food recollections inspire conversation, and this is the point of terroir: the fla-vor, conversation, and poetry of place. Terroir and cuisine suggest that we can know, epitomize, and experience the essence of the local through the filters of spoken words and sometimes tangible souvenirs ranging from unsnapped wishbones to next year's sweet potato "seed." Terroir and cui-sine, then, are not only about the flavors of place but also about how we choose to locate, consume, and remember the essence of place through food and story.

Folks on the Eastern Shore of Virginia rhapsodize over Theodore Peed's turtle party, dispute the merits of clam fritters, extoll the rise and fall of the strawberry. They narrate the near-forgotten taste of oyster pies and talk of meals driven by the necessity of getting by and yet remembered with grace and affection. They savor yeast rolls and the reputations of local bakers. They remember gunning for marsh hens and fishing for spot and drum and fatbacks. They celebrate figs and sweetness in a southern land-scape, proclaim the virtues of Hog Island mutton *barbacoa* and tamales, recollect fish stews cooked on parlor stoves, offer loving recitations of duck or chicken and dumplings, recite genealogies around sweet potato varieties descended through families since Reconstruction, connect food to spiri-tual praise and ministry, and more. They position stories about and around food in ways that evoke laughter and togetherness, instilling lessons about history, the natural world, and the very essence of knowing community.

Kenny Marshall, descended from a long line of Hog Islanders, sits in his Willis Wharf decoy carving shed and smiles as he links summertime crab feasts to community and conversation: "We had crabs steamed every Saturday night. That was a big thing. We knew a lot of neighbors that would come around. A big old pot of crabs with everybody sitting around picking the crabs and talking, gossiping. Just a social thing, but that was almost every Saturday." Terroir extends to the literal consumption of place and how, when we consume place, we become an embodiment of that locale. On the Eastern Shore of Virginia, food stories chart the contours of be-longing and difference—and they began to take shape long, long ago.

Reading through *The Countryside Transformed*, a massive digital archive created by Brooks Miles Barnes and his colleagues, I come across a tongue-in-cheek news item printed in 1895 in the *Peninsula Enterprise*, published out of Accomac, the county seat.

WACHAPREAGUE.

Those of our towns-people who had proposed to breakfast last Monday morning, on hot oyster-stew, were suddenly and unexpectedly called upon to change their bill of fare. At an early hour an unusual commotion was discovered in the lower part of the town, centering mainly about the shucking establishments at the foot of Main street. A few moments [later] it was realized that a band of strikers had charge of that part of the town, and the wheels of our busy marts were brought to a stand still. The tie-up speedily extended through all the ramifications of the oyster industry. Boats at the wharf lay with battened hatches, others in the stream were afraid to haul in, those about to go out postponed sailing. A few dissenting shuckers who attempted to mount their stalls were seized by the strikers and hustled out under escort. Oyster measures, buckets and wheel-barrows were overturned and placed under strong guard. Indeed so silently and effectively was the blow struck that almost before our citizens were aware of it, they stood confronting one of those awful upheavals of discontented labor, already known to the experience of some of our sister cities. As time wore on, numerous reports gained in credence in the streets; some asserting that telegrams had been sent to Norfolk for scab shuckers, and that a bloody fight would be the result; others contending that a sheriff and posse should be summoned at once; a few suggesting an appeal to the Governor to call out Col. Jones and the 1st Virginia Regiment. Meantime a committee from the strikers marched up the street in a body, demanding an interview with the proprietor, and the citizens held their breath with suspense, trying to recall all they had read about the past Chicago and Brooklyn strikes, and fearful of what the end might be. Cigars were offered the committee which they peremptorily refused to smoke, and the situation looked ominous. But negotiations finally began, the strikers fixed their ultimatum at two cents advance per gallon. After parley these terms were finally accepted by the proprietor and the strike was declared off—much to the relief of our business stagnation. But the end came too late for the oyster stew.

The anonymous Seaside correspondent who submitted this report to the editors setting type just a few miles to the northwest limns perfectly the ways in which local anxieties around labor are made visible at the table. The labor dispute is resolved more or less to everyone's satisfaction, but oyster stew breakfasts are disheartenedly disrupted. The upending of custom and convention at the table is the deeper measure of the significance of the oyster shuckers' job action. If the writer and the editor, however, had truly wished to instigate violence in their readers, they would have published a recipe and labeled it "the best." Labor disputes could be reconciled for pennies; oyster stew preferences were intractable points of contention.

The local practice of establishing truthfulness through detail reaches back to the early 1600s, figuring prominently in the depositions of witnesses in local court actions ranging from adultery to death by misadventure. "Experience which is passed on from mouth to mouth," wrote the German expatriate Walter Benjamin in 1936, "is the source from which all storytellers have drawn." Benjamin continues, elaborating on characteristics that stories of all sorts hold in common: they contain "openly or covertly, something useful. The usefulness may, in one case, consist in a moral; in another, in some practical advice; in a third, in a proverb or maxim." I would add entertainment, novelty, emotion, and feeling. Benjamin terms these useful outcomes "counsel," noting that "counsel is less an answer to a question than a proposal concerning the continuation of a story which is just unfolding." Terroir and cuisine offer counsel. That certainly holds true for the 1895 newspaper report on the shuckers' strike and the loss of oyster stew for breakfast as well as for the greater Eastern Shore of Virginia in the present day, where cooking and telling are living practices refined and revised in a constant flux of convention and invention.

The chapters that follow flow from a combination of ingredients, recipes, remembrances, and natural histories. There is an order in the sequence of foods and stories. I begin with the dishes that enjoy a wider geographic circulation but possess an Eastern Shore of Virginia twist. Dumplings, figs, crabs, panfish, and marsh hens populate those conversations. More distinctively local ingredients and preparations follow: Hayman sweet potatoes, oyster pies, clam fritters, and swelling toads. Although a measure of terroir and cuisine may be taken on the plate, its true heart is discovered in the culinary lives of people and the events that bind them: the Wachapreague Volunteer Fireman's Carnival cake wheel, drum head soup, "Cook" Ross's yeast rolls, mutton *barbacoa* and oyster crab *mengue*, and the autumn parties thrown by H. M. and Mary Lou Arnold and Theodore and Kathy Peed.

I think of the foodways that map the terroir and cuisine of the Eastern Shore of Virginia as an undiscovered culinary country. Encountered at home or festival, signature dishes, for instance clam fritters or baked Hayman sweet potatoes, are deceptively straightforward and plain. Like the Carolina Lowcountry fifty years ago and the bayou country of Louisiana before that, Eastern Shore dishes are notably plain—and filled with possibilities for experimentation and invention. It is a cuisine that invites the future even as it reveres its past. With that in mind, I reached out to friends valorized for their creativity in the kitchen and at the table, asking them if they would each imagine recipes that place the culinary distinction of the place within reach of cooks near and far. The chapters are interspersed with recipes for the home cook. Consider them blessings gratefully recited at table.

Some readers will look for certain "iconic" foodways, for example, blue crabs. It would seem that there's just not much to say after William W. Warner's extraordinary *Beautiful Swimmers* of 1976. But watching watermen unload bushels of crabs from workboats at the Bayford wharf, I discover a lexicon for crabs that demands translation. As for oysters, I have a shelfful of books filled with natural and culinary histories of the oyster. But oyster pie, that's a different story, and it is here. This book is not intended as an encyclopedia on Eastern Shore of Virginia foodways. It offers, instead, a series of meditations on provisions and preparations that convey the distinctive terroir and cuisine of a place and the people who make it their own every time they step into a boat in quest of drum fish, tread in a field to set sweet potato slips, hunker down to a clam fritter dinner, or share a story over a Sunday breakfast of salt fish and pancakes.

The rapture of Eastern Shore of Virginia terroir and cuisine resides in the recollections and stories that frame those favored recipes and legendary meals. As things go, one story leads to the next. What emerges might take the form of a single anecdote—or, one telling leading to the next, yielding a cycle of stories. The sequence of linked tales depends on the situation of each telling and may involve several storytellers each contributing to a larger narrative. Food stories on the Eastern Shore tap a wellspring of individual and shared experiences. They are not always about growing, harvesting, hunting, fishing, cooking, and eating, but those actions are almost always present. They lend believability to narrative—even through wild exaggeration. As H. M. Arnold put it one sweat-soaked summer afternoon down at the Bayford oyster house, "You can't make it up." His friend Theodore Peed nodded in agreement, "Yes sir, especially if everybody tells the truth. Lot of people tell a damn lie. I tell the truth, boy." And, that is, in fact, the truth of it.

A Taste for Dumplings

Ron Crumb, the former proprietor of Paul's Restaurant in the old railroad town of Cheriton, lists a veritable ark of wildfowl his family consumed with dumplings. Remembering how his mother cooked wildfowl, he begins with affection, "The main way they cooked ducks was in a big roasting pan—a big pan with a cover on it. She would put like an inch of water and maybe an onion or two in the bottom and that would flavor it. And, you see, it was six of us when we were growing up, it would be six ducks and everybody got a duck. My sister Kate was the baby, and she usually got the butterball or the teal or, you know, the smallest one. The trick of it was eating it without breaking a molar or hitting a shot that was in the duck." He grins, "Right at the end," he turns back to his mother's technique, "she would do the dumplings into the onions and everything. And a big pile of mashed potatoes. Greens of some sort. Anywhere from cabbage to kale to collards. Collard was probably the most predominant one. Sometimes you'd just get a big old plate with mashed potatoes and right next to it was a big old plate of dumplings, and greens. . . . Yeah, that was the last thing made, was usually the dumplings. The greens and everything else was all there."

Taste is one of those words that covers a lot of territory—and partitions it, too. We think of taste in its physical sense as flavor—the play of sweet, salt, bitter, sour, and savory unique to every ingredient and every dish. Taste in this sense is about bodily sensations. Taste also entails social knowledge. A connoisseur uses specific knowledge about food, wine, art, literature, and just about everything else to render acts of judgment. Taste in this iteration is about discernment and sensibility, and it is very much about creating and policing the borders of community and distinction. Taste, then, is on our tongues and in our minds and in how we comport our lives in the company of others. Terroir and cuisine make taste

Buck Doughty at Riggins's clam house, Red Bank, Virginia.

visible. Taste is a function of habit: it is learned and cultivated as something that is known through the body and measured in the mind. We could think of taste as the acts of knowing that lie at the crossroads of consumption and conversation, a posturing about what we eat and why we like it for high intellectual purpose. Or we could pine for a plate of black duck and dumplings—and the grand universe of dumpling types and preferences found on the Eastern Shore of Virginia.

You have to start with basics. What is a dumpling? Food historians have expended extraordinary effort in sorting out this problem. In short, the *Oxford Companion to Food* defines the dumpling as "a term of uncertain origin which first appeared in print at the beginning of the seventeenth century, although the object it denotes—a small and usually globular mass of boiled or steamed dough—no doubt existed long before that. A dumpling is a food with few, indeed no, social pretensions, and of such simplicity that it may plausibly be supposed to have evolved independently in the peasant cuisines of various parts of Europe and probably in other parts of the world too. Such cuisines feature soups and stews, in which vegetables may be enhanced by a little meat. Dumplings, added to the soup or stew, are still, as they were centuries ago, a simple and economical way of extending such dishes." The *Larousse Gastronomique* adds: "A ball of dough, originally savoury and served as an accompaniment to meat or as a dessert . . . made by shaping small portions from a batch of bread dough before specific mixtures were developed using flour, cereals, pulses, stale bread, potatoes or cheese, sometimes with a raising agent added or enriched with fat in the form of suet, were developed."

Eastern Shore cooks distinguish two broad dumpling categories: "slick" and "puff." Ron Crumb explains, "There were a couple of ways they do dumplings around here. One of them is a skinny slick dumpling. And that's the main one that the family does." Other cooks, he explains, "using Bisquick or something, get a fatter dumpling." "They would just make the dough," he summarizes, "and roll it out kind of thin and slice it up and put it in for so many minutes. . . . And just kind of turn it so they didn't stick together." Emory Ross of Onancock preserved family recipes for both, slick and puff, in her typed personal cookbook from the early 1960s:

DUMPLINGS—ROLL OUT
1 Cup Flour
¼ Teaspoon salt
½ Teaspoon baking powder
½ tablespoon shortening
Enough liquid to just mix well
Roll out and drop in liquid and cook about 15 minutes

DUMPLINGS—DROP
1 Cup Flour
1½ teaspoons baking powder
¼ teaspoon salt
½ Cup Milk
Drop in broth and cook about 15 minutes

The generality of her instructions "enough liquid to just mix well" speaks to dumplings as a culinary commonplace so familiar that cooks presumed their readers' ability to fill in the blanks.

Phyllis and Hooksie Walker of Bayford associate puff dumplings with Maryland foodways. Hooksie begins: "We used to call them Maryland dumplings. My mother was from here, but father's family all came from Maryland. My mother, when she made them, called them Maryland dumplings. My grandmother used to make them, and she, of course, was from Maryland. That was the only kind she made." Phyllis adds, "I like them, too. They're delicious. . . . A lot of people do puff dumplings around here. But my mother always made slick dumplings, we called them, and they're thin and you made them from scratch and you rolled them out. Real thin. And then you cut them and then you cooked them in the juice where you baked your chicken. And you added water to it and you dropped your dumplings in there and you'd cook them for fifteen minutes I guess, they'd boil. . . . I used to make the dumplings. He'd roll them out. Then I'd cut them."

In Bessie E. Gunter's 1889 *Housekeeper's Companion*, the first Eastern Shore of Virginia cookbook, one correspondent provided a recipe for dumplings that could be applied to both slippery and puff variations.

PLAIN SUET DUMPLINGS.

One pound of flour, two teaspoonfuls of yeast powder, one pound of fine suet well rubbed together. Wet with milk, make into balls or cakes or roll out on the cake-board, cut in cakes half-inch thick. Drop in boiling water and boil twenty minutes. Eat with sauce.
  — Mrs. V. C. P.

Still, as H. M. Arnold notes, the preference was for slippery or slick dumplings: "We used to have dumplings, but we used slick dumplings. Flat ones. I like them better anyway than the round ones. . . . I like slick dumplings better than I do the drop dumplings. They slide down good with that old black duck." I should confess at the outset that I've never savored the delight of black duck and dumplings — but I'm hopeful.

Taste and memory are cultivated things. Storytelling unites them. Consider Buck Doughty's "epic" recollection of his mother's black duck and dumplings. The black ducks, residing somewhere near the heart of this layered tale, are among the most favored wildfowl that migrate through the vast Atlantic marshes between the mainland and the barrier islands. Sport hunters pay serious money for equipment and guides that provide the questionable pleasure of crouching in blinds, shivering over salt water, waiting for dawn and an errant bird. I guess it puts the freeze in frisson. In a bygone age, hunters provisioning their family's tables tended to be a bit more direct and businesslike in the quest for an entrée, trapping, baiting, and night shooting. Jean Doughty shared her directions for what remains a favored dish:

BLACK DUCK AND DUMPLINS

Cook your black ducks first make sure you stuff his butt with onion and salt then cut some up in the water. Then after they're done you put the dumplins in. While the duck or goose is cooking you make the dumplins with flour and water a little salt and mix together then roll dough out and cut the dumplins out and throw them in the water with the ducks don't forget to salt and sprinkle old bay seasoning in it.

Except for the Old Bay, a recent addition to local spice racks, Jean Doughty's recipe is as timeless as the coming together of wheat flour and local wildfowl in the 1600s. But this recipe is not just about how to make a Sunday supper, at once special and basic. It is about a series of seemingly unconnected conversations coming together in a multilayered story about family, misadventure, and memory. The challenge is where to begin. There is no established sequence for this story. Rather it starts, develops, and concludes according to the occasion on which it is told. Jean Doughty gifted her handwritten recipe in the wake of a conversation that her son Buck and I shared that emerged from an unlikely set of coincidences that stretch back over a lifetime. Our story goes like this.

Not so long ago, on the advent of the winter holidays, I came into possession of what was presented to me as a pair of "barely legal" black ducks. I interpreted this lovely gesture as someone having overshot their limit and, motivated by necessity and generosity, passed them along to me, a neighbor known to cook and eat just about everything. I accepted the black ducks late on a bitterly frozen afternoon, carried them home, and undertook the task of cleaning them in the woodshed near the barn. It doesn't take long for fingers to burn with cold and knuckles to go red and stiff from pulling the chilled innards out of a duck and plucking through layers of feathers and down. Fortunately, I was already late for a holiday party down the lane. Plausible excuse to abandon the task at hand was all I needed. The ducks weren't going anywhere, and it was as chilled as a walk-in refrigerator in the woodshed. My thoughts turned with relief to the prospect of festive lights and overheated conviviality.

The celebration was in full swing when my wife, Rebecca, and I walked in the door carrying our contributions of smoked bluefish and whole fig preserves, two of my favorite summertime tastes best resurrected in the cold months of the year. Hélène Doughty occupied a seat at the end of the kitchen island and we fell into conversation. Her father, a retired Parisian fish chef, was coming to visit and, she lamented, they had had no luck in procuring any ducks or geese for his culinary pleasure. "How fortuitous," I thought, looking at my fingers still bright and raw from addressing the transition of those black ducks from wildfowl to ingredient. "Hélène," I smiled aglow with thoughts of my own largesse in passing along these increasingly orphaned ducks, "I happen to have two partially dressed black ducks in the woodshed and would be very happy to contribute them to you for your father's holiday!" "Lovely," she exclaimed, "I'll send Buck when he gets here." I had known Buck, Hélène's husband, since he was about nine years old and running around the house while I interviewed his late father, Kellam Doughty, a deputy sheriff and Hog Island descendant. Kellam passed away shortly after our last conversations. Buck and I hadn't connected then, but recent events had aligned to bring us together.

A couple of summers earlier, Rebecca and I had to have some tree work done so that a mammoth water elm wouldn't topple onto the house during one of the storms that rumbles by on a regular basis. After consultation with folks who keep up with these matters, we found John Marshall, who arrived one stifling morning with his bucket truck and bucket man on just about the hottest, most humid August day imaginable. At ten o'clock in the morning the temperature was already closing in on ninety degrees and the cicadas were screaming their mad, screeching songs of lust with deafening abandon. It was that kind of hot. The bucket man whizzed around overhead while John, a huge man with a voice like a bull fiddle, and I surveyed the proceedings. John noticed that the bucket man was running low on chainsaw fuel, took his leave, and headed off to town to buy a gallon of gas. I went inside the house for coffee to the accompaniment of the thud of heavy limbs falling onto soft earth. The bucket man continued his flight through the canopy, threading branches, dropping dead boughs. Shirtless, he ran rivers of sweat.

John returned an hour later, clambering out of his pickup truck carrying a gallon milk jug in a hand the size of a prize-winning ham. The bucket man swooped down, reached over, snatched the jug, unscrewed the cap, and guzzled several big gulping swallows. And then realized that what looked like iced tea was chainsaw fuel with the gas and oil combined. The result was spectacular—in an unfortunate way. The bucket man ran for the undergrowth along the creek bank. John and I stood together in amazement, listening to the retching in the bushes and vines. This went on for what seemed a long time. Every now and then the bucket man would stagger forth, look around, grab his gut, and careen back into the brush. There was plenty of time for chat.

John and I spoke of folks we knew and the bygone communities of the barrier islands that lie off Virginia's Atlantic Coast. Remembrance of Kellam Doughty came up and with it the news that his son Buck still lived in the community along the Seaside Road above Eastville, the county seat. Buck, John offered, would very much like to have copies of the tapes that preserved his father's recollections, in part for their content related to family history, but just as much for the sound of a voice he thought he would never hear again. I said, "Consider it done." Just then the bucket man came out of the scrub, fished a cigarette from a sweat-stained pack, and began to flick his lighter. We could smell the gas on his breath twenty feet away. John turned to me, wincing, "Sure hope he don't explode. A good bucket man is hard to find."

So that's how we came to be sitting at our dining room table with Buck Doughty, who had been dispatched by Hélène to secure the two partially cleaned black ducks in the woodshed. We talked about Kellam and Buck's mother, Jean, and then I asked him, given my interests in Eastern Shore of Virginia recipes and ingredients, how he would cook the ducks awaiting his French father-in-law's impending arrival. Buck spoke without hesitation or equivocation, linking cooking instructions to genealogy to connoisseurship.

"Black duck and dumplings," he began. "Oh, Pop-Pop [Buck's grandfather Albert Coe Wallace] used to get them all the time over in Wachapreague." And then he launched into a recitation that placed the dish on the table: "Mom-Mom [Buck's grandmother Jeannette Sue Groton Wallace], she pretty much cooked them for him every time that he would get them. Everybody would bring them over. He ate everything that wouldn't eat him."

Buck digressed, outlining how his grandmother taught her daughters to cook, assigning each her own signature culinary domain: "She taught all the girls to cook everything the same way, so Mom became the fryer and everything else. She was the one who could do the wild game. Aunt Darlene seemed like she was really with just the meals, the turkey and everything else. Aunt Barbara became the baker. She could do all the desserts and cakes. She was all about the breads." Buck held the opinion, though, that it was his mother, Jean, who "was really the kingpin behind it all." He veered in the course of his story to locating cooking in the character of his seaside lineage: "Jeannette Groton [Buck's mother] was really earthy. She learned everything through Pop-Pop's side of the family. The Wallaces, they were just traditional Seaside people."

Buck tacked back to the preparation of black duck and dumplings: "The way he [Pop-Pop] liked black duck and dumplings, I asked her how to make it. She said, 'You boil your duck. . . .'" At this juncture, Buck makes the recipe his own: "I think you boil it for the first shot, and then you change the water and you salt it up real heavy. And you go ahead and boil it a second time down. Cook them up until it starts coming off the bone and everything. Then you start making your dumplings. You just roll them out really, really thin. Just keep rolling the dough. Cut out your squares. You take what's leftover, keep rolling it out flat and just—as thin as you can get them."

Buck praises the extraordinary fineness of his mother's dumplings, marveling at her hand strength and technique. Given Buck's impressive physical stature and the obvious power of his hands developed through a lifetime as a welder and metalworker, his testimonial to her abilities carries real weight: "Mom could always cut them out really thin, I don't know how because I've tried pressing it out, and it really hurts my hand to get it that thin. I don't know how she would get the dough to a consistency where she could get them that thin. They were really tight, and they would stick your teeth together. She knew . . . they were just right when you didn't have a doughy effect inside of them. It wasn't like cake and thick. But they would stick your teeth together. They didn't go to pieces in the water. That's the consistency you're after. You want them nice and dry when you're rolling them out, not too thick. So it's the sweet spot that you got to hit. And she showed me a little bit about how to get the flour just right. That's probably the key."

I am mesmerized by the passion underpinning Buck's story. He loops on around to the black ducks: "Cooking duck—I think she puts a lot of onion in with it when she's boiling them down. When she gets the water to the right spot when it's got a lot of the duck coming off and floating in it, and you see the little flecks of meat and stuff, that's when she'll throw in the dumplings. When the duck is done, you stick a fork in there, and you know, the meat comes off the bone and everything is kind of falling apart. That's when you go in with your dumplings. If you go with them too early, you'll cook them too much. So, you go ahead and get about a good fifteen-minute, twenty-minute boil on the dumplings, they're about ready. The gravy gets really dark from the meat itself," he explains. "It's like a dark consistency. Not like turkey gravy or anything, that's kind of brown. Black duck will get kind of brown, maroon brown. Almost like a blooded brown. And it's really a different flavor. Black duck and dumplings, it's always been my staple favorite. I love it!"

Buck, always forward thinking, happily anticipates leftovers. "Reheated, they're even better. They'll sit there cold, the flavor goes through them, then you heat them back up and then they're good. But you reheat them too many times, they start going to pieces. When your duck gets cold and after you get the dumplings all ate up, whatever. We always just made mayonnaise black duck sandwiches. You just take it, cut it where it's so dry. Even when you boil it, it's pretty dry. We'll just slice it up and make a black duck sandwich with a little bit of mayonnaise. Moistened it up a bit."

Buck gets back to the details of black duck and dumplings, "Peppered it up real heavy. You got to pepper the hell out of it. You got to pepper a black duck. Black duck is just strong. It's got its own duck flavor. It's really not like a Muscovy duck or anything like that, it's really a dry, dry gamy taste, but it's a good taste. I love black duck. Mallard, all of it. It kind of tastes the same, but black duck is really dry. Dries your mouth up. It's almost like a Guinness versus a Beck's, you know. It's really the ultimate dry duck."

"Damned by faint praise," I think to myself. Buck is almost drooling. There's a hungry, faraway look in his eyes and he laughs his big laugh, "You just go for it!" We are all laughing!

Then Buck's telling veers in an unexpected direction, and he launches into a story that on the face of it has virtually nothing to do with black duck and dumplings. In retrospect, though, I realize that Buck has made a strategic narrative leap that serves up black duck and dumplings as a centerpiece of a story larded with reminiscences, adventures, laughter, and wistfulness. "Black duck is just really dry and really strong," he begins. "It's just kind of gristly and no fat in it at all. It's really, really dry." His father, Kellam, he elaborates, "loved black duck. Loved it to death." "But, truth be known," Buck adds, "he actually liked goose more than anything that I remember."

Kellam apparently relished goose enough to risk uncertain futures, taking actions resulting in unintended consequences. Buck sets the scene as we listen: "Mom was out on the horse with Jeanne [Buck's stepsister] on Cimarron [Jeanne's horse] where we lived in Eastville. And, she [Buck's mother, Jean] told me, I remember it when I was younger, but she told me what happened. I was wondering why she broke her back." Where is this going, I wonder? "She went out there," Buck forges ahead, "and got on this horse this one time. Jeanne finally talked her into getting up on it. Dad heard geese flying over. He went over there with his pistol, or I think it was his pistol. She said it was his pistol. He went there and nailed a couple of them while they were flying over." I can see Kellam stepping out of the house, ready for work in his deputy's uniform, hearing the oncoming geese as they skim over the fields, unholstering his service revolver with the aim, as they say around here, of hailing himself down a few.

Buck plows ahead, "Well, the horse bucked her off the back, and she ended up going and getting her back fused. She was all tore up! She had to go to Salisbury, Maryland, to stay at the hospital, and they fused her back. In the meantime, he [Kellam] was babysitting us. Well, I was helping him on the farm. I wasn't too much in the way, but Jennifer [Buck's younger sister and still a toddler at the time] was crying a lot, crying and crying and crying. So he went and get her to Sweet's, who lived across the street." Sweet and Dink Moore were an older childless couple residing near the Doughty household. As Buck presented their situation, Sweet and Dink longed for a baby of their own but had resigned themselves to a life without children. Then a miracle happens; Kellam "rode up there on the tractor one day and said, 'Here. Take her. I can't take it no more.'" Sweet and Dink Moore take possession of the baby Jennifer, believing that Kellam has gifted her to them! I'm wondering how this fits in with black duck and dumplings.

Buck continues, "Mom comes home and wonders where Jennifer was at. And he [Kellam] says, 'Uh, . . . I kind of took her over to Sweet's, let her take care of her for a while.' Mom went over to get her." Sweet, it appears held a very different view of the situation, "She says, 'That's my baby! You can't have her back! Kellam gave her to me!' My god, it was a mess!" We are all laughing harder. "So, he technically gave my sister away when we were little. Sweet, she'd raised her for two weeks, like her own little kid."

I can no longer think of a plate of black duck and dumplings without recalling the baby Jennifer's odyssey between households. I realize that, although the full recipe for the dish may start with the barely legal black ducks in my woodshed and the prospect of homemade dumplings, an abundance of narrative seasonings stocks the cupboard of Buck's memory.

Listening to Buck recount his tales of black duck and dumplings, I am aware of other stories that connect each to the other in a series of culinary episodes that invariably speak to terroir, not as the taste of place, but rather as how memory lingers on the palate. I am mindful of a late summer day thirty years earlier, thunderstorms moaning and clattering their way across the Chesapeake Bay, traversing the Eastern Shore, blasting a path across the Atlantic marshes before crashing over the islands and out to sea. I was with my friends Jack Robbins, who would become county sheriff, and Buck's father, Kellam, in the oystering village of Willis Wharf. Concerned with the progress of my schoolwork, they agreed that there was someone I had to meet and we went in quest of Earl Doughty, long retired from the lifesaving service on Hog Island and known for his musical prowess in playing the spoons and telling a good story. We found Earl driving his truck through a driving rain squall in Willis Wharf, pulled him over, and retreated to a nearby oyster house. As the rain rattled the metal roof, Earl regaled us with stories of Hog Island—including one that evoked, in a roundabout way, the power of dumplings.

> See, in that '36 storm, it was Mr. Revell and Mr. Tom Phillips watched Ballard's oyster ground. Had a watch house down there by High Shoal Lump. Well, they had planted clams down there, and of course, they watched them both. Well, this storm come along and taken the shanty off and they both got drownded. So Captain Harry Bowen found Mr. Revell at the south end of Orville Shoal, and he was up there. Had some oyster ground around in there. So he stuck his pole down, what he usually used to stick his oyster scow down along a rock. He stuck his pole down, take a short piece of line, tied it around his leg, and tied [it to] this pole and come on down to the Coast Guard station.
>
> Well, the picket boat, I was in her—I was off here [at Willis Wharf] to the mainland. Randolph, Clark Thornes, and myself. So, we didn't know nothing about it, you know. So we was going on out the creek, got down there by Baron's Slip, and the wind was southeast. So, run across that vane of wind that done blowed by that lifeboat that was

carrying him in in the scow. I'd just been back after going in the pilot house. Well, they had the pilot house windows up. I said, "Did you two smell what I just smelled?" Randolph says, "Yeah, goddamned right. I never smelled nothing like that before in my life!"

Emphasizing the moment, Earl Doughty inhales sharply,

That one sniff was all you got because we was going this way and the wind was blowing that away. So, when we got down below beyond the woods so we could look out on Hog Island Bay, we seen the lifeboat coming with the scow in tow. Well, we met them between the Crab Hook and the Elbow Light.

We figured they'd found some drownded man, but we still didn't know what the story was. They went in that lifeboat back to that station in case they had to go to sea, because she was the only sea boat that we had. We take the line and come on in here to Ballard's Dock. Of course, there was enough of them who knew Mr. Revell to know that was him. Evidently the Coast Guard had done called Ballard from the station that they were sending this body in. They'd done called Mr. Fred Mapp, who was the undertaker, to come down and get him. So, the tide was down, so they had to put him in a tarpaulin. You know, they runned it under him and two or three men got hold of each end and just brought him in, water and all, and then they covered him up. Well, tide was down and getting him out, there was two or three men at each end, because he was a right good-sized man and still soaked with that water.

I was standing there and Randolph, all of us helping to get him out. I don't know whether if it was his head was up higher than his feet or vice versa. There was something or other inside him that said, "Shiioosh."

Earl makes a wet, blowing sound. "God Almighty knows!" Earl mutters and shudders with the recollection of gas escaping the body, "Well, Randolph he let go of everything and started puking! He puked everything he had in him and then he begin to puke blood! So, we got him straightened away, so going back to the station, he said, 'Goddamn it, don't say nothing about that old man when we get down there.' He says, 'I spewed up everything but my asshole.'" Earl, remembering the conversation, chuckles. "When we got down there, Bill Marshall, he was the cook, had a chicken pot pie and the skin on that chicken looked exactly like Mr. Revell where he'd been in that water."

I can see where this is going. Earl presses on. "Arthur Morris, he reaches over—had it in this old big roaster, enough to feed twelve or fifteen head. So he got his tablespoon, got some potatoes, dumplings, and gravy. And he taken his fork and reached and got the short joint, and about the time he got ready to put it on his plate, the skin dropped off—the meat dropped off! Randolph says, 'Son of a bitch!' He pushes that plate aside, went down to Stanley's Store. He bought two cartons of almond Hershey bars! That's what he eat for thirty days."

Imagining Randolph Higby's gut-wrenching encounter with chicken and dumplings, Buck's father "hailing" geese with his service revolver, and the circumstances of my coming into possession of two barely legal black ducks reminded me of other stories. I recollected Claudia Ballard's narrative of her father's illicit black duck haul one Christmas perhaps fifty years earlier. Sitting at her kitchen table one evening, she offers: "My father, growing up, I've heard quite a few tales. I can tell you one tale if you'd like to hear it. It involves black ducks, I don't know if you want to hear it." I'm energetically nodding, "Yes, I would!" She begins, "We had a lot of duck, too, and my father was a big hunter. Not too much venison, but we had duck and goose a lot. Down at Cherrystone was a salt-recovery pond. This was before it was turned into a campground. Indian salt-recovery pond. It's still there now. But he, and I'm not sure who the other individual was who was in this, set out a duck trap."

"When they went to check it," Claudia resumes, "they had no idea that it would be as loaded down with black duck as it was. So loaded down that I remember being four or five years old, and I remember hearing all this commotion in the kitchen. I went out into the kitchen and I'm looking. My mother is standing there looking at my father, going, 'You are going to end up at the federal pen in Georgia! I just hope you know this.' When I looked over, there was a washtub, a galvanized washtub. The big one! With a mound of cleaned, not feathered, cleaned duck." She pauses for emphasis, "Just like this, right before Christmas, and Dad said, 'Bess, stop worrying about it. I'll get them out of here.' And indeed he did. Two cleaned black duck fit very nicely in gallon oyster cans—and the majority of those ducks were shipped to his customers up north. The game wardens love for me to tell that, because nobody believed it. That kind of thing went on. He never trapped another duck after that. A lot of what was oysters supposedly went out of here containing ducks, so they had a good Christmas up north."

Buck has finished his story and drives off into the blackness of a moonless winter night with the black ducks destined for Hélène's father. I am relieved to see those ducks gone to a better home.

A month later, just before Christmas and in the wake of the first winter northeaster of the season, I am puttering around out of doors when our neighbor Al Minio from across the shell lane walks up to the house. "Where's Becky?" he asks with his south Philadelphia accent. "Out and about," I reply. "She alright?" Al presses. "She was when last I saw her"— I am mystified as to where this line of questioning is going. "When did you last see her?" "A couple of hours ago," I answer with rising curiosity. "Well, there's a drowned woman on the beach," Al reports. "What?" "Really," he says. Off we go to witness the scene. I'm puzzling over Al's connection between the body on the beach and Becky's whereabouts, concluding that he harbors some vague suspicion that I might not be as harmless as I think I look.

Al and I reach the shore, where we stand off to the side, taking in a sad tableaux of law officers erecting a temporary screen of sheets in an effort to provide some final measure of privacy and respect for a corpse roughly abused by wind, surf, sun, and birds. It is the clearest evening, the kind of chilled sharpness in the breeze that follows on the heels of a December storm front when the air has been cleansed. The sun is setting into the waters of the bay. Al and I wonder aloud about what has come to pass. In this moment of extreme human sadness and brilliant natural beauty, one of the officers breaks away from the group along the shoreline, striding up to question us about what we may or may not have witnessed. She's wearing the uniform of the Virginia Marine Resources Commission police, carrying a holstered sidearm, rubbing circulation into her hands as she steps up from the beach. She looks us over. "You don't know who I am," she says to me. I read her nameplate and I'm taken aback, "Of course, I do! I do believe you are the baby Jennifer." And she is. I am inappropriately thinking of black duck and dumplings. I am thinking of food and stories.

I'm reflecting on the larger intricacies of black duck and dumplings. The black ducks at the center of Buck's recollection are a storied game bird. Dwight W. Huntington, writing in *Our Feathered Game* in 1903, shared several observations regarding the black duck. First, he notes its range from the Mississippi to the Atlantic and from the Canadian Arctic to the Gulf Coast. Second, "The dusky duck or black-duck," he remarked, is "often called black-mallard in the West, the *Canard noir* [in] Louisiana." Noting its shared qualities with the mallard, he adds, "These birds are so much alike that the difference may be regarded as local or climatic, and for the sportsman they are one and the same." More to the point, as far as fitness for the table was concerned, Huntington found the black duck inferior to other wildfowl. Polk Kellam, who grew up duck hunting with his father on the Eastern Shore of Virginia, qualifies Huntington's opinion on the question of taste and flavor: "Black ducks have been, over the years, one of the most plentiful ducks on the Seaside. They could be really good—or maybe not so good depending on what they have been eating. If they eat bull minnows, periwinkles, animal matter, they're strong. They can be really bad. If they're eating grain, there's nothing any better. They're good birds, a very good bird."

Polk turned to the subject of black duck and dumplings: "I've had duck and dumplings. That's an old traditional Eastern Shore way of having them, where, instead of using the oven, you put the duck in a pot on top of the stove and boil it. Some people pour off the first water after it comes to a boil. If there's any mess there, you want to clean it up a little bit more. You basically cook it until you get that level of tenderness you like. It would be sort of like slow-cook, because boiling is 212 degrees. You might boil it two or three hours. Take the duck out and put your dumplings in the pot. I used to have them, but somebody else cooked them. That's a good way to have black duck, too. Black duck and dumplings."

Polk turns to how the dish connected with other memories of people and places. "When I was a boy and hunted with Daddy, he had a houseboat that he kept at Revel Island. He and Sheriff Hoke from Accomack—Sheriff Hoke died and that old houseboat went and Daddy built another houseboat with Elmore Ballard from Willis Wharf." Elmore Ballard was Claudia Ballard's father. Terroir, I realize, is about connections.

Polk recollects, "I'd go down when I was in school on vacations with them at Christmastime and stay with them aboard the houseboat—and they'd often have black duck and dumplings. Wade Long, who worked with Daddy for years, he was the black duck and dumplings man. They were good. They developed a very convenient rule, which was that the youngest person in the party cleaned up the dishes. I got to do that every time. I didn't mind. Used to love it. We had fun." Polk laughs softly with pleasure and adds, "I remember some years ago. It was actually at our company and somebody asked this gentleman who worked for us what his favorite meal was. He said, 'Black duck, Hayman potato, and turnip greens.' And you talk about an Eastern Shore menu, I mean that's three things that may not be unique to the Shore, but black duck and Hayman potatoes are almost unique."

Slick or puff, dumplings rendered meals more filling and provided a medium that absorbed the flavors of the main ingredients. Eastern Shore cooks added dumplings to a variety of dishes, including cooked blackberries, garden peas, stewed tomatoes, and drum fish. Arlen Church, looking back on a lifetime of home cooking, summarized the range of dumpling dishes for her daughter-in-law Teresa Church, who noted with affection, "Dumplings were a big deal for Mom Church's family. She also told me about bean dumplings, strawberry dumplings, and blackberry dumplings. Bean dumplings are made with white navy beans cooked until almost done and seasoned with condiments to suit the taste. Then dumplings are added. Cook until beans and dumplings are done. Blackberry and strawberry dumplings call for ripe strawberries or ripe blackberries sweetened and cooked until almost done. Here again the desired sweetness can be achieved by adding more sugar, if needed. Add dumplings and finish cooking." Dumplings in the Church family's recipes extended the substance and flavor a dish—and in that purpose they resonate throughout the community.

Pete Terry, Willis Wharf native and an owner of Sewansecott oysters and clams, spoke of fruit and dumplings served with duck: "Mother would fix blackberry dumplings. . . . I guess it's like—it's not a slick dumpling. It's like one of those puff dumplings, you know. I don't know how you make them, but Mom used to. A lot of time we had them with duck. . . . You know, you make gravy and dumplings with duck. Sort of offset the taste of the duck a little bit. It's been years and years since I even thought of that. Most of the time black duck is all we had, because that's a Seaside duck. We didn't have a lot of mallards."

H. M. Arnold recalls blackberry dumplings served as a dessert. His mother made these dumplings by mixing blackberries in the dough and then dropping the dumplings into a hot blackberry sauce: "I remember them. They looked like they were round dumplings. They were almost like a biscuit. And she'd just set them in there. They were on top. . . . They were more boiled, I guess. Drop them in like a dropped dumpling almost. They were good. That was the dessert. Of course, you had the blackberries in there, too. Well, you know, almost like a pie but with no crust. You'd dip the dumpling out with the juice—with the blackberry juice—and ate it like that. Well, back then we used canned milk to pour over the top of them. That was our—I guess you'd want to say—Cool Whip." He stops, then adds, "She might have cooked the dumplings first. Baked them or something, and then dropped them in the juice. They just floated around and absorbed the juice. They were good!"

The fruit dumplings remembered by Pete Terry and H. M. Arnold resonate with a recipe from Bessie Gunter's 1889 *Housekeeper's Companion*:

SUET DUMPLINGS (WITH FRUIT).

One pound of grated bread, one pound of suet, one pound of sugar, four eggs, half pound of currants, half pound of raisins, lemon. With your hands well floured make into balls the size of an egg. Roll in flour, drop in boiling water. Boil twenty minutes. When done they will rise to the top of the water. Wine sauce.

—Mrs. V. C. P.

Gunter's fruit dumplings in wine sauce were far more polite and refined than the remembered dessert dumplings of everyday Eastern Shore fare. Sweet dumplings map only a small corner of the dumpling universe.

Savory dumplings, often in combination with seasonal vegetables, were commonplace. One variation favored by many cooks was the doughboy—a small dumpling dipped out with a teaspoon and dropped into boiling liquid with tomatoes or peas. Speaking in the shade of a tent at a local art fair, Connie Zahn, Danny Doughty, and Sam Taylor evoked the pleasures of "peas and doughboys." Sam Taylor began "Peas and doughboys? Dumplings! You call them doughboys. You work and shell the peas and get them all ready. Then you put them in some nice water and get it boiling. Put a little salt in there and a piece of fat meat. And boil them maybe ten or fifteen minutes, and then you make dumplings, which are flour and lard, little bit of water. Roll them out nice and thin. And when it's boiling water, you dump them in." What Sam describes are miniature slippery dumplings. Then Connie inserts the puff dumpling alternative, "Or dip them in with a spoon. Make them little balls. We like them little doughboys." Sam adds, "You do little fat boys. If you like them light, you put a little baking powder in them." Danny, an experienced chef who ran a café in Willis Wharf, breaks his silence, "If you want some thickening with them, leave all the loose flour on the dumpling when it drops in there because it thickens it naturally. It absorbs the taste of the pea so that the peas and the dumplings become cohesive together. They create this taste between the two of them. The combination that just is really, really great. A lot of people would never think of it. Usually you put a piece of meat in with dumplings, but peas and doughboys are unbelievable." Then, hedging his bets, "or flat dumplings, or round ones. Whatever you prefer."

On another day in a different conversation, Kerry Paul, working the Wachapreague Volunteer Fireman's Carnival, paused in his labors. His sister, he noted, "she made peas and doughboys. I was the one that—I was the only one they would let pick the doughboys out because I wouldn't eat the peas, but since I was the baby, they'd let me do it." He smiles happily at the recollection. For Marilyn Sharp and her sister Hurley Mae, sitting in her pickup truck parked next to her produce stand by the highway, the magic pairing is peas and dumplings with Spam. Cars whiz by as Hurley begins, "You got to cook the dumplings before you put the peas in there, now I know that because I cook them myself." Marilyn jumps in, "I'm going to tell you what. Now you can go in the store, and if you don't want to make your own dumplings, you can get Miss Annie's dumplings that come in a red box in the freezer." Hurley clarifies, "Called 'old-fashioned,' 'old-fashioned dumplings.'" Marilyn concludes, "Miss Annie's Dumplings,

Connie Zahn's peas and doughboys, Onancock, Virginia.

and take them and drop in there. You know what I do with my peas? I put onions in my peas. I get me some Spam, the light Spam in the can, and I chop that, I dice it up, and I put that in my peas. Let me tell you, it's good!"

Dumpling dishes abound. Arlen Church's tomato and dumplings, for example, follow her grandmother's preparation: "Well, my favorite way to cook tomatoes would be to wash those tomatoes good, peel them, and slice them, and put them on into a little pan. Put some sugar into them, and cook them. And after they got done, if you want tomato and dumplings they used to call it, you then make the bread. Roll it real thin and then cut it in little pieces, about an inch square, and put it in there and let it cook. Then you'd cook it fast and that was her dumplings. That was tomato and dumplings. She put a little bit of sugar into them, and I don't know what else she put into them. I never did see her do that, if she had something else she put in there. I think she put a little bit of pepper in there." Tomato and dumplings was distinct from stewed tomatoes. Arlen Church describes the difference, "Stewed tomatoes don't do nothing but boil until it gets real tender."

Fairy Mapp White wrote and compiled her 1958 *Foolproof Cook Book* from a lifetime of experience and with a strong sense of local history. In her introduction, she links her effort to three Eastern Shore food histories. White places her collection squarely in the context of family, thanking her sisters and locating her book in a generational chain between her mother, who helped her "learn to cook in the kitchen at Woodland," and her daughter: "This was done for my own use, but meant eventually for my daughter . . . in answer to her frequent question, 'Mother, how did you make this?'" To answer those queries, White dipped into the diversity and distinctiveness of Eastern Shore cooking, offering dishes that reflected ordinary fare.

MEAL DUMPLINGS
1 c. Old Time corn meal
⅓ c. flour
1 tsp. salt
1 egg
1½ c. boiling water
1 tsp. grated onion
Process:
  1. Add meal and salt to boiling water, stirring all the time, remove from fire and stir until smooth. Add egg well beaten and onion.
  2. Drop by spoonfuls on floured waxed paper, roll around on flour on paper to make balls. Drop balls into boiling turnip green water, cover tightly, and boil 10 min. Serve with jowl and greens.

There were other kinds of dumplings as well. H. M. recalls, "My grand-mother Parks used to make a dumpling, a dry dumpling. She always had the slick dumplings. They rolled them out, but she would bake—I never cared for them too much—but they were the same thing. She baked them, so they were hard. Just a hard dumpling, so you ate them like that. She'd have them on the table with everything else. You could put gravy on them with stuff, but they were hard. She'd roll out the slick ones, cut them, put them in with the gravy. They'd be slick and soft. She'd slice them the same way and put them on a sheet with flour and put them in the oven. They'd just taste like dough, that's why I was never crazy about them. But, my granddad and them, they'd always just grab them and ate them. She always had some baked dumplings that were hard. I remember that well. If I was going to eat one of them, I had to dip it in the gravy. It was just dry! They just ate them like they were. They didn't put butter on them or anything like that. They just kind of ate them with the meal. It was just an old-fashion way, I guess. I never asked my wife to make them—not unless they've got gravy on them!"

Dried dumplings, I suspect, are descendants of hardtack, a form of bread baked to the consistency of a concretized cracker with the advantage of a long storage life and the ability to stretch soups and stews.

HARD TACK RECIPE [gone-ta-pott.com]
2 cups of flour
½ to ¾ cup water
6 pinches of salt
1 tablespoon of shortening (optional)
Mix all the ingredients into a batter and press onto a cookie sheet to a thickness of ½ inch.
Bake in a preheated oven at 400°F (205°C) for one hour.
Remove from oven, cut dough into 3-inch squares, and punch four rows of holes, four holes per row into the dough (a fork works nicely).
Flip the crackers and return to the oven for another half hour.

The dried dumplings recollected by H. M. Arnold and hardtack or ship's bread may well relate to beaten biscuits, a dense bread linked in local memory to the Eastern Shore of Maryland, but also produced in Virginia kitchens like that of the long-vanished Plantation Inn in Cape Charles.

Newly wed, Amine Kellam, born and raised on the Eastern Shore of Virginia, spoke of the challenge of making beaten biscuits for her husband, Polk, in the late 1930s. "I didn't like beaten biscuits," she begins. "Beaten biscuits are a Maryland dish," she says dismissively, "and Polk's family were all from Pocomoke, Maryland, and Polk was crazy about beaten biscuits."

Despite her best efforts and deep misgivings, Amine acceded to her husband's desires: "One day he said that he had a cousin named Mabelle Bull. She was the only one in the family that knew how to make beaten biscuits, and he had sent for her to come down and teach me, and I didn't even want to learn. But I had to get excited about it." The reluctance in her voice is palpable even after years of marriage and Polk's passing, "So Mabelle came. I didn't realize until later that she had to be bribed to come, because she liked to keep her recipes all by herself. Polk promised her a hindquarter of beef if she would teach me how to make beaten biscuits. We were raising beef cattle at the time, so she couldn't resist that."

Amine revisits the day. "She came and walked around the kitchen, and she said, 'You sit here.' And so, I had a lesson. She said, 'Now, you've got to beat them.' I said, 'What do you mean, beat them?'"

From her supervisory seat in the kitchen, Mabelle instructed, "Get a hammer or a sledgehammer or a rolling pin." Amine's neatly typed and well-worn recipe card specifies "a dull hammer or similar instrument" with the annotation, "I do 600 strokes." Mabelle directed, "'You've got to beat them until they blister.'" Sufficiently battered and hand rolled into little balls, the biscuits were baked "in [an] oven with fluctuating heat—first hot, then cooler, and so on. Like an old woodstove would cook." "Then," Amine concludes, "she turned me loose. That was how I learned to make them. The beating is very tedious and very hard!" Amine, haunted by memories of beaten biscuits, repeats, "It is a Maryland thing."

Not so for black duck and dumplings—that is an Eastern Shore of Virginia thing.

A CHEF'S RECIPE FOR HOME

PAN-SEARED (OR SMOKED) DUCK WITH
SWEET POTATO DUMPLINGS AND PRESERVED FIGS

Kevin Callaghan, Acme Food and Beverage, Carrboro, North Carolina

Kevin Callaghan takes the idea of Eastern Shore of Virginia black duck and dumplings as a starting point and reinvents the dish, turning it into something quite unique. What lingers, though, is the constellation of duck, dumplings, sweet potatoes, and figs.

Makes 4 servings

For brining the duck

    1 gallon cold water

    ½ cup kosher salt

    ¼ cup brown sugar

    2 bay leaves

    12 black peppercorns

    1 teaspoon dried thyme

    1 teaspoon red chili flakes

    4 duck breasts

For the dumplings

    1 cup White Lily self-rising flour

    1 tablespoon brown sugar

    ½ teaspoon kosher salt

    ½ teaspoon freshly grated nutmeg

    2 teaspoons minced fresh thyme

    ½ teaspoon ground black pepper

    1 cup cooked sweet potato purée

    2 large eggs

    2 tablespoons half-and-half, plus more as needed

    1 tablespoon bacon fat

For the preserved figs

    2 bottles inexpensive Madeira, divided

    2 pounds brown sugar

    ½ cup sherry vinegar

    4 bay leaves

    2 tablespoons whole black peppercorns

    3 tablespoons whole allspice

    ½ cup minced fresh ginger

4 sweet onions, thinly sliced

1 quart ripe brown turkey figs, quartered

Salt and freshly ground black pepper to taste

For cooking the duck

2 tablespoons butter or extra-virgin olive oil

For garnish

Freshly ground black pepper

Thyme leaves

To brine the duck

Mix together the brine ingredients in a large nonreactive bowl until the salt and sugar have dissolved. Place the duck breasts into the brine and allow to cure for 4 hours. Remove the duck from the brine and wipe off any brine residue and pat dry with paper towels. With a sharp knife, score the skin side in three places.

To make the dumplings

Combine the dry ingredients in a clean, wide bowl. In a separate bowl mix together the wet ingredients until well combined. Add the wet ingredients to the dry ingredients, mixing well. If the dumpling mixture seems a bit dry, add more half-and-half, 1 teaspoon at a time. Form the dough into gnocchi-size (1 × 2-inch) dumplings. Set aside.

To make the preserved figs

In a stainless-steel Dutch oven, combine the Madeira (reserving ¼ cup), brown sugar, vinegar, bay leaves, peppercorns, allspice, and ginger and bring to a simmer over medium heat until the volume is reduced by half. Strain the mixture through a sieve and put the cleaned liquid back into the Dutch oven. Bring to a simmer and add the onions. Cook over low heat until the liquid begins to thicken and the onions are translucent. Carefully add the figs and continue to simmer for 30–45 minutes, gently stirring occasionally, being careful not to beat up the figs. When the liquid has the consistency of syrup, remove it from the heat and season with salt and a liberal amount of pepper; set aside.

To cook the duck

Heat a skillet until quite hot. Place the butter or oil in the pan. When a small drop of water added to the pan sizzles, reduce the heat to medium. Add the dumplings to form a single layer, making sure not to crowd them. Shake the pan gently after about 30 seconds to make sure the dumplings aren't sticking. If any do stick, gently use tongs to dislodge them. Continue to cook until the dumplings are well browned. (At this point, they can be placed on a plate covered with a paper towel or put in an oven-proof pan and kept warm in the oven on a low temperature.)

Salt the skin of the duck breasts and place them in the skillet, skin side down, over low heat. *It is very important that the skillet is not too hot.* The goal is to render the fat from the duck skin without deeply cooking the meat. When the skin is brown and rendered, turn the breasts over and sear them quickly, no longer than 1 minute. Remove the breasts from the heat and let rest.

Bring the temperature of the skillet to medium. Pour the reserved Madeira into the pan to deglaze, using a wooden spatula to scrape up all the tasty bits. Add 1½ cups of the preserved figs and stir them into the fat with the wooden spatula. Reduce the heat and continue to cook for 1–2 minutes or until the liquid in pan becomes very thick. Keep warm for serving.

To serve

Using a very sharp knife, cut each duck breast into 5 slices. Place several warm dumplings into the middle of 4 plates. Fan the duck slices on one side of the dumplings, then spoon the hot fig mixture on top of the duck and dumplings. Top with pepper and a few fresh thyme leaves. Serve immediately.

Figs
Sweetness in a Southern Landscape

Among the saddest, most dispiriting photographs I have viewed is the snapshot of the ruins of Eunice Crumb Glaxner's garage following a fire ignited by an unattended batch of fig preserves. Vivid yellow caution tape cuts across the image as if drawn by a censor's hand. Collapsed roof timbers crush the car. Everywhere there is the debris of charred wood, melted plastic, scorched metal, shattered glass—and somewhere in the bitter ashes of disaster lies a lost batch of homemade fig preserves that had been intended for the annual bazaar hosted by the Trinity United Methodist Church in the former railroad and ferry town of Cape Charles on the Chesapeake Bay. Eunice Glaxner's nephew Ron suspects that the fire broke out when his aunt went into the main house and turned the burner under the figs up instead of down. The result was catastrophic. The number of jars of preserves consumed by the flames is unknown, but Ron estimates that the blaze immolated as much as twenty-two quarts of figs collected in big metal pans—that amounts to dozens of finished half-pint jars. Whatever may have been insured, it's a certain bet that those figs were not indemnified. Penned in a shaky hand on the back of the photo, Eunice Glaxner recorded, "In the awful fire we had [been] cookin figs for church." I feel the horror of her loss.

Ron Crumb and his sister Kay Crumb Downing recall their aunt Eunice's fig preserves with palpable affection. "My mom did it a little bit," Ron recollects, "but my aunt Eunice, she was the preserver of the family. That kitchen they had out in the garage is where they did all of this canning. And she did this right up until her early nineties." Through the height of the late summer fig season, Ron collected figs from the family trees: "You had all these figs. . . . My aunt Eunice, for about ten or fifteen years, during the middle of August when the figs were ripe, I would pick one to two large basins every other day." He continues, "Every two days I would take the figs to my aunt Eunice, and she would make two to three dozen pints that would be sold at several church bazaars, or she would give them away to family and friends at Christmastime." According to the running tally she kept in her recipe notes, Aunt Eunice's production of fig preserves was prodigious, numbering tens of dozens of jars each year. "The ones that my aunt used to do," Ron notes, "were a little more syrupy. The syrup content was kind of like maple syrup. It wasn't real thick." He adds, "They would do little half-pint jars, but mainly they were pints. And at the end, if you always had one or two pints that were just the syrup."

Ron and Kay share their aunt Eunice's detailed handwritten recipe for fig preserves:

FIG PRESERVES

7 lbs. Figs — little brown ones. Cut ends off. Scald hot water. Wash under hot water to clean them from dust, bugs, & the Birds.
Put 5 lb. Sugar
3 pts water
In large Kettle make syrup. Drain water off scalded figs. Put by hand full in syrup. Start to boil on high heat. Let cook 1 hour on high. Skin off the foam. Test 1 fig. some syrup will tell you all most done. I do cook mine 1 hr. 45 min. I have jars rings all ready to put Figs in Jars. Makes 7 pt. I do put wax to help seal them for a long time keeping and I have kept some 4 & 5 years still good.

Just to make sure the directions are clear, she emphasizes, "7 lbs. Figs, 5 lbs. sugar, 3 pints water."

Ron confesses, "I had some of the last ones she did. They last three to four years really good, and after that they start to get a little dark. I had a whole case of them I forgot I had. And I was doing something and found them and felt terrible." I wince at the memory of a time I waited too long to open a bottle of wine and lamented the vinegar it had become.

Figs encircle the Crumb family home on what local folks recognize as "Crumbs Hill" in the fishing village of Oyster. "Crumbs Hill," Ron remembered, "is where both my grandparents lived at one time. Kay and I grew up in a house our father purchased for $1,500.00 in 1945 the year I was born. The house was on Broadwater Street in Oyster. The locals called it 'The Block,' being it was the only block of houses in Oyster. The house is still there overlooking the Seaside landscape. It was a great little town to grow up in, full of large families and friends, all two-hundred-plus of us."

Ron's and Kay's recollections of figs from their Seaside childhood at the edge of the vast Atlantic marshes sweeping toward Cobb Island extend

Hooksie Walker, Bayford oyster house, Bayford, Virginia.

well beyond their aunt's beloved preserves. Kay begins, "We had a huge fig tree in the backyard. My cat and I used to lay up in that tree. I mean the branches were huge. Sir Puss and I used to sit up there all the time in that tree, until the wasps took over and then you had to vacate the premises." Ron steps in, "Now if you missed a couple days and the wasps, the bees got in there, then it was a war. But if you kept them picked so they weren't growing too ripe, you could work on the trees." Angry, jealous wasps are a terror, but few surprises are more startling than reaching into the shadows cast by a fig tree's massively spatulate and deeply lobed leaves and riling up a cluster of feasting June bugs rattling their wings, swarming with false ferocity.

The associations with figs and summer childhood are broadly shared. Oneida Wade Smith, in her nineties, remembered the ancient fig tree in a family cemetery near her home in the oystering village of Willis Wharf: "I'll tell you one thing. This is true, sounds like a fairytale, but this is true. It's a graveyard with the fig trees. Fanny would come across the field to play with me and I'd go back across to play with her. My grandmother, she'd get tired of us being around her, if we wore her to death, she'd say, 'You two go on out into the graveyard there and ask Miss White what she died for.' I said, 'Oh gosh.' She said, 'They'll say nothing at all.' I said, 'Mom, they won't be able to say anything.' She said, 'I told you they'd say nothing at all.'"

Following her mother's instructions, Oneida and Fanny went to the cemetery and addressed the grave under the fig tree. "Fanny and I'd go out into the graveyard." Oneida recalls their adventure, "I'd say, 'Miss White, what did you die for?' Fanny said, 'She's not talking.' I said, 'She's not going to talk either.' Well, we said it again, and still she didn't say anything because she was dead. We went back to the house, and I said, 'Mom, we asked Miss White what she died for, and she said nothing at all.' She said, 'I told you she'd say nothing at all.' I said, 'I don't understand you.' She said, 'You asked her what she died for, and she said nothing at all.' Oh, I said, 'Shoot.' She outwitted me." That graveyard and its sentinel fig endure.

Ron provides details on Crumb family figs. "We called them plum figs. My dad liked figs. I can't remember who gave him a cutting, and he planted four in the backyard. And only one of them made it. If all four of them had made it, we would have had to move out of the town because this one was huge. It just got big."

Enormous fig trees reaching the eves of a two-story house flourished in home gardens the length of the Eastern Shore from the early colonial period onward. Sometime during his sojourn in Virginia from 1712 to 1719, the English naturalist Mark Catesby visited the Eastern Shore. "*Accomack* is a narrow slip of Land in *Virginia*," wrote Catesby in his *Natural History*, "having the Sea on one side, and the Bay of *Chesapeck* on the other, here I saw Fig-trees, with Trunks of a large Size, and of many Years standing, without any Injury received by hard Weather. On the opposite Shore were only Fig-trees of a very Small size, occasioned by their being often killed to the Ground." A century later, a correspondent for the *Norfolk Herald*, describing the recreational delights of Cobb Island, reported, "There are also a large number of fig trees, bearing the largest and most delicious figs ever seen in this country—some of which have measured 11½ inches in circumference." Then there is my friend Pooh Johnston's Only Farm fig tree, which towers just outside his second-story bedroom window, enabling him to reach out sleepy-eyed for his breakfast while still in his pajamas. Pooh, who planted that tree nearly twenty-five years earlier, has always been a forward-thinking individual.

Confusion embarrasses the fig. In Genesis the fig feeds Adam and Eve in their innocence and clothes them with its leaves in the awakening of their self-knowledge—the first recorded instance of "too little, too late." Commentaries aligning the new United States with an Edenic state defined by plenty and tranquillity cited 1 Kings 4:25: "And Judah and Israel dwelt safely, every man under his vine and under his fig tree, from Dan even to Beersheba, all the days of Solomon." Nineteenth-century African Americans regularly drew on the same passage as the rhetorical measure of freedom and equality, often in contexts of new church building from Louisiana to Liberia: "I can say for the first time since our existence as a church that we assembled in our own church and held quarterly conference; and partook of the Lord's Supper on the Sabbath, under our own [vine and] fig tree." Christ in Mark curses the fig into barrenness, a signal action given the fecundity of the fig in the time and region. Gustav Eisen, the nineteenth-century authority on figs, traces the fruit's origins to Arabia and the earliest perfection of its cultivation to the valleys of the Tigris and Euphrates in present-day Iraq. The fig entered the Mediterranean world with the ancient Greeks and over the millennia found its place as commodity, staple, and luxury around the world.

Native to Asia, the fig (*Ficus carica*) came to the Americas in 1520, imported by the Spaniards to Hispaniola, five years before the plant made its way to England from Italy. Captain John Smith noted its existence in Virginia by 1621, the cultivar having been transplanted from Bermuda. Jane Pierce of Jamestown was the fig's first Anglo-American devotee, harvesting one hundred bushels in 1629, an amount that suggests the presence of a sizable orchard and preservation endeavor. By the early eighteenth century the cultivar had run feral. John Lawson's 1709 account describes an import gone native in the Carolinas:

> Of figs we have two sorts: One is the low Bush-Fig, which bears a large Fruit. If Winter happens to have much Frost, the tops thereof die, and in the Spring sprout again, and bear two or three good Crops.
>
> The Tree-Fig is a lesser Fig, though very sweet. The Tree grows to a large Body and Shade, and generally brings a good Burden; especially, if in light [sandy] Land. This Tree thrives no where better, than on the Sand-Banks by the Sea.

Almost two centuries later, an unknown photographer captured the portrait of a Hog Island, Virginia, family with a fig tree of staggering proportions overshadowing an outbuilding in the background. Visitors to the Virginia barrier islands frequently remarked on the local figs as a delicacy. "Some 300 people inhabit this island and throughout the year, and excepting those employed in the lighthouse and life-saving service, gain a livelihood from harvesting sea food," a guest wrote in 1911, continuing, "The unique features of the place are luxuriant fig trees, which bear abundantly season after season, the great number of ever present musical mockingbirds and also the primitive customs of some of the natives." Newly reelected president in 1892, Grover Cleveland enjoyed island figs as the conclusion to a hunters' banquet: "The big kitchen attached to the club was turned over to the best island cooks. There were oysters from the shores of the island, terrapin, turkey, roast beef and wild fowl of every variety, prepared in every culinary style. At dessert some preserved figs, raised on the island and the club's special pride, were served."

The *Cyclopedia of American Horticulture* describes the fig as "a warm-temperate fruit" that, with protection from cold weather, can be grown in most parts of the United States. The fruit, the *Cyclopedia* continues, "is a hollow pear-shaped receptacle with minute seeds (botanically fruits) on the inside." In essence, what is taken as the fruit of the fig is its flower, a blossom that grows inside out and is pollinated by a specialized wasp that enters through the tiny opening at the base of the "fruit." Like the fig, the wasp is an exotic import, and the fertilization of figs for seed in the United States is historically quite limited. Thus, the propagation of the fig from its earliest introduction into the Americas has relied on various strategies for rooting branches either clipped from the tree or bent to the ground and covered. In many areas of the South, the fig went native to the extent that commentators on the countryside saw it as a natural and incidental element in the domestic landscape. Left in the wild, the fig sends out runners that can be cut for new plants. Significantly, figs with documented nineteenth-century and earlier histories are essentially clones of even older root stock—arguably making it possible to locate and continue an early American cultivar with some measure of genetic integrity.

The resilience of the fig in warmer environments, its ease of propagation, and its productivity inspired one southern author to group it in an 1857 gazetteer of "Fruits That Never Fail!": "This delicious and healthy fruit—of which we have many varieties—grows almost spontaneously everywhere," adding the caveat that "fig trees are not entirely hardy here—they need a slight protection of pine tops or similar shelter, while young, succulent and tender—severe winters often nip them quite sharply, but their recuperative power is astonishing." Gardeners of all persuasions cultivated a variety of figs. Favored strains in the southeastern United States included Black Genoa, Black Ischia, Brown Turkey, Brunswick, Green Ischia, Celestial, Lemon, Havana, Large Blue, Alicante, and White Marseilles. Many of the varieties listed for sale by nineteenth-century nurseries survive in southern gardens. The Celestial, Lemon, Brown Turkey, and other figs have been documented on the Eastern Shore of Virginia and Maryland, where they sport local names—sugar figs, Crisfield white, Hog Island, and Westerhouse green. Each variety, black and green, possesses a distinctive appearance, ripening schedule, and flavor profile. Intensely sweet and favored for preserves, sugar figs (a variety of Celestial) appear in early August. Westerhouse green figs mature in late September and offer a complex flavor at once sweet and floral. Hog Island figs, with their rich and slightly musty flavor, are well suited for preserves and are harvested in late August and early September.

Fig culture in the American South offers a conflicted narrative, one that blurs lines between the exotic and the everyday, the fragile and the hardy, slavery and freedom. Figs all too often anchor sentimental childhood recollections of antebellum plantation life in the South. Samuel Williams, writing under the penname Samuel Aleckson, grew up under slavery in the South Carolina Lowcountry. His memoir of his life as a slave evokes the sweetness of the fig. Aleckson reminisced:

> There were fruit trees in our garden; peaches, apricots, pomegranate and figs. We loved the figs most, of which there were several varieties. Our especial pride was the large black fig tree. There were six of us, three girls and three boys. Four of us were white and two were Negroes. . . . Every morning in season would find us at our favorite fig tree. The boys would climb into its branches while the girls stood below with extended aprons to catch the fruit as we dropped them.

Tom Gallivan with Hog Island figs, Hog Island, Virginia.

Some times there came a voice from above in complaining tones— "Now Jennie! I see you eating." "Oh," would be the reply. "That one was all mashed up." "All right, now don't eat till we come down." Then when we descended we took large green fig-leaves, placed them in a basket, laid the most perfect fruit thereon, and one of us would run to the house with it. . . . "Don't eat till I come back." "We won't." . . . When the messenger returned we went to our favorite nook in the garden and after dispatching about a dozen figs apiece we rushed to our breakfast with appetites as unappeased as if we had fasted for a week.

Concealed within Aleckson's nostalgic constructions of the fig and summer idylls is a continuing link between the Garden and the Fall, slavery and freedom.

The enslaved people of Monticello likely found little of Edenic solace in

Thomas Jefferson's offhand observation that saw the ripening of the fig crop as an occasion for light labor. Writing from France in 1787, Jefferson recorded his observations on a tour through the south of France, "The fig and the mulberry are so well known in America, that nothing be said of them. Their culture too is by women and children, and therefore earnestly to be desired in countries where there are slaves. In these, the women and children are often employed in labours disproportioned to their sex and age. By presenting to their master objects of culture, easier and beneficial, all temptations to misemploy them would be removed, and this lot of the tender part of our species much softened."

The reality of picking and processing figs on other southern plantations did not accord with Jefferson's sensibilities. James Roberts, born into slavery on the Eastern Shore of Virginia and sold south to a southern Louisiana plantation, described in his 1858 memoir the labors of harvesting and pressing figs, "First a layer of sugar, then a layer of figs. The figs are gathered off the bush when ripe, and the box is filled up as described. Then the box is put under the hand-press, and the press is screwed down upon them. What the women and children gather in the day, the men pack at night. In the morning, at the blowing of the horn, the women and children go out again to the wood; then at night, after a heavy day's work, the men must pack all they have gathered; and that is the rule while the figs last, which is from the first of August to the first of September." Unlike Jefferson's vision of gender-appropriate labor, Roberts's account placed fig culture in a context of heavy seasonal labor.

The art of drying figs invited periodic submissions to nineteenth-century American agricultural papers. Earlier contributions tend to emphasize the political and economic advantages discovered in the cultivation and preservation of a homegrown exotic. A correspondent to the *Southern Cultivator* in 1850 succinctly addressed core themes linked to fig culture including its ever-increasing presence in the gardens of poorer families, its underutilized abundance, and its political connotations: "Considering how cheaply figs may be grown, to any desirable extent, in the Southern States, and how many poor families there are who might cure and put them up for market, it does seem wrong that this country should pay from one to two millions of dollars a year to foreigners for Smyrna and other Mediterranean figs." Thirty years later the same lament reappeared in the same paper, "Among the many varieties of fruits adapted to our Southern zone, the fig has not received all the attention it deserves, viewing it for commercial purposes. True, few gardens throughout the country are without a fig tree, but beyond supplying the table with the fruit in a fresh state, no use is made of it. No attempt seems to have been made to grow it on a large scale, for the purpose of drying the fruit and bringing it in competition with the imported article." The response to these declarations was modest at best. Occasional correspondents submitted various approaches to drying figs for market, but in the end the southern fig thrives as a dooryard staple for seasonal family tables, yet to achieve the status of a valued market commodity.

Phyllis Walker of Bayford speaks of women who dried figs in the town of Cape Charles. "I told you about the lady," she whispers in my ear, "who many, many years ago used to dry them on the roof of her sun porch. It was a tin roof, and she'd put them on this big pan. She'd cover them up so the birds couldn't get to them and dry them with the sun. My mother and daddy's neighbor, she used to do the same thing. Put them out in the sun and dry them." Phyllis, evoking visions of rampaging birds from a Hitchcock movie, repeats her warning, "You have to put something over them so the birds don't eat them up and take them away." Celebrating her ninety-second birthday that evening, she appends, "That was an old, old thing from down the road. These old people down the road—these people I'm talking about lived in Cape Charles." Then she speculates, "I guess old people up the road did it, too." Time and geography map terroir.

During the Civil War years, southerners desperate for increasingly scarce commodities as diverse as food preservatives and ink turned their attention to the possibilities offered by the fig. "The juice of the skin of our *blue fig* is abundant," noted Confederate surgeon Francis Porcher in 1863, "and of a deep, brilliant red color; a half-page written with it a few days since had the appearance of having been done with red ink. . . . I have seen blue cakes resembling indigo, intended for dyeing, and marked fig blue—probably extracted from the skins of the fig." Porcher also recommended the fig stems for use as pipe stems and the fig itself for molasses. "Figs," he added, "are excellent pabulum for vinegar" and advised that "vinegar should be constantly replenished with over-ripened figs." A correspondent to the *Southern Cultivator* in the same year suggested fig pickles as a military ration: "Figs, properly pickled, are generally preferred even to cucumbers by those who have tried them; and large quantities should be put up for army use." The principal advantage of fig pickles lay in their medicinal qualities. "The sharp acid of this pickle renders it a very grateful addition to the table, in spring when the bilious state of the human system demands vegetable acids, and early fruits are still unripe." In the decades following the Civil War, the *Southern Cultivator* continued to note the medical efficacy of the fig, generally in syrup, beneficially acting "on the kidneys, liver and bowels, effectually cleansing the system, dispelling colds and headaches and curing habitual constipation."

Ron and Kay Crumb share a story about the efficacy of figs as a digestive. Ron begins, "I had an uncle Dick. He was a common laborer, one of the nicest guys you ever met." Kay adds, "a big old teddy bear." Ron goes on, "He loved them. I was coming down towards the end of the pickings and my aunt had had enough and I happened to run into him down at the dock and I asked him, 'Uncle Dick, do you like figs?' 'Oh my Lord, yes.' So I picked a big bowl that afternoon and took them to him. About three or four days later, I saw his wife, Eleanor. I said, 'Aunt Eleanor, did Uncle Dick eat all those figs?' She looked at me and laughed, 'Eat them? He went out on the porch with a half a gallon of vanilla ice cream.' She said he ate that whole bowl and a half gallon of ice cream. He didn't have many teeth, and he ate that whole bowl! Bet he was pretty regular for the next few days."

Brother and sister break into laughter, "I remember giving it to him. And he smiled, all you saw was gums."

In the later decades of the 1800s, the preservation of figs turned increasingly toward methods of putting up the fruit. "Putting up" recipes generally fell into one of two categories: preserving figs in a spiced sugar syrup or, less common, pickling. Although directions for pickled figs appeared in nineteenth-century publications, it was the less favored approach. An 1855 recipe for pickled figs published in the *Southern Cultivator* begins, "We do not know of a superior pickle or relish, nor one which will 'keep' with so little trouble," and conveys something of the sense of their tartness and crisp texture: "Select figs of a fair size and good quality—the common large white variety is excellent. When they are just swelling to ripen, but not soft, pick them without bruising, and let them stand in salt and water for two or three days. Then take them from this pickle, put them in a glass or earthenware jar, (not glazed) and pour over so as to entirely cover them, scalding hot vinegar, sweetened with good brown sugar, at the rate of one pound to the gallon, and highly flavored with mace gloves [cloves?], pepper and allspice. (The sugar and spices should be put into the vinegar before it is set over the fire to heat.)" The author enthuses, "Let every good Southern housewife try it." I did. They were tasty in unexpected ways.

The overwhelming abundance of figs that arrive in late summer demands invention. Eastern Shore cooks collected instructions for sweet pickled figs, fig syrup, fig jam, candied figs, and more. Amine Kellam, who maintained a wonderfully large fig tree at her home, preserved and pickled figs using her mother's recipes transcribed onto ruled three-by-five-inch index cards:

SPICED FIGS
6 qts. figs
1 cup water
1 gallon boiling water
Let stand for five minutes. Drain and Rinse.

SYRUP
5 lbs. sugar
3 pints vinegar
3 tablespoons cinnamon
3 tablespoons cloves
Boil figs in syrup for ten minutes.

And:

FIG PRESERVES

1 teasp. lemon juice

1 cup sugar

⅓ cup water

2 cups figs

Cook syrup until sugar is melted. Add figs. Remove when tender. Boil syrup longer until thick. Pour over figs. Seal.

Carrie Polk Kellam, Amine's mother-in-law, recorded multiple fig recipes in a black-bound composition homemade cookbook most likely begun in the early 1930s. A frayed and yellowed insert offers directions for Fig Pudding:

Take 1 cup milk

1 cup molasses

1 cup suet chopped fine

3 cups flour

2 eggs

1 teaspoon cinnamon

1 teaspoon soda

1 heaping tablespoon brown sugar

1 lb. figs chopped fine

Mix together molasses, figs, sugar, spice and suet. Beat eggs nice and light. Dissolve soda in milk. Then beat milk into eggs, adding and beating in good the flour. Beat two mixtures together. Boil 5 hours.

Then there were Sweet Pickled Figs:

5 lbs. of ripe figs—washed and pricked with darning needle. Drop into boiling salt water made by using 2 tablespoons of salt to 1 quart of water. Simmer 3 to 5 minutes. Have a syrup hot and drop the well drained fig into the syrup. An open metal spoon should be used as it drains all salt water from the fruit.

In a second recipe, Carrie Kellam adds cinnamon, cloves, and allspice to the syrup. And she includes Candied Figs, a recipe that calls for two syrups.

Select ripe firm figs. Wash and drain. Have two syrups ready and boiling.

1st syrup:

4 cups sugar

2 cups water

3 tablespoons Karo

2nd syrup:

6 cups sugar

2 cups water

6 tablespoons Karo

Drop the figs into the first syrup and simmer until tender, then with an open spoon drain and drop into the second syrup. Simmer until clear. Allow the figs to stand in the syrup overnight or several days is better. Remove from the syrup, drain well and dry on platters.

Concocted in the early 1900s, Karo corn syrup replaced sugar as both sweetener and preservative—as if figs weren't sweet enough.

As an ingredient, figs appeared in nineteenth-century desserts, for instance fig cake. Bessie Gunter included instructions for two variations on fig cake along with a recipe for an elaborate Fig Ribbon Cake in her Eastern Shore collection. Ribbon cakes originated, contemporary to and not unlike crazy quilts, as a Victorian display of domestic virtuosity and extravagance. An early layer-cake variation, cousin to the stack cakes of the Chesapeake Bay and Outer Banks regions, the ribbon cake was a fancy confection composed of three or more layers of contrasting colors like gold and white or red and white. An icing or a fruit preserve separated each layer, and the completed cake was frosted. Gunter's recipe uses fresh figs in her Eastern Shore variant:

> *White Part.* 2 cupfuls sugar; ⅔ cupful butter, creamed together. Add ⅔ cupful milk; 3 cupfuls flour, alternately; 2 teaspoonfuls of baking powder, and then the whites of eight eggs (beaten lightly). Bake in two layers.
>
> *Gold Part.* Beat a little more than half a cupful of butter and a cupful of sugar to a cream. Add the yolks of seven eggs and one whole egg (well beaten), half cupful of milk and one and one-half cupfuls of flour (mixed with one teaspoonful of baking powder). Season strongly with cinnamon and allspice. Put half of this gold part into a pan, lay on it halved figs closely, previously dusted with a little flour, then put on it the rest of the gold cake and bake.
>
> Put the gold cake between the white cakes using frosting between them, and cover with frosting.

Chef Amy Brandt, who cooks in her catering kitchen near Cape Charles, resurrected this recipe for a dinner party late one summer evening to the delight of all. The texture of the soft pastry combined with the flavors of figs harvested from trees with century-old histories amazed the assembled company. Some forsook all pride and restraint and pressed for seconds.

Still, figs preserved in sugar syrup remain the enduring favorite in southern larders. Bessie Gunter's *Housekeeper's Companion*, compiled from recipes contributed by Eastern Shore of Virginia friends and their families, contains a representative example for preserves: "Scald the figs and let stand till cold. Make a syrup of one pound of sugar, a half pint of water to each pound of figs. Let the syrup come to a boil, then drop in the figs and cook slowly until done. This recipe is for little brown figs." The quality of fig preserves in syrup varies considerably despite the fact that the basic recipe is nearly universal. On the Eastern Shore of Virginia, where many families put up fig preserves at summer's end, home cooks use their own variations on the standard nineteenth-century combination of boiling sugar syrup, spices, and figs. Violet Trower of Exmore does not peel her figs and cooks them slowly until the syrup is a deep caramel brown. Phyllis Walker of Bayford peels her figs, and her syrup is considerably lighter in color and viscosity. Fig syrup, Ron Crumb observes, did not go to waste: "At the end, you always had one or two pints that were just the syrup. And, it was two or three folks like John Harlow's wife, Mary [friends of our family], she loved the syrup. She didn't like the figs, but she loved the syrup. Give her one of those at Christmastime and she thought she was in heaven.

Hooksie Walker, former proprietor of the old oyster house in Bayford, and his wife, Phyllis, locally celebrated for her homemade rum cake, walk step by step through the process of making fig preserves. Phyllis begins, "Hooksie, what is it, seven pounds of figs and five pounds of sugar? That's what he says. And some lemon. We peel our figs. To me, that makes a fig so good. He peels them." "I can't peel them," she explains, "because it breaks my hands out, but I could peel them if I put gloves on. But he does that." Theirs is clearly a collaborative recipe: "We take and we measure and we weigh, like he just said, seven pounds of figs to five pounds of sugar. You cut up a lemon, take the seeds out. Don't put a whole lemon in there, maybe a half one. Just cut it up into little pieces. You put it on and if they're too dry, you put one or two drops of water in there." In the pot and on the stove, "You put them on and as soon as they come to a rolling boil, you start timing them, and you don't let it go real high on your stove. Maybe medium high. You have to skim off this white stuff that comes off the top. You let them boil about twenty minutes and that's it. Then you let them calm down, but be sure you skim off all the white foam. And when they cool, you just put them in the jar and either freeze them or put wax on them and put them in sterile jars and put them on the pantry shelf." Hooksie adds, "Generally it has a lot of liquid leftover, and some people like just the liquid." "You save the juice," Hooksie appends, "and let it boil down until it gets sort of thick. All I want is the fig, but if you cook it down enough, it's good. I like it on my pancakes." Hooksie looks out the window in the direction of a small copse of fig trees near the house he has lived in since he was born, "Those old fig trees we have, I don't know how old they are. Somebody gave my father some cuttings from a tree. I think you just cut it and root it and that's where these trees come from." He concludes, a note of wistfulness in his words, "I don't know how old they are. My mother used to put up a lot of fig preserves. We don't put them up like we used to. I don't know why." Making preserves is a lot of work.

Marilyn Sharp, working their Exmore produce stand, offers additional insight. "I used to do fig preserves," Marilyn says. "Take them and cook that up and then cook it down." She details her process with an economy of words, "I take and peel my figs, put them in a saucepan, add a little sugar to them and cook them down until they thicken up. Then I take them out and jar them up. Put my jars in the hot water and boil them for a while until the lids seal on them and put them up and then I've got fig preserves." The reward for labors, she concludes, "I cook me some hot biscuits—some hot sweet potato biscuits or regular biscuits—and put that fig on there. Let me tell you, it's some kind of good!"

Local cooks also put up fig jam, a technique that requires chopping or mashing the fruit. Emory D. Ross, a home cook in the Bayside town of Onancock, memorialized two preparations in her 1960s recipe collection:

8 c figs—chopped
6 c sugar
2 whole lemons—sliced *thin*
Bring to a boil & continue to stir occasionally while boiling until proper consistency. May add ½ c ginger chopped.

Then she recorded a "variation":

4 c. figs
3 c. sugar + ⅓–½ ginger chopped
1 lemon sliced thin
1 pkg. pectin (MKP)
Mix all together. Bring to a boil. Stir occasionally & continue boiling & stirring til ready to seal.

To this recipe, she appended the annotation, "Excellent!"

The Ribbon Fig Cake originated in the parlor cuisine of Victorian America, but it also speaks to a continuing culinary engagement with the everyday landscape. When Gunter published the *Housekeeper's Companion* in 1889, the fig was a common fixture in the kitchen yards of rich and poor, black and white. Its summer bounty provided pleasure for all. Fig preserves, though, were the staple. Packed in jars, they occupied a special place in family pantries. As Ron Crumb remembers, watermen included them in their provisions when they worked the shellfish and fishing grounds in Hog Island and South Bays, "Everybody around here used to preserve stuff to take out to the watch houses."

Describing her mother's fig preserves translated from Veracruz, Mexico, to the Eastern Shore, Laura Gonzalez speaks to newly arrived culinary traditions: "She makes a preserve, but she makes them whole and they are sweet." Laura notes, "She has her own version of that, too. She makes them really good." "I used to have a fig tree at my house, and we were getting a lot of figs," Laura confesses. "I didn't know how to cook them. We will eat them raw because we didn't know." Laura told her mother about the figs. "Bring them to me," she said. Laura marvels, "She makes a preserve, but they were whole figs. I mean they were really good. . . . It's different flavor. I bought fig preserve from the local vendors and it's a different flavor."

Her mother, Irma Ramirez, adds, "I'm going to make them the way this man would make pumpkins, but I do it with figs. I wash them. . . . And I put a little bit of lime. It's just a little bit, in the water. It's just like when you make it with pumpkins but you switch it with figs. You prick little holes all over the fig and drop it in the water with lime. After that you dry it and put it in the syrup, and it will stay whole, it doesn't fall apart. . . . Like ten minutes . . . they are rinsed again." Laura picks up the thread, "She rinsed them again and let them dry and then she cooks the sugar." Irma clarifies, "*Piloncillo* and cinnamon." Laura glosses, "It's like the sugar cane, they sell that at the Mexican store. It's like a block of sugar cane, or *piloncillo*, that's how she called it. . . . She makes the sugar with that, and then once the figs are dried, she drops them in the sugar and let them cook. And they are like truly cooked and they are sweet but they are kind of hard. They don't melt as easily." Irma adds, "These are to eat like in three or four days." "I imagine," she says, "that the process is the same like when you preserve tomatoes and you get them hot and put them in a jar to preserve them, I imagine you could do the same with the figs." Sounds like a plan.

Violet Trower grew up in the African American community without access to figs, discovering them later in life. Sitting on the porch of Ellen Rue's house in Belle Haven where she works as a caregiver, Violet explains, "Didn't have access to them." "Then when I met her," she glances to the sitting room window, "all these figs! I said, 'What in the world!' So, I said, 'Ms. Rue, this is the thing, I'm going to start making fig preserves, and when your friends come by to visit you and see how you're doing on holidays and stuff, this is what we're going to do. We're going to put out figs in a jar. We're going to label them, and when they come, before they go out the door we'll always give them fig preserves to carry home with them.' Every year people see me, they say, 'Violet, you doing fig preserves this year?'" Violet laughs, "Yep!"

Violet recites the story of Ellen Rue's niece, displaced by Hurricane Katrina, "She's coming from New Orleans, this month, September. She loves figs. Oh, my goodness! She always ends up, she says, 'I can't get nothing in my suitcase, but I'm going to get these figs in my suitcase to take back.' She was with the Katrina, when they were refugees, and, I guess she stayed about a month and they told her they could come back. And she said, 'Violet, I got my fig preserves in my suitcase.' I told her when she comes in September, I'll make sure I have some. But I don't like to start on mine till it starts getting cool." Violet describes the process: "I just figured it out on my own. Let them cook slow. Make sure they don't burn. Keep stirring them and keep watching them. You don't have to have a recipe for stuff like that. You just put things together, what you think it's going to need. That's how I did it. But I never used a recipe for nothing I cook." Violet's fig preserves remember a healing sweetness of a southern countryside. Resurrecting a taste of sun and warmth from a bygone season, her fig preserves erase the somber chill of winter, anticipating all the summers yet to come.

A CHEF'S RECIPE FOR HOME

SURRYANO HAM–WRAPPED HOG ISLAND FIGS

Walter Bundy, Shagbark, Richmond, Virginia

Walter Bundy notes: "Hog Island figs are famed for their concentrated sweetness, complex flavor profile, and their historical significance to agricultural practices on the Eastern Shore of Virginia. To bring the simplicity of the fig to the forefront of this dish, the Hog Island figs are simply stuffed with a local cheese and wrapped with country ham. This dish takes an already amazing Hog Island fig and brings it to another level."

Makes 8 figs

4 ounces Grade A maple syrup (preferably from Highland County, Virginia)

1 ounce aged sherry vinegar

2 tablespoons European-style butter, cubed and softened

8 Hog Island figs, perfectly ripe and soft to the touch (Black Mission figs also work)

2 ounces Meadow Creek Grayson cheese or any firm and great melting cheese (such as smoked Gouda, a blue, or even a semifirm brie), cut into 8 cubes

4 thin slices Edwards Surryano ham (prosciutto-style ham also works great; smoked prosciutto is even better)

2 slices Sally Lunn bread or 2 slices buttery brioche

2 tablespoons melted butter

Preheat a convection oven to 375°F. (Note: If you don't have a convection oven, the figs can be broiled.)

Warm the maple syrup and vinegar in a small saucepan over medium heat until it reaches a gentle boil. Remove from the heat and slowly stir in the butter, one piece at a time. Store this mixture in a warm place until the figs come out of the oven.

Lay a fig on its side and cut it lengthwise starting just below the stem and slicing all the way through the body of the fig, keeping the fig attached firmly to the stem, and open the fig like a book. Repeat with the remaining figs.

Using a melon baller or small spoon, remove just enough of the inside of the fig to create space for the cheese. Place a cheese cube inside each fig and close up the fig. Repeat with the remaining figs.

Spread out the slices of the ham on a cutting board and cut each slice in half. Gently wrap each fig with a slice of ham and squeeze with gentle pressure to ensure the fig will not come unwrapped.

Place the figs on a baking tray, stem-side up, and bake until the ham is slightly crispy, the cheese has slightly melted, and the fig has softened just a touch, 5–7 minutes. Or broil on high until golden and the cheese has melted.

While the figs are baking or broiling, cut the bread into quarters. Drizzle the bread squares with the butter and toast them in a pan over medium heat until golden brown on both sides.

To serve: Place the bread pieces on a plate, rest a warm fig on top of each, and pour a tablespoon of the reserved glaze over top of each fig. Eat immediately or the magic will be lost!

Busted Sooks, Rank Peelers, and White-Belly Jimmies
Mudlarking Words for Crabs

It's an early summer afternoon at Bayford. A breeze kicks up, the air is clear and fresh, the sunlight on bright white boat hulls and shimmering water is blinding. Crabbers tie up at Bayford wharf in succession. Each boat with its two-man crew offloads bushels of Chesapeake Bay blue crabs. Andrew Bunce is there tabulating and fulminating about catch, quality, and people who can't count. In the shadow of a seafood truck, he's created an office furnished with a bushel basket stuffed with blue crabs just caught and landed. The crabs wriggle and scratch in their packed confinement as Andrew fields and confirms orders on his cell phone and writes down the catch counts hailed from the wharf. The sound of motors shutting off and voices drifts into the oyster house. H. M. Arnold, the oyster house proprietor, grabs a bushel basket and heads out to the dock. H. M. is there for the peelers that he will shed into soft-shell crabs. "Docking fee," Andrew smiles.

Folks come and go exchanging greetings, one-liners, and rough good humor. Drivers load their refrigerated trucks, consolidate the contents of bushel baskets, and organize their cargo by the crabs' sex, size, and condition: number ones, number twos, number threes. . . . Listening to the back and forth, there is, I realize, a code for crabs and a lot of words to complicate it.

Walter Brunk works with his father, Russell, unloading their boat.

"So, what's the count?" Walter shouts to Andrew.

Andrew calls back, "I got you for three and two-thirds ones."

Russell affirms, "Yep."

Andrew adds to the inventory, "Two and two-thirds twos."

Russell, "Yep."

Andrew Bunce tallying crabs, Bayford, Virginia.

"Two threes. Two and a third fours," Andrew hollers. "And one busted."

Russell confirms, "Yep. Sounds good to me." He turns to his son, "What've you got? Three threes, Walt?"

Walter replies, "Two threes."

Russell asks, "What's this here?"

"Busted sooks," Walter responds.

Andrew confirms, "You got two threes, two and two-thirds twos." Andrew cautions, "They got to be hard and five and a half."

Walter stakes his reputation, "I stand by them today, because I touched them."

I ask about fours and busted sooks. "White crabs," Russell enlightens me, "are fours and busted sooks are fives." Then he says, "They've got a different system here." I take his word for it. Russell senses my confusion and helpfully explains, "Number ones are five and a half and on up and a hard crab. A good full-meat crab. The twos are five inches and a good hard crab. The threes are clean sooks, shedded sooks. Fours are just white-belly jimmies — shedded ones. Ones that are hollow, ain't got much meat in them, are fours." He illustrates, "Like these. See, they're just shedded, they're not real hard. They're still a little soft under there. There's not much meat in them." A five, he clarifies, "that's a busted sook." Referring to the watermen of Tangier Island further up the bay, he elaborates, "Tangiermen call them lemons because they've got that yellow sponge on them. Cushions. That's a busted sook, too. That's what Tangiermen call them — cushions and lemons." The number system, he notes, "They've always had that for going up the road and selling them. That's what they go by." A glossary, I speculate, could be useful. Russell agrees, "So people understand what the hell the lingo is. They've probably got a whole other language up there in Maryland."

William W. Warner's masterful and poetic book of 1976, *Beautiful Swimmers*, chronicled the crab industry, concentrating on the Crisfield area and its environs on the Eastern Shore of Maryland. He provided sidebars to the crabbing industry in Virginia with a particular emphasis on winter crab dredging, when boats would work the bottom for dormant female crabs slumbering until the arrival of the springtime mating season. Andrew Bunce remembers crab dredging without pleasure: "I was crab dredging, which used to be our winter fishery. I ain't the only one this has happened to. You pull these big steel dredges on the bottom that dig the crabs out when they're hibernating for the winter and the hydraulic hoses broke. My hand was caught in the dredge and I went straight down to the bottom with the dredges. It wasn't fun! It was winter! It was January! We were working in a fleet of probably sixty or seventy boats. Some people rode right by me because they didn't want to miss a lick on the crabs." He laughs grittily.

"Of course," Andrew continues the tale of his journey to the bottom of the bay, "the boat looked like it was about a mile away, although it was probably only fifty yards. I guess I was panicking. The guy I was working with, he picked up one arm and threw me right over the top of the dredge into the bottom of the boat. I think he was more scared than I was! Still had my boots on. Some people drowned with that happening." He looks out over the creek on this warm afternoon, "Hell, that was about one of the commonest jobs you could mate on was crab dredging. You were working grass. You were out in the cold. It's just nonstop work. It's a labor-intensive job. They've cut it out, trying to make the crabs come back. I don't care if they bring it back or not. You won't see me doing it!" Our conversation stutters and breaks on a rising breeze. Later I tell the tale to Steve Bunce, Andrew's older brother, and he shakes his head, "He's hard. You can't kill that son of a bitch!"

The trade in blue crabs remains an important part of the Eastern Shore economy, and it traces its origins back to the arrival of the railroad and advances in food processing and preservation in the late 1800s. A correspondent to the Accomac newspaper the *Peninsula Enterprise* enthused in 1888 about "the possibilities of the crab industry and the source of revenue it opens up to many of our people at a season of the year when they are comparatively idle." Offering proof, the editor quoted an Onancock businessman, "'This is our second year in the crab business at this point, and on last Monday and Tuesday we bought about 13,000 crabs and on those days shipped to New York 860 dozen soft crabs. . . . The wages of the 'crabbers' amount to from $1 to $6 a day." A subsequent contributor to the *Peninsula Enterprise* wrote in 1896, sharing the particulars of another firm, that "has engaged quite extensively in the soft crab trade, and also utilizes thousand[s] of hard crabs. He has the hard crabs steamed and the meat picked out, which he ships to market in gallon tin cans. He has employed in his crab factory at Franklin City from 15 to 25 women and children." Little remains of Franklin City today, and crab-picking operations on the Eastern Shore of Virginia are a dwindling enterprise.

There is much to be learned from words for crabs and how vocabulary expresses the taste of place at a point where natural history, commercial enterprise, and community life come together. Words for crabs break down into overlapping categories. First, there is the Latin (*Callinectes sapidus*), which translates as beautiful swimmer with the afterthought of savory appended. There are words that describe the crab through the arc of its life cycle. There is an abundance of words, some overlapping, that place the crab in its market and kitchen histories. Kenny Marshall, retired waterman and decoy carver, cuts to the essence of the labor those many words for crabs perform. "There is no such a thing as a crab," Kenny Marshall announces. "My dad," he says, "used to get on me if I said, 'I sent my ball into that tree.' He'd say it landed over by that maple tree or that black walnut tree or that cherry tree. It's not just a tree! Call it what it is. Same thing as with a hammer. There's no such thing as a hammer. It's a claw hammer, a ballpeen hammer, a carpenter's hammer, a rip hammer." Kenny is laughing, "You don't just have a crab!" Point taken. Precision seasons the language of terroir.

Writing on the crab industry in Maryland for *Field and Stream* in 1905, Winthrop Roberts provides some basic terminology that serves as a starting point:

> There are six stages of a crab's life, commonly classified as follows: First the "hard crab," or one [in] its natural condition; second, a "snot," or one that has just entered the shedding stage; third, a "peeler," when the old shell has begun to break; fourth, a "buster," when the new shell can be seen; fifth, the "soft crab"; sixth, a "paper-shell," or "buckram," when the new shell is beginning to harden. During hot weather it takes from two to three days for a "snot" to become a "peeler." One tide will often change a "peeler" to a "buster," and another from a "buster" to a soft crab. A few hours after shedding the crab has reached the "paper shell" stage, and within three days the hardening process is completed.

I grasp the process, but the term "snot" is news to me. I need help and turn to H. M. Arnold.

H. M. tutors me on the Eastern Shore of Virginia crab lexicon. Cleaning spot in the cool interior of the oyster house after a summer dawn of gill-netting on Nassawadox Creek, we listen to radio news reports of the rarity of a tornado that hammered the shoreline just to our south a week earlier. H. M. lays out the crab basics that others will embroider in conversations to come. He begins, "You got the he-crab, the he-peeler, then you got the jimmy. Number one jimmies are five and a half up. Then number twos, they're five to five and a half for the jimmy." In the progression, H. M. provides, a he-crab is an immature male, and the mature males, jimmies, are classified by size for market. Andrew amplifies this point, "Males, they're called jimmies. They grade them out different sizes. You have your number ones, which are five and a half and up. You have your jumbos, which are six inches and up. Your number twos, which are five- to five-and-a-half-inch crabs."

Words for female crabs are a bit more involved, but the fundamental principles of categorizing crabs in the lingua franca of the marketplace holds sway. "The female," H. M. starts, "she doesn't have to have any size. Once she's mature, the female, she's done all she's going to do as far as getting any size. Could be a small one; could be a big one." Andrew helps out, "You have your females, which they call them sooks, and they go any size. When they have their eggs, they call them busted sooks, lemons, and sponge crabs and cushions. They're the ones that are getting ready to rub their eggs off." Kenny Marshall elaborates, "A sponge crab, that's an adult sook who has dropped her egg apron out and you can see the eggs in under her apron. They'll start off real pale orange and get darker and darker and darker until they're almost black just before they hatch out."

Andrew explains, "Then you have your immature females, which are called she-crabs. I've heard the immature ones called virgin females. I heard that one last year when some guys from Carolina sent a bunch of she-crabs up, and they told the truck driver they were virgin females," Andrew laughs. "A crabber will pull your leg in a second to sell his stuff," he snorts with good humor. Under the umbrella of the female crabs, I learn of the she-crab (in addition to virgin, I've heard sally), sook (a clean sook for market is a number three), busted sook or lemon or cushion or sponge (an egg-laden crab for market is a number five). Dizzying!

I wonder about the smallest crabs. H. M. sometimes refers to them as bugs but notes that there is no real terminology for the smallest. Kenny Marshall underscores this point, recalling that there were no words for the small crabs he found up in the guts, "They were inconsequential. You didn't talk about them. They didn't exist as far as anybody was concerned." No market, no name.

Number threes, the just shedded jimmies, are known variously as white crabs, paper shells, buckrams, and buckys. Kenny Marshall clarifies, "A buckram is a soft crab that's stiffening up getting ready to get hard shell again. . . . We call them buckrams. Some people call them paper shells. It's poor. It's not good to eat, for steaming or anything. They're real white. They haven't had time for the weather or the water or whatever to brown them up. Easy to pick, there's not much meat to them." A buck all but hardened is a white crab or number four. A hardened crab—sook or jimmy—grown heavy and dull in color, on occasion even barnacled, is "rusty." Words for crabs are piling up.

Their existence crosses a threshold into the universe of soft-shell crabs. Crabs emerge from winter dormancy in a "first run" in May or, as Oyster waterman Jack Brady times it, "If they were picking the strawberry field, we'd start mudlarking the next day." These crabs, crowded into their old shells, ready to forage, and starved for sex, are set to shed their old armor—an event that provides procreative opportunity around a moment of vulnerability. As H. M. teaches me, you can see the process unfold through signs discerned in the back fin, or swimmer. It commands a practiced eye. All crabs entering the molting or shedding phase are peelers. Peeler crabs become the soft-shell crabs favored by gourmands—or serve as fish bait.

H. M. introduces the phases of a peeler. "We call him green if it could be

H. M. Arnold peeler potting, Nassawadox Creek, Virginia.

a week or so away or it could be two or three days before he starts showing sign. If you keep him, nine out of ten times, if he doesn't have a sign and you put him in that float, he'll go back." "The next sign," H. M. continues, "you'll see is a white sign. It's the same place. Instead of pink or red, it's white." Andrew Bunce notes that "the white sign is a real green peeler." H. M. explains, "We keep them. In the spring, definitely, he'll turn. In the spring, they all do it. If he's got any sign at all in the spring, you can keep him. I'll say over 90 percent will turn into a good peeler, which is pink or red sign." "Pink or red," H. M. says, "he's within a day or two. When he's really red that's when he's ready or rank within a day."

Andrew fills in details, "Pink is when it's not quite red. With a rank peeler, it's real red. They're the ones closest to ready to shed out. They'll start out as a white sign, and then they slowly start turning colors right up to until it turns red." Andrew's crewman Mike contributes, "Then you've got busters. They're busted open already." Andrew picks up the overview, "He's coming out of the shell. We call them busters." Mike adds, "We shed them out in a bucket on the boat. They turn into soft crabs while we're crabbing." Andrew: "Then we bring them in to H. M." Words for crabs keep piling up—white, green, pink, red, rank, buster, soft-shell. Those that don't make the grade are culls; those that die in the process of shedding are stills.

Culling is its own art. "A lot of people," Andrew begins, "have to flip the crabs over to see whether a male or female, but the longer you do it, you can just look at the tops because you know jimmies got blue claws and the sooks got orange claws. You get where you can tell just by looking at them. Like peelers, you look at the fins for the signs. But H. M. and I can damn near look right at the crab and see how it's fat-looking and all that—it's a rank peeler. Just by the looks of it." Andrew explains his expertise, "That just comes from years of looking at them." He pauses for an instant and dismissively adds, "It's a lot of all back and no brain. You don't have to be too smart to do this job." I could not disagree more—experience and a fine-tuned sensibility with nature are rare gifts.

Soft crabs possess their own words rooted entirely in market value and desirability based on size. H. M. runs down the list beginning with the smallest. "Hotels," he launches in, "that size is pretty much eliminated now, because the size of the crab. "To be legal," he notes, "they've got to be three and a half inches. That's pretty much eliminated the hotel." "A prime," he continues, "is four inches. Four to five inches. Three and three quarters, four inches, and a hotel was under that. Of course, back then they had a medium. He was even smaller than a hotel. That's definitely gone." The thought of a medium evokes a description of Eastern Shore cocktail parties in the 1950s, when mediums and even smaller soft-shells, labeled "tinies," were fried and served on sweet potato biscuits as cocktail canapés.

"Five inches is a jumbo," H. M. moves to the larger, most marketable soft-shell crabs. "Got to be five inches point to point." Whales top the inventory. "If you go five and a half, you can actually go to a whale. I don't mess with whales too much. I put them in the jumbos. I don't catch that many, and you can't get that many in a box. So really, unless the price is a whole lot different, you're really not doing a whole lot. Sending less crabs in the same box. Sometimes the whales are a lot higher, but most times only a dollar or two difference, and that ain't really a whole lot to mess with." As for me, my preference aligns with H. M.'s and a taste for the smaller primes.

There are other words for crabs—some unsuitable for polite company and others simply insider references. Out on the creek, setting a line of pots, Andrew notes, "Everybody talks that stuff. Everybody's different on the boat." By way of example, Mike offers, "You ought to put Timmy Jimmies in there." Andrew clarifies the reference, "All the dead rotten ones. That guy I had to fire. When we see a dead rotten one, we call that a Timmy Jimmy." They laugh, "There's a lot of sarcasm out here on the boats. Some stuff you can't record; some stuff is funny. You've just got to be here. If you're out here on the boat, you'll hear stuff we don't think of telling you." Mike pitches another crab pot off the stern as we motor along. The glossary grows.

Listening to words for crabs, I realize how many relate to the business of shedding, grading, and selling soft-shell crabs. I am struck by the complexity of peelers and wonder about how all those crabs about to molt find their way into the shedding houses and, as soft-shell crabs, onto the menu. The present quest for peelers that will become soft crabs is hard work that involves setting peeler pots, chicken-wire mesh traps baited with live jimmy crabs that entice sooks into their artificial lairs, where the sooks shed their armor and in that moment of softness "double" with their mate. I've seen the lothario jimmies abandoned, dead and bleached, in their pots along the wharf at Saxis Island. Clearly, the wages of sin (if invertebrate lust is sin) is death. Before the introduction of peeler pots, especially on the Seaside, mudlarking was the way.

When it comes to words for crabs on the Eastern Shore of Virginia, mudlarking is a word with a history worth knowing. Long before its Eastern Shore associations took root, Victorian London social reformer Henry Mayhew famously defined the mudlark in his encyclopedic *London Labour and the London Poor*: "There is another class who may be termed river-finders, through their occupation is connected only with the shores: they are commonly known by the name of 'mud-larks,' from being compelled, in order to obtain the articles they seek, to wade sometimes up to their middle through the mud left on the shore by the retiring tide." "The mud-larks," Mayhew reported, "collect whatever they happen to find, such as coals, bits of old-iron, rope, bones, and copper nails that drop from ships while lying or repairing along shore." They sold their gleanings to buyers that included neighbors, ship chandlers, and the proprietors of rag and bone shops who stocked their premises with scavenged goods. Eastern Shore mudlarks sold their haul to the shedding houses.

Billy Bowen, who worked a lifetime on the water out of Willis Wharf, recalls mudlarking. We sit on the comfortably plush sofas in Billy's front room. It's a bright and sunny morning, the temperature mild, the day breezy after the big thunderstorms of the evening before. Billy smiles (he smiles a lot), cradling a paper coffee cup in his hands. "It's a godforsaken job," he laughs. "It started after Mother's Day, about last part of May, first part of June." "You'd sink, and it would be over your ankles and halfway up to your knees sometimes. You do that three or four or five or six hours, it'd wear you out! But you made a dollar."

Others echo Billy's summation. "Mudlarking," H. M. states, "was for soft crabs, for peelers. That was only thing I ever knew it for. Some of them places was, my god, muddy. You had to be a man!" "As a teenager," Ron Crumb reminisced, "I tried it twice. My recollection is you've got to be protected with the only thing sticking out, your nose, your eyes, because you're in the sea oats or the marsh grass where it's muddy. You've got gnats *and* horseflies after you. The sea oats are poking you in the face. It was a really rough way to do it." Ron concludes, "Guys used to come in that were fishing or crabbing or whatever. Used to be kind of proud of their catch and all—and the ones that come in from mudlarking were just glad it was over." "They never seemed like a happy bunch of guys," he laughs. "It was a nasty job."

Oyster and clam grower Steve Bunce declares, "I did it for one day. Never again!" There are three bad things about mudlarking, he says, chorusing Billy and Ron: slogging through mud, trying to wrest a she-peeler from under a belligerent jimmy, and struggling through more mud. Surprise encounters with a protective jimmy were painful. "One of the worst things to me," Billy recalls, "you'd have a nice deep hole there and you know there's going to be a peeler and you reach in there and there was a jimmy in there with his mate. He would cling to you and you pull your hand out and sling him thirty or forty foot right in the air. He would bite down on you, Cap'n! That I didn't like. I didn't like that at all! But you knew there had to be a crab in there. You had to go try for it, because every one counted."

It wasn't all bad. Kenny Marshall, a Hog Island descendant and waterman out of Willis Wharf, knows about mudlarking. "I did a little mudlarking when I was a teenager with my dad. Even as a child, go along with him and play in the mud. In the early spring, maybe in May, right around Mother's Day, most every crab you see in the marsh will be a shedder crab, or a peeler as we call them." He describes the ecology of the hunt, "When you're going up these little guts in the marsh. . . . These little guts branch off from the bigger creeks and along the edge you have a tall marsh, but behind that is a lower muddy, muddy, muddy bottom. That's where the crab will bury. You can just see the outline of their eyes and face. You go along with a lard tin—a five-gallon lightly made bucket. You had to punch holes around the bottom edge of it so that water would drain out. You put a handle across it, so that when you stepped down in that real soft mud you could almost use it to support yourself, pressing against it." Almost.

"You'd see these little crabs—little peelers—in the marsh. Pick them up, rinse them off, throw them in the tin, and carry it back to your boat—

Unloading crabs on the Bayford dock, Bayford, Virginia.

pushing skiff," Kenny continues, "and you had what we called a crab float in that—a little old box made out of plastering laths so the water could run through it. You'd dump your lard tin full of crabs in that. You'd only get about half full. Then you'd go out and get another bucketful. It was hard work! You had to pull your socks up over your pants and hold them together and tie them up some kind of way so that mud wouldn't suck them off, which it would do if you're not careful."

H. M. echoes Kenny's observations on the qualities of different kinds of mud, "It's a lot softer down in the guts. On top of the marsh where the grass is, it's harder ground." The peelers, he says, "they go up on high tide. Then when the tide goes out, they'd be in those little holes." Jack Brady, born into a working life on the great Atlantic marshes, knows about mud.

"One day, me and Mama went up this creek. It was a little, teeny trickle—
we call them. Went through a little piece of mudflat. I said, 'Now, Mama,
don't go over there because you're going to get stuck!' And like a cow, she
had to graze and graze. She went over there. She buried her basket. She
lost her boot! I looked, and she was setting on the basket, trying to get her
boots out of the mud!" Jack laughs, remembering his mother's predicament, "It was just plain soft. You couldn't walk on it!" "A mud pot! That
would be like jelly when you got close to it. That's what we used to call
them. There's one down the road here on the Scott farm. A little gut goes up
in the marsh, but there's one certain place when you get close to it and jar
the bottom, you'll see it. It will quiver." "You step in that, you don't know if
you're going this deep or this deep," he gestures heights from knee to chest.
"It just depends on how soft it is. You've got to watch it up under the land."

Jack should know about "ploughing around in the marsh." "What we did
on the first run of peelers," he remembers, "one of us would have a car, and
we would get somebody to take us down to the Scott farm and we would
crab all the way back up to Oyster. We had to work our way back home. I
guess it's three or four miles from there up to here. When you get your tin
full, you'd dump it in—we call them clam sacks. They had kind of holes like
that," he measures a quarter-inch weave with thumb and forefinger, "big,
thick sacks. Lay them in a drain, where the water could be to them. Then
you would crab up a ways and come back and dump them, and you'd take
the sack on up to where you had stopped at. That was hard work because
you had to bring the sack all the way from there up here to Oyster in order
to sell them. You worked your way back home! If you got all you could carry
before you got home, then you just took your time. You would have most of
the time at least two tins of crabs in a bag plus your tin full—and you had
to drag that bag. That's rough! Plus, you've got to fight the horseflies, the
gnats. Yessir, I loved it!"

Danny Doughty, recalling his father's mudlarking days, paints a grim
picture of the work. "Mudlarking. They'd walk along through the marsh—
and you could only imagine the greenheads, the heat. It was really horrible doing it. You'd get stuck in the mud and lose your moccasins. You'd
see welts all over them where there were horseflies. They would tear you
up!" Danny's mudlarking story takes a dark turn. "My dad was going up in
one of the guts he had gone in for years. He knew every little place to find
what he was looking for. Up ahead of him, he saw this little skiff. They'd just
had a bad thunderstorm. The hail was so horrible! It was like pummeling
hail. He goes plugging, plugging, plugging along, and he pulls up and when
he gets up to the boat, there's an older man—and he knew who it was—
dead. He'd evidently had a heart attack, and when that storm come, it just

pummeled him! He was laid out in the boat—and there was not one place where you could stick your finger that there wasn't a horsefly stuck to his body. They had pretty much pulled the blood right out of his body. It took him forever to get hold of him and turn him around in those guts, because he was in a bigger boat, and to pull him all the way back to the dock and get him there, but he died. I was just a little boy, like six."

Kenny Marshall's and Jack Brady's mudlarking childhoods were much happier. "I used to go with my dad in the summertime every day," Kenny says. "Wherever he went, I was with him from maybe three years on up. I'd go out with him mudlarking, and I thought that was fun because you had those steep mud banks and I could slide down those just like an otter. Have all kinds of fun. Didn't have my mom never telling me not to get muddy. My dad, he was muddy, too!" Jack, who invariably prefaces his reminiscences, "I loved mudlarking!" shares a story of his first outings with his cousin Herbert Moore. "I went with him when I was about eight, nine years old every summer. I looked forward to doing it. Every summer! I can hear Mama telling him right now, 'Herbert, you're going to lose him out there!' And Herbert, he cussed a lot, he'd say, 'Well, damn, Ruby, you think I'm going to leave that young one out there? I can find whichever way he went through the marsh. I can walk down behind him and find him!'" Jack laughs and adds, "I wasn't as tall as the grass."

Robert Bridges links knowledge of the natural world to the hand-in-hand education of watching and helping his father, Bobby. "So we had to write a paper in the fifth grade, and I wrote about things I was proud of or that my dad had taught me," he smiles, "that I knew what a jimmy was as opposed to a busted sook or a sook, and I knew how to tell a rank peeler from a green peeler."

Kevin Abrahams links words for crabs and mudlarking to play and coming of age as he recalls his boyhood adventures on Tangier Island. "I'm sixty years old, been doing it all my life. It started when you're a little boy. Messing with it. Then you fall in love with it. Messing. Just going, playing. Having fun as a kid. The older you get, the more fun it becomes, especially when you start making a little money. You start out as a kid just enjoying fun. Something to do while you're out of school. Mudlarking, walk the meadow with a crab net in your hand. Picking them up with a dip net." "You start learning the words for crabs from the time you step foot on a boat," he explains. "Little kid. You hear it and learn it. You know what they're talking about. Just like a little boy following his dad on a tractor plowing a field, you just learn. You start following your dad. The older you get, the more serious it becomes. Each year, you just learned a little more. Until next year, he says, 'You're going to start working with me. If you ain't going to

Soft-shell crabs packed for shipping.

want to go to school.' You learn that language because you hear it at home, you hear it at the docks, you hear it on the boats. The next thing you know, we're talking like we're pretending to be watermen. Then we are one. We pretend when we're seven, eight, nine years old. Sailing our little boats off the dock. Pretend that we're crabbing. Our little handmade boats, pulling them with a string. That's when you start using all them words! Exactly."

Kenny and Kevin reveal two seasons of mudlarking. First, there is the pursuit of peelers in the spring of the year and through the summer months. This is nature's season. Second, there is the experience of learning the work and ways of water and marsh. This is the season of coming of age. Andrew Bunce relates his passage, "I was nine or ten years old when I first went. When I was young, I used to go with Billy James. At first, I just started watching. Then they'd let you cull, which is sorting out the crabs. I learned everything there was to learn. Then when I was thirteen or fourteen, I got my fifty crab pots and I had an old wooden bateau skiff with a 25 Evinrude. I can swim faster than she'd go, but I was proud of her."

An accomplished mudlarker possesses three abilities: navigating the marsh, spotting the peelers hiding in little pools of water, and collecting sufficient numbers to make a living.

Walking the marsh begins with knowing the lay of the land. "Where your tallest marsh grass is," Billy explains, "you're going to find softer mud. Shortest grass is going to be a harder mud. You're going to find your crabs in your softer mud." "If you get up to grass like this," he gestures a foot or so high, "you're on turfy ground, and it's just like walking on this floor. You get up to grass like this," he raises his hand to a point two to three feet tall above the floor, "then you're walking in soft mud. Every step!" As for technique, "When you're mudlarking, you depend a lot on that lard tin to put your weight on to help you get out sometimes. That lard tin helps you a lot as far as walking in the mud! It really does."

Moving through the marsh, Billy elaborates, "Some people could not do that—and there was some walking across there, you'd think they were walking on a stone road. They had a talent for it. Some people just cannot walk in mud. They just cannot do it!" "You just walked, but what you would do was take your foot and push the marsh grass over and stand on that," he demonstrates a skating-style stride, "so you wouldn't sink as deep. You never put your foot down toe first. You always tried to put your foot down flat or step on grass." Then Billy repeats a joke, "It was a hard job. You're walking in mud all the time. Some people would say, 'Well, how do you do that?' I said, 'You put your weight on the foot you're picking up.' Well, that's a pretty good trick if you can do that!" Then he turns serious, "You can't imagine walking in mud for four or five or six hours at a time. That was hard on you. You earned what you made." He repeats for emphasis, "You earned what you made!"

Finding peelers in the marsh depends on how and where you look. Ed Bell remarks, "I've talked to guys who used to do it. They would look for the crab's eyes. He would kind of be a little bit under the mud. They would see the crab and just grab him and just throw him in the bucket. They were trying to find peelers, not hard crabs." "Always," Billy says, "you did better after the second or third day, because you could go back where you'd always walked and there was more holes there. Before that there wouldn't have been holes for the crabs to be in. They kind of laid in teeny little sinks. This way would give them some water, too, because of your footprints."

Knowing how to navigate the mud and spot a peeler made it possible to catch enough crabs to make a living. Accomplished mudlarkers are remembered and admired. "Back before the pots came along," Ed Bell smiles, "there were guys that could catch two or three thousand crabs on a tide! One guy—they called him 'Biddie'—Biddie Bennett, he was one of the best ones around. I'll never forget, I was a teenager at this point, but he said, 'I'll show you how it's done.' He took a bucket out one tide and he came back with about five hundred crabs. This was before everybody was peeler potting, so it was hard to believe that he would find that many crabs, but he knew where to go and how to do it. Of course, when pots came along, it was so much easier. I can't imagine going up to the heads of those creeks in the hot summertime with those horseflies. Couldn't have been fun work! Muddy!" Billy adds the perspective of lived experience, "I remember the first time I ever done it, I was about eight or nine years old, and I caught one hundred crabs that day, and they were a penny apiece. I made one dollar! But it was a dollar!" Even as he laughs at the recollection, I'm thinking about how hard he labored in the mud to make that dollar. "As time went on, the price went up a little bit," Billy notes, "so you could get to the point that you could go out there and catch six or seven hundred crabs at five or six or seven cents. You were making a nice day's work. A real nice day's work!"

The introduction of peeler pots in the late 1950s marked the final days of mudlarking. Robert Lamb witnessed the arrival of peeler pots, "That happened in my time. Everyone thought that was a miracle. I don't know who thought it up, but somebody had sense enough to understand the way crabs lived. The way nature is with crabs, the females are looking for a mate. Somebody figured out, put him in the pot for bait and they'd come— and they do. They come and go in there trying to get to that male crab. They usually put two or three in a pot." He relates his own experience, "One spring I used to put them in Cherrystone Creek. After that would just get finished up, the Seaside would be time, and I would move the pots over there. This one spring (I just had a small boat—I could only carry twenty pots at a time), I put the first twenty out and went the next day to check them. Had a man with me. He pulled the pot up. I couldn't believe the amount of peelers that was in it. Doublers. It was eighty some! He said, 'Lord Almighty, I'm going to count these!' He counted them, and it was like I said—eighty some. We went to the next pot, and it had more! I never did get anymore pots overboard. Those twenty pots caught me all the crabs I could handle and keeping nothing but the best."

For Billy, the introduction of peeler pots changed the landscape of labor. "Nobody, since they come across with the peeler pots," he declares, "goes into the marsh anymore! Nobody goes mudlarking!" With peeler pots, Billy says, "People got to the point, if they didn't have peeler pots, they bought peeler pots. It was so quick—and easier for you. When we first started doing it, Daddy and myself, we didn't have no peeler pots, but we talked to Pete West over on the Bayside, and he had them, and he allowed us to take and use his pots, and we worked out a deal. We used his pots to start off with, and after that we got some of our own for the following year." "I remember we set some pots down under Hog Island," Billy recollects, "my daddy and myself, and we went back the next day. You put four jimmies in the upstairs. I went to pull the pot. I said, 'Gee-my-knee, Daddy, this must be caught in an old tree or something here,' because we were down underneath Hog Island. Pulled that up, and that was nothing but loaded with peelers. That was a pretty sight! Two pots overrun a basket! Got a basket and a piece out of two pots." "At one time, mudlarking was a good way to make a living," Ed observes, "but once pots came along, it became a thing of the past."

H. M. tells a story about peeler poaching that marks the moment of change. His friend Alfred Nottingham and I listen. "I remember one time we were peeler potting out at Hog Island. I mean they were there, buddy! They were fifty to a hundred in a pot. This fellow we know comes out of the marsh. We'd put pots in holes. Put two right beside each other, and usually they were loaded. We come to one every once in a while, and there wasn't much in it. But here comes this fellow out of the gut there. He'd been mudlarking!" Alfred and H. M. shake their heads. "He had about a thousand! Got you!" H. M. exclaims, "What are you going to say? You didn't see him. I mean I was crabbing, but something looked fishy! He was known to be a little shady." It was the rare moment when you encounter the end of an era.

Mudlarking for peeler crabs at the scale described by Robert Lamb, Billy Bowen, Ed Bell, and others was linked to the introduction of new markets to the Eastern Shore. The extension of the railroad to Cape Charles in the 1880s and the advent of motorized trucks in the 1920s made it possible to move highly perishable commodities with speed, efficiency, and safety. Advances in canning and food preservation made it possible to cook, pack, and ship crabmeat west of the Mississippi River. The invention of the outboard motor and its rapid adoption by Eastern Shore watermen facilitated movement through the vast marshes as well as in and out of landward villages. New technologies opened new markets and reshaped old practices. Eastern Shore folk—Native American, European, and African—foraged through the marshes for hundreds of generations. Rising demand led to new practices around old things. A metropolitan hunger for soft-shell crabs and the ability to feed it transformed the soft-shell crab from an occasional local delicacy into a full-blown commodity. If mudlarking was the extractive industry that mined the marshes for peelers, the soft-shell crab pounds served as the processing plants and refineries that translated raw materials into a pan-ready product. Words for crabs: green, white, pink, red, rank, and buster had to be translated into hotel, prime, jumbo, and whale.

Robert Lamb introduces the history of the soft-shell crab fishery. "At that time, the only way they knew to shed crabs was in the water in what you call crab floats," he locates his story in the 1930s. "My father-in-law was big in that. He had a place down at Cherrystone at the end of the road. He would have over a hundred floats. You just can't throw these crab floats overboard and let them be exposed to the storms and stuff. You had to have like a breakwater." "What they usually did, they just put in pilings in an enclosure," he explains. "They used back then, sawmills would have these slabs, where the bark comes off first, and they would use them like a fence. Put it on the poles, and it would stop the waves. It was a crab pound."

Jack Brady traces the process from the mudlarker's hands to the buyers waiting at the dock. "The buyers were honest. You didn't have to worry about them cheating you." "Lot of times there would be so many crabs there," he describes the transaction, "the buyer would lump them—what we call lumping them—and he would pay you. When they took them up the road to where he shedded them and counted them, if it was more, he would pay you for them the next day. He was an honest man." Jack explains lumping. "Look at a size float or a bag—they had wooden boxes about that long," he frames a four-foot between his hands, "they dumped them in so they could count them and separate them—the rank ones and the green ones. He would just say, 'What do you think, Jack?' You'd say, 'Well, I got two lard tins. I figure there's probably two hundred, two hundred fifty to the tin.' He would pay you for five hundred. If it was short, he would take it out of your next. No money transferred. He would just say, 'Well, you were fifty short.' First fifty crabs was his. And that's the way it was worked."

The buyers conveyed the peelers to the crab pounds where they were shedded out as soft crabs. Robert Lamb remembers the volume of crabs that flowed into the market through the 1950s, "During the peak of the first run, he would have enough soft crabs to send a six-wheel truckload to market every day. Now most crab-shedding operations wouldn't send a truckload in a whole season. He would send a truckload every day. He had ten people working in the crab pound. They had to work twenty-four hours a day."

"George Spence and them," Billy Bowen says, "they had floats, all of them were outside. You had to fish them day and night. When you're shedding out crabs, it's a twenty-four-hour job, just about. You'd be lucky to get three hours of sleep a night. But it's a short season, and they were making decent money at it, so that's what they chose to do." "Captain Harry Brad-ford," he adds, "right down to the wharf here, he had fifty or sixty floats overboard. That was a lot of floats, but he had his boys. They fished them day and night, packed them up, and shipped them out. That's what he done year after year."

Robert Lamb shares photographs of his family's shedding operation on Cherrystone Creek. The first provides an overview of the crab pound in the off season. A narrow walkway runs straight to a crab house supported on heavy poles and cribbing. Two parallel board tracks laid across the walkway decking provided smooth passage for the carts that crab hands shuttled back and forth between waiting trucks on shore and the plain vertical-sided, metal-roofed work building. Taller poles carried electrical wires that powered lights for night work and kept the refrigeration running. The piling and board "pen" stand in the background. A pair of floats tied to slender poles forced into the creek's muddy bottom bob in the still water. The sec-ond photograph depicts two men working the floats. Bent at the waist, the pair have lifted the wings of the lath-sided float onto the gunwales of their workboats. Working through the crawling mass of peelers, they harvest soft-shell crabs one by one, placing them in low wooden boxes.

Jack Brady, who witnessed the operation, completes the picture. "They had people hired. Haney Smith had three or four people over there. One man would stay in the shedding house or packinghouse, and the others would go out there in little teeny boats just big enough to paddle, because most of the time they didn't have to paddle. They just pulled from one float to the other, and they would dip the soft crabs out. And when they had got a certain amount and they had put a little bit of time out there, they would bring them back where they could be packed in the boxes with a little bit of ice sprinkled on them. In the boxes that they shipped them in, they put newspaper over them—wet—and just flipped a little bit of ice on them, because if they wasn't alive when they got where they were going, they wouldn't buy them."

A shift from crab pounds to shedding houses occurred in the late 1960s and early 1970s and was as seismic as the advent of peeler pots a decade earlier. Pete West, who worked a lifetime on Nassawadox Creek and is cele-brated for having tried to eat at least one of everything he ever caught, elaborates on what the change brought to the soft-shell crab infrastruc-ture, remembering an older, quieter time of the floats moored along creek-side docks. "Soft-shell crabs," he says, "I've done that for sixty years." "They were all overboard, and now you put them in the houses," he nods across the creek toward H. M.'s setup in the old oyster house, "put them in where you want them. You brought the crabs in in the floats and you separate them in the different stages in the floats. Crabs who'd shed in three or four days; crabs who'd shed within a week; and then, if there were green ones, some would shed and some wouldn't. You'd just repeat that in your operation. You'd take them every four or five days — you'd cull them. If they had a green sign, it was a week, maybe ten days away. If they had a pink sign, that'd mean he was a few days away. It still hasn't changed. It's just people put them in houses now. In fact, there's not many people doing that anymore like they used to. That way of life on the water's gone. I suppose everything has moved to the aquaculture."

Billy Bowen recognizes the shift as a distinct improvement. "When it rained or when it was dark outside, they had lights inside and they didn't have to go out there and get in a little boat and go out there and raise the float up and get the crabs out." As H. M. observes, "Overboard floats, I don't know of anybody now. Pete West was one of the last ones in this creek who did it — and that's been quite some time. I don't blame them either." "I think that even Donny Miles," H. M. refers to a working waterman on Nassawadox Creek, "if he had to go back to that, he'd quit."

Because a shedded crab begins to harden almost immediately, the floats are monitored once very four hours around the clock. H. M. goes tank to tank with a short-handled dip net and scoops the soft crabs into a small pen in the tank that enables the crabs to harden enough to survive the trip to the live seafood market and protects them from the cannibal predations of their fellows. A crab that's advanced in the hardening process is a buckram, buck, or bucky. H. M. describes the buckram, "After he's shed and he starts hardening up, we call him a buck." "Then the next thing," H. M. charts the crab's development, "he's back to a hard crab again. Bucks, they don't have a whole lot of meat in them when they first shed." A crab just shedded is lean and ravenous. "He'll eat everything up as soon as he comes out." H. M. tells me that buckrams pan-fried without their upper shell are quite tasty.

All those words for crabs, all those reminiscences of mudlarking and shedding houses bring to mind recipes for crabs and the language that attends their culinary possibilities. When it comes to recipes for crabs, diversity of opinion and taste prevails. Kenny Marshall offers, "We had soft crabs more than anything else. Steamed crabs was like a Saturday evening thing where you had company over. Everybody'd sit around a big old pile of crabs dumped out on the middle of the table. Everybody had a beer or a soft drink. Just sitting around. Eight or ten people sitting around a table picking and eating crabs and eating them as you pick them. That was a

Saturday afternoon or evening thing. All the cousins and uncles and aunts come together." More often than not, local cooks steamed and picked their crabs. Professional pickers produced neatly graded crabmeat for market in ascending order as claw, special, backfin, lump, and jumbo lump. Home cooks mixed the meat together. I don't know of a name for the blended meat, but that's what I use for everything from crab cakes to tamales.

Late June, the soft-shell crab season is done; the height of the hard crab is kicking in big time. H. M.'s peeler pots are cleaned, stacked, and stored for the year. The cooling hours of evening begin to break the day's heat. I ask folks gathered in the Bayford oyster house to name their favorite way to eat crabs. Jim Arnold, H. M.'s uncle, "Fried soft-shell." Joy, "Claw meat in butter." Major, whose family has resided here since the early 1600s, "Fried soft crab," then adds crabmeat-stuffed flounder—then adds steamed and picked with friends. There's no restraining Major. Steve smiles, "H. M.'s cleaned soft-shells fried in butter." "Mustard free," he emphasizes, referring to the greenish-yellow crab fat. "Crabmeat-stuffed flounder," Hank, H. M.'s son, contributes, referring to the local legendary entrée served at the old Candlelight restaurant, long vanished in all but memory and desire. Mary Lou, H. M.'s wife, seconds Hank. H. M. adds, "a pound of crabmeat mixed, seasoned with Old Bay, fried in butter." Major's back to soft-shells, "I like hotels, no jumbos." Uncle Jim, "Stills are my favorite." Earl walks in the door, "Crabmeat that somebody else has picked—no shell bits—in a crab dip."

Kenny Marshall mixes his crab along with the occasional dividend of eggs gleaned from cleaned sooks: "Steamed crabs. Pick the meat out and do what you want with that—crab cakes or crab casseroles. I used to mix them in with scrambled eggs for breakfast. Real heavily mixed in. A lot of it. Just enough scrambled egg to hold them together and fry it out for breakfast. The crab eggs were good. I liked the eggs! In fact, they were marketable for a while, but not anymore." "As you're picking the crab out," Kenny continues, "you save the egg, and I just threw it right in with the meat and stirred it together. If you made a crab cake, the egg was all mixed through it. The egg was fairly stiff. I scrambled crabmeat with scrambled chicken eggs, but the crab eggs, if I ran across them, just mixed right in with the meat, and whatever I was doing with it they would be right in there." He emphasizes the rarity of the treat, "You didn't ever have hardly enough of them to cook them separately. You could take a whole bushel basketful of sooks, full of crabs—probably wouldn't have over a cup of eggs—if that. Once they're busted, you don't want them. These were very immature sooks. They have a few right up under the tip of the shell, and they move down apparently when they get ready to bust and some right between the two halves where you break them in half. You get a lump maybe the size of a nickel and then another little speck out of each end of the shell itself."

Words for crabs offer an excess of language. For frying soft-shell crabs, the opposite holds true. Bessie Gunter's 1889 recipe consists of one sentence, "Raise the back of the live crab, remove the dead men, fry in butter," followed by an equally succinct serving suggestion, "Serve in cream gravy seasoned with salt and pepper." The simplicity and incisiveness of Fairy Mapp White's directions for fried soft crabs seventy years later rely on a deeply shared knowledge about cooking: "Prepare crabs by removing dead men, eyes, and flap on shell. Wash crabs and salt and pepper. Dip in flour and fry in hot fat. Keep pan covered while frying crabs." Gunter and White omit a few crucial details. Dead men are the gills under the crab's upper shell and arrayed along both sides of its body. It's a good idea to press excess water from the crab lightly to prevent the creature from exploding when moisture hits hot oil. And the crabs, as Gunter wrote, are alive when their gills, apron (the flap), and eyes are removed. Not for the faint of heart.

Kenny Marshall's approach was more barebones, "Soft crabs, deep fried. Just breaded them and fried them. Some people did more cleaning than others. I always liked to clean them right well. Get the lungs out of them— dead men. Then you cut them in half and clean them pretty good. I like some of that greenish-looking fat. Gives them a little flavor. It's like a sauce almost." As for buckrams, "Used to be you could go around to these commercial shedding places and get them at no cost. They'd give them to you. If they were too hard to ship, it wasn't any good to them, so they'd give them away to you. You'd be surprised how hard a crab can get after you fry it that you can't tell the difference hardly. The back you can, but you throw that away. The legs and the claws and the rest of the body, it can be pretty papery, really."

Fairy Mapp White provides instructions for ten crab preparations in her *Foolproof Cook Book*. Half of those dishes, she acknowledges, reflect inventions from "away" and include Crab Louis, Crab Burgers, Crab Jacques, and Crab Mousse. Steamed crab, except for its service as an ingredient, is not on her menu, but White does offer three distinctly Eastern Shore recipes of which fried soft-shell crabs is one. The others are crab cakes and fried hard crabs.

I think of crab cakes as a Maryland creation and more specifically a Baltimore invention that are glorified fritters. The associations with fritters are apparent in H. Franklyn Hall's 1901 self-published *300 Ways to Cook and Serve Shell Fish*. Hall, apparently in desperate financial straits, drew on his experience as the chef of Philadelphia's Boothby Hotel and created a compilation that included a paltry seventeen crab recipes—crab cakes in butter sauce among them. "Make a stiff, rich cake, batter thin, mix in enough crab meat to make stiff," he instructed. "Cook on grid-iron or in a smooth bottom fry pan same as griddle or pan cakes; serve with drawn butter for breakfast or lunch." His hand-molded crab croquette, made with onion, egg yolks, celery salt, and red pepper, more closely resembles the modern crab cake.

Like Bessie Gunter's advice, White's guidance economizes on language and relies heavily on the reader's familiarity with ingredients and process.

1 pt. crab meat
1 egg
1 small grated onion (or cut fine)
1 c. bread crumbs
3 tbs. mixed mustard
1 tb. mayonnaise
Pepper and salt
Blend all ingredients and shape into croquettes or cakes. Fry in deep fat until golden brown. If dusted with flour, they will cook and brown better.

The bread crumbs and mayonnaise, as well as the reference to croquettes, are surely polite affectations for a dish that likely flows out of African American cookery. Gunter's recipe links the crab cake to its older history as a fritter. For "Crab Patties," she instructs, "pick the meat from the crabs, add the fat, season with salt and pepper, and to each dozen, add one beaten egg. Mould in flat cakes and fry in butter. . . . Dip the crabs in flour before frying." A gravy accompanied these crab cakes: "Add cream and chopped parsley to the gravy. Serve over the crabs in a gravy boat." The idea of a gravy is a marvel to me, but the creation of a crab cake composed entirely of crabmeat bound by a minimum of egg is perfection in a contemporary moment where fussy excess is its own kind of heresy.

White presents her recipe for fried hard crabs as "a very old recipe given me by my mother-in-law," adding, "it was used frequently in her kitchen and in mine."

FRIED HARD CRABS

1. Prepare hard crabs as soft crabs, but leave only about ½ in. of claws on crabs, remove back shell, saving fat and eggs, if any, in shells.
2. Scrape crabs and wash well. Roll lightly with a rolling pin to break shells a little. Salt and pepper crabs, flour well, and fry in hot fat.
3. Put crab fat and eggs, from top shells in a small pan, add a little

water, vinegar, dry mustard, pepper, and salt. Mash as mixture cooks down, thicken with a little flour, add a little of the fat in which crabs were fried.

4. Serve gravy in a bowl. Some prefer to eat these hard fried crabs with their fingers and put gravy on the cornbread served with them.

Fairy Mapp White's recipe owes a great deal to Bessie Gunter's preparation, but there are some notable differences. For "Hard Crabs Fried," Gunter directs, "take off the shell and claws, while alive. Take out the fat and put in a dish; take out the dead men. Roll the crabs with the rolling-pin to break the shells. Sprinkle them with salt, pepper and flour." This mirrors White's recipe, but then ingredients and process diverge. "Fry in butter," Gunter instructs. "When done, take from the pan, add to the gravy more butter, the fat, and the meat picked from the large claws. When they have fried a while, add a cup of cream, stir well a few minutes, then pour over the crabs. If parsley is liked, add a little to the gravy, chopped fine." Where White goes for the piquancy of vinegar, mustard, and pepper, Gunter emphasizes savoriness or umami through butter, cream, and crab fat. Tastes evolve and terroir, a living entity, morphs with those changes. As an afterthought, Gunter notes helpfully, "I kill the crabs by steam before breaking them; do not cook them."

My favorite recipe, though, comes from Kenny Marshall. The scent of cedar chips is rich in the air of his decoy-carving shed, where we sit. Our conversation winds down to its conclusion and lunchtime is imminent. I'm thinking of soft-shell crabs at the Exmore Diner. Kenny smiles with his recollections of mudlarking, words for crabs, and pan-fried soft-shells. Then he surprises me. "I used to take the shell off the back and fry that separately," he says. "Clean it up. I'd call those crab chips. They'd get crunchy deep-fried." Crab chips! The elegance of ordinary things! I am at a loss for words.

A CHEF'S RECIPE FOR HOME

SAUTÉED SOFT-SHELL CRABS WITH
GARLIC, CAPERS, AND LEMON

Seth Kingsbury, Pazzo, Chapel Hill

Seth Kingsbury shared this very simple and quick dish with me. Seth is all about respecting the character and integrity of ingredients, and this is a great example that celebrates the salty freshness of soft-shell crabs.

Makes 4 servings
- ¼ cup extra-virgin olive oil
- 4 live soft-shell crabs, cleaned and patted dry
- 2 large garlic cloves, thinly sliced lengthwise
- ¼ cup dry white wine or Pernod
- 1½ tablespoons fresh lemon juice
- ½ tablespoon drained capers
- 2 tablespoons chopped fresh flat-leaf parsley
- Kosher salt and freshly ground black pepper to taste
- Shredded greens of your choice

Heat the olive oil in a large heavy skillet over medium-high heat until it is shimmering hot. Add the crabs, shell side down, and sauté until browned, 2–3 minutes. Turn the crabs over with tongs and continue to sauté until milky when pressed, 2–3 minutes more. Remove the crabs to a plate.

Add the garlic to the pan and cook for 1 minute to color slightly. Add the wine or Pernod, lemon juice, capers, and parsley and let boil for 1 minute. Season with salt and pepper.

To serve, arrange a bed of greens on 4 plates, place a crab on each, and drizzle with the sauce. Serve immediately.

On Strawberries

Considering strawberries, chef Amy Brandt, sitting at the kitchen table on a perfect blue-sky mid-May afternoon, begins, "They were really good this year." She assigns the excellence of those strawberries to a combination of circumstances: varietal, timing, and weather.

"I think," she muses, "the most important thing is finding someone that you like who you get your strawberries from, and figuring out what variety they have. I don't love a big strawberry . . . , the best berries are smaller berries. I'm not sold on a big berry."

Her preferred berries are the Sweet Charlies sold from William Baines's farm stand next to his fields along the main road that transects our county. Mr. Baines, she observes, harvested "a new crop, a new planting this year. If I'm not mistaken. It looked like they took everything up and replanted."

She cautions, "You kind of have to watch the weather. So if it's rained, and then you have a dry period, and then they start harvesting, it is a bonanza! I mean it was just beautiful."

Timing, she concludes, is everything: "Just been picked, they're red through and through, which really seems to happen at the third-of-the-way point in berry harvest. So, it's like not the very beginning, but like a third of a way to, like two-thirds of the way, to me seems like the optimal time to get them."

Amy gifts us two jars of her preserves, one infused with wild chamomile. I'd been conjuring images of strawberries long before our conversation, beginning with the purchase of several packets of old strawberry pickers' tickets from a shop in the venerable railroad town of Exmore. Those tiny paper rectangles imprinted with the farm owner's name and the number of quarts picked spark questions of how the strawberry business from cultivation to gustation actually worked. And those queries generate more questions about the origins of strawberries as we know them. Nothing is ever as simple as it seems, and strawberry histories are no exception.

The modern strawberry is a made thing, an artifact that traces its genealogy to a plantsman's experiments in northern France in the early 1700s. Striving to domesticate the strawberry for the garden and finding the wild woodland strawberry of Europe uncooperative, attention shifted to the berries of the Americas. Thomas Harriot, inventorying in 1590 the abundance of what is remembered as the Lost Colony of Roanoke, praised the strawberries he consumed "as good & as great as those which we have in our English gardens." George Percy, reprising his adventures at the founding of Jamestown in 1607, marveled at "a little plat of ground full of fine and beautifull Strawberries, foure times bigger and better than ours in England."

Strawberries, it seems, were linked to fabulations of promise and plenty. Just over a century later, specimens of the North American *Fragaria virginiana* were crossed with the southern hemispheric *Fragaria chiloensis*. Their romantic encounter was nurtured in the hotbeds of northwestern France; love blossomed. The offshoots of this first union were introduced to the Americas and are the ancestors of the modern garden strawberry. As eighteenth-century amateur botanists and sophisticated gardeners bred and crossbred the descendants of the "first" strawberries, they developed more and more varieties with different attributes defined by yield, flavor, size, and shape. When I eat a strawberry, I imagine the flavors of discovery and the Enlightenment.

A century later, in the waning decades of the 1800s, the advent of railroad transportation and food distribution networks made it possible to ship strawberries — delicate commodities in their moment of perfection — with dispatch and in quantity to urban markets. A Gilded Age promoter of Eastern Shore agriculture breathlessly chronicled the strawberry's journey from field to table. "There were 200,000 quarts of strawberries in 5,000 crates," he set the scene. "While the city sleeps certain of its population are wide awake, and preparing for the appetites of thousands more." Then he shifts his narrative into high gear: "During Sunday night up to 12 o'clock 125 cars, making up special trains from Cape Charles, Delaware, Norfolk, and Salisbury arrived at the new market station in West Philadelphia, and were all unloaded before 4 o'clock in the morning." Then:

> Towards midnight the station begins to take on the appearance of life. The depot men are waiting for the special produce trains to arrive from the south. . . . Before the midnight hour all is in readiness, for upon the arrival of the trains the scenes of bustle enacted before that

time are lost sight of in the great activity which follows. When the trains roll in long lines of cars are tracked beside ample platforms, and their contents handled with trained quickness by the entire force of the depot. Then the commission merchants and their men arrive, and affairs move faster than ever, and hundreds of dollars change hands as soon as the consignments are placed on the platform. It is rush, push, and bustle for three or four hours. By that time the cars are unloaded, and their contents on the platform, or other places designed for them. Tons of produce have already been sold, and on the way to stores and distributing points through the city. Many of the first sales are made to hotels and large restaurants, in order that they may be in time for early breakfast. Then the grocers' wagons begin to arrive and the business goes faster than ever.

Strawberries purveyed across the city, the reporter concludes, "by 6 o'clock in the morning things are quiet again; the vast business has been done, and half an hour later the fresh products of southern fields and patches are on the breakfast tables of thousands, from one end of the city to the other." As the city awakes, the market drowses, catches its breath, girds for the coming night.

The 1944 Farmers' Bulletin No. 1028, *Strawberry Culture: Eastern United States*, offers an "outline map of the United States, showing the approximate shipping season for each strawberry-producing section," emphasizing "the most important producing areas." The Eastern Shore, including Delaware, and southern New Jersey easily claim title as the preeminent growing areas. The bulletin records how strawberry farming changed over time, "In years past the strawberry was grown only in the home garden and by gardeners located within a few miles of the market." Developments in transportation, refrigeration, marketing, and varietals changed all that. "Since about 1860," the bulletin's authors reported, "the period of its consumption has been greatly extended, and in large city markets strawberries can now be obtained throughout the year." Given the all-too-often capitulation of flavor to the aesthetics of appearance and durability, the modern year-round strawberry does not necessarily constitute a happy culinary conclusion.

At William Baines's strawberry patch and stand, where customers pull off the highway to buy two or three or four just-picked quarts, his friend George packs baskets as Mr. Baines greets the trade. He presents an eight-quart flat of strawberries just harvested and, sample strawberry in hand, invites, "Go ahead, try one!" Fabulous! And in that moment of delight, I consume the long arc of the industrial and transportation revolutions.

Amy Brandt with her father, Paul, Cheriton area, Virginia.

Strawberries are big history. But they hold intimate histories of everyday life as well. That's where the strawberry pickers' tickets enter the story—small bits of cardstock creased and frazzled from their hand-to-hand transit through field labor and local commerce.

Delicate things, strawberries are picked one by one—and that is the connection that holds my attention when I look at the strawberry tickets handed out to strawberry pickers. In the scrip from what seems a distant past, now neatly arrayed on my writing table, I see Mr. Baines's pickers kneeling, sitting, bending between the long, low rows, reaching into the greenery, turning leaves, plucking individual berries, placing them in one-quart containers of folded, stapled wood streaked red with the juice of overripe renegades. Berry pickers talk but don't sing; they slide, scoot, and shuffle across on the pale brown sandy loam between the rows. Theirs is work without cadence or rhythm. I look at the 1½-by-2-inch-rectangles, red, gray, blue, green, imprinted with farm owners' names, Drummond, Johnson, Mason, Somers, Moore, Bloxom, and the amount harvested, ranging from two to twenty quarts. Odd numbers are rare. The tickets are pocket-worn, some to the suppleness of cloth, and sweat-creased through innumerable transactions between pickers and owners and local shopkeepers. They are the tangible reckoning of speed and delicacy. They are the finger-softened currency for vanished, all-but-forgotten nations of labor.

The strawberry pickers' chits intimately evoke an intricate infrastructure of things embracing specialty boxcars, field bowers, recipe books, urban markets, and the sensorium of early summer. Farmers the length and breadth of the Eastern Shore as well as in the outlying agricultural districts of Norfolk across the Chesapeake Bay kept accounts by chit in much the same way. Pickers picked the rows, runners carried the berries in trays to temporary stands or "bowers," where the quarts of berries were tallied and tickets returned to the field hands in the strawberry rows. In the bowers, the strawberries were often repacked, with the best strategically layered on the top. A wagon or truck would retrieve the berries from the bowers at regular intervals and convey them to the "block," where they were auctioned, packed in specially designed crates, and shipped by rail or boat to Baltimore, Philadelphia, and other cities. The process, though, began with pickers in the fields.

Mary Onley, a minister and an artist in papier-mâché and paint known to her friends and followers as Mama Girl, builds elaborately detailed tableaux of oyster shuckers, crab pickers, cotton pickers, and the Last Supper, in her house west of the old railroad hamlet of Painter. She's never fashioned a scene of strawberry pickers, but it has been on her mind as she recollects her younger self at work in the fields. Crafting all those berries from paper would be a lot more work than picking them.

"I remember working in the strawberry field, it was one morning, early in the morning . . . early in the morning, and I think our grandparents—I lived with my grandparents—taking us out in the field, and I can remember right from there, I said, 'Boy, I love going to the strawberry field.' Because, boy, you get ten quarts, you got a dollar!" She laughs, "It was ten cents a quart then. You got a dollar. I said, 'But they're so big, it don't take long to make a dollar.'"

Looking back, Mary Onley forges ahead, "I don't know how many crates I picked, and then after that day, see I didn't go in the strawberry field no more. That was through the week before I went to school, early in the morning, mosquitos and gnats biting you and scratching your head, everything, you might even scratch blood off yourself, you itchy. Then after that day I didn't go no more until on Saturdays. Matter of fact, to tell you the truth, it just came to me, I didn't go no more until I was grown!"

There is pleasure in Mary Onley's reminiscence, but her children did not share her enthusiasm for fieldwork: "They hated it!" She describes how her son and daughter would wear work clothes over their school clothes and their embarrassment at the berry stains on their hands and arms. "If you were going to school," she says, "you didn't want to get nothing on your clothes because sometimes you put some clothes over what you already had because you know that bus is going to be coming and you going to have to get out there fast." She continues, "Put on some clothes so the stains . . . so you wouldn't get to school and look up and say, 'Ugh! That's strawberry stain on my arm!'" Where Mary Onley loved working the fields and running her harvesting crew, her children felt shame. For them, strawberry stains were the stigmata of class and necessity, "You know, and the children would laugh at you."

"I think," she adds, "most of the families could have worked in the field, they did what they had to to survive."

Mary Onley recollects a strawberry world in a composite vignette. "Picking strawberries is easy work, if you can put up with the gnats," she laughs. "It's hard for me to hassle being in the field, because I loved it." She offers details, "There in the early morning and you'd pick the strawberry, then you came up with this big, I call them slats. You'd tote the quarts in these slats and you came up, they'd either give you a ticket or give you the money right then. But if they give you a ticket, then, after you finish picking, you go ahead and cash your tickets in. Sometimes more when the strawberry was good, and sometimes there was nothing. Sometime when they were good, you came home with a pretty piece of money. And it was fun. It was fun. Because it was more than just one group of children, or one family group." "Most of the time," she explains, "the family carried the children with them. My grandmother, grandfather, and all three of my cousins, we would be there, then there'd be my uncle with the other cousins, you know what I'm saying? My mother, you know what I'm saying? All of us!" "It would be like a family there picking," she continues, "and it wouldn't just be my family there picking. You'd look over and there's another family you know picking strawberries. It was more like family . . . with the different families. You could talk and have fun."

Mary Onley speaks directly to a connection between work crews and family, between field labor and social pleasure in a seasonal turn: "It was families. Family. Let me see, it was the Reed family, the Walker family, oh god, I can't recall the families out there. And the families—didn't just get to meet the families that was up in Accomack County. We branched out in Northampton County, so we'd get to meet other families. Then up in Maryland, you'd get to meet other families. Different crew leaders with different groups of families." She adds importantly, "What I call family, it's the people that we know, that we connect as a family."

Mary Onley ascended, in time, to the role of crew leader, recruiting family, friends, and neighbors to work in the strawberry fields as well as the hand harvesting of other crops. Strawberry picking remained among her favorite seasonal occupations. They were comparatively easy to harvest, the pay generally was rewarding, and the pickers' conversations as they worked the rows were enlivening. She recalls the continuing use of tickets to keep accounts even as the tickets themselves changed from custom-printed cards to those peeled from a roll: "Either the farmer would pay us, or either the gentlemen I was working for would give me the money. Then I paid the people. The man would have to pay whatever I told him." The latter-day tickets, she noted, "It wouldn't be no number on it or nothing, it would just be a little ticket, just like the ticket like when you were raffling off something." The folks on her crew received "one ticket per quart. One ticket." Her crew members, she concluded, "They know what that one ticket automatically would bring you."

Theodore Peed, relaxing with his great friend H. M. Arnold in the shade of the Bayford oyster house on a breathtakingly hot August afternoon, spoke of his own experiences in the strawberry fields. Peed nods to H. M., "He don't know about strawberry fields, but damn if I don't! You get them suckers in the morning when everything is wet, and it's cold, too, because you start picking in May. Man, your hands down there will freeze, boy! And them gnats come out of them bushes! Man, you'd be on fire, boy! Your hands were cold and you'd be beating your hands on your body, like your fingertips, trying to get them warm. I was going to school. Go to school. Fingertips was red." "Them gnats," Peed chokes and coughs, "they would burn your ass up, boy! You'd be out there in the strawberry field at daybreak. Nine o'clock it was over with."

H. M. agrees, "Yeah, you were done."

Peed explains, "Because they had to carry them to the market. They had to get them while it was cool. Pack them and everything, carry them to market in Exmore."

H. M. interjects, "Getting ten cents a quart."

Peed continues, "Ten cents a quart. Ten cents a quart."

H. M. chuckles, "Pick about ten quarts before you went to school and had a dollar, you were doing good."

"But me," Peed presses on, "I used to get by the fastest pickers. My aunt and another guy, right? If they pick a hundred, I could pick about eighty some. So I had about eight dollars. But we didn't keep all of that money. You had to carry some of that money home. You kept a little bit. Maybe your parents—I take it to my grandmama, because they fed you, bought you clothes and everything."

As for the portion Peed kept, "I was trying to get that little bit of money before I went to school. That's all there was to it. . . . That girl, you'd go to the school and buy her a carton of milk or something, you know what I mean, or lunch every now and then. You was a man! You was a man!"

A remarkably detailed 1899 account of the strawberry harvest near Norfolk resonates with Mary Onley's and Theodore Peed's recollections:

> I had just one chance to see strawberry-picking going on in the regular business way. Mr. Trotman had received intelligence from Boston that berries were up to 12 cents, and, in fact, I believe he had kept picking right along. You see when the fields are once abandoned they cannot very well start again, because rotten or overripe berries would get among the good ones in spite of the pickers; therefore the proprietor of a strawberry-field must keep the pickers going till he decides to stop, and then he must stop for good. When I saw the pickers in the field I said to friend Stebbins, "There must be very nearly a hundred people who are gathering berries." I have been so much in the habit of estimating the number of hives in an apiary by simply a casual glance that I thought I could guess pretty nearly at the number of people scattered through the patch. Friend Stebbins counted them, and reported 104. There were all sorts of people—big and little, old and young, black and white; but for all that, every thing seemed to go on very harmoniously and quietly. Little colored boys, who seemed hardly big enough to carry a quart of berries, would march in with a tray on their heads, and offer their filled quart boxes and get their tickets. Some of them did not have very elaborate clothing, but they always arranged to have a pocket that would carry their tickets safely. A smart colored man received the boxes on a sort of counter, letting the picker take his tray back to the field. The proprietor's son was stationed near by with tickets of different values stowed in handy pockets; and he always had the proper ticket or tickets to hand out just as soon as the picker was ready to go back.

Artist Howard Pyle reported a similar scene on the Eastern Shore of Maryland in the 1870s. "The berry-pickers, mostly negroes," he began, "are a peculiar class of people, holding the same relative position that the hop-pickers do in England." In the romanticized Jim Crow voice and perspective of his day, Pyle rhapsodized, "They are a merry, jolly, happy-go-lucky tribe, taking no thought of the morrow, finding food in the berry fields, where they work for a mere pittance, finding raiment in a motley of tat-

William Baines with the morning harvest, Machipongo area, Virginia.

ters and patches." Pyle turned his attention to the business of berry pick-ing: "In the berry-house, where the packing of boxes is done, a huge pile of empty crates reaches nearly to the roof, the loaded ones being placed in a large berry wagon standing near at hand. As the fruit is gathered it is brought into this house and placed on a deal shelf along its length, the pickers receiving tickets for the amount of quarts they bring in, good for the sum of two, four, six, or more cents, depending on the quantity they have gathered." He ends, observing: "It is amusing to watch the various characteristics as each receives his or her tickets: the trusting one, who thrusts his 'keerds' into his apology for a pocket as he receives them, with-out a second glance at their amount; the cautious one, who puzzles over his account, striving to master the problem of how much nine, minus two, multiplied by two, amounts to; the generous one, who treats the 'colored ladies' to cakes; the selfish, who devours all the cakes himself, and so on through the list of human characteristics."

This was Pyle's perceived world of strawberry tickets imbued with the romance of local color, framed through a wistful curiosity of an American primitive. Strawberry tickets are more deeply haunted than that.

G. Fred Floyd Jr., owner of an eighty-acre farm fronting the Chesapeake Bay on Church Neck, details the mechanics of the strawberry harvest: "We'd plant about three acres every year and do away with three acres every year. You got to harvest those strawberries about three seasons, and then they deteriorate." "I can remember all the people," he reflects, "African American people that lived in villages around there, and of course the ones on the farm. There was many a morning when I'd wake up early and look out there, and it would still be dark, not really dark, but not really bright, and there would be people sitting at the end of the row, waiting for it to get light enough to go in and start picking." Their payment took the form of the same species of farm scrip Pyle reported nearly a century earlier, "You weren't paid cash. You were given a ticket. And you could take that ticket to one of the stores at Bridgetown and use it just like money. Or then, come Saturday or whenever, you could go to the owner and cash them in." Those stores are all gone now.

Fred linked the work to children's work, "Before you'd go to school, you'd go out and pick two or three quarts, get two to three cents a quart for them . . . and you'd have your tickets, and you'd show them to your buddy, 'I picked this morning.'" Fred's son and namesake, "Gee," remembers his time in the fields with far less affection. The gnats that bloodied Mary Onley and Theodore Peed plagued him, too. He recalls the use of smudge pots in a futile effort to lessen the assault. In first grade, he missed school to lend a hand in the harvest, and he often did the heavy labor of an adult. For his father, the tickets signified pride of work; for him, they represented rough labor. For Mary Onley's son, the tickets encoded shame, coming from the fields in the crew van: "He wouldn't even go into the store if he was hungry. He'd cover up his head. He didn't want nobody seeing him." For Theodore Peed, the dimes and dollars he earned contributed to his family's income and funded the opportunity to impress a girl.

Moggie Marsh's grandparents grew strawberries for market. Like other children, she picked through the height of the harvest. Strawberries, fragile things, cannot wait.

Barry Marsh turns to his wife behind the counter of the antique emporium in the old railroad town of Exmore, "Your mother remembers you getting up at four in the morning. You and your three sisters. Dressing them, because it would be chilly, and going out to the fields."

Moggie adds, "Dressing us warm, and going out and pick strawberries." Her mother would humor them: "'Probably, you ate more than you picked.'" "This," Moggie says, "was all before school."

Barry Marsh shifts his attention to the larger workforce. "Most of the strawberry pickers, I imagine, were local, because that was a good time in the year to make a few dollars if you were young and didn't mind back-breaking work," he chuckles. "Getting down and picking them strawberries, because I remember some of them pickers, they were fast." "They picked them and put them into the strawberry containers," he explains. "Put them on a flat. A flat would hold probably sixteen or so smaller berry crates."

Moggie observes that the field was organized in rows or lines and that "you would walk through the lines to pick them. A field full of lines and lines of strawberries. They started at one end and worked their way up, but nobody was assigned a row." The pickers in the rows would fill quarts and place them on flats. They would then run the filled flats to the ends of the rows, where they would be picked up and carried to the shed or bower for packing and transport to the block or auction house.

George McMath's grandfather and great-uncle, successful nurserymen and agricultural entrepreneurs, not only developed new strawberry varietals in their test fields next to the railroad line at Onley but also invented a special crate for rail transport and operated the produce exchange. He spoke of how, even in the brevity of the season, strawberry culture was central to Eastern Shore agriculture and rural life. "The season is very short,' George estimates, "probably about three weeks. It was the focus of Shore living during that period."

In full swing, the season dominated farm life from field to market. G. Fred Floyd, who worked with his father through the 1940s, 1950s, and 1960s, recalls: "We had a strawberry block at Bayview, and there was one at Exmore further up the shore. And we picked those strawberries, we picked half of the field—half one day and the other half the next day. Picked them in quarts. And we packed them. When I was a very young child, they actually packed them in thirty-two-quart crates. Then they went to, later on, twenty-four quarts. Then, toward the last, they got them packed in sixteen quarts." He continues, "You haul them to the block. I remember one time we had a car, and we had a trailer a lot of people used, that was before we had a pickup or small truck. A lot of people had a trailer, back of an old vehicle of some kind, an old car, and we hauled them that way. And they would be auctioned and there would be plenty of buyers."

A clear grasp of the dynamics, differences, and fluctuations at the block proved key to the successful sale of strawberries: "There would be quite a lot of strawberries. We had a couple of vehicles. One we pulled on the back of a car. One was an older pickup. One of us would go to Bayview block; the other would go to Exmore block." Having tested the murky market waters,

Strawberry pickers, Machipongo area, Virginia.

"We'd still have some left over from those two loads, and we'd come back, having been to the block and disposed of those berries, and we would confer as to who got what kind of price where, and then we'd make a decision what to do with the residue. Which block to go to. And that was kind of the gist of the whole thing." Nodding with the memory of the number of farmers selling their loads of strawberries, he added, "I'm telling you, the number of vehicles that had strawberries on them, it was amazing. The buyers would buy those strawberries, send them all over the East Coast. And that was mostly before refrigeration. A lot of them went to the eastern markets. Of course, some went further to New York and Boston and Baltimore and Philadelphia."

"A lot of times," he continued, "you'd ship right directly, the farmer would, to a commission merchant. Most of the strawberries were sold to people that were in the produce business. It wouldn't be any problem for twenty-some loads of strawberries to leave the shore, even maybe more than that, on a daily basis."

Cracking into that final jar of last season's strawberry preserves, I inhale an essence of bright white flowers, damp straw, and sandy earth. I look forward to drum fish, asparagus, early soft-shell crabs, and the last gasp

Strawberry picker, Pickett's Harbor Farms, Townsend area, Virginia.

of winter oysters—and then I consider the culinary limits of strawberries. Fresh from Mr. Baines, they are sweet things and best eaten fresh, often as strawberry shortcake—or put up as preserves, an art in itself.

H. M. Arnold remembers, "My mother would make that homemade shortcake." He sighs at the recollection, and Theodore Peed does, too. "Slice that in half and butter that. Put strawberries on that. Hot dang!" "She'd make a cake and cut it and butter it in the middle and put it back together. Slice a piece off and put it in your bowl. Make sure you got plenty of juice and strawberries."

Theodore Peed connects the memory to a larger story of home cooking that he sees slipping into the past. "Them old ones knew how to cook, boy. I tell you one thing, the poor people cooked better than the rich people could. But they had to know how to save," Peed emphasizes. "Stretch that food. They could stretch it, too, boy. Coming up, you didn't find no bad cooks."

H. M. concludes softly, "That's all they did."

George McMath remembers strawberry ice cream. "Mother did make strawberry ice cream and I loved it. It was wonderful. I'd come home from school and she was saving some frozen strawberry ice cream, which I loved. Made with Pet milk, I believe. Condensed milk. I can taste some now!" he laughs.

Barry Marsh reprises the more recent invention of strawberry pie. "We were involved with the Pungo Strawberry Festival [on the other side of the Chesapeake Bay] for about three years, four years. We had a strawberry pie tent. We did real good with strawberry pies. You'd have about four women in the back, and we'd have a pallet of strawberries that would be this high." He gestures about seven feet in height. "Easily that. A couple of years we even had two pallets."

"A week before the festival," he gets down to details, "you would have women who were taking shells and baking the shells and stacking them and restacking them. Then on the morning of the festival, you'd have four women back there, and they'd be capping strawberries, transferring them from the pallets, capping them and washing them."

"Slicing them," Moggie, his wife, glosses. "Then you had another group of women that would be placing them in the shell, and then you'd have the Cool Whip or something over that."

George McMath knows his way around strawberry pie but observes, "I don't recall strawberry pie growing up. We have it now. But I never had a piece of strawberry pie until ten or fifteen years ago. That's a whole new thing for here."

And then there is an 1888 julep recipe from the across the Chesapeake Bay, one surely emulated in local gentry households:

> In the early spring, gather the young and tender mint, have your demijohn three-quarters full of the best whisky, and into its mouth drop the mint, rolled into little balls, and well bruised—about a quarter of a peck, loosely heaped up, to each gallon of liquor. Next, enough loaf sugar is saturated in water to melt it, and sweeten the whisky *ad lib*. This fills the demijohn, which is then sealed tight, and kept for the future, being rarely opened for at least two years.

The preparation of the drink is simple, and yet artistic. First, a julep ought never to be mixed but in a silver flagon—there is such a thing as a "perfect accord." The demijohn being opened, the fragrant liquor is poured into the mug, with a double handful of *crushed* ice—not pounded, but crushed until it is like hail or snow ice—(a stout towel and a few blows against a brick wall will accomplish this result); add a few sprigs of fresh mint, a few strawberries, a tablespoonful of Jamaica rum, and you will have an elixir worthy of Jove to drink and Ganymede to bear.

Strawberries may have been relegated to a julep garnish—but they crowned the concoction, bestowing color, flavor, and freshness in a surely near-lethal alchemy. Still, strawberry preserves and jams dominate the menu.

Bessie Gunter's *Housekeeper's Companion* offers two approaches to preserving strawberries on the Eastern Shore in the late 1800s. Both require sugar and heat:

TO PRESERVE STRAWBERRIES.

Put in a bowl alternate layers of a pound of strawberries and a pound of sugar, till you have in each bowl three pounds of fruit. Let it stand an hour or two. Put it on the fire, and in twenty minutes from the time it begins to boil, it will be done. Keep them in glass tumblers.
—Mrs. S. S.

Gunter's second entry, collected from a resident of Onancock, instructs the cook: "Put three quarters of a pound of sugar to a pound of fruit, just putting enough water to cover the sugar, and let it boil. After skimming, put in your berries and let boil fifteen minutes. Then put the berries on shallow dishes, covering with half the syrup. Set in the sun for two days, the second day add the other half of syrup."

Fairy Mapp White, whose *Foolproof Cook Book* furnished newlyweds' kitchens through the 1960s, reprised a method using stoneware crocks that concluded with a childhood memory. "Our good neighbor," White wrote, "always made us welcome to get all the strawberries that we wanted to eat and to preserve. Her children wanted to eat the berries as soon as they were preserved, when, I agree this kind are at their best." Recalling her mother's pantry, White penned, "I can see now the stone crocks filled with preserves lined up in my mother's storeroom. We children were given turns to name the preserve we would like for supper. Each crock was covered with cloth and paper, carefully labeled."

Amy Brandt, in quest of the perfect consistency for strawberry preserves, explains her approach in detail. She begins with an overview of how a cook gauges the readiness of preserves: "It's this timing thing, or a visual prompt. Like it should look when you put the spoon in and you lift it out. The mixture should be sheeting off of the spoon."

The problem jam makers encounter, though, is one of individual subjectivity combined with the inevitability of variation in the strawberries themselves. "Visual is interpretable by your own self," Amy observes, "and timing is dependent on fruit all being exactly the same, which it is not. Some berries are big, some berries are waterlogged, some berries are small, and you know drier, which is the ultimate kind of what you want."

As she speaks, it is apparent that Amy has developed a strawberry preserves philosophy that braids the registers of science, art, and invention: "I really was thinking about it a lot, and I said, 'There has got to be a scientific way to do this.' Because there's way too many people doing this as a production item, that they can't be standing there looking at it or just timing it. So, I thought about it, and it came to me, temperature." Amy continues her account, and I am struck by the ways in which her experiments placed local custom in tension with imported science. For generations, season after season, local cooks produced their strawberry preserves by sight and touch through practiced craft. Each jar of preserves contained not just a taste of place but the taste of knowledge as well. What Amy set forth is something very different. First, she speaks to the problem of sweetness, "You're essentially making candy and you don't want to end up with that cloying taste where you don't taste fruit anymore." When the candied quality takes over, she summarizes, "it's just gone too far." The goal, she says, is "how do I make it taste like fresh fruit?"

Amy's answer synthesizes demonstrated practice with a deep knowledge of culinary science—exactly what you would expect from an established and respected chef. "I always use lemon zest because the zest is where most of the pectin is. I think most people use juice," she elaborates, "I use both—I use lemon zest and lemon juice."

Then she turns to science. Jam sets, she explains, at 200 degrees, elaborating, "I do everything that I have to do to my jam before the temperature reaches 220. And I have a digital thermometer that I insert into the vat of jam, and at like 216, I put in a mixture, I just put the juice and the zest together." At 219 degrees, Amy goes on, she sprinkles dried pectin into the mixture and stirs, bringing the mixture to the magical 220 degree mark. "I turn it off, and I process the jars," she concludes, "and that's worked out really, really well."

An afterthought occurs to her: "Another thing that I think has made a big difference is that I have two copper preserving pans. One was my grandmother's on my dad's side, and then one I purchased. And both, they really make a big difference in being able to speedily reduce and also have evaporation." One pan for family and heritage, one pan for increased production.

Amy, who creates jam in large batches, follows a system. "I put my sugar in first into the pan dry. And then I put the berries in." Speaking to scale, she adds, "I did a lot this year, and originally I was cutting them up, and I said, 'This is a lot of time that I'm wasting.' So we hulled them, and then I have a big potato masher, like a commercial size, that has a handle that's about two feet long, and then the mashing disc is about six or eight inches in diameter. So essentially, I just mash the fruit in the pan with a potato masher, and it makes like a quarter-inch slice and also helps start to release juice. And I stir it together, and I turn it on high until it's about 215 or 216. And then I just keep cutting it back incrementally . . . and you're stirring frequently, as you start to feel like maybe things are starting to drop to the bottom and stick a little bit. Then it's time to turn it down, turn it down, turn it down."

She continues, "The other thing that I did, too, is that, you know when you're canning, especially doing a lot, you don't want to have to go into the water bath with the jars and then take them out and then take the lids out . . . and I read that this girl washes and rinses her jars, puts them on a tray, and puts them in the oven at like 225 degrees. And that's what I did. And then you just take them out on a half-sheet tray and you fill them up, and then I do the same things with the lids and the bands, and it has worked out really well. I still process them with the water bath because I want that big change in heat from when they come out of the pot, sitting there, you really get an aggressive sealing of the vacuum, the vacuum seal."

More to the point, Amy's strawberry preserves are delicious.

The science and empirical observation underpinning Amy's analysis of the sweet spot for strawberry preserves represents a rarified refinement of an approach that is at its heart simple. Catherine Kellam's strawberry preserves, reprised in her self-published cookbook, are pretty much those made by folks in a seasonal moment. Her ingredients combine one quart of strawberries, four cups of sugar, and the luxury of one and a half lemons:

> Place all ingredients into a heavy saucepan.
> Let them come to a rolling boil.
> Cook for about 20 minutes.
> Ladle into sterile jars and seal.

Her abrupt declarative sentences scan poetically, a culinary quatrain underscored with the observation that strawberry preserves are great with biscuits—an observation she surely doesn't need to make. When I align

Kellam's instructions with Amy's narrative, I am mindful of the extent to which the "scientific approach" codifies and captures practice—as if a kind of worry about lost knowledge lurks on the outskirts of tradition, replacing practiced invention with regulated instruction.

Amy's rendition of processing strawberry preserves evokes similar ways of knowing in the cultivation, harvesting, and marketing of strawberries. Agricultural commentaries from the mid-1800s onward extol scientific method in the breeding, cultivating, shipping, and marketing of the fruit. I think of the unruly European woodland strawberry of the 1600s resisting domestication and the birth of the modern strawberry, born in France of parents from North and South America—four hemispheres in one bowl— with cream.

Nobody captures the way that dipping into a jar of strawberry preserves evokes a distant season than Amy Brandt: "If you eat a strawberry that you've picked or just went and picked up and it's warm out and they're warm from the field and you eat that, it's an incredible experience." Tears seem to well up in her eyes as she speaks. "It really captures that beautiful essence of that fruit at its prime. I've got a soft spot for homemade things like biscuits that are so simple, and then you put strawberry jam on it in the wintertime, and you're instantly transported back to this time when the earth was waking up and the leaves were coming on the tree, and it was getting warm, and you know, seeing people at the stand and seeing Mr. Baines."

She speaks longingly as if winter has already arrived and the world outside her kitchen window has gone dormant and sere. Strawberry preserves, she says, are "a nice way to be transported, you know a time machine, to be transported back to another place." I know that feeling all too well. What I imagine, though, is something different. Reflecting on the recollections of Mary Onley, Fred Floyd, Theodore Peed, and Barry and Moggie Marsh, I see strawberry pickers in the gray instant before dawn clustered at the ends of the long, low rows. Heads wrapped to ward off the plague of gnats, chilled fingers and hands slapped and snapped into warmth, strawberry pickers bend to their harvest. The thumb-worn cardstock tickets I hold in my hand offer testimony to their labors.

A CHEF'S RECIPE FOR HOME

PEACH CHIPOTLE JAM

Rebecca Y. Herman, Westerhouse, Virginia

Rebecca Herman's inventive jams bring together Eastern Shore of
Virginia flavors in new combinations that include locally grown fruit such
as strawberries, figs, blueberries, and blackberries. Her jam bridges the
long arc of growing imported fruit trees that began in the 1630s with the
recent explosion of Latin American flavors and ingredients.

Makes 7 eight-ounce jars

Special equipment: water-bath canner; 7 eight-ounce canning jars

> 3 pounds ripe peaches
> 2 tablespoons fresh lemon juice
> 1 box SURE-JELL fruit pectin
> ½ teaspoon butter or margarine (optional, to reduce foam)
> 5½ cups sugar
> 1–2 chipotles in adobo, finely chopped and warmed

Fill the canner halfway to three-quarters of the way full with
water and bring the water to a boil. Lower to a simmer. Wash the
jars and screw bands in hot soapy water; rinse with warm water.
(Alternatively, wash them in the dishwasher.) Place the flat lids in a
saucepan and pour boiling water over them. Let stand until ready to
use. Drain well before filling.

Peel, pit, and finely chop the peaches. (I use a food processor.)
Measure exactly 4 cups of the prepared fruit into a 6- to 8-quart
saucepan. Add the lemon juice and stir until well blended. Stir in
the pectin. Add the butter, if using. Bring the fruit to a full rolling
boil over high heat, stirring constantly (the mixture should not stop
bubbling when stirred). Stir in the sugar and return to a full rolling
boil and boil exactly 1 minute, stirring constantly. Remove the
pan from the heat. Skim off any foam with a metal spoon. Add the
warmed chipotles and mix thoroughly.

Immediately ladle the jam into the prepared jars, filling them
to within ¼ inch of the tops. Wipe the jar rims and threads with
a warm wet cloth, cover with the flat lids, and screw the bands
on tightly. Place the jars in the canner rack and lower it into the
canner. (Water must cover the jars by 1–2 inches. Add boiling water,

if necessary.) Cover the canner and bring the water to a boil. Process the jam for 10 minutes. Remove the jars and place them upright on the rack. Tilt the jars gently to evenly distribute chipotles and fruit if necessary and cool completely. After the jars cool, check their seals by pressing the middle of the lid with your finger. (If the lid springs back, it is not sealed and refrigeration is necessary.)

Panfish Spot On!

Late summer the phone rings in the Bayford oyster house on the Eastern Shore of Virginia. "Bayford," H. M. Arnold answers. "Yes, Ma'am," he says a few seconds into the conversation, "I don't have any spot today. They don't seem to be running. Nobody I know has them. I have some hardheads though, if you want to drive down and get them. Thank you." H. M. shakes his head and sits down in his plastic chair by the stainless-steel counter where he shucks oysters for the winter trade from Thanksgiving to New Year's. The afternoon steams August hot, a bit of breeze ruffles the water on Nassawadox Creek outside the door. The tide is rising, and soon enough will seep under sills and into the dock end of the venerable shucking house, sheeting over the old concrete floors, compelling H. M. and his visitors first to walk on boards and then to slosh their way past the soft-shell crab shedding tanks now all but closed down for the season. Tank, the monumental Chesapeake Bay retriever who lives up the hill, stands in the boat launch with a chunk of pine branch clenched in his jaws, waiting for someone, anyone will do, to seize the wood and pitch it into the water. Strangers shy away from the large dog, regulars ignore him. Tank perseveres. And so do the callers seeking spot, a panfish deeply savored in this corner of the world. The phone rings. "Bayford," H. M. answers.

Spot, it seems, have diminished in their numbers since 1890, when a fish census noted: "Large numbers of young spot from 3 to 4 inches in length were seined in the bay at Cape Charles City. They were present in abundance, numerous schools being seen. . . . As a pan fish, the spot is the most highly prized of all fishes sold in the Norfolk market." Writing from North Carolina, Hugh M. Smith reported in 1907, "The spot, which gets its name from the round mark on its shoulder, inhabits the east coast of the United States from Massachusetts to Texas, and is one of the most abundant and best

Spot freshly caught, Nassawadox Creek, Virginia.

known of our food fishes." Smith concludes, "The spot ranks high as a food and is by many persons regarded as the best of the salt-water pan fishes. There is a good demand for North Carolina spots in Baltimore, Washington, and other markets of the Chesapeake region, and the fish is also rated high as a salt fish for local consumption." Spot, another observer reported, "are the smallest members of the croaker family that are sold with any regularity. Most specimens weigh only about ¼ pound. Spots are easy to recognize by their spot right behind the gill opening." The spot's distinguishing markings, asserts Pooh Johnston, oysterman, raconteur, and cook in Onancock, are the marks of Christ's fingertips imprinted when he divided the loaves and fishes for the multitude in Mark 6:41. Communion of a different variety causes H. M.'s phone to ring.

Uncommonly common in the lower Chesapeake and North Carolina's sounds, the spot (also known regionally as Jimmy, chub, roach, goody, and Lafayette) lives inshore from late spring through autumn and winters in deeper offshore waters during the winter months: "The waters of the Chesapeake Bay off Norfolk, Virginia, are such prime spot fishing grounds that out-of-town menus often list this small, sweet fish as 'Norfolk Spot.' As early as the Revolutionary War, Norfolkians were enamoured with the little fish. . . . Prior to spawning season in the fall, the spot takes on a golden color much like its cousin the croaker. At that time the fish are often referred to as 'Ocean View Yellow Bellies' because they congregate to feed off Ocean View, a Norfolk neighborhood on the Chesapeake Bay." When spot run, H. M.'s phone rings with unrelenting frequency.

The spot's culinary associations are tightly knit into the history of place, but over time its associations with class have become more generous. A late 1880s survey of the diets of African American families in the Virginia tidewater recorded spot (or roach—the venerable name by which spot are still known by some folks on the Eastern Shore) along with other fish, including croaker (or hardhead) and salt or smoked herring. Along with sturgeon heads (used for fish chowders) and snapping turtles (also cooked in stews or soups), the spot lacked august historical associations. Danny Doughty, whose family ran a fish store on the highway near the railroad town of Painter, spoke to the close associations the fish held with the African American community: "Spot was one of the staple fish, one of the cheaper, you know, fish that a lot of people—if they wanted their fish filleted or they didn't want bones in it, or whatever that was really considered in bad taste because the best part of the meat was the closest to the bone. If you were a real fish eater, you knew how to get to all the good meat, and just leave the bones, you know. It was kind of frowned upon if you were to fillet or waste any of the fish, if you didn't eat every bit of it and didn't clean it to its full potential to get the most out of it."

Charles Amory of Amory's fish wholesaler in Hampton, Virginia, remembered one of the few instances in which spot successfully climbed the social ladder. A Washington, D.C., fishmonger, he recollected, "called me one day, and he said, 'I've got a special order I need to go to the White House.' He said, 'I want you to handpick them, mark the box so I know which one it is.' And we did it, and sent them up there. That was the only high-dollar, white tablecloth that I knew directly about. And, you know, years ago, I'd send spot over to the yacht club, and they'd cook them for lunch. We didn't usually send very many because there weren't that many of us that would eat them. We didn't even try that this year. The cooks that graduated from the culinary institute in Norfolk didn't know how to cook them." Over a century later, the spot plays a leading role in a culinary social imaginary centered on nostalgia and authenticity.

Commentaries on spot tend to be notably incisive. "The spot," one 1880s source details, "is generally similar in appearance to the Atlantic croaker, but the body is shorter and deeper and there are no barbels on its lower jaw." It concludes, "There is no commercial fishery for this species, but considerable quantities are utilized as panfish by sport fishermen." "Spot," cookbook author Alan Davidson observed with equal concision and a century later, achieves a "maximum length about 35 cm; common length 15 to 25 cm. This fish is blue-grey above, with golden gleams, and silvery below. Its range is from Texas to Cape Cod. It frequents sheltered bays and estuaries and is of some commercial importance in the Chesapeake Bay area. Cuisine: A good pan fish." And with greatest rapture, a spot fan succinctly enthused in a regional cookbook, "Though small, rarely over a pound in size, the spot is considered the best pan fish around. Many Tidewater Virginians salt the tiny fillets down in crocks for later eating during the winter months. Nothing, however, quite beats a spot fresh from the water and into the pan. Rolled in cornmeal and quickly fried in hot fat is the traditional way of cooking them."

Panfish, something of a dismissive term, is defined as "fish suitable for frying whole in a pan, especially one caught by an angler rather than bought." Panfish could be purchased in seafood markets throughout the South, for example, at Young's Fish Market far from the Atlantic Coast located in the mountain town of Asheville, North Carolina, where the proprietors advertised in 1900, "For Frying—Smelts, Small Trout, Croakers, Perch, and Panfish." The designation, with its associations with the "amateur" fisherman, carries connotations of a "simple" preparation lacking the status of a recipe and outside the scope of a cuisine. P. G. Ross of the Virginia Institute for Marine Science and a decoy carver, after inspecting a stretch of oyster ground, leaned over the back of his truck and recalled fishing for spot as a boy. It was the one fish he could count on catching. Carrying spot home to his grandmother made him feel as if he were contributing to the family larder in a meaningful way.

Panfish on the Eastern Shore of Virginia simply refers to a host of small fish including spot, croaker, sand mullet, jumping mullet, hogfish, swelling toads, and more. The idea of the panfish relies on four characteristics: size (they fit whole into a skillet), status (they tend to be associated with less desirable fish—often linked to qualities of oiliness or boniness), procurement (although netted, seined, or trapped commercially, panfish are commonly associated with amateur angling), and preparation (largely fried). In essence, panfish, spot in particular, are notable for their everydayness, remarkable only in the moments of their absence. When folks call H. M. Arnold for spot, it's about layers of memory and association that transcend the culinary specifics of the fish they eat. Spot are an acquired taste in the sense that they are a learned delicacy about place and identity.

When it comes to spot, nobody knows the history of the market like father and son Charlie and Meade Amory. Meade, who runs the family fish and trucking company, sits between "a hundred years of experience" with his father, Charlie, on one side and Richard Coughenour on the other. A single shared desk runs the length of the room, fronting a picture window that looks out onto the loading docks where workers navigate small forklifts, rocketing around pallets of seafood, loading orders into refrigerated trucks destined for the Midwest. The open timber-framed structure smells of brine, fresh fish, and the chill of refrigeration. In the distance the warehouse ends at the water, where fishing boats dock and deckhands offload their catch. Amory's workers, well gloved, work through the fish piled on sorting tables, distributing them quickly onto beds of crushed ice packed in waxed cartons. The fish arrive clear-eyed, pink-gilled, and scented only with seawater. They are so fresh that Meade boasts, "They're still kicking." Iced, a portion of the haul goes directly onto the waiting trucks and to market; the remainder of the fish are hauled across the wet concrete floors and into a walk-in freezer where they await demand.

Amory's Seafood is the last business of its kind along a waterfront increasingly confronted with urban renewal schemes, new houses, condominiums, and acres of recreational boats. Only Cooper's, the equally venerable marine supplies store on the opposite side of King Street in Hampton, keeps it company, remembering the vitality of the seafood trade when a remarkable variety of fish was readily available, including a number of species long out of favor. Spot, according to Meade Amory, who surveys the packing room bustle, have always been a seasonal staple: "Spot run out of the bay in the fall, and that's the big run of fish, and that's when everybody catches them in gill nets, haul seines, pound nets for the most part. . . . People will set up anywhere along the shore with gill nets, mostly. It can start as early as the middle of August or as late as the first or second week of October, and when it starts, it usually lasts for anywhere from four to six weeks. Sometimes it can last as long as eight weeks. The fish leave the bay, and that's when you catch them. . . . They get ready to run, something signals them—Mother Nature—usually a good north wind gets them mov-

Spot fried with sweet potato and greens, Exmore Diner, Exmore, Virginia.

ing. . . . The fish are white all summer, and then, when they go to start running, they are gold—shiny, pretty gold. Gold belly, the fins are bright, shiny gold, and the customers know that's what they're looking for and that's what they're asking for. They used to call them Norfolk spot, and I don't know if it has to do with when they leave the Chesapeake Bay, as they go around Cape Henry and come through Ocean View area and out and down the beach—that's when they're the prettiest color."

Meade Amory continues as his father listens: "There's a very small market for spot. It's pretty much just East Coast, and pretty much just the middle states. We do send some to Boston, and some to Miami, but mostly New York to Atlanta, and probably, I'd say 60 or 70 [percent] of it is Maryland, Virginia, and North Carolina." The spot once landed were tallied by weight and number and boxed for shipping: "Everything used to be weighed in wooden fish boxes, and they were a hundred pounds. One hundred pounds of fish, put ice in the bottom and ice on top—that's one hundred pounds. When you hear people talk about a count, particularly with spot or croaker, they talk about a head count to the hundred pound. A two-hundred-count spot is a half-a-pound spot."

On an autumnlike blue-sky July early morning, the sun lighting up the quiet surface of Nassawadox Creek, H. M. in oilskins and I in a heavy rubber apron push off from the Bayford oyster house dock in search of spot. His dog, Mick, curled in the bow, dreams to the rhythmic slap of water and the outboard's grrr. We skim past lines of crab pots and staked marsh clam and oyster grounds, where growers are already at work culling their crop, heading toward the deep hole where H. M. set his nets in predawn darkness. A black flag fashioned from a ruined plastic trash bag flutters above the cork that marks one end of the fifty-fathom net. A red float marks its terminus in the distance. H. M. idles the motor, sets out two baskets for sorting the fish, and neatly hooks the marker, hauling it into the boat. "You pull the cork line, Cap'n," he says to me—and I jump to. Hand-over-hand, we haul the net. The fish are scarce, but they are here. "Bluefish," H. M. remarks, slipping it from the mesh and dropping it into the orange basket. "Croaker," flipping the grunting fish into the blue basket. More croakers. More blues. We encounter a handful of menhaden: "Carolina spot," H. M. smiles, tossing it back into the creek. More croakers and bluefish—and then we begin to pull in a few spot. They are beginning to show some size after a summer of grazing the bottoms of the creeks and bay; a couple have the first golden tones of the fall run on their underbellies. We're done. Two hauls of the net yield fifty pounds of croakers, maybe two dozen bluefish, a sea trout, and perhaps a dozen spot. "It's not like it was," H. M. observes as he revs the engine and we head back to the dock.

Casual fishermen go after spot with rod and reel outfitted with a bottom rig baited with bloodworms. Inshore commercial fishermen, on the other hand, generally pursue three approaches: haul seines, gill nets, and traps or pound nets. Haul seines consist of large nets run out from shore and then circled back to capture fish running parallel to the shoreline. Haul seines are rare now, but in the 1950s and 1960s news of a seine traveled in the community, and folks turned out with burlap bags to retrieve the bycatch when the fishermen's labors were done. The dark rolls of the snake-like net lay on the silver-bright sand of a moonlit beach, the doomed fish gasped wrapped in its folds, the bystanders gleaned its length. Pound nets consist of a line of heavy wooden stakes planted at right angles to shore that extend into a penlike configuration. Nets are hung from the poles in a configuration that leads the fish into the pen and a trap known as the heart. The fish migrating along the shoreline hit the net and follow it out to get around the barrier, only to find themselves entrapped in the heart. Gill nets are run laid out with the tides and marked at either end with a buoy. Following the turn of the tide, the fisherman hauls the net onboard, shaking the fish out of its mesh and into baskets.

H. M. Arnold reprises gillnetting for spot on the Eastern Shore: "The boys that really gillnetted years ago, they would, at the end of the season, like August, end of August, if they knew a northeaster was coming, they would grab their gear and go to the Western Shore and anchor their nets out because northeast [winds] blew them up against the shore over there. And they'd have big catches, and they did this year. . . . And they'd catch them in fish traps over there, too. I mean by the tons. Over here [on the Eastern Shore] you don't." He continued, noting that spot tend to segregate themselves from another favored panfish—the croaker. "When they mingled, though," he began, "you'd go to one net and it would be nothing but croakers, and you could have a net by that barge and it would be nothing but spot. And that's what I wanted—spot. You can have them croakers. They fall out of the net; those croakers, you pick them." He laughs and then recalls how another Bayford waterman needed help on one memorable occasion: "Steve Bunce one day, I had fished and come in. I mean, everyone was catching them. I had probably fifteen hundred, two thousand pounds. Of course, they were fishing a lot more nets. And I came in, went up to Ches-Atlantic [a seafood wholesaler in the railroad town of Painter and now closed] and unloaded and brought my ice back and everything." Steve, H. M. smiles, "was on VHF [radio], and we're sitting in the store and he called, and goes, 'What're you doing?' 'Nothing.' And he said, 'Man, I got so many fish, can you come out here and take one?' And, I mean, just out here. Not two miles off. . . . And I said, 'Well, we got a couple of them in here. We'll come out and take one.' So, went on out and I pull up to him. And he had a load of croaker or spot in that one. I think it was croakers. I said, 'Which one you want me to take?' And he goes, 'Well, I got two of them. There's one here and one there.' I said, 'OK, I'll take that one.' So, we're getting ready; we're getting our oilskins on and everything, and we pull that net. It had all spot in it. He got through that one and went to the next one, and it had all croakers in it again. In about three hours we were done, man. We probably had about fifteen hundred pounds in that net. It was a load!"

Spot, H. M. explains, could also be netted through a technique known as sounding that fished the space between offshore sandbars and the shoreline:

Inside the shoreline there used to be two or three sloughs. They were about four foot deep. And we'd go out there on the flood tide, just take one net—about fifty fathoms, three inch, three-and-a-quarter mesh back then because they were nice spot—and run the net out. Of course, we didn't have a big boat then, a little old scow was all we had. And we'd go around the net, maybe ten yards from the net, and as we did it, we'd take a pole—and it was hard sand and there was some grass out there then, too (ain't too much grass out there now)—go around that baby two or three times, fish the net, and you'd have yourself a basket of nice spot. And you'd run it back again, or if you didn't even take it up and you just ran it over the boat, you could do that most of the flood tide. I just run the motor and the boat, and somebody would be up front there hitting it, sounding it with a pole, unless you were by yourself, then you did it. Go around it maybe two or three times. I've tried it two or three times, but it hasn't worked like it used to. We'd catch two or three hundred pounds of them.

The taste for spot is linked to time and place, H. M. muses. "The old generation is gone," adding that the current market wants "round or square fish." "It used to be," he concludes, "I could make a living selling them here and not even going to Ches-Atlantic." The home consumer market, Meade Amory agrees, has aged: "I would say the average age of most people that buy spot now is probably sixty. Nobody young comes in this door and buys a box of fish. We don't sell retail—we sell wholesale—so it would only be a fifty-pound box as the smallest amount, generally, other than maybe frozen twenty-five-pound boxes of spot. People don't come in and buy that anymore. The older people—fifty-, sixty-year-old people—still do, but no young people." Meade Amory adds, "There are a few grocery chains that still carry them. I don't think you'll see them at your high-end chains. It's the old-timers. People come in here and buy fifty pounds at a time in the fall when they know. They'll buy them and take them and split them up with their neighbors and salt them or have a fish fry for their church or that sort of thing. A lot of people used to salt them. That was before freezing. We still do a little bit, because it's tradition and we're used to having a breakfast like that. My grandmother used to make it, a breakfast for my dad and uncle and I." Besides spot, Eastern Shore folk also salted croaker, mullet, and bluefish.

According to the Amorys, there is only one way to cook salted spot. Meade speaks for them both, "My whole life I only had it one way, and that was the way my grandmother cooked it." They explain, "You take them out of the water the afternoon before you're going to cook them, and you soak them in fresh water, let some of that salt come out of them. You can rinse them off before you go to bed and put fresh water in them, and then rinse them off again. Put them in a pot of water and boil them. Fry some bacon. When you take the spot out of the water, lay them in a platter with just a little bit of the juice from the pot, and then pour your warm bacon drippings over the top of them. It's a lot of sodium and a lot of bacon fat; it's a miracle we're still here talking about it." Tom Walker, whose family has run a clam and oyster business in Willis Wharf since 1889, declares the spot the tastiest of the inshore fish, noting that they are bony, possess a strong, rich flavor, and are "a little irregular." In quest of a more healthful outcome, he cooks them on the grill: "I'm still trying to find a way to keep the damn things from sticking on the grill. . . . You have to start them on a cold grill and bring the heat up." Salting the fish, he adds, helps keep the skin from coming off. When the spot is done and the side pricked with a fork, clear oil from the fish runs out. Still, he acknowledges that there is work to be done on refining his technique.

H. M. Arnold speaks with authority, "The only way to cook a spot is fry them." Danny Doughty seconds this point of view, remembering how African American women would have their purchase scaled, gutted, and cleaned before frying: "We would prepare them, clean them in the fish market, like, everywhere you could think of. And most of the black culture there would have them cleaned—the older women especially—with the head left on and split down the back, which you took a sous knife. . . . And you would cut right down the back of the head after you scale it, and slice all the way through the head, the eyes, and everything, the gills all the way down the backbone to the tail. Then you'd open it up, just like butterflied it wide open. And then we'd take the knife and scrape from the inside of the head—leaving the eyes in because they loved to eat the eyes—scrape the gills, and then all the insides out of them. Once that was done, then you'd rinse some off, and usually for the most part they would fry them in lard, most of them in a cast-iron frying pan at a really high temperature, and they were really, really good."

Although spot can be cleaned by gutting the belly, most Eastern Shore diners prefer their fish split down the back—and more often than not with the head and tail left attached. Tracey Rasmussen cleans spot to order in her seafood shop by the highway in Keller, Virginia. She scales the fish and then, pressing the fish with her palm against the cutting board and deploying a flexible fillet knife, she makes an incision along the top of the dorsal fin. Gently working the point of the blade into the body, she delicately rides its edge along the curvature of the ribcage, being careful not to pierce the abdomen. With the cut complete, she stands the fish upright and brings the steel down through the skull, neatly bisecting the fish the entirety of its length. She completes the operation, laying the spot open, extracting its viscera, and cleaning out the black body fat (the last step being anathema to some old-school gourmands). H. M. dresses his spot in the same manner but with the head off. Both techniques produce a fish that can be laid flat in a pan of sizzling oil and fried to order.

As far as size and flavor go, H. M. notes: "A pound is big. . . . Really, when he gets that big, he's not as good as a twelve or fourteen ouncer. Kind of gets a little stronger. . . . The thing with them is, if you really cook them right, you eat this side of them, and all you have to do is pull the backbone out. And there's no bones anywhere else, so it's like pulling them all out, and then you eat the other side. That's how we always did it. Of course, most of them like the tail fried crispy. They like that." As an addendum, he states, "When people cook a big spot, they strike him about three times with a knife on each side, so he can go ahead and cook quick, quicker."

Danny, who also operated a restaurant associated with the family fish store, expands on the basic preparation: "We would just wash them off, salt and pepper, and usually use pancake flour because—or we'd use regular white flour—pancake flour has a little more sugar content in it. It makes it brown a lot more even and quicker. Because fish it doesn't take that long to cook, so, you know, at a higher temperature, quicker time, that's the way you cook good fish. It sears the outside of them. People that fry fish like you fry chicken, it's not good fish. It just soaks up the grease, so that was a big deal with him. And they use a lot of cast iron, especially if they're doing the outside kind of deal with a reunion or something. Then we get a fifty-pound box of spot, or a bushel basket of spot or whatever, and clean them all and put them in—wash them off and clean them in some salt water, and then salt and pepper and a little bit of flour, pancake or mix the two together was a good way to do it, because you get a little bit of the sweetness of the pancake flour and then the regular flour mixed in with it."

When you get right down to the nub of the matter, though, people fry spot, and frying spot or any other fish is so elemental that it receives scant mention. Back in 1899, in her *Housekeeper's Companion*, Bessie Gunter wrote only:

TO FRY FISH.
Have a hot pan and some boiling-hot lard in it or the drippings of fat meat (equally good). After the fish have been properly prepared, dredge them in flour and put them in the pan to fry.
—G.

Within those simple instructions resides a universe of variation and personal preference. The greatest distinctions are between spot fried hard or soft and spot fried head on or head off.

Danny Doughty, like many others, savored spot fried hard and head on:

Danny Doughty with a "bake sale" painting.

"Fried hard, yeah, that's the way because they were so crisp on the outside, and then the inside—it would steam the inside. The meat was just—spot has got a real kind of sweet, nice, moist consistency. It isn't dry fish. And the fat in it would just even, just really go through the meat. You wanted to get them in a hot temperature and back out, and we used, like, early on in my life, fried everything in lard and then Crisco. Then using a cast-iron frying pan, you get a hot temperature and roll them in there. You usually cook 75 percent on one side, flip it, the other side the other 25 percent, flip it out, it's done."

Mary Onley, artist and minister, describes much the same practice, comparing the spot to its cousin the croaker, or hardhead: "They taste better to me than croakers. But they have a little bit more bones, little small bones in it. But they're good. And so what I do, I make me a batter. After I done clean them, soaked them, I make me a batter, and in my batter I don't put nothing but salt and pepper and flour, and I put them in a plenty hot grease and let them fry, and I get them after a good ten minutes in that hot grease, and they is ready to come out of the frying pan and eat it. I fry them hard. I love them hard. I love to hear the crunch in them." Hers is a voice in a choir. A conversation with a visitor to the Bayford oyster house elicited, "There's something about him when he's fried, you leave that skin on, cut him, and just eat him from the inside out. Spot is good, buddy, I can tell you that." And Katie Luray White, who cooked with Danny Doughty, stated with near religious devotion, "I fry mine hard and eat the bones, the tail, and all. . . . I always cook that head because I like crunching on it. I love crunching on it! I leave the tail on. The head and tail, I leave on."

The delectability of spot fried hard lay in total consumption: "Oh my gosh, it was so good it was like, I can just see it now, taste it now. Like, when they were crisp, just chomping the tail right off, eating the tail, every bit of it, all the fins, the eyeballs, the gills—even though we didn't eat the part that we throw away, the outer sides of the gills. There was nothing thrown away but the actual bone that run through the core of the fish and the outer bones that come off from it. Everything was eaten. That was one of the beauty parts of it being real fried hard, because you could eat every-thing."

When Addie Sue Smith of Exmore says that she savors her spot "fried soft" and adds, "there's a certain taste in that head if you want to go in and fool around with it," she reveals discernment. Danny Doughty spoke to the positive qualities of spot fried soft, "It was a thing—and if you had children in a family, they'd say, 'Cook one of them soft. I'm going to fix the baby some fish,' or whatever. So they would kind of, you know, pull the skin off real easy, and then kind of slide the meat off the bone onto a little plate to itself so they wouldn't get choked on a bone." Spot fried soft, he noted, also appealed to "some of the older folks, if they didn't have teeth or if their teeth weren't very good. They'd say, 'Fry them soft! I don't want them hard. They're too hard on my gums, my teeth!' You know, it was kind of funny, but it was so true. I mean, they were telling the truth. Their teeth weren't good, and they didn't want to be crunching on spot."

Fairy Mapp White, author of the *Foolproof Cook Book*, which was often presented to Eastern Shore brides for their trousseaus on the eve of their vows, offers little direct commentary on the spot, simply grouping it with other local fish. Under preparations, she codifies what Mary Onley and others described, "Most fish heads are cut off, spot, perch, and other small fish are often left on." Where she speaks directly to the place spot occu-pies in Eastern Shore cuisine, it is as a salted and boiled fish: "1. Salt trout, croakers (E. S. hardheads), fat back, or spot, heavily and let stand overnight or longer. (Any of these can be put in brine in the fall and used until spring. . . .) 2. Rinse in cold water, cut in medium size pieces, place in a heavy frying pan, cover with cold water, and bring to a good boil. 3. Lift out of water with a pancake turner and put on a flat-dish, draining off all water. Pepper well and season with bacon fat and place some of the strips of the fried out bacon or salt pork on fish. 4. Serve at once on hot plates with meal cakes, cornbread, or hot rolls, with plenty of good coffee." Her closing recommendations remind us of the importance of side dishes.

Danny Doughty, who always speaks lovingly of spot, associates it with his favorite sides: "Fried apples, they were, like, unbelievable!" He then described their preparation: "Cut up, leave some of the peeling on, take the core out, and tons of sugar and butter, and fry them in a cast-iron frying pan on top of the stove until they cook down into a, almost an applesauce consistency, a little bit of the body of the apple left, but just a little bit of tart and sweet and kind of a golden brown. I mean, that combination of that little bit of saltiness of the spot, and you slip a little bit of the apple on that and then take a bite. That salty sweet mixture, mmm, that was really unbelievable." "Also, sweet potato, great with it, too," he enthused. "Then, of course, you had to have fried white potatoes. Either fried white potatoes usually with onions, peeled, of course, a little salt and pepper, little bit of Crisco fried up, and that was a staple. You lived off of potatoes quite a bit. Then to have the spot and the apple and the potato together was the real deal. . . . We had fried sweet potato, too, which was just a sweet potato sliced in slices about a quarter-inch thick, and just fried in a frying pan with a little bit of oil or shortening, and then sprinkle a little bit of sugar over top of them." Other diners cite greens, stewed tomatoes, and spoon bread as favored sides for spot.

Whatever side dishes may have been preferred, Danny Doughty distilled the essence of the experience: "Spot is that old-school staple food that was cheap, good, available, and it was just a great-tasting fish. People enjoyed the art of eating fish, which is not conducive with people in today's culture. To see some of the older people do it, it was like—you learn from them how to pick and separate and be able to lift a part up just right, and then a hint of the apple, a little bit of potato, whatever. It was just really a little symphony, you're kind of playing with over the plate." Danny stopped, a thoughtful, wistful, hungry look in his eyes.

The phone echoes through the old oyster house. "Bayford," H. M. Arnold answers. "No, Ma'am, they're all sold out, but I have some hardheads."

A CHEF'S RECIPE FOR HOME

GRILLED SOY-AND-SPICED "BONE IN" SPOTS

Ricky Moore, Saltbox Seafood Joint, Durham, North Carolina

Makes 2 servings
2 large spot, scaled, gutted, and gills removed
¼ cup soy sauce
2 tablespoons brown sugar
1 garlic clove, minced
1 tablespoon minced fresh ginger
2 tablespoons finely julienned orange peel
2 tablespoons fresh orange juice
¼ teaspoon crushed red pepper flakes
2 tablespoons melted butter
4 scallions, thinly sliced

Prepare a charcoal grill until it is hot to your palm positioned 5 inches away from the cooking surface.

Place the fish in a large bowl. Combine the remaining ingredients and pour the mixture over the fish. Marinate for 30 minutes.

Place the fish on a grill set about 5 inches away from the heat for about 10 minutes per inch of thickness of the fish, turning once halfway through the cooking time and basting often with the marinade.

When the fish is tender and flakes easily, remove it from the grill and serve hot.

Note: The fish can also be cooked indoors by placing it on a broiler pan and broiling about 5 inches from the heat for 10 minutes per inch of thickness, turning once halfway through the process.

A Freezer Full of Marsh Hens

"Yeah, man," forearms on the truck rail, fingers laced, Tom Gallivan leans against his pickup, its bed filled with the workaday flotsam of aquaculture: scraps of clam net, saltwater-rusted chunks of rebar, plastic oyster baskets of red, blue, purple. "I was driving up the road this morning, the tide was running high," he continues. "It was a marsh hen kind of day."

I could imagine the flooded marsh at Quinby Bridge where it spans the Machipongo River that flows out to Hog Island Bay. "I heard from one of my crew," Tom adds, "about this woman, Jeanette Spady, on the Seaside Road, who used to make a marsh hen liver and gizzard pie." That would require a lot of livers and gizzards, I thought, and, by extension, a good many marsh hens. "You should go talk to her," he prompts. "I'll do that," I promise.

Marsh hens, mud hens, sage hens, clapper rails, rail birds, whatever you call them, are as much a part of what flavors the Eastern Shore of Virginia as Hayman sweet potatoes, Accomack broccoli, Hog Island sheep, drum, toads, and oysters. Their histories—natural, cultural, culinary—are legend. They are the emblem of marshland worlds of men hunting vast wetland meadows of salt grass, cooking together in clam houses and garage kitchens, bragging sotto voce of wild escapes from vigilant wardens, recalling great hauls of birds and even greater feasts.

"Marsh hen hunting," H. M. Arnold begins, "I don't go much anymore because the law's pretty heavy." It's a mild late April afternoon, and we're sitting in plastic lawn chairs in the Bayford oyster house, where I've come to collect eels for smoking. Salt water scents the air as the tide rises just outside the door. "We used to run a motor," H. M. recounts, "and you'd shoot them that way. Get your limit and come on in, but if you go now you're pushing."

Pushing or poling a boat through the marsh is real work.

H. M. eases into what will develop into a near-epic tale. "Hayes Angle, my partner, and Glenn Stevens—we were at the Exmore Diner one morning and the tide was coming up—Hayes said, 'Let's go marsh henning.'" "Glenn," H. M. sets his story in motion, "hung around the old boys who didn't mind trapping ducks and shooting ducks. They'd get a couple of tickets here and there, but nothing anybody else wouldn't get. Glenn said, 'Yeah, we'll go.'" Decision made, H. M. and his compatriots rise from their booth, exit the diner, and set forth on their spur-of-the-moment hunt. "I had an old dog named Pup," H. M. continues, making sure all the actors are accounted for. "We got our guns and stuff. Went down to Willis Wharf and got Glenn's boat and went up the Machipongo River there. Tide was up. We looked, there was this bird right there in this tump. We rode right up to the tump."

As an aside, a tump, it is worth noting, is a subtle feature in the vast landscape of the Atlantic marshes. Ron Crumb, who grew up in the fishing village of Oyster on the edge of the Atlantic wetlands, explains, "A tump is basically a little bit of higher ground. I think most of them are old reefs of oyster shells that have just silted up and grass has attached to them." Scattered throughout the marshes, tumps vary in size from small mounds to large areas dozens of yards in breadth and length. They are not islands. Ron explains, "They were just spotted here and there, mainly down in Mockhorn Bay, and there's a couple behind a couple of the barrier islands. There's not a lot of them, but it's higher ground than the normal area. It's not high enough to grow trees or stuff on them, but it's high enough to grow a wild sharp grass on it."

I ask about the orphaned dead cedars I see out on the Seaside. Ron explains, "That's a form of a tump. The ones that we're hunting on are the lower tumps. It takes an extreme high tide to cover them. Some of the tumps that you're talking about were probably a little higher and actually a tree tried to grow on it, but it eventually can't handle it." High tumps and low tumps—a subtle geography, a world of salt water and marsh hens.

H. M.'s story resumes. "Glenn started shooting. Birds everywhere!" And then things go wrong. The hunters hear the hum of a light airplane and look to the sky: "There's the man in the airplane!" H. M. begins to laugh, and his story rolls on. The three friends resolve to make a run from the airborne game warden: "We go to Quinby Bridge." Before they flee, though, H. M. notes, "We picked up a bird—we might have had ten or fifteen in that one bunch right there." The chase is on, "Go up to Quinby Bridge, Junior Spence's crab house, Hayes and myself take the guns, the dog, the birds—jump out. We look way up out the creek there, here comes a boat, boy! It's in high gear coming."

The situation looks rough, but then an avenue of escape opens up.

Pete Terry on the clam grounds, Hog Island Bay, Virginia.

"Hayes's cousin worked there for Junior Spence—'Tony,' he says, 'Tony, get us out of here!' We get in Tony's truck—dog and everything—we're going out the road." One of the hunters, though, heads back to the boat. "Glenn goes back out in the boat, and he's going back. They stop him. Game wardens. Plane's still buzzing!"

H. M. and Hayes tune into the CB radio in Tony's truck, eavesdropping on the wardens' chatter: "They got the radio on and you hear the pilot going, 'They're going up. They're going to Painter.' They were following the truck!" Laughing more, H. M. relishes the saga. "Going to Painter, well, we cut through back of Painter—a wooded area. I jump out with the birds, the guns, the dog, and hide in the woods. Hayes goes on with Tony. The airplane was still talking until Hayes got to Exmore. I think that's when they cut off, but Hayes didn't know it. They're going through the middle of Exmore. They slow up—there's some traffic there. Hayes just steps out of the truck. The truck never stops. It goes on!"

Hayes is on foot. I'm listening to a screenplay for a high-speed chase in slow motion: "He gets down to Willis Wharf, where our trucks were. Here I am in the woods. I guess I'm there for about an hour. Here comes Hayes— he comes and picks me up. We go back to Willis Wharf. Well, about that time, Glenn was going through the marsh a hundred miles an hour and there was a boat behind him! He throws his birds up there in the woods somewhere. They get the birds anyway." Their fugitive apprehended, the wardens ticket Glenn for hunting marsh hens under power.

H. M.'s story has yet to run its course: "They write Glenn up for running the motor. Hayes and I, we didn't hear about anything for about a week. Well, Tony was going into the marines. They knew who drove the truck. So Hayes and I were doing something one day and Hayes went home, and he said he hadn't even been in the house a second when somebody knocks on the door. He goes and there's the game warden."

"Uh-oh!" The warden says, "'I know it was you with Glenn marsh henning. I've got a ticket for you. If you don't take this ticket, we're going to stop Tony from going into the marines.'" Loyalty among hunters is everything: "Of course, Hayes says, 'Okay.' He took the ticket. I don't know how I got mine, but I got one, too."

H. M. moves toward the conclusion. "Anyway, Glenn, he had to go to federal court. So, he went across the bay. His fine was, I don't know, $150 or whatever." H. M. and Hayes, however, were destined for local justice at the court in Eastville, the seat of Northampton County for the last several centuries: "We just had to go down there to Eastville, so we called down there to pay our fine. The clerk, she was not a very personable woman, took the money. She said it was $45 or $56, I can't remember. Hayes and I ride down there and we go in there and she's sitting at the desk, kind of a heavy-set woman, goes, 'What are you all here for?'"

H. M. and Hayes respond, "'We called. We've got a fine to pay.'" The clerk chides the pair, "'Well, I guess you all should have known better!'" H. M. is still laughing. I sense that the moral of the story is just around the corner, "She looks it up: $24! Well, Hayes and I had the $56 or whatever it was right there counted out, and we looked at each other. We shelled $24 and signed the receipt, and we're walking out the door and here comes the game warden."

"His face is as red as that sign there," H. M. points to a bright red advertising sign nailed to the oyster house wall, "'You all didn't pay the right fine!' I said, 'But we did. We got a receipt that says, 'Paid in Full.' Oh man, he didn't care for that at all! There wasn't much he could do and we walked on out the door!" H. M. laughs again. "That was our day of marsh henning. Can't outrun the law!" he concludes with smiling irony. H. M., Glenn, and Hayes didn't get to eat their marsh hens. I wonder who did.

The tale of a chase through the marsh, down back roads, and on foot through woods and town speaks to a moment that describes much more. It is a story of a brotherhood of hunters, adventure, and a world that seems to many increasingly distant. Marsh hens mapped a man's universe, but not always. Women, Kay Crumb Downing for one, hunted on occasion. "First time I ever went," she recollected, "I was dating Barry, my husband. Daddy took us and Barry had a 28-gauge that he loaned me. And the first bird I ever shot at, I killed, and I thought my father was going to fall right overboard. If he got tickled, he wouldn't laugh out loud. He would get weak. I mean, you had to see it to believe it." The affection in her voice is as apparent as the pleasures of memory in H. M.'s great adventure.

On a bright early November morning, Pete Terry and Heather Terry Lusk introduce me to Billy Bowen. Billy greets us at the kitchen door and invites us into his sitting room, which looks out to the main street running into Willis Wharf from nearby Exmore. Pete launches right in: "I'm going to tell you a quick story on Billy before we get started. It was blowing, I'd say thirty to forty miles an hour northeast, spitting rain, terrible day, when I came to Billy and I said, 'Billy, what do you think about going to shoot a couple marsh hens?' And he said, 'I think that's a good idea.' I said, 'Alright.' He said, 'Let me get my gun and my shells and we'll go.' Well, I went home and I got my gun and I got a box of shells. Billy went home and got his gun and he got three-gallon containers of gun shells."

At this point, Billy is laughing so hard he's hunched forward wheezing. Pete presses on: "And I said, 'What are you going to do with all those?' He said, 'When I'm done shooting, we're done.'"

"My mistake was," Pete says, "I thought he was kidding." Billy can barely contain his laughter at this point, and still Pete presses on. "And listen," Pete pauses for dramatic effect, "I'm not going to tell you how many birds we shot because you're recording this, but I'm going to tell you this: after he shot all the shells that he had, he had one shot left. I said, 'Billy, there's a bird.' He said, 'No, I'm going to save this last one for a doubler.'" "Is that a Hog Islander for you, or what?" Pete asks and ends, "You know the truth is I'll lie, but that's a true story."

Billy cannot let the story rest here and, still laughing, presents an explanation for his hunter's zeal. According to him, his shooting above the daily limit of fifteen birds was an informed and sensitive act of environmental awareness.

"That is a true story," he says looking at Pete. "You know, I love shooting marsh hens. I don't hardly ever go anymore, but I never could see this, going out there getting fifteen birds, burning five or six gallons of gas and getting fifteen birds. I believe in going and getting all you can, you don't have to go no more." He builds his case. "You go ahead and you kill 150, 200 birds, and you don't have to go no more. That's the way I looked at it then." By going out just the one time, Billy reasoned, he cut back on the outboard exhaust emissions and struck a blow against climate change. Because he didn't motor in and out of the marsh channels repeatedly, his wakes didn't constantly undercut, collapse, and erode the banks. Billy smiles; Pete shakes his head in feigned disbelief. "Like now," Billy concludes, "I don't hardly go at all. I got too old, don't do it, I got decrepit." Judging by the Harley parked out back, Billy Bowen's claims to decrepitude lack substance. His love for marsh hen gunning and time spent in the vast expanse of Hog Island Bay runs deep, and so, too, does his appreciation for a good tale well told.

Few stories inspire as much delight as those of shooting marsh hens as they rise from flooded tumps, flying with all the awkward grace of rubber chickens thrown into a high wind. Few tales generate as much laughter as epic narratives of harrowing and hilarious, often failed, escapes from wardens. Few stories inspire as much pleasure as gustatory accounts of sitting down to marsh hens fried, stewed, or baked in pies and served with greens and sweet potatoes. Marsh hens, simply, are as much a part of the Eastern Shore of Virginia's food histories as Sunday breakfasts of fried salt fish and pancakes, black duck and dumplings, oyster cakes, clam fritters, greens so bitter that, as Theodore Peed claims, "They taste like your momma smacked you," and spot fish, fried head on and as crispy as a cracker.

Migratory denizens of salt marshes from Florida to New Jersey, clapper rails or marsh hens have captured the attention of naturalists, hunters, cooks, and diners since at least the early 1700s. The conservationist T. Gilbert Pearson, a visitor to Cobb Island in 1901, succinctly described the species: "The clapper rail is about fifteen inches in length, including its short excuse for a tail. Its body is very slender, which makes it admirably adapted for threading its way through the labyrinthian pathways of its marshy haunts. Its legs are slim and the bird is a good runner. It can also swim with ease. It is a poor flyer and as a result seldom takes to wing."

Naturalist and hunter Dwight W. Huntington amplified Pearson's representation about the same time: "All the rails have long, slim bodies, and seem to be built especially to move quickly through the rushes and wild rice where they are always found. They run with remarkable rapidity, and it is difficult to put them up. The rails have short, rounded wings and fly with an apparent effort just above the tall reeds, often dropping back into them after going but a few yards. So labored is their flight that it is not easy to understand how they make their long migration north and south." There it is: the lowly marsh hen, clumsy in flight, a migratory wader with a wedge-like body adapted to slipping through the marshes without ruffle or ripple.

The iconic American naturalist John James Audubon, in his *Birds of America*, published piecemeal from 1827 to 1838, adds, "During ebb, the Clapper Rail advances towards the edge of the waters as they recede, and searches, either among the grasses, or along the deep furrows made by the ebb and flow of the tides, for its food, which consists principally of small crabs, a species of salt-water snail attached to the rushes, the fry of fishes, aquatic insects, and plants. When the tide flows, they gradually return, and at high-water they resort to the banks, where they remain concealed until the waters begin to retreat."

Audubon sketches the marsh hen habitat: "They confine themselves entirely to the salt-marshes in the immediate vicinity of the Atlantic, the islands and the channels between them and the main shores, but are never seen inland or on fresh waters, unless when, during high tides, they remove to the margins of the main, where, indeed, during heavy gales and high seas, these poor birds are forced to take refuge, in order to escape the destructive fury of the tempest that, notwithstanding their utmost exertions, destroys great numbers of them. On all such occasions the birds appear greatly intimidated and stupified, and as if out of their proper element."

Closer to home, a Depression-era visitor to the Virginia barrier islands wrote, "The clapper rails, called locally marsh hens, were abundant on Revels Island, but they lived such secretive lives in the tall grasses that, despite their harsh, cackling notes, they were rarely seen except when one made a painstaking search for them. Each spring they returned from the South in extraordinary numbers, and skulked about among the grasses, rising and flying only a short distance when startled. . . . Their nests, neatly hidden under the overarching grasses, contain from 10 to 18 pale eggs that are comparatively large for so small a bird." Residents and visitors alike esteemed the eggs a delicacy and gathered them with relentless energy. Even Audubon, who regretted the unrestrained hunting practices that diminished marsh hen populations, confessed, "As the eggs are in request as

Theodore Peed's fried marsh hens, Hare Valley area, Virginia.

a delicious article of food, they are gathered in great numbers, and I my-self have collected so many as seventy-two dozens in the course of a day." That would be 864 eggs—and a great many potential marsh hens vanished.

"You'll see them on shorelines," Buck Doughty says with the knowl-edge of generations living on the verge of the Seaside marshes, "You'll hear them out there." He makes a clucking, squawking sound, imitating the bird's call: "You'll hear that all going on." Reprising a soundscape created by marsh hens pushing through the grass, Buck adds, "It's almost like a high-pitched chuckle almost. I used to hear them every morning I'd wake up on Webb Island. You'd hear them out there just kind of talking and get-ting going. You'll hear them roar up, a few of them, and they'll quiet down for a little bit." Concerning their habits, Buck speaks with a naturalist's eye and a hunter's purpose. "They kind of just sneak around and they eat them fiddler crabs and everything else—all that stuff in the tumps. They hide up in there really good. They're not going to move around much. Black ducks will fly right up. They jump and go. But a marsh hen will sit there. He'll let you ride up on him. That's why a lot of people like to hunt them. They'll lay until you just, you can hit them. They'll just ride up there and get them."

Marsh hens, Buck notes, may be easy shooting, but they also possess a powerful determination. "You got to hit them good because a marsh hen— if you don't hit him good, a lot of times, they'll swim down. They'll hide. They'll get underwater, and they'll get themselves down there and hold on until they drown themselves. They won't let you get them. They're very, very determined to evade you."

Marsh hens court more enemies than the hunters who shoot them over the flooded marshes of autumn. Kenny Marshall, a lifelong waterman, recalled one particular predator that went after the newly hatched "biddies." "Herring gulls eat most of them. . . . Once they are hatched in two or three days of the nest. She doesn't feed them, she takes them around and shows them how to get bugs off the marsh grass and stuff. But she'll be, the female, the mom, will be swimming around and these four or five little black biddies behind them. And the herring gull come," he makes a swooping sound mimicking wind and wings, "just pick them up one or two at a time." Gone in a dusting of feathers and down.

Philadelphia artist Thomas Eakins famously depicted gunning for marsh hens in the New Jersey marshes along the Delaware River shore. His 1874 painting captures the vastness of golden-grassed marshland of early autumn and the sky rising from a white horizon to a pale blue cloud-flecked heaven. The painting depicts three boats, each propelled by a guide and poised at a crucial moment in the hunt. Gentlemen hunters dressed in their rustic best come together in a dance of loading, watching, and shooting. A marsh hen attempts its escape, but I am not optimistic about its imagined fate. Eakins's scene could as easily record marsh henning on the Eastern Shore of Virginia, described by Polk Kellam over lunch one late September afternoon.

It's marsh hen season. Polk speaks, and I see Eakins's painting in my mind's eye. "Marsh henning is still popular," he says. "Clapper rail, that's the book name for the bird. I think they're migratory and local—and they are very common in our salt marshes, Seaside and Bayside." But, he adds, "They're more common on the Seaside. More abundant. More marshes. And more huntable because of the tides." Polk summarizes the moment in the painting, "You need a high tide to hunt marsh hens. They are very good hiders, and they don't fly readily like a lot of game birds. You have to hunt them when the tide is really making up full. Storm tides. They gather or cluster in high tumps. Tumps of grass that are the last to flood."

"You have to pole the boat. Shoving, as we say. Shoving. That's what Eastern Shoremen call typically a ten-foot oar that's flat so it will slide through the water. You push the boat forward and it knifes through and you take another stroke," Polk explains. "That's how you shove a boat. You'd go on the flood tide when it's getting up high, and hopefully you'd have a storm tide like we had a few days ago, and you'd approach these tumps that still haven't inundated. One man shoves and one man is in the bow doing the shooting." Time sometimes stands still.

Celebrating the great days of wildfowling on the Eastern Shore, Richard Parks waxed nostalgic, reflecting on days gone by when great flights of ducks, geese, brant, and shorebirds ruled sky and marsh. Black ducks and redheads were the prize. Marsh hens definitely perched on a lower rung of his version of the hunter's ladder. "In early fall," Parks wrote, "the place is alive with Clapper Rail but each year they meet the same fate—the first bad northeaster sweeps the tide completely over the marsh and they drift helplessly to mainland to face a battery of hunters, intent on getting a potful."

Ron Crumb deepens the story, "Usually the season started in September. You needed a high tide because the birds were up in the marsh and you were chasing them down." Referring to the work of guiding, he explains, "Most of them would get in the boat, and they would go to different blocks of marsh out here and drop off the hunters. They would go up these little creeks and try to get their limit of fifteen, come back to the boat, and come in. They would clean them as they came in." "The favorite way I do it," he elaborates on a second hunting strategy, "on a couple tumps sitting around Mockhorn Island and different places, pull up on to one end of the tump and just walk and chase the birds up and shoot them."

The most common method, Ron wraps up, is from a boat, engine off, drifting toward the tump where the marsh hens hide. Billy Bowen describes the process: "It's about one of the simplest huntings you can do because you've got to have a high tide in order to do this. The tide has really got to be above normal. Because they're in the grass, they get on the surf grass, you know, marsh grass, and they can run, fast. What you usually do, you're going up a gut, you're running your outboard, you're supposed to, when you see one, you're supposed to cut your outboard off, be sure she ain't got any forward motion at all. So you usually put the bow in the marsh so she'll stop, and then you shoot." He pauses to catch his breath in the telling, "They'll fly, and they can run fast. They can swim pretty decent, too. But if it's raining, they don't fly as bad. That's why sometimes you wait until it's misty raining, so they won't fly. You're allowed fifteen birds per person."

Gary Kellam's recollections mirror Billy's. "Well, you got to go when the tide is right. You got to have a real high tide, and it's best to have a wind out of the northeast. Like what we had the other day, that northeaster, that storm that came through, made the conditions perfect for it. Once the tide gets high enough, the birds don't have anywhere to hide. If you go out there when you don't have a high tide, they hide down in that grass. And you won't ever kill one. But when the tide is high and they don't have anywhere to hide and they don't know what to do, they might find one place where there's a little tuft of grass and all kind of bunch up in there. Then, when you get up on them, they flush up and fly, and you shoot and they're easy to hit because they're slow and they're not very smart."

"We just go and pick them up," he finishes. "The tide's so high that you can ride the boat pretty much anywhere. You don't have to worry about running aground. We take a net with us, it's like a crab net, and we cut the handle off of it so you can dip them up out of the water."

Buck Doughty rounds out the details of the hunt, whether from boat or stomping through the marsh. "If he gets underwater, you're not going to find him. It's like they'll move around and they'll hold onto some grass or something until you go away, or die. So, you get up there and you get a good shot on them. You hit them on the head or whatever you can to knock them down good. They'll just float on the side, and you go out there with a net, a crab net. Just scoop them up, put them in the boat. Sometimes you've got to walk in for them if you're up on the marsh and you can't get the boat to it. Last time we went, because the tide didn't make it out very good, we had to walk for a lot of them. That was my job. I'm long-legged, and I'll get overboard instead of going out with a net." Buck footnotes his instructions, "Just don't sink over your neck, and just keep a basket so you can push out with." It's easy enough to get bogged down in a patch of soft marsh mud. Hauling yourself out of the muck with a basketful of marsh hens is the challenge.

I follow Tom Gallivan's recommendation and visit Jeanette Spady at her home on the Seaside Road not too far from Webb Island, where Buck remembered waking to marsh hens cackling in the high salt grass. Walking to her front door, I pass her son's welded-steel oyster roaster and the ruins of a feast from the previous night. Mrs. Spady welcomes me at the door and leads me past sleeping revelers into her kitchen, where we sit at her kitchen table. Coffee is ready and presented along with a gift of homemade pomegranate preserves. I am there to learn about cooking marsh hens—and in particular marsh hen liver and gizzard pie.

Jeanette Spady declares, "I'm a scratch cook. When the marsh hen comes," she explains, "I go at him on my cleaning table and strip the feathers off of him. Cut the head and feet off, and cut him up like you would a chicken. You split the breast, and when you split that to get to the feathers, you can skin the whole bird because the bird feathers come right with the skin. Usually, I just split them right down halfway because they are so small, and then boil them." As for cooking, "You just fry them. Now, a lot of people don't like them if they are not fried, but I tried to stay away from fried foods. That's why I make a potpie out of them. You take and soak them overnight in salt water. Clean the blood and stuff out of them." "A rabbit or a squirrel," she draws a parallel, "you would do the same thing."

Translating marsh hens into entrées begins with cleaning the birds. Mrs. Spady describes her process in the form of recipe preparation. Billy Bowen presents his as a history lesson: "The old way we used to do it, you'd nip your little place. You'd take your thumb right by the neck and you rip them on down and you skin them right off. That's the way you do it," he stresses, "the old way they used to do, they'd cut the legs off, cut the neck off, and cut the back part of them off, and then you cut right down the backbone and you split them." With the old style, he explains, "You're frying the ribs, the backbone, too. Well, as time progressed, what you do, you learn to cut the legs off, you popped the breast off. You didn't have no ribs, no neck to cut or nothing like that, which is very, very simple. Then you had the livers and the gizzards."

Danny Doughty, who ran a café in Willis Wharf and grew up in the family fish house, remembers prepping marsh hens with considerably less affection: "I didn't like cleaning them." On occasion, however, a fish house customer requested, and Danny's father, Kenneth, would do his best to oblige. "Some of our people we dealt with, they'd say, 'Can I get me some marsh hens?' Well, my father wasn't a big hunter really, but he would go marsh henning and he'd bring back a load and we'd have to clean them damn things. And skin them!" Danny shudders a bit at the recollection of confronting a mound of marsh hens that needed to be dressed for cooking. "After a while it didn't bother me," he says, "but skinning a bird like that, especially a little bird, it wasn't the funnest thing to do." But, there is good news, "Marsh hen was all dark meat. The reward was very well worth it. For sure. It made it a little more tolerable."

"My mom," he says, "was not a big kind of wildfowl person, but that's one thing she absolutely loved to get, were marsh hens." He remembers flavors almost as elusive as the bird secreted in a sheltering tump: "I don't know, now it's almost like a fleeting thought of what they even taste like. It's been so long since I've had any."

"What about the pie?" I ask Mrs. Spady. "Yeah, well you can put them in a pie, too. I mean the liver and gizzards. I always fixed marsh hen pie by pulling the meat after I cook it off of the bone so it won't be no bone in the

Jeanette Spady with pomegranate preserves, Webb's Island area, Virginia.

pie, and put a pack of frozen vegetables in there with it. Put a crust over top of it." I'm taking notes. "Put it in a piecrust unbaked," she says, "and then put your vegetables over it and put another crust over top of it and bake it. Bake 375 or 400 degrees." I ask about the gravy. Mrs. Spady patiently and laughingly offers an unaccustomed level of detail: "You put the gravy on the stove and boil it, which it takes a little longer for the gizzards, but I dump them all right together and boil them." "Make sure I have enough water in there to put some dumplings in, and let them cook." "When the gizzards get almost done," her instructions take an unanticipated but not unfamiliar turn toward dumplings, "that's when I make my flat dumplings and drop them in there. Just let them boil a little while and then cut the burner off and let them set in that juice." "If the gravy's not thick enough," she cautions, explaining, "you can't put too much thickening in them because if you make gravy and then put a thickening in, it thickens up after it gets cold." "So," she completes the lesson, "then they're ready, but you put salt and pepper in them like you want." Watching me scribbling in my notebook, she remarks, "I never write a recipe down. I want to tell you that to start with." I'm wondering if this is one of those recipes that might carry the warning "For experts only!"

Some home cooks roasted marsh hens. Drummond Ayres, who left his hometown of Accomac to write for the *New York Times*—and returned— hunted marsh hens, wading through the marshes in early autumn. He wouldn't shoot many, but he brought home what he bagged. "I'm sure Mother cooked him just like you'd cook a duck," he says. "You might put an onion inside or maybe a piece of apple and run it under the broiler with some, maybe some cooking oil or rub it with butter. I don't remember exactly what she would do. Essentially, we cooked marsh hens the same way you'd cook quail or a duck. Put something in the cavity. But marsh hens taste good. They don't get fishy like some ducks do." Marsh hens fried and stewed were the go-to options.

Billy Bowen recounts, almost salivating, "What you did do, you cooked the potatoes. Then you'd fix the dumplings, with flour and stuff like this, water like that. First off, you'd put your legs and your breasts in there, and you'd put the livers and gizzards right in there. You would boil them. That's when you would start putting your dumplings in to kind of thicken it up so it wasn't real thin, it was like a gravy. That was some cooking." "You know," he pauses, reflecting on extended stays in watch boats anchored in the ditches and drains of the Atlantic marshes, "when you used to cook eggs you used to have grease a half-inch thick in the frying pan. They don't do that no more. All you want to do is spray a little stuff on there and fry. Well, that was good cooking down in that bay."

"As far as cooking them," Ron Crumb emphasizes, "probably 95 percent of marsh hens around here are fried. They do take the gizzards and livers, and some people fry them up. I have had a couple of people I know that do a big stew. Put them in a big pot and just cook them right down and put the potatoes and onions in there and it's almost like chicken and dumplings." Almost, but not quite. "I mean they all have unique different tastes, but it's either fried or cooked down. They would make a big pot of mashed potatoes, and then the dumplings right in there. And you just go for it. Pretty tasty."

John Marshall agrees, "The way I like to do it is fry them. Put a layer of flour on them and salt. Put them in that grease. You could fry cardboard and it would probably taste good." As for marsh hens with dumplings, John observes that his cousin Buck, "he likes to stew them. I think that's what we're going to do with the ones we just killed. We'll put them in that great big old cast-iron kettle over the fire and just roll them—and maybe even do dumplings with them. You ought to come down." I respond brightly, "Give me a call!" And they do.

H. M. Arnold enthuses, "Oh man, they're good fried! Fry them up." "Peed," he says, referring to his good friend Theodore Peed and his legendary community turtle dinner, "cooks them at his party. They're just a good-tasting bird. It's just a good-tasting fried bird," he says, adding that "some people, I guess, potpie them." I love the idea of potpie as a verb. H. M., referring to a former marine resources officer and game warden, concludes with a note of discernment, "I know Randy Widgeon, he saved the livers and gizzards out of them. He liked them. I just never did, but I could eat them." For Kenny Marshall, viscera were an added bonus: "I always save the gizzard, the liver, and the heart and just threw that in if I was frying them or stewing them. I kept that. That was always a part of it." "Marsh hen livers and gizzards offered a treat," as Alfred Nottingham, sitting in the Bayford oyster house on a winter evening, remarked. His young nephew, something of a picky eater, discovered pan-fried marsh hen livers, a savory snack that he devoured with great avidity.

John Marshall recognizes a diversity of taste when it comes to marsh hen, "They're good eating." Speaking for himself, he observes, "To me that's probably the best bird you can eat—a mix between a duck and chicken, sort of. It's tender and it's not that gamy." Then, nodding to his wife, Crystal, who is listening with a faint air of disgust, he adds, a tinge of sadness in his voice, "She doesn't like the smell of them when you clean them, but I think they're great."

John's father, Kenny Marshall, raised to eat everything, is a bit more discriminating in his connoisseurship. "What they used to call a potpie

wasn't a pie at all. It was like stewed chicken and dumplings. You can make that with most any bird. My mom had done it quite often with railbirds or shorebirds, curlews. Curlews are tough." Good to know. Young marsh hens, Kenny says, are "fairly tender. If you get an old bird it can be tough." Also good to know.

Billy Bowen speaks first to his preference for fried marsh hens and then addresses the pressing question of side dishes: "Marsh hens," he goes step by step, "you would flour them up, salt them, put a little pepper on them if you wanted pepper. Then you'd fry them in the grease. When it came time for the livers and gizzards, if you had enough of those, what you would do, you fry them. You take most of all your grease out, make a little gravy, and then let them sit there and just stew in that and spread that over bread. It would make your tongue slap your jaws every time. Boy, that was some kind of good." He's on a roll. "Cream potatoes. Have a little cream potatoes there and gravy. You'd take that marsh hen there and you sometimes you put it right in with the gravy and take a bite of him. You don't get no better! It just don't get no better." His voice rises with excitement, "We used to fry them like that and then let them simmer in the gravy, and it was just like they would melt in your mouth. It's unreal!"

Vacationing in Utah with a group of friends and partners in the oyster and clam business, Billy Bowen thought that his traveling companions, especially those unfamiliar with Eastern Shore of Virginia cuisine, would benefit from some marsh hens. "We went snow skiing one time," he sets the stage, "and I carried about five packs of marsh hens out there. There were eight, ten of us guys out there and some of them had never heard of a marsh hen or nothing. I fried them up, we had a big platter, and I had it piled up with marsh hens. It was a big platter, a foot and a half, and they were piled up at least a foot on there." Billy gave his all for his friends' delight. "I fried them until my back got hurt. I stood up there so long frying them marsh hens. Doggone, I had two frying pans going at one time." He laughs, "You don't leave marsh hens on the plate. What you cook, you eat. Them guys never had it, man they loved them, too. They were really, really good. That was one of the very, very few times that I never had gravy with marsh hens because my back was hurting." Maybe so, but marsh hens without a liver and gizzard gravy?

Terroir is memory; cuisine is storytelling. When it comes to marsh hens, Danny Doughty gets right to the point: "My father being from Hog Island and all his family, and us living in Willis Wharf, if you didn't eat a marsh hen or you didn't like them, there was something genetically wrong with your coding." Marsh hens on the menu celebrate connections that reach across time but are deeply rooted in the specifics of place.

Father and son, Kenny Marshall and John, recall those connections. "I started out marsh henning with my dad," John recalls, "when I was ten or eleven years old. That was one of the first hunts I ever went on with him. When the tide comes up, as the tide is rising, the birds run to the higher tumps of marsh, and if you get enough tide, there's just a few tumps left, and the birds are all gathered up in those tumps. You ease your boat up into them, and then you get close enough, they just pop up and pow! pow! I enjoy it. I've been doing it ever since he took me the first time." Then John appends a story. "The first time, your nerves are all up, you're excited to kill a bird. . . . He took us up to Fowling Point at the head of the gut there." Kenny instructed the two first-time hunters on the techniques and etiquette of the hunt. "He told us, 'Now the way we're going to do this, guys, is one guy going to stand up to the front. He'll have his gun loaded and he'll be ready, and when we see birds, he'll go ahead and unload the gun, and then the next guy will come up, he'll shoot. We'll rotate like that.'" John tells his story, "We opted to let my buddy Chip go first. We come up on that first tump of birds, and here they come flying up!" John makes the sound of a shotgun ejecting cartridges: "He unloads his gun. He misunderstood! Dad meant unload the gun on the birds! I rushed up there. They were flying away! I don't know if I got a shot off or not. I don't remember. We finally got that straight. We had a good day."

But the larger story is one of a past of plenty and a present of absence. "It was enough birds," John says, "that we could kill them with a paddle. We could come up there with the boat and hit them with the paddle. You don't even have to waste the gun shells on them, there was that many."

Kenny Marshall taps into the theme on plenty and loss from his own youth. "Clams, oysters, birds, fish, shorebirds," he says, "just shoot them by the hundreds. Skin them, fry them up, and one bird would be about a mouthful. Fry them real, real crisp and you could eat the bones and all. Except for the breast ribs. That was normal. We did that all the time. One thing about it, though, my dad taught me, we never killed more than we could eat or give away. There were a lot of retired old water folks and widows, and we always made sure that they got plenty of game. And fish. Anything we had, really. Don't take any more than you can use or get rid of. Don't waste it."

John Marshall preserves that lesson. "Dad told me that I had to have a bird for every shell I shot. If I missed one, I had to double up. If you could bring back more birds than shells spent, you did good. That's what you're trying to do." His grandfather John steps back another generation, "used to get two shells—he had a double-barrel shotgun. Walk down to the E. L. Willis Store in Willis Wharf and buy them out of a big crate. There was an old big crate of them. Buy two at a time, put them in his gun, and walk down to the marsh. Whatever jumped up, that's what they had for dinner that night. You didn't waste shells, if you just pow-pow-pow, you didn't eat that night. They could have been marsh hens, they could have been black ducks, or they could have been any kind of yellowlegs or any kind of shorebird. Crankies. Whatever. I think they were just food for them back then. They were hopeful for the better stuff, but whatever jumped was probably what they were going to have. Those days are over."

Danny Doughty agrees, "My family, being from Hog Island, they made all kinds of stuff. I didn't eat a lot of it myself. They'd make marsh hen pie," he looks sadly toward a receding family history. "They had to be resourceful with anything they had." Danny mourns, "Marsh hen is one of the things, I'm pretty sure, in a short period of time, you will no longer be able to even get any of them, I would think, the way things are going, I guess."

Billy Bowen brings it all into perspective as an ecology cultivated in work on the water. Like Kenny Marshall, Billy sojourned "down the bay" in a watch boat for days at a time: "That was good cooking down in that bay. You used to go up on the beach and get light wood," he recollects, "which was knots out of trees, and you'd take a hatchet and split it. You'd put that in the stove, and that's what you'd cook with. You didn't have the modern conveniences down there. You laid down there for a week at a time, and you'd eat basically what you caught or shot. Clams, oysters, ducks, marsh hens. Marsh hens were one of the easiest things to shoot or to get a hold of, so that's one of the main things that you get to eat down in the bay. You'd stay for a week at a time, sometimes you'd stay for a week and a half, sometimes two weeks. You didn't take a lot of groceries with you, you didn't have no refrigerator to keep things cool. What you caught and what you killed, if you caught fish, that's what you eat down in the bay," Billy says. "That was it. You took lard and flour with you, that was the main two ingredients." He extends his list of provisions, but it remains modest, "and molasses and salt and pepper. But like I said, you caught it or you shot it, and that's what you lived off of."

Those times may be in the past, but the stories thrive in the present. Marsh hens remain on the menu, and they are devoured with joy, not regret. Billy glances over to Pete and Pete's daughter Heather as we sit in his sunny sitting room. "Ham and cabbage," he augments his recollected menu from a life on the water. "But," Billy completes his thought, "I would say overall my favorite meal is marsh hens. Without a shadow of a doubt, I love marsh hens." There is joy in his voice, he pauses and bursts out laughing, "I do!" A beloved dish remembered.

A CHEF'S RECIPE FOR HOME

OYSTERS WITH WILD MUSHROOMS

Bernard L. Herman, Westerhouse, Virginia

I like to keep it as simple as possible, and this dish, based on one of the 750 oyster recipes recovered by Katy Clune for the period between 1885 and 1915, meets that criterion. The use of nutmeg in this update of a 1907 recipe is a revelation. A spice that has been around for centuries, nutmeg has slipped in popularity for savory dishes. This recipe argues for its rehabilitation.

Makes 4–6 servings
2 cups wild oyster mushrooms or other large-cap mushrooms
2–3 tablespoons butter
1 pint shucked oysters in their liquor
¼ teaspoon freshly grated nutmeg
Salt and freshly ground black pepper to taste
2½ ounces Madeira
Flat-leaf parsley, for garnish

Gently clean the mushrooms with a damp cloth. Remove the stem and shred the mushrooms by tearing them along the gill lines. Melt the butter in a skillet over low heat and add the mushrooms. Sauté slowly until the mushrooms are reduced in size and browned. Set aside.

Place the oysters with their liquor in a saucepan over medium heat and bring to a gentle boil until the oysters plump and the gills curl, 3–4 minutes. Turn off the heat, add the nutmeg, and season with salt and pepper. Add the Madeira and gently stir it into the oysters. Ladle into hot bowls and garnish with parsley.

Mr. Hayman On Sweet Potatoes

 Margaret Young, Anne Nock, and Billie Mason gather in the front room of the Accomac cottage where their friend Sara "Cook" Ross lived out her later years. Their thoughts turn to the prospect for Hayman sweet potatoes in the coming autumn. They speak with a hint of desperation.

Margaret declares, "Hayman potatoes are so hard to find now."

"They really are," Ann agrees.

"I've been cooking Haymans, and you throw away half of them because . . ." Ann doesn't complete her sentence as Billie jumps in.

"They are nothing!" she exclaims. "They're awful! You remember last year, they were awful."

Ann responds with indignation, "And some people are calling things that aren't Haymans, too! You buy something that's not quite a Hayman."

"I hope," Margaret says with a tinge of sadness, "that's not going to be a dying thing."

Amine Kellam, an Eastern Shore native and descendant of the first families on Cobb Island, echoes a sense of the local and the lost. She begins, "Hayman potatoes, they're green on the outside. And that is why a lot of people in the North don't know about Hayman potatoes because they think they're not ripe. When you take them to friends up north, they'll say, 'Well, how long will it take these to get ripe?' But this is the color that they are. They're a greenish color."

"People don't grow them anymore," Amine says, "and we haven't had a one this year." Her son, she explains, "usually buys a big thing of them to send them to his northern friends." There will be, she says flatly, "none of that" this winter season. Amine speculates on the dearth of Haymans, "I've heard, maybe one reason is that they take a lot of ingredients out of the soil. That may not be true. It may be because they're fragile and don't like bad weather. I don't know why." She is unhappily resigned to an absence of Hayman sweet potatoes from her dinner table. "They are so good." She repeats, "They are so good—everybody misses them." I feel as though I've been tasked with following up on the report of a fugitive sweet potato.

Terroir is about much more than the taste of place as an expression of soil, climate, varietal, and process. Terroir, as an idea, encapsulates particular forms of memory and knowledge. It's a connoisseur's word that speaks to the passion and possession of knowledge as a means of understanding the essence of a place and its people. Terroir can be defined as the expression of belonging and the capacity to understand and respect what that sense of belonging means in its most intimate iterations as food sustained by stories. It is a concept that is always there in the food worlds of the Eastern Shore of Virginia but never articulated with self-conscious precision.

William Harmon, among the last growers of the Hayman sweet potato, extolls the virtues of the variety two days before his seventy-eighth birthday. His Haymans are in the ground and flourishing in the August heat. He's hopeful for a good yield. Mr. Harmon has grown Haymans all his life, as did his father and grandfather before him. "Now Hayman potato, he won't grow fast. He take his time in growing." I appreciate Mr. Harmon's use of a personal pronoun for this locally beloved sweet potato. He periodically refers to the potato as Mr. Hayman, a designation that incorporates respect and affection. "But you give him time," Mr. Harmon adds, "and he is definitely as good a potato you will ever eat if you ever ate any." I assure him that I've been known to eat a sweet potato or two—and that Haymans are near and dear to my heart, which, it seems, is never far from our kitchen.

Although the Hayman (*Ipomoea batatas v. Hayman*) did not debut on the Eastern Shore until the second half of the 1800s, sweet potato culture had been long established. An account of the first sweet potato shipment for market appeared in 1891 under the headline "Chapters of Unwritten History" written under the pseudonym Septuagenarian. John W. A. Elliott, the septuagenarian in question, recounted a merchandising experiment and sea voyage he experienced as a thirteen-year-old boy. "The first cargo of sweet potatoes sent from the Eastern Shore to New York was shipped in 1837," he began. "The experiment of testing the market of New York with 200 barrels of potatoes was considered at that day a dubious venture, and many doubts were expressed in regard to the result." "The 200 barrels of 'sweets' making up the cargo were grown by probably a hundred farmers of Accomac and Northamp[ton] and loaded at various landings on each side of Macapungo creek." Freighted with sweet potatoes, the schooner *Providence* set sail and, after an encounter with bad weather, arrived in New

William Harmon with his Hayman sweet potato harvest, Hare Valley area, Virginia.

York—cargo intact. "Though small lots of Carolina 'sweets' had been sold in New York, the arrival of a whole cargo from Virginia was an event which stirred the market with no little excitement."

What followed was sweet potato pandemonium, as Elliott relates, still excited sixty years later: "The deck of the Providence was soon thronged with a motley crowd and our skipper pressed with many curious inquirers. The price of a single large sweet potato was placed at a shilling and many sold for curiosities. When the rush had subsided, Capt. Mathews took a sample of his cargo to Mr. H. P. Havens, at that day the only commission merchant known to the E. Shore. The idea of a whole cargo of sweet potatoes evidently took his breath, 'Two hundred barrels of potatoes?' he exclaimed; more than enough to glut the whole market of New York. The people here do not known [*sic*] what to do with sweet potatoes." Nevertheless, something had to be done. "Advertisements of this remarkable importation were sent to the morning papers, and clerks dispatched to solicit sales with the corner groceries and market-men." Still, a surfeit of sweet potatoes remained. "Eventually we opened our hatches to the wholesale trade; some of the market-men taking a whole barrel, a few of the bolder ones two. Meanwhile the Captain had ordered the 'old-wife' potatoes spread out on the quarter deck where a brisk retail trade was carried out at the rate of a shilling apiece." The venture took two weeks, but at its conclusion all two hundred barrels had been absorbed into the larders of the great metropolis. "Thus," Elliott beamed, "ended the first venture in a line of trade destined to open up a new era in the industry and prosperity of the Eastern Shore."

Elliott bore witness to the transformation of Eastern Shore of Virginia agriculture—and the arrival of the Hayman sweet potato. The year before the local *Peninsula Enterprise* printed Elliott's reminiscence, the New York *Sun* celebrated the Eastern Shore of Virginia as "New York's Great Sweet Potato Patch. Millions of Bushels Raised Every Year." "The one crop that takes precedence of all others on the Virginia peninsula is the sweet potato," the author hyperventilated. "The sweet potato patch rules the peninsula. Everybody plants sweet potatoes, and on the product and price of that crop depend the welfare of two counties." Well, close, but not quite considering the almost thirteen million bushels of Irish potatoes grown in 1924. Sweet potato production stuttered along in a distant second place at an annual rate of roughly a mere three million bushels. Chronicled by William G. Thomas III, Brooks Miles Barnes, and Tom Szuba in *The Countryside Transformed*, the 1884 opening of the railroad that ran down the spine of the peninsula made it all possible. In 1928, for example, fourteen thousand boxcars carried Irish potatoes to market. Following a detailed accounting of sweet potato culture, the *Sun* correspondent offered an additional observation that at its height at the turn of the twentieth century, cultivating sweet potatoes was largely the labor of African American hands whether as tenants, field hands, or the owners of small farms. Somewhere in that great wave of sweet potato fever, the Hayman arrived and established itself first for market and ultimately as an emblem of local identity.

R. H. Price, professor of horticulture, botany, and entomology at Texas Agricultural and Mechanical College, provided a staccato description of the Hayman sweet potato in his 1896 *Sweet Potato Culture for Profit*: "Foliage

pale green, abruptly conical with prominent notches on the side; vines vigorous, root profusely, length seven feet; tubers oblong, large and white. A
promising variety but easily affected by drouth." He then reprised the Hayman origin story: "In 1856, Capt. Dan Hayman was master of the schooner,
'Harriet Ryan,' freighting between the West Indies and Elizabeth City, N.C.
While on one of these trips he purchased a supply of sweet potatoes at
one of the West India Islands. A Methodist clergyman on visiting the ship
after its arrival in Elizabeth City was attracted by the fine appearance of
the potato, obtained a few and propagated them. From this source came
all the Hayman potatoes now grown in this country." Given the number
of Methodist chapels in towns and along country roads, I have little doubt
that the Hayman made its debut on the Eastern Shore of Virginia in a moment of evangelical fervor.

T. E. Hand and K. L. Cockerham observed in their 1921 sweet potato
treatise, "It is a very early, unusually productive and is considered one
of the earliest varieties to keep in storage. It is much improved in eating
quality by storage and though not a very choice eating potato in fall and
early winter, it becomes very good indeed in late winter and spring. It is of
a very light color outside, presenting a grayish-white rather than yellow appearance. The flesh is pale yellow. The vine growth is heavy. The tubers are
inclined to become over-large in rich soil, unless early digging is practiced."

Relying on correspondence from the Virginia Truck Experimental Station, Hand and Cockerham clarified some of the considerable confusion
around the identity of the Hayman. "The Hayman and Southern Queen
are identical, having whitish skin and creamy flesh." They continue, "This
variety and the Nancy Hall are the only 'yam' kinds grown in the eastern
shore production section." Marketing changes everything: "The Hayman
has long been well known in that section but years ago it was taken up by
B. K. Bliss, then a leading seedman in New York City, and sent out as a new
potato under the name Southern Queen. It is now known in many sections
by the latter name." The quest for market share did not conclude with one
name change. The Hayman or Southern Queen or West Indian White or
Bahamas Sweet Potato or, around Baltimore, the White Yam were apparently all one and the same.

Rebranding the Hayman as the Southern Queen was well established
long before Hand and Cockerman provided their account. James Fitz, a
sweet potato promoter based near Charlottesville, Virginia, cribbing his
commentary from an unidentified correspondent, blurs distinctions even
more. His 1908 commentary aligns qualities of the Hayman aka Southern
Queen with his favorite, the Nansemond, as well as the "Spanish Potato."
The Hayman, Fitz states, "is the earliest of all Sweet Potatoes. It was intro-

Planting sweet potatoes, Machipongo area, Virginia.

duced some years ago from South America. It is in eating condition here, near Baltimore, usually by the middle of July, and when first dug is generally in good eating condition. As the season progresses, and during the fall and early winter, they are generally too wet to suit Southern palates; while during this time the Yellow potatoes are in their glory. It is for keeping qualities that the 'Southern Queen' stands unrivalled. As a variety to begin and prolong the Sweet Potato season, there is nothing to compare with the 'Southern Queen.'"

The connection Fitz draws to the Spanish potato coheres around the observation, "In tide-water Virginia, particularly on the eastern shore of both Maryland and Virginia, every farmer grows, besides the main crop, a few 'Spanish Potatoes' for home use, though they are not usually eaten until the depth of winter, when they become 'fat,' as it is termed. Those who have never eaten a 'fat' Spanish potato, do not yet know the capabilities of the Sweet Potato."

"A white-skinned greenish-yellow-fleshed sweet potato," David Shields, 143

Sweet potato field newly planted, Machipongo area, Virginia.

author of *Southern Provisions*, summarizes in the nomination of the Hayman to the international Ark of Taste maintained by the slow food movement, "has rounded, spade-like pale green foliage with purple stems. The leaves, usually whole, sometimes possess occasional prominent notches, [and] grow to five inches across at the widest point. The vines are vigorous, extending seven feet in length, and root profusely. The tubers are regularly oblong, smooth, large and white—blunt at the ends, or spindle shaped. The variety bears prolifically—one reason for its quick adoption by commercial seeds-men. When baked the flesh of the Hayman turns dull yellow or grey-greenish—not the most alluring of colors." Adding insult to injury, he adds, "The potato enjoyed equal popularity as livestock winter feed as it did as table fare for humans."

A tattered promotional flyer archived in a tin filled with recipes introduces Eastern Shore of Virginia sweet potato culture in its heyday: "Sweet potatoes rank as the second most vegetable crop in Virginia, and about three-fourths of Virginia production is located in Accomack and Northampton Counties, where approximately 12,000 acres are devoted to its production." No longer. The bulk of sweet potato production shifted to the southeastern reaches of North Carolina and southern Delaware. The four-page brochure provides recipes for sweet potato biscuits, sweet potato pie, and "Sweet Tater Puffs." The yellowed, creased, and stained handout lists five sweet potato varieties: Nemagold, Allgold, Yates Golden, Sunnyside, and Puerto Rican. Haymans are conspicuous in their absence. The taste of place can be the taste of absence.

The Nottingham cousins Addison and Butch sit at a long conference table in an office building on the edge of the tiny airport near Melfa in Accomack County. They grew and marketed sweet potatoes all their lives, and their fathers founded the original Nottingham Brothers produce concern. Their friend Richard Dryden, who worked his way to the top in John W. Taylor's sweet potato cannery near Oak Hall, close to the Maryland line, joins in the conversation.

Butch gestures toward a kaleidoscopic display of sweet potato brand labels. "In 1960, I think, we had two-hundred and thirty-some sweet potato growers, and some of them were awfully small, but we had that number." Now, he says, "Six? I don't know, ten?" Richard comments, "I don't think you'd fill up both hands counting them on your fingers." "And," Addison steps in, "as far as the big deal, there is nobody really growing a real large acreage of sweet potatoes. We don't have that. It's gone."

And it's not just sweet potato culture that has faded. Richard describes the arc of the cannery where he worked. "John W. Taylor's was the first to can. He started in 1904, I think. He started canning sweet potatoes, and he got into tomatoes and other stuff, too. He went bankrupt, I guess, when the Depression hit." "He paid off all of his debts and got back going," Richard emphasizes the importance of honoring debt. "He died in 1946," Richard establishes the cannery's genealogy of ownership and his place in it. "He had passed away before I went there. He had four daughters, and they continued to run the company. It was family stock. When one daughter had no children, when she passed away, she split her stock up, and she gave Ed Porterfield and I the stock." "Ed Porterfield and I were the only ones that was not a Taylor family member to own stock," he says with pride.

"When I started there in the early seventies, they were canning about twenty tons an hour. They were Jewels [a sweet potato variety] about that time, too. That was about the heyday on Jewels—all local grown." He describes an armada of farm trucks loaded with sweet potatoes parked around the perimeter of Railroad Square and down all the side streets. His memory of the scale of production resonates with a local booster's account from the 1920s: "A Shore sweet potato cannery tunnels its way clean through twelve hundred barrels of golden sweet potatoes in one day. In other words it takes the crop of a big farm to satisfy the ravenous appetite of the machinery of the average cannery for just one day." Not to mention the two hundred plus workers, many of them seasonal hands from North Carolina and the interior of Virginia.

Richard chronicles the end of an era through the story of his career. "I started there greasing equipment and mechanic's helper, and somebody would pass along or retire or whatever, and I'd kind of fall into that. One thing led to another, and when the plant manager retired, they asked me if I'd take that position. I kept that position until they closed in 1992. That was the last vegetable canner in the state of Virginia. It closed in May of 1992." When it came to canning Haymans, Butch adds, "They didn't can well. They kept trying to can them, and they'd turn dark when we canned them. Nothing they could do about that." The canneries may be shuttered and the big sweet potato farms of the past converted to the cultivation of soybeans, winter wheat, and feed corn, but still, a few modestly scaled growers endure—and they all cultivate Haymans.

Butch and Addison speak with authority and humor. "We were the largest Hayman grower in the world," Addison says. "I think we had thirty-five acres. I do like growing them." "It just got where we couldn't grow enough to justify all the expense," he tempers his enthusiasm, "because they're expensive to grow." Butch adds, "And they don't yield. They're an old variety. You can get four hundred bushels of something like a Covington, and you'd be probably lucky to grow one hundred fifty of the Haymans." "And," he nods to his cousin, referring to W. T. Nottingham, a grower near the tip of the peninsula, "Let me tell you, he's getting forty dollars a bushel for them. I don't think he's getting rich with them." "He's not growing very many of them," Addison observes.

Cultivating Haymans or any other sweet potato, Addison explains, "it's a thirteen-month crop. You never get any time off when you're growing sweet potatoes. There's always something to do." He walks through a sweet potato year step by step: "You start at harvest, which would probably be September, October. Early potatoes would come off in August, even. But September and October would be when you harvest potatoes. We always used to store potatoes. We had a storage house with heat in it that we would put them in and store them and cure them. The curing process would take probably a month, two months. The skin would set on where you could go through the machinery and pack them and get them ready to ship."

"During this whole time," he explains, "we're still selling potatoes while we're harvesting and storing them. We were able to sell some, and we didn't

Sweet potato harvest, Machipongo area, Virginia.

want to sell them all at harvest time because you don't get as much money, because that's when the most of them are available. So we hold them to sell along during the winter. We usually shipped a few every weekend to go to a place like New York and Philadelphia and Baltimore, close-by markets. And we had a man with a truck that would come by and pick up any small amount that you had. One pound or forty boxes, he'd carry them to New York or Philadelphia for you. During the winter, we usually packed them on maybe a Friday or Saturday morning, and the guy would come by on the truck and pick them up and make the market for Sunday night. That was almost every week during the winter."

Addison describes the next phase, "Once you've got through shipping the marketable potatoes, usually that was around Easter. You'd get through shipping." "It was another good little spot in the deal when you could sell that many at one time," he offers as a sidebar. "Always tried to have potatoes for Easter, because you've got a premium for them now. They weren't as plentiful." "Then," he picks up the chronology, "we had seed put away, which were ones that were too small to sell to ship. They were picked up separate and stored separate. You would warm them up and then we'd go to the field with them probably end of March, first of April. And put them in these hotbeds."

The conversation moves from harvesting to storage and curing to marketing and shifts to starting the new crop in hotbeds. The hotbed, Butch elaborates, "it would have sides on it and some slats, and polyethylene over the top of it. You'd have to ventilate them. There was a lot of labor involved in them." And vigilance, too. Addison explains, "If you had a real sunshiny day in the spring, the sun had a lot of strength to it, so shining through those covers would really heat up, so you'd be cognizant of what the sun was doing all day long." Butch picks up the story, "And how hard the wind was blowing, because you could roll the cover off a little bit and let out some of the heat." "If the wind was blowing," he looks at his cousin, "I mean, I tell you! I was coming home from church on a regular Sunday morning and seeing these covers all up in the air where I had to go back and change clothes and go back out there and deal with that."

In recent years, though, bedding techniques evolved. "Here, within the last, I guess, fifteen years, we basically cold bed. We put them in the ground and put clear plastic over them. It's the same type of plastic, except it's clear. You put them in there, and when they first start coming through, you take a little hole punch that would punch holes in it so you wouldn't get too hot over there, and they keep growing. You go back six or seven weeks later and cut the plants and plant them in the field. And then you got all summer to grow them."

Planting or "setting out" the new crop, Addison spins out the thirteenth month of the year: "Sprouts. We call them sprouts. Or draws." I've heard them called slips as well. "Once they get tall enough . . . if you had them in the beds, you had to keep them watered, too, because they're drawing all this water with this heat—and a little fertilizer. Not much. You really had to keep an eye on them because something could go wrong at any minute. Later in the year, we had trouble with deer."

The intense labor continued. "Before you had any kind of a weed control, that meant you had a weed-pulling crew," Butch notes, and Addison affirms, "All summer." Butch resumes, "All summer long! When I was a kid, I had the pleasure of pulling some. We had four or five other boys from the neighborhood, and Louise—she helped us weed. We would maybe weed fifty acres, or something like that, and by the time you got through going through one time, it was time to start back on the first ones again."

Addison segues into the harvest as the sweet potato year rolled into autumn, "It's quite a deal. Once you've got them grown, they'd cover everything up, then it was time to go, and you mowed the vines off and take a turn plow and plow them up. We always got them up by hand. What they called 'shake them out.' We'd go shake them out and lay them up on the 'lift.'" The lift, he explains, is the long mound of earth built up beside the furrow, "like a pyramid, but a little wider at the top." The field hands, including the cousins, "they'd come through and sort them according to size. The smallest, of course, would be for seed or for the canner. The marketable ones would go separately into a crate and be carried to the store." Butch summarizes, "You couldn't throw them around. You'd set them up there and then people would, what they call, shake it out. They'd put them up on top of the lift, and they would take a box or basket in between the two lifts, and they would just put potatoes in that basket."

The digging process has changed. Field hands no longer stoop and bend in the furrows hand-packing sweet potatoes in individual crates and baskets. Instead, a field crew rides a moving platform pulled behind a tractor. A chain conveyor belt rolls the potatoes off the lifts and past workers who cull the potatoes, dropping them into large wooden bins. Dead vines and bad potatoes simply roll off the end of the belt, falling back into the soft earth, where they will be plowed under. Addison elaborates on current practice, "It didn't make it any less expensive to dig them, but it made it better for the help to be able to deal with. Rather than being down on the ground in the dirt, you're actually standing up and picking them off the table. It was just better for the workers and better for the potatoes because you didn't bang them up. You had more control over what went on."

The sweet potatoes went from field to storage. As the old year rolled into its thirteenth month, a new one was already under way.

Butch and Addison keep their sweet potato disasters in perspective—wet years, sudden winds, overheated or dried-out hotbeds, sharp cold snaps. Still, some stand out in their lifetimes of shared experience. "We try to forget about the disasters," Addison begins the tale of an unfortunate sequence of events. "We had sweet potatoes in the storage house one winter. We had a bad storm come and blew the roofing off. This was in the middle of the winter." Butch contributes, "All we had was plywood on top." Addison resumes, "So if it rained and it wouldn't hold the heat either. We went to a nurseryman and said, 'We need some plastic to cover this roof up. We lost the roof off our potato house. We're going to lose the potatoes if we don't.' The man said, 'I got plenty of plastic. You can come down here and we're going to give you what you need and get it all straight.'"

"Then his partner showed up," the story progresses, "and his partner said, 'Hold on here a minute. We might need this plastic ourselves. You can't let these boys have it.' They about had a fistfight right there, but we wound up with the plastic to cover up the roof on that storage house. It was a pretty good-size house, too. We didn't completely save the crop, but we saved a lot of what we had in storage. That was a disaster we kind of skimmed by." It is also a story that speaks to underlying values of mutual support in a corner of the world where recollections of assistance in a difficult situation endure—and memories of self-interest and denial often come home to roost.

William Harmon, the Nottinghams' neighbor and a fellow sweet potato grower, adds his expertise to the cultivation of the Hayman. Mr. Harmon preserves his planting stock every year by cutting slips from producing plants and planting them in special rows he designates for "seed." His Hayman stock has descended through the Harmon family over generations. Grown from slips, these Haymans remain genetically constant from year to year. Only in recent years has their nature changed, reportedly as a result of research in experimental stations. As far as many Eastern Shore cooks are concerned, those improvements have not benefited their taste for Haymans. The potatoes they remember with the greatest affection, the Nottinghams say, "were something that was just kind of passed down. People would save their own seed ever since I can remember. That's really the only source they had until research stations got into it. You'd buy them from so-and-so, and if anything was a good line of Haymans, we'd buy some seed from them. It was never much trouble selling seed when we first started selling it. If you had some you wanted to sell, somebody would want them."

Jack Robbins, the retired sheriff of Northampton County, expresses his doubts about the integrity of the Haymans he's encountered in recent years. "The quality of the Haymans you get nowadays are way different than they were when I was growing up. I got some this year that are better than they have been, but they're still not like they used to be. When I was coming up, they were just as juicy . . . ," his voice trails off for a moment. "The ones I got this year," Jack resumes, "I got from that little country store in Pungoteague." "There's a guy—actually he got in trouble and he was in jail while I was still sheriff, and of course he's gotten out, and he's growing vegetables and stuff, and he sells them at his farm." Clearly, you need to know someone to find a good Hayman these days. "I was going to get Haymans from him this year, but he lost his whole crop. It got too wet, and he was planting them in flat rows and not hilling them. He lost the whole damn crop. He's the one who told me about the guy in Pungoteague at the old store who had them, so I bought some from him." With

Sweet potatoes for sale, Machipongo area, Virginia.

some resignation and reservation, Jack looks forward to next year's supply from his Pungoteague source. "Supposedly, he's going to change his farming method on growing his Haymans, and I'll try him again next year."

"Supposedly he found a strain of potatoes that is the original strain." Jack emphasizes pedigree: "Now most of what they sell for Haymans around here are what they call O'Henrys. They're not really Hayman potatoes. They kind of look like Haymans. I mean they're the same shape." Jack associates the culture of Haymans with small-patch farmers in the African American settlements scattered throughout the two counties. "There was a couple of them down Cheriton area that had them. When they died, I guess their potato seed stock—nobody preserved it or did anything with it, and it died when they did." Not quite. Mr. Harmon still cultivates Haymans on his farm near Franktown, and when it comes to Hayman sweet potatoes and preserving the strain, he is both authority and source.

"To get the plant, you got to bed them," Mr. Harmon reviews his process. "I bed them any time after the twentieth of March. I put them in the bed. Then you put the cover over them and you keep the bed moist. And then after eight or nine days, the slips come up." He monitors the heat and moisture of the hotbeds, bending down and inserting his hand into the sandy loam. Too warm or too wet, he vents the bed. Just right, he settles the top back into position. "Any time after the ninth or tenth of April we cover them with cloth, after the ninth or tenth of May, you put that whole potato in the bed and you put about an inch and a half of dirt on top of it. Then a plastic cover that you put over that bed with an arc to it so that the water will roll off. That plastic will draw the heat when the sun is shining and heat up them potatoes in that bed and make the plant come."

Mr. Harmon adds some background history. Before plastic, he says, "they would use unbleached muslin" sewn into strips. "If you want to make a nine-yard bed, you sort of have to make three strips. Then you put linseed oil on that muslin. You soak that with oil and it would draw heat just like the plastic would." "But that plastic," he observes, "is dangerous." Heat would build up inside the plastic, and the tender potato slips would dry out, cook, and perish. "The heat will burn those plants to the ground," he cautions. "You will lose your plants in one day's time."

"I put down two hundred-foot beds at ten feet wide, and we get around five or six thousand plants from each bed. When you pull him out of that bed, he's got about that much root that you put back in the ground." Mr. Harmon illustrates, forming a caliper between thumb and forefinger into a two-inch gap. The part of the potato that gets planted is roughly two inches in length and white, with tiny rootlets sticking out. "That part," he says, "you put back in the ground and make sure he's tight. If you put him down and the air gets around him, he's gone." On average a plant will produce six to eight potatoes per hill. William Harmon harvests three or four hundred bushels and sells every one of them locally to his neighbors as well as residents throughout the county who purchase them for the winter holidays. He also sets aside a hundred bushels of seed potatoes for the coming year.

After the potatoes are planted and have rooted in the ground, the principal task, as the Nottinghams noted, is walking and weeding the rows to keep grasses out of the field. "When the vines are about two, two-and-a-half, three feet long," Mr. Harmon provides detail, "then you can't work them no more."

Mr. Harmon's Hayman sweet potatoes are ready for digging around the second week of September when the potatoes actually begin to break the ground, but, he's quick to warn, you cannot eat them right away. "You have to put them up and cure them," he says, "put them in the potato house somewhere, keep the heat around 65 or 70 degrees. Keep him warm like that for a couple of weeks. You'll see sugar come out on the end where you break the stem. The sugar will come out kind of black." "And," he adds, "if that softens up and the more sweetness you want, then he be good to go. But don't try to cook them when you first dig them." I never do.

Every Hayman sweet potato grower stresses the importance of curing— the practice of letting the sweet potato rest after harvest until the skin hardens a bit and thin trails of black sugar appear. Before the advent of sweet potato houses and later through lack of access to the amenity of heated storage, Mr. Harmon's family and others in the African American community stored their potatoes in "kilns," insulated pits excavated next to the fields.

"It was quite a few years back," he recounts, "but colored people was tending to them. My two farms had eight or ten rows, and that made plenty of potatoes for the winter months. Back then they made a potato kiln and put the potato in there and cover them up with pine needles, pine shatters, and then cover them up in layers about two, three, six—and you could keep them potatoes there all winter." "Always go to the southern side, you had people who would go to the southern side—the warm side—in wintertime and make that kiln there," Mr. Harmon advises. "Go to your hole, dig out what you want, cover it back, and keep potatoes for all winter. Most of the time we would go down to the woods and get on the sunny side of the woods, on the south side of the piece of the woods you would have. Any place that would block that north wind, that is where they would make the kiln." "That was years back," he says. "See, we don't bury them in no kiln now, you just put them in a house. See, you got heat you can put in there now. Back then, there wasn't no heat unless you had a fire." Now, he says, "I got a room there in my shed on the end there where I put them when I dig them."

Fred "Picky" Weatherly, who worked the Seaside oyster grounds with the Terry family, recalls a similar arrangement for families who didn't cultivate potatoes. "Yeah, people used to take like white potatoes and sweet potatoes. They'd dig a hole, put shatters in it, put stuff in it, then they cover it. Then they just leave a hole at the top where you stick your hand in to get in and out. And they would keep it cold in a cold kiln is what they called it. But those potatoes would not rot in it."

Chester Satchell, a neighbor stopping by to purchase some Haymans from Mr. Harmon, adds another step to the process. "I usually let them sit in the sun until the syrup starts to come out of them a little bit. I let them wait in the sun, let the sun hit them for a while. I just set them out there. I try not to let them get wet. Like sometimes I'll lay them out. When it's a day like today." It's a blue-sky autumn morning, warm and breezy. "I'll take them home today, and these will lay out the rest of the day," Chester says, "then maybe tomorrow. They green up, and then they're nice and sweet. Rub them down and wash them off, rub them down in some grease or oil or something. Stick them in that oven. Mmmm."

There's an art to curing Haymans. Butch and Addison Nottingham did their best to communicate this to their customers, providing curing in-

Laura Dennis, Franktown, Virginia.

structions for folks who came to them for their Haymans: "These Hayman Sweet Potatoes have not been put through the curing process, which converts the starch in the potatoes to sugar, giving them their sugary taste. You can cure them by putting them in a place where the minimum temperature does not fall below 55 degrees F. for several weeks or until they begin to show signs of piping (small sprouts will begin to appear on one end of the potato)." "If you are still in doubt about the eating quality," they added helpfully, "bake a couple [of] them. If they don't cook soft and sweet, try again in a week or so. Repeat this process until you are satisfied with their sweetness." Or run out of Haymans, I think dispiritedly.

Addison and Butch associate their Haymans with the winter holidays and homecomings. "We sold a lot of them out the door," Addison says. "A lot of people came and got them. So you got to see a lot of people that you really wouldn't see all year. People call up and hit you up to get their box of Haymans ready." When the customers arrived, "you got to visit with them a little bit. It was kind of a social activity as much as it was a business. We really liked doing it." His cousin and business partner, Butch, explains the circumstances in greater detail.

Another partnership sold Haymans at their feed store. When they shuttered their doors for the last time, Butch says, "that gave us an opportunity, and we picked up on what they were doing. Kept some hand-packed back there all the time so people could come in and get them. It was fun because mostly it was the holiday season anyway. You got to see people over Christmas and Thanksgiving that you probably wouldn't have seen any other way." Addison continues, "People would always want to come get something that they couldn't get anywhere else. They'd come and you'd visit with them, and it was a lot of fun. It really was." He concludes, "The help liked doing it, too. We had a couple of ladies that worked with us, and they'd keep them packed up, and they'd be there, if we weren't going to be there, we'd have somebody there to help folks that came to get them."

It's hard to imagine a more passionate diatribe castigating a universe of sweet potato villainy and abuse than the one offered by the Eastern Shore Farm Credit Administration in 1901:

But the cooks of the country ever have been and are to-day its worst enemies. By every conceivable method have they attacked and robbed this tuber of its attractiveness and of its valuable and delightful qualities. They have peeled it, and drowned it, and boiled it, until it was nothing but a sodden, sticky, nauseating mass of insipid pulp, and they are doing just this same thing with it all over the North and West today, and this by the highest priced "chef" in the finest hotel as well as by the housewife in the hillside cottage, notwithstanding she pays 60 cents a peck for them; and yet it survives this murderous treatment and grows in popularity everywhere. The potato roasted in the ashes or in the oven with its "jacket" on; the potato sliced thin and quickly baked to a light-brown and served hot with butter; the rich and golden potato pie; the hot and crisp potato biscuit and the delicious potato custard, are all unknown to these murderous cooks of the North and West. What a wonderful change would be wrought by good cooking in the present position of the sweet potato in the markets and in the homes of these sections! With an Eastern Shore cook in every household there, the sweet potato would take those sections by storm; the supply would not half equal the demand. To enjoy a sweet potato in its perfection, it should be grown in the right soil, handled in the right way, and cooked by the right cook.

There you have it.

Sweet potato recipes abound. When the Virginia Sweet Potato Commission created a promotional compilation of recipes sometime in the 1960s or 1970s, they turned to the "homemakers of Virginia's Eastern Shore." Contributors submitted directions for delicacies that included "Mother's Sweet Potato Croquettes," "Sweet Potato Fluff," "Sweet Potato Waffles," and "Sausage and Sweet Potato Skillet Supper." The mainstays, though, were the nine variations on sweet potato pies, five for biscuits, five for pudding, and eight (minimum) for baked and glazed.

The editors justified repetition: "At first glance some of these recipes appear to be the same—but upon reading you will find that each home-maker has her own proven method for a successful sweet potato dish. We have included all these methods with the hope that you, the cook, will be able to develop your own dishes when you see how easily it is done." The empowering generosity of editorial inclusiveness also yielded a recipe for sweet potato diplomacy with no contributor shunned.

Reading through the alchemy of nearly seventy sweet potato preparations, I am surprised by three absences. First, there are no instructions for baking sweet potatoes, by far the most common preparation. Second, there is no acknowledgment of the African American cooks who surely developed and perfected many of the recipes. Third, "Mr. Hayman," prized by so many local cooks, is curiously AWOL. That was not the case when Fairy Mapp White shared a narrative recipe for roasted Haymans (or Hamans, as she spelled it) in her 1958 *Foolproof Cook Book*.

Headlined "Baked Sweet Potatoes, Hamans and Spanish," White's recipe provides instructions for oven roasting enriched through brief vignettes. "The Eastern Shore of Virginia variety of potatoes, not really yellow, are hard to find now, but there are none better when properly baked," a sentiment that remains current over a half century later. "Potatoes should be put in hot oven dripping wet, reduced some in about 15 or 20 minutes," she instructs. "I learned from a substitute maid Christmas 1953 that greasing Spanish and Haman potatoes with left-over sausage or bacon drippings made them bake and peel better. Both are hard to peel as soft inside." White then appends a note that captures a sense of terroir as a fusion of local knowledge, memory, distinction, and feeling: "So far as I know Haman and Spanish potatoes are raised only on the Eastern Shore of Virginia. As late as 1957 Alonzo Mears (a tenant of my father's over fifty years ago) refused to dig them until there had been a frost, and I know we never ate them until they had been dug long enough to mellow, that is become lusciously soft and sweet. Home from the public school, known as Grange Hall, on the old Keller Fair Grounds, nothing was more satisfying for a snack than a homemade sausage and a juicy Haman or Spanish potato."

When it comes to Haymans there are four recipes forever lodged in my culinary imagination: roasted, pies, biscuits, and candied. None are specific to the Hayman alone, but the peculiarities of the Hayman influence the outcome.

Oven-roasted sweet potatoes were a staple. Bessie Gunter provided the simplest instructions in her cookbook published at the advent of the Victorian golden age of Eastern Shore agriculture:

TO BAKE SWEET POTATOES.
Wash them perfectly clean, wipe them dry, and bake in a quick oven.
Do not open the oven while baking, unless it is necessary to turn
them. Roasted or baked potatoes should not be cut, but broken open
and eaten from the skin as from a shell.
    —G.

Annie Reed prefaces her memory of roasted Haymans with the recollection of her family farm: "I was born and raised on the Eastern Shore. Lived here most of my life. My father was a farmer, and from that we just kept right on. My father has now passed, but my sister, myself, my brothers— we do a little farming. We plant sweet potatoes, string beans, different items, tomatoes, different things like that on the farm, squash, things like that." They have grown Haymans off and on for as long as anyone can remember. As far as Haymans go, she says, "I'm still at it." "It's got a nice, sweet taste to it," she explains, "when you broil them right. We broil them, yellow yams and the Haymans. We usually just put ours in the oven and just cook them until they're soft enough for you. We grease ours, we put a little oil on them, and then bake them." When she retrieves the potatoes from the oven, "We put them in a little basket and put the damp cloth over them and just leave them stay there for a while." Haymans need to sweat a bit, "That keeps the moistness to them."

Roasted, Haymans complement just about everything on the menu. Polk Kellam, reflecting on his family's culinary legacy, shared, "Somebody asked this gentleman who worked for us what his favorite meal was. He said, 'Black duck, Hayman potato, and turnip greens.' You talk about an

Eastern Shore menu." Richard Dryden makes the point with equal concision. Sweet potatoes, he says, go with "just about anything and just about any way you can cook it. I like a sweet potato." His friend Addison Nottingham agrees, "Pie is good. I like a baked sweet potato, and I like them with spot, spot fish. Spot, sweet potato. Pretty good eating there, buddy." Charlie Weatherly of Willis Wharf also connects roasted sweet potatoes to fish, fried and baked, "Loved that drum. You take drum fish, fried drum fish and sweet potatoes." His brother echoes the sentiment. "They had that, and it was a nice meal," Charlie says, and then remembers hard times. "But all meals was nice, because we didn't starve."

When folks roasted Haymans, they always baked a few extras to eat cold the following day. "I remember my father telling me when he was a boy, he'd take off and go quail hunting," Jack Robbins remembers, "and most of the time what he had for lunch was a cold Hayman potato he just carried in the pocket of his hunting coat. When he got hungry, he'd sit down and peel it and eat it." Kay Crumb Downing, who grew up in the Seaside village of Oyster, recalls, "You always had sweet potatoes on the table," adding that "even Daddy ate sweet potatoes for breakfast if we had them. He was a fanatic about his sweet potatoes." "Sweet potatoes," her brother Ron offers, "they'd just bake them and put a little butter on them—and Mom made sweet potato pies."

The subtlety of sweet potato pies is not lost on me. Every home cook bakes them, and they do so in signature ways that revolve around the tiniest details in proportion and sometimes the addition of a wildcard ingredient—cardamom or pineapple, for example. Gloria Harmon, married to William Harmon, whose family has cultivated Hayman sweets for generations, makes a different sweet potato pie, a confection that draws its accent from the lemon juice she adds.

"SWEET POTATO PIE"
2 X-large eggs
2 Cup sugar
1 Stick butter
3 Cup cook[ed] potatoes
½ Cup whole milk
1 Cup canned milk
2 Tbsp vanilla
2 Tbsp lemon
½ Tsp salt
Mix ingredients together. Bake at 375°. Use unbaked pie shell.

The instructions are simple enough. Collect the ingredients, blend them thoroughly, pour the filling mixture into the piecrust, and bake until the pie is done. There are no steps but these; there are no intervals but those defined by practice. I've made this pie according to these exact specifications and in doing so discovered the pie as the craft produced from a deep reservoir of knowledge achieved through practice and the most literal acts of consumption. At heart, sweet potato pie is an idea encountered on a plate.

Sara "Cook" Ross of Accomac kept her recipes in a blue cookie tin that held two small file boxes and a handful of loose papers. Her handwritten recipe consists only of a list of ingredients with no instructions for a crust and no directions for mixing and baking the filling. Cook Ross presumed that if you were going to make something as familiar as a sweet potato pie you were already fully versed in the lingua franca of pie central to the enterprise. The enumeration of ingredients told the experienced baker of sweet potato pies all they needed to know. Her ingredients, consistent with those listed for other sweet potato pie recipes, vary in proportion from Gloria Harmon's, but the alchemy of evaporated milk, sweet potatoes, butter, eggs, spice, and sugar is much the same.

"SWEET POTATO PIE"

2 cups potato
1 large can milk
1½ cup sugar
1 stick melted butter
pinch salt
4 eggs
1 teaspoon vanilla

Laura Dennis recalls her mother's pie and cake business in the town of Cape Charles during the Great Depression: "Mother was most famous for her pies. She had the best recipe for piecrust, and it was just as flaky, never soggy. She made lemon and coconut pie. Butterscotch, cherry, apple, mincemeat, pumpkin, sweet potato." As a little girl of nine or ten, Laura had the job of delivering those pies to customers in the community. "They would order the cakes and the pies and the rolls. She would take orders during the week. And we would deliver the goods, and we had a little wagon that my uncle fixed. It had a little cage on it with two shelves, and we put the pies in there and pulled the wagon around and deliver. And that's how she made her living." The one pie Laura Dennis never made, though, was a Hayman sweet potato pie, inscribed in a recipe in her collection, which included many from her mother, with the caution "will be slightly greenish in color, and very, very rich." Undaunted, I baked and ate this sweet potato pie, and it is, in fact, both slightly green and exceedingly rich.

WHITE HAYMAN SWEET POTATO PIE
3 cups cooked white Hayman sweet potatoes
1 stick butter
1 pinch nutmeg
1⅓ cup sugar
4 eggs beaten
1 tsp vanilla
1 (13 oz) can evaporated milk
1 unbaked pie shell, large, or 2 small
Combine potatoes, butter, sugar, vanilla and nutmeg. Combine beaten eggs and milk; mix with potato mixture until blended. Pour into pie shell or shells. Bake at 350° for 1 hour or until knife inserted comes out clean. May take 20 minutes longer in large pie.

"Oh my, sweet potato pies," Margaret Young recalls the pies of her Accomac childhood, "out of the Hayman potatoes, not just the red-skinned, but Hayman the green sweet potato the Eastern Shore is known for." Billie Mason's mother created many of those pies: "She did it at Ms. Mapp's with the Haymans. At home she did it with the red-skinned, what we called them Puerto Rican potatoes—that's when she made them at home." Billie, too, made those pies for the Mapp family. "When I came there I had to make them like Mother. I told Mrs. Mapp I couldn't and Mr. Mapp didn't think I could do anything." Mrs. Mapp intervened, "said, 'George, just give her time! She could do it if we tell her do something!'" She and Margaret laugh. Then Billie finishes, "And I could do anything that Mother did. Because I had seen her do it."

Billie Mason's sweet potato pie lineage doesn't end there. Her grandmother, she states with pride, made the first sweet potato pies served on the ferry boats that ran between Little Creek on the Norfolk side and Kiptopeke on the Eastern Shore before there was a bridge-tunnel across the Chesapeake Bay. Travelers purchased pie by the slice from a concession on the upper deck. "See, I was young," Billie states, "and I seen the picture on the wall and Grandma was holding the potato pie. I said, 'Grandma, what is this?' She said, well, she was the first, the first lady—black lady—that made sweet potato pies on the ferry coming from Norfolk to Kiptopeke. I guess she fed them to somebody, that sweet potato pie, and they said, 'Wow, this would be good!'"

Thoughts of sweet potato pies—especially Hayman sweet potato pies—

slide easily into reveries of sweet potato biscuits. Sweet potato biscuit recipes are legion on the Eastern Shore. It's one of those things where everyone holds an opinion and they show no reluctance in pressing their case for the best. As far as I'm concerned, the best sweet potato biscuit is the one that's on my plate in the moment. Still, folks argue their preferences with no small passion. The best sweet potato biscuit, some might say, is made by Tangier, who cooks at the roadhouse down the road. Another might claim the crown for a grandmother or great-aunt long passed but whose sweet potato biscuits endure in memory. Bessie Gunter makes no mention of sweet potato biscuits in her 1889 *Housekeeper's Companion*, but Fairy Mapp White includes a single recipe in her 1958 *Foolproof Cook Book*:

SWEET POTATO BISCUITS

3 c. flour sifted with 6 level tsp. baking powder

1 tsp salt

2 c. mashed sweet potato, mixed while hot with 3 level tbs. lard and
½ c. sugar

Process:

1. Combine these two mixtures.

2. Roll out not too thin (as it does not rise as much as plain biscuits).

3. Bake in 400° oven only what you want to eat at once. Store balance in ice box. It will be even better than first baking.

Sweet potato biscuit recipes multiplied. A generation after White's compendium, the Virginia Sweet Potato Commission's promotional booklet offered four variations. The recipes, much the same, vary only in details of proportion, oven temperature, and baking time.

Dee Spady, formerly an assistant to the chef at a local restaurant, recounts a call she received from a coworker unskilled in the ways of sweet potato biscuits. "I told him when you make it you can't take the potatoes and throw it in the steamer," she says. "That don't work. When you make a sweet potato biscuit, you put it in the oven. You wash them and put a little grease on them or oil so they can slide out of the jacket better." "When you're cooking them," she admonished the new arrival, "you cook them like 85 percent. You don't want to cook them till they're mush. That way you still have some little hard pieces in there." The result is obvious, "That way when you make them up and a person's eating them, 'Oh, these are homemade,' because you can see the pieces of sweet potato in it."

Dee elaborates, "A lot of people, when they are making bread and stuff, they put it in the mixer. You know what the best kind of mixer is that you can buy? This!" She holds up her hands and laughs, "Clean the fingernails out. Go to work. This is the best thing!" Dee's expertise was called upon more than once: "They call and ask me about showing the girl how to make sweet potato biscuits. I showed her and I said you need more flour and a pinch more baking powder. Then I taste it, and a pinch more salt. I know. I can just feel it. I can just feel it." "Oh, gracious. They are so good!" She smiles and offers an afterthought, "And they good, too, with turkey gravy. Yes!"

I ask Dee if she ever made Hayman sweet potato biscuits. "Yes," she says. "Yes. I made some not too long ago. They're good. They're good." "But," she amends, "I also put my sweet potato biscuits and my Hayman biscuits — I always put a little bit of heavy cream in them, and I cut them out, they're good." "After I bake my potatoes," Dee explains, "while my potatoes are baking, I got a bowl here with butter and Crisco, and when I peel them, I dump them in there like that. And then I mix them up by hand so they melt. Then I set them aside, because I don't mess with them while they're hot." "I either make them that day, later on that day, or the next day," she says. "The next day I put my salt in, and flour, put my salt and flour and mix it up. Then I put my sugar in it till I've got it just right. The last thing I put in it is cream." "No," she corrects herself, "before I put the cream I put my baking powder in. If the recipe calls for, say, four teaspoons of baking powder, I put two more extra so they be fluffy." Is this because Haymans are heavier and denser, I ask. "Yes. And I add my flour to it, and you've got to make sure, with the Haymans I always do a sample, because you got to put it on a little plate, put it in the oven and see. Because they stay wetter longer than a regular potato, I add more flour to it, and I make a sample. If the sample is just right, then I go on with it."

Tradition is invention grounded in the many ways in which people know and inhabit the world around them. Tradition creates opportunity, imagines culinary possibility, and sometimes leads to excess. Consider candied Hayman sweet potatoes (candied yams by any other name). Gloria Harmon offers straightforward instructions, "I just slice them and I put them in the pan. I cook mine — some people put theirs in the oven — but most of the time, I cook mine on top of the stove. Put sugar and butter. And cinnamon. That's how I cook mine." She acknowledges that many cooks boil, peel, and slice the sweet potatoes into rounds and then bake them in the oven. "That's the way they do it when they put it in the oven," she says dismissively, "but most of the time, I cook mine on top of the stove." People also have a tendency to add frills. Directions for candied or glazed "sweets" collected in the Virginia Sweet Potato Commission's recipe booklet include the addition of cloves, lemon juice, marshmallows, butterscotch sundae sauce, and orange marmalade.

More to the point is Jack Robbins's variation that he learned from an elderly cook in the African American settlement near Bayford Crossroads. The way I remember Jack relating the recipe many years earlier is in the context of a lost hunting dog that required Jack to canvas from door to door before he located his wayward hound, dirty and exhausted from three days of running deer in the forests and fields. Jack claims to have no memory of this, but he recollects the recipe with precision. He begins with a lament, "I just wish we could get Hayman potatoes like they used to be when I was coming along." "The sweet potato recipe, I don't know if it had anything to do with the dog being lost or not," he qualifies, is a "lady's recipe for cooking Haymans—different from just rubbing Crisco on them and baking them. She would boil them, then peel them, then of course cut them, put them in a Pyrex dish or something, then put some butter and brown sugar on them." It's enough to send you into shock, I think. "I've made them that way lots of times," he says. "In fact, I've done it a couple of times this year. I've baked some and peeled them and eaten them that way." The leftovers, "I do three or four that I put in the refrigerator and then peel. The next time, I usually just put them in a Pyrex pan with butter and brown sugar on them." Easy enough—and no fussiness.

"I tell you the truth," Jack shakes his head, "I think you could eat a shoe cooked that way, to be honest with you." But it would be tastier if the shoe was a Hayman sweet potato.

CHEFS' RECIPES FOR HOME

COAL-ROASTED SWEET POTATOES WITH BARBECUED VIRGINIA PEANUTS AND SORGHUM

Jeremiah Langhorne, The Dabney, Washington, D.C.

Makes 6 servings
  6 small- to medium-size sweet potatoes or 3 large ones that can be
  cut in half
For the spiced peanuts
  1 teaspoon coriander
  ¼ cup sweet paprika
  ¼ cup brown sugar
  3 tablespoons black pepper
  2 teaspoons garlic powder
  2 teaspoons onion powder
  2 teaspoons celery seed
  1 cup roasted Virginia peanuts
For assembly
  1 bunch chives or scallions
  2 tablespoons extra-virgin olive oil
  1½ teaspoons of finishing salt (such as J. Q. Dickinson, Amagansett,
  or—closer to home—Barrier Island salt)
  2 tablespoons sour cream
  2 tablespoons sorghum
  1 tablespoon Virginia Heritage Vinegar Works chardonnay vinegar
  or lemon juice

To cook the sweet potatoes
  In a charcoal grill build a small fire with a few coals. Gradually add
  more coals until you have a medium to large pile that will burn
  for at least 2 hours. Once the coals are burning brightly, arrange
  them in one corner of your grill, leaving room to position the
  sweet potatoes around the edge of the coal bed. Cook the potatoes
  for 1 hour, rotating them a quarter turn every 10–15 minutes,
  remembering that you want them to be exposed to an even amount
  of heat from all sides over the course of cooking. When the hour
  is up, begin to check them for doneness—they should be firm but
  yielding and the skin will be blackened and charred; depending

on the size sweet potato, this could take up to 1 hour longer. Meanwhile, make the spiced peanuts.

To *prepare the spiced peanuts*

Toast and grind the coriander and combine it with the rest of the spices; set aside.

Warm the peanuts in a skillet over medium heat, shaking them constantly so they don't burn. Once warm transfer them to a small a bowl. Sprinkle 2 tablespoons of the spice mixture over the peanuts and toss well; rough chop them and reserve.

To *serve the potatoes*

Chop the chives or scallions into small rings and set aside. Line up the potatoes on a tray and, using a knife, split them lengthwise, then use a fork to mash and fluff the insides. Sprinkle the potatoes with the olive oil and salt, then top with the sour cream, dividing it evenly among the potatoes. Drizzle with sorghum and sprinkle the peanuts, to taste, over the potatoes.

For the final touch, sprinkle with the chives or scallions and a splash of vinegar or lemon. They are ready to serve!

HAYMAN SWEET POTATO BISCUITS

Amy Brandt, Amy B Catering, Cheriton

Amy Brandt is always experimenting with local ingredients, historic recipes, and new opportunities, including the rise of Hispanic cuisines on the Eastern Shore of Virginia. Her miniature Hayman sweet potato biscuits are much sought after. For the best outcome roast the sweet potatoes.

Makes approximately 3 dozen 1½-inch biscuits

2 cups peeled and mashed Hayman sweet potatoes (about 3 medium potatoes)

3 cups cold buttermilk

5½ cups all-purpose flour

3 tablespoons plus 1 teaspoon baking powder

2 teaspoons salt

1 teaspoon baking soda

¾ cup (1½ sticks) cold butter, diced small

Preheat the oven to 400°. Line a baking sheet with parchment paper. Roast the potatoes until they are fork tender.

In a large bowl whisk together the sweet potatoes and

buttermilk. In a separate bowl whisk together the dry ingredients and then transfer them to a food processor. Add the butter and pulse until the mixture looks like coarse meal with a few pea-size pieces of butter remaining.

Add the flour and butter to the sweet potato mixture and stir just until combined. Scrape the mixture out onto a lightly floured work top and knead the dough just until it comes together. Less is more! Roll out the dough to 1-inch thickness. Cut out circles with a 1½-inch biscuit cutter. Place the circles on the prepared baking sheet and bake for 18–20 minutes.

A Nice Dish for a Bad Time
On Oyster Pie

"Oyster pie?" Buck Doughty laughed his rumbly laugh. "Never heard of it." "Buck," I pressed, "How could that be? I've run into all sorts of folks around here who recall oyster pie with a tear of sentiment and a sigh of memory." "Not us," Buck says, "and we were Seaside folk who ate most anything we could catch or forage." He glanced at the empty beer bottle in his hand and headed to the cooler to retrieve a fresh one. I felt a similar, but unrequited sense of absence. Buck's lack of recollection left me perplexed, feeling as if something had slipped away. Undeterred, I asked H. M. Arnold down at the Bayford oyster house: "Heard of it. Never ate it." Hank, his son, added, "Sounds like something eaten by old heads."

Considering the possibility that oyster pie might be a dish with African American connections, I visited Theodore Peed and Chester Satchell. "Could be it's something those water people eat out on Tangier or Saxis," Chester suggested. Mr. Peed shrugged his shoulders. Marilyn Sharp looked up from her Exmore produce stand, "No. Who makes that?" I turned to the professionals. The shuckers at Steve Bunce's oyster house on the Bayside Road professed a distant familiarity, but none had concocted or eaten oyster pie. Louise Sunkins, head cook at the Exmore Diner, said no—but helpfully added that she would ask around.

Still, the disappearance of oyster pie from Eastern Shore tables, although palpable, is far from absolute. Catherine Kellam included a recipe in her self-published cookbook of 2004:

OYSTER PIE
1 pint fresh oysters
3–4 Tablespoons butter
Salt and Pepper, to taste
1 baked pie crust
Make pie crust and bake until golden brown. Reserve

some dough to make a lattice crust on top of the pie. Heat the oysters slowly in a shallow pan. Bring to boil and add some butter, salt, and pepper. Add oysters and a bit of liquid to the pie shell. Dot with several lumps of butter. Criss cross with strips of the extra dough to make a lattice top. Bake 325° until golden brown.

Her basic recipe resonates with one published in Bessie Gunter's 1889 *Housekeeper's Companion*: "Fill an earthenware pan three-fourths full of oysters. Season with butter, pepper and milk. On sides of pan and on top, place rich pastry cut in thin strips and laid across each other so as to form squares."

On the heels of our first conversation, Buck couldn't shake thoughts of oyster pie and talked to his mother, Jean, and his aunt Darlene, both born and raised near the fishing hamlet of Wachapreague. Oyster pie, he learned, was a childhood dinner staple made by their mother and neatly topped with a lattice crust. John Marshall, Buck's cousin and a Hog Island descendant, asked his father, Kenny, if he'd eaten oyster pie. Yes! But it had been a while. "Oyster pie is basically oyster stew thickened with a roux, put in a pie dish, covered with rolled-out biscuit dough," he explained. "Same as the periwinkle . . . 'pennywinkle' pie. Only with oysters instead of 'pennywinkles.'" I like the sound of periwinkle pie, but the prospect of collecting enough of the tiny snails in the spiny marsh grass while fending off ravenous insect swarms blunts the edge of my culinary determination.

Cory Watts, Mr. Peed's nephew, recollected that his grandmother baked oyster pies but added that he would have to check on the details. Still, I had leads on oyster pie—and oyster pie was, I knew, once an Eastern Shore culinary mainstay—a dish with the cultural resonance of shrimp and grits in the Carolina Lowcountry or gumbo in the bayous of Louisiana. Its purchase on the culinary imagination of Eastern Shore of Virginia cooks, however, was slipping into forgetfulness. I resolved that now was the time for an apotheosis of oyster pie.

Kenny Marshall's recollection of the pie as a thickened oyster stew laid in and topped with a pastry crust provides a start—something of a departure point in what seems to be a territory largely lost to gastronomic amnesia. Oyster stew, though, remains a dish long savored in this part of the world and, in its day, one that aroused no shortage of opinion. If there was going to be an oyster pie renaissance, I knew it would require a multipronged approach just to get it into the oven and onto the menu.

In pursuit of its historic origins and variations, I also knew that some oyster pie archaeology was in order. Given Kenny Marshall's observation that the base of the pie was oyster stew, I had to determine which of a near

Seaside oyster rock, Quinby area, Virginia.

infinite array of possibilities worked best as a pie filling. Given the extreme partisanship around oyster stew recipes, this would require no small measure of sensitivity and diplomacy. And I had to be mindful of the history of scalloped oysters, a layered casserole-like dish with pie attributes. In search of expertise, I would have to recruit the assistance of gifted and adventurous chefs to bring oyster pie to the table. How hard could these tasks be? Easy as pie, I thought.

The heyday for oyster recipes predictably coincides with the turn-of-the-twentieth-century boom in oyster harvests. The peak in landings (the quantity of oysters harvested and brought to market) in the late 1880s and on into the 1920s inspired the creation of hundreds of recipes that appeared in a host of popular publications that ranged from newspapers to specialty cookbooks. In 1914, Swepson Earle, a noted Chesapeake country antiquarian and secretary of the National Association of Shell Fish Commissioners, presented an inventory of "100 economical, wholesome and palatable dishes . . . furnished by the chefs of some of the great hotels and restaurants of New York and Chicago." Published in the Raleigh, North Carolina, *Farmer and Mechanic* newspaper, Earle's oyster rhapsody appeared under a layer-cake-like stack of editorial headlines that tested basic rules of grammar: *Oysters Are a Healthful Food; Should Have Prominent Place on National Dietary, Biologist Thinks; Their Food Value Great; Nearer in Composition to Cow's Milk Than Do Most Other Meats; Sea Salts They Contain Useful in Regulating Nutritional Processes and Aid Digestion.* Clearly, the editor was deeply vested in the oyster business and eager to whet the popular appetite. For his part, Earle enshrined four pie variations in his catalog of oyster recipes: oyster pot pie, oyster pie, Yankee oyster pie, beefsteak and oyster pie along with oyster tartlets, but no recipes. Still, a bit of dedicated sleuthing discovered Earle's sources—and then some.

Hoping to resolve his financial woes, H. Franklyn Hall, "Chef Boothby Hotel Company," in 1901 self-published *300 Ways to Cook and Serve Shell Fish*, a hundred of which were devoted to oyster dishes. His oyster roll call concluded with Oyster Pie a la Boothby, Oyster Pie Baltimore Style, and Oyster Pie Family Style. The Oyster Pie a la Boothby, likely Hall's invention, is a fussy affair with ingredients extending to canned French mushrooms, mace, hard-boiled eggs, and cream sauce. His representation of a family-style oyster pie sounds closer to home: "Prepared and served the same as oyster pie, Baltimore style, except that you cook and thicken the oysters before putting them in the pan to be covered." The Baltimore style recipe includes only oysters, butter, salt, and pepper—with a parsley option. The difference is that the family-style oyster pie mandates precooking the oysters before placing them in the pie shell—an approach that aligns with Kenny Marshall's recollection and is preserved in Bessie Gunter's alternate preparation, which seems to be little more than an oyster stew poured into a crust and placed on the table: "Line a deep baking dish with rich pastry rolled thicker than for fruit pies, stick with a fork and bake. Pepper and salt the oysters, dredge them with flour, add lumps of butter, fill the dish three-fourths full, pour in the oyster liquor, cover with pastry and bake." "Or," Gunter veers in another direction, "you can stew the oysters, while the pastry is baking, pour in hot and serve immediately."

When it comes to oyster pie recipes, however, Olive Green surely holds the record. Her 1907 compendium of 215 oyster recipes describes eight preparations that evoke a veritable atlas of Virginia, English, Rhode Island, Maryland, and Boston pies.

VIRGINIA OYSTER PIE

Make pastry according to directions given for Oyster Patties II.
Line a deep pie-plate with the paste and fill it with bread-crumbs or raw rice to be removed later. Fit on a top crust, buttering the edges underneath. Bake the crust. Prepare the oysters for filling according to directions given for Oyster Patties II, take off the crusts carefully,

remove the crumbs or rice, fill with the hot oyster mixture, and serve at once.

Her instructions for the filling run: "Prepare Creamed Oysters according to the first recipe given, adding the beaten yolk of an egg. Have the patty cases piping hot, fill with the hot oysters, put on the cover, and serve immediately."

Green's recipe for creamed oysters directs: "Put one heaping tablespoonful of butter into a saucepan. Cook until it froths, add two tablespoonfuls of flour, and stir until the mixture leaves the sides of the pan. Add two cupfuls of cream, and salt and pepper to taste. Stir over a slow fire until the sauce thickens, then add a pint of oysters, simmer until the edges curl, and serve immediately."

Forget the flour and egg, and you have oyster stew in the style my old friend and former Northampton County sheriff Jack Robbins sought to re-create. "The best oyster stew I ever ate was at the old Etz's restaurant in Cape Charles," he says. "When you asked him how he made it, he would say with evaporated milk, that was it. I have been trying to make it as good. I am close with the following":

One pint of oysters (or more) fry the big ones, use the small ones for stew
Half gallon whole milk
12 oz evaporated milk
One stick real butter
Salt and pepper
Melt the butter in a good sized sauce pan. Add the oysters (do not wash them but strain and save the juice) and juice and cook until solid. If your pan is big enough add whole milk all but about the amount of the evaporated milk. Add evaporated milk.
Season with salt and pepper and simmer for about two hours. It gets the oyster flavor into the stew. Make sure it does not boil. It will make a good amount and will be better when you warm it up for the next meal. Not an old family recipe but an evolving one.

Jack's comment on an "old family recipe" raises a larger question about the genealogy of Eastern Shore of Virginia oyster pie.

As it turns out, folks have been assembling oyster pies for a very long time—pretty much since the invention of pie. Even in antiquity a Roman concoction of a steamed, custardlike fish "pie" made with anchovies and smelts concluded with the observation, "When done sprinkle with ground pepper and carry into the dining room. Nobody will be able to tell what he is enjoying." Mindful of the well-documented Roman appetite for *Ostrea edulis*, the European flat oyster, it is easy enough to imagine an oyster substitution. Still, a pie is baked in a pastry shell, and the Roman dish may be recognizable, although not as a pie—at least one recognizable on the Eastern Shore. The observation by the ancients that diners will be unable to discern the qualities of the object of their pleasure is another matter.

Whatever its dim, primordial origins, oyster pie was on the menu by the Renaissance and a European standard by the 1600s. An Italian variant offered in 1570 by Bartolomeo Scappi, private cook to Pope Pius V, in the *Art and Craft of a Master Cook*, describes a pie that Eastern Shore gourmands would recognize with wariness if not outright disdain:

> **TO PREPARE PIES OF OYSTERS *EN CROÛTE***
> **FOR SERVING HOT.**
> Get oysters, removing them from their shell either after they have sat a little on a grill or while they are still raw. Set their water aside. Coat them with pepper and cinnamon, and put them in a pastry shell with a little butter or sweet-olive oil. Cover the pie over and bake it like the other ones. When it is almost done, have a flavouring made up of other oysters ground in a mortar, a little *mostaccioli* and spinach tips moistened in the water [likely the reserved oyster liquor] and a little malmsey, orange juice and sugar; put all of that through the hole in the top of the pie. Finish off baking it.

More familiar antecedents for Eastern Shore oyster pies, however, appear in seventeenth- and eighteenth-century England and northern Europe. English cook Robert May, who trained in Paris and worked in the households of minor English aristocracy, gave directions in 1685 for an oyster pie that resonates with the simpler versions prepared on the Eastern Shore:

> Now for the other Pies you may fill them with several Ingredients, as in one you may put oysters, being parboild and bearded, season them with large mace, pepper, some beaten ginger, and salt, season them lightly, and fill the Pie, then lay on marrow and some good butter, close it up and bake it. Then make a lear for it with white wine, the oyster liquor, three or four oysters bruised in pieces to make it stronger, but take out the pieces, and an onion, or rub the bottom of the dish with a clove of garlick; it being boild, put in a piece of butter, with a lemon, sweet hearbs will be good boild in it, bound up fast together; cut up the lid, or make a hole to let the lear in, &c.

Similarly, R. Smith's *Court Cookery: or, The Compleat English Cook* of 1725 records two types of oyster pie. The first required cooking the oysters and

Tom Gallivan with oyster harvest, Bayford, Virginia.

then mincing and mashing them in a mortar with pistachios, nutmeg, sweetbreads, marrow, and more before placing the pasty mixture in a crust and baking. Not around here! But "An Oyster Pie another Way" rings true:

Take a Hundred of Oysters, or more, according to the Bigness you would have your Pie, and blanch and bard them; then take a Handful of Parsly, and shred it small, add to it, three or four spoonfuls of grated Bread, half a grated Nutmeg, as much pounded Pepper as will lie on a Shilling, and an Anchovy chop'd, and about the third part of a Pound of Butter; make all these together like a Paste; then sheet your Pan you design to bake it in, and put half of your Seasoning under your Oysters, and half at top, with four spoonfuls of the Oyster-Liquor, and a thick slice of Lemon without the Rind; lid it and bake it half an Hour, take it out, and squeeze in the Juice of a Lemon, and serve it to Table.

Get rid of the aristocratic affectations expressed through May's and Smith's ingredients such as marrow, anchovy, nutmeg, ginger, and lemon, and the result is an oyster pie of passing familiarity. Despite all the pomp and pretension that season these ennobled pies, the likelihood is that they are the descendants, not the progenitors, of the common oyster pie. Given the possibilities for an apotheosis of oyster pie, mindfulness of the ordinariness of its origins and the uncertainty of its place in the ever-expanding universe of gourmands seems like the meanest measure of respect.

Before turning to the oyster pies flickering on the receding horizon line of Eastern Shore culinary memory, we need to account for the changing status of oyster pies from delicacies concocted for the popes and monarchs of Europe to the one-dish entrée served in the homes of Eastern Shore families from watermen to wealthy landowners. And we need to address, briefly, the culinary cousin, scalloped oysters. Scalloped oysters, first.

Scalloped oysters, indeed scalloped anything, involves crumbs and layers. Before the introduction of the modern cracker (think Saltine) in the 1870s, cooks used bread crumbs for scalloping. Oyster pie recipes, in all their many variations, often appear in cookbooks and near to preparations for scalloped oysters. North Carolina Pamlico Sound country celebrant Bland Simpson offers, "My history with oyster pie is decidedly simple: lift fork, apply to pie, eat & repeat!" and observes that the dish was "more like a pot pie and pretty close kin to a casserole dish of scalloped oysters." That doesn't translate scalloped oysters into oyster pies, but it does establish a relationship between the two baked dishes that gets murkier when the scalloped oysters are prepared in a pastry shell. A passage from Mrs. Mary Mason's 1875 *The Young Housewife's Counsellor and Friend* settles some of the confusion:

SCOLLOPED OYSTERS.

Cover the bottom of a baking-dish with bread-crumbs, mixed with butter, pepper, and salt; add a layer of oysters, then another covering of bread-crumbs and butter, sprinkled with salt and pepper, then oysters again and bread-crumbs, till the pan is full. Let the last layer be of bread-crumbs, butter, etc. Bake brown, and send them to table hot.

Scolloped oysters are sometimes baked in scollop-shells, prepared as above, and thus has the name been obtained for this mode of dressing oysters. They may be prepared in little patty-pans.

OYSTER PIE.

Cover a baking-dish with puff paste, fill it with oysters, butter, pepper, and salt; the butter rubbed up with a spoonful of flour. Cover the dish with puff paste, and bake of a light brown. You may ornament the top crust with paste leaves.

From a Linnaean perspective, recipes for scalloped oysters differ from pies in two key respects: oyster liquor is not used, and oysters and crumbs (topped with butter) are arrayed in layers. Same family, different genus. As with everything else in the pie universe, exceptions abound.

The social status of oyster pies is no less ambiguous. In fact, when it comes to oyster pie, its fundamental truth is its equally fundamental paradox. The solidity of oysters, flour, and evaporated milk baked in a pie becomes fluid in recollection; the material certainty of pie yields to its changeable place in memory and identity. The primary social indicators for oyster pie fall into three categories: ingredients, association, and occasion.

Picking steamed blue crabs one summer evening, Buck Doughty asked his mom and aunt Darlene about oyster pies and received a tutorial on the subject. Buck recalled the conversation: "I said, 'Have you all ever heard of oyster pie?' 'Yeah, we had oyster pie when we was little. Yeah, everybody was eating it.'" Buck followed up with a series of questions, asking, "'How often did you all have it? I mean, was it a normal thing? Did everybody eat it?'" Buck, recounting his mother's words, continued, "They'd make it once like every two weeks. Mom said she'd have it once every two weeks, I mean, growing up. Because it was easy. It was one of those things—it was a kind of filler food." He laughed and added, "Old people's food, that's what she said. It was a nice dish for a bad time. It cost nothing to make. Baking powder they'd used to get that in cases, whatever. Everybody had it. And, flour, you know, everybody grabbed flour. . . . Everything was cheap to make it." The oysters, Buck observed, were the cheapest ingredient, "They'd just go out there every day and catch them."

Kenny Marshall echoes Buck's reprise of his mother's memory of oyster pie as an everyday dish, placing it in the context of other home menus. "It was really pretty ordinary fare, really," Kenny explains. "It wasn't anything unusual at all. We had all kinds of seafood of course and garden vegetables, but for dinner, or even lunch, which we called dinner and dinner we called supper, you had fish, clams, oysters—chowders, fried, all kinds of ways. Clam fritters, crab cakes. They didn't have crab cakes very often, because they had a lot of soft crabs in season. But it was just ordinary. On weekends the special meal was chicken. You had fried chicken on Sundays or a baked hen, maybe, or sometimes even a baked ham."

Kenny Marshall and Buck Doughty remember two strikingly different variations on oyster pie in terms of crust and finish. The top crust in Kenny Marshall's pie was "fairly thick" and "it didn't always use a bottom crust."

Shucking oysters at Steve Bunce's oyster house, Franktown area, Virginia.

"Most of the time my mom did, and rolled it out very thin," he elaborates, "but the top crust was perhaps a half-inch thick of dough which you put on there. It would bake, the top part of it would be like a biscuit when it came out of the oven, but the bottom part that was touching down on the roux would be like a dumpling, sort of . . . and the biscuit would raise a little bit. When you put it in half-inch thick of dough, it probably would come out an inch or three-quarters of an inch or something like that."

Buck Doughty describes his mother Jean's recollected pie, "You make a crust up, you know. You get your crust made however you all make crust. She'd roll out two big circles. You know, you make your first pie. You put your bottom in. Lay that in there nice and tight, and then they'd fill it with the oysters. They'd put the oysters, but you strain it and of course save your juice. You just put the oysters down in the bottom. Fill it up pretty good. Then they'd take the oyster juice and boil that with cream."

Buck, possessed of an astonishing memory, works up an appetite in the telling: "They'd cook that all together and roll it into a boil, and then in the meantime they'd whip up some cornstarch to thicken it. You'd do that with a little bit of water. You'd pour that in at the end once it started boiling really good and hard. You'd pour that in and mix it, and when it started mixing, you'd pour that right into your oysters. And the last piece of crust that you had, you cut strips and you'd lattice it. Lattice it out and paint it with butter. Throw that in the oven and finish it out. That would cook the oysters and it would cook the crust. Man, they had it all the time!" The salivating catch in his voice testifies to a newly discovered spirituality.

Danny Doughty does not share in Buck's romantic, wistful longing for the dish: "With us, it was utilitarian—more the everyday fix-it, and it was hearty and it tasted good, but it was not like a delight to the eye as much. It was looked upon, the way I grew up, as something they had. It didn't take very much to add to it to prepare it, and it didn't take a lot of cooking time to fix it. So I saw it through that filter of everyday life. It wasn't like we're having a party, 'We're having an oyster pie'! It was more like 'we're having an oyster pie tonight.'"

When Danny Doughty speaks to "nouvelle" oyster pies glorified and gussied up with other ingredients, I imagine he's referring to recipes for preparations, for instance the "ultimate oyster pie," that combine finely minced smoked salmon, sherry, eggs, and the subtle accent of a single clove. Or maybe he's backing away from Cajun oyster pie, with roast pork "sliced and shredded," scallions, cayenne pepper, and "flaky pastry." Or "Virginia Ham and Oyster Pie," with cured ham, fresh mushrooms, and a biscuit top. It is hard to envision anything further removed from everyday life than the confection the renowned chef Charles Ranhofer sets forth in the 1912 edition of his monumental treatise, *The Epicurean*:

OYSTER TART OR PIE, SMITH STYLE
(TARTE AUX HUITRES À LA SMITH).

Poach in their own liquor three dozen medium oysters, drain and remove the muscles or ligaments. Fry in two ounces of butter, four ounces of bacon cut in three-sixteenths of an inch squares, two ounces of onions cut the same size, and half a pound of peeled and seedless tomatoes cut into five-eighths of an inch pieces; add the oyster liquor, reduce the whole with a pint of velouté sauce (No. 415), and when well done and seasoned nicely, add the oysters. Place all of this into a deep pie dish (Fig. 183), and lay on the edge, after slightly wetting it, a narrow band of puff paste (No. 146) an eighth of an inch thick and half an inch wide; moisten the top of this band, and cover the whole with a layer of paste made of fragments of puff paste; cut away the extending edges, and decorate the top with bits of the paste rolled out to one-eighth of an inch in thickness; pinch the edges round the border, and egg over the surface twice, then cook the pie in a hot oven for twenty to thirty minutes, and serve on a folded napkin. Either salt or smoked bacon can be used.

Ranhofer's fusion of French and American culinary practice, built on his celebrated career at Delmonico's at the height of the Gilded Age, cross-references three additional recipes, advocating a near-manic level of precision. His oyster pie also recalls the ennobled pies of aristocratic tables in the 1600s and their place on menus for fancy dinners in the early United States, such as the preparations for a 1909 event in Washington, D.C.:

> Dinner-parties demanded a large variety of dishes. They were not served *à la Russe*. Two table-cloths were *de rigueur* for a dinner company. One was removed with the dishes of meat, vegetables, celery, and many pickles, all of which had been placed at once upon the table. The cut-glass and silver dessert dishes rested on the finest damask the housewife could provide. This cloth removed, left the mahogany for the final walnuts and wine.
>
> Three o'clock was a late hour for a dinner-party—the ordinary family dinner was at two. The large silver tureen, which is now enjoying a dignified old age on our sideboards, had then place at the foot of the table. After soup, boiled fish appeared at the head.

The author, Sara Agnes Rice Pryor, then described the negotiations with the hostess's caterer over the culinary lineup: "An interview has been preserved between a Washington hostess of the time and Henry, an 'experienced and fashionable' caterer. Upon being required to furnish the smallest list of dishes possible for a 'genteel' dinner-party of twelve persons, he reluctantly reduced his ménu to soup, fish, eight dishes of meat, stewed celery, spinach, salsify, and cauliflower. 'Potatoes and beets would not be genteel.' The meats were turkey, ham, partridges, mutton chops, sweetbreads, oyster pie, pheasants, and canvas-back ducks." This was not the oyster pie served to everyday working families but something that marked an unspoken sense of refinement and status in concert with other native delicacies that included game birds: partridge, pheasant, and canvasback.

It's not that Danny holds any animosity toward pies of pretension. It's just his view that they are creations that speak to luxuries of time and ingredients that were not part of his upbringing: "Basic, simple, it wasn't looked at in my environment as anything over the top or glamorous about it like you hear people say today, 'Oh, my god, we're going to have oyster pie!' When someone tells me that, I don't have that wonderful tingle about it. It never was presented to me that way. Like with a lot of other dishes, too, other people had like the help come in and do it. People with privilege and stuff, and they had a whole different take on it. I was in the grit of everyday life—and my family coming from the barrier islands and the mainland and being very poor."

Danny elaborates: "The whole element of it really translated into the food so much because, as we all know, being of privilege changes everything right down to every bit of food you had consumed and how it was prepared, and the ingredients. You could go in someone's house and not pay attention to anything about the house, or education, or wealth, or whatever, and see the plate and tell where they stood in society. How they connected with what they fixed. How it was presented; how it was prepared. Everything." He adds: "It just was what it was, because I know at times I've had it when it was way more oysters in it because having oysters not as diluted down with some of the fillings in it, and then I've had it when you spruced it up to the point where you throw like some onion or other stuff in it to help kind of stretch it. I look at them just as utilitarian. It wasn't like you were going to get excited that night that you had oyster pie."

Danny brings his oyster pie narrative to its close: "You could look at it without knowing anyone or somebody'd just bring the dish into a generic room and set it on the table—you could tell the family, you could tell from that one thing pretty much how they stood in life. I know that sounds bizarre to some people, but it truly isn't. It was one of our report cards in life, and not like your bank account, is how you ate. . . . It's right in your face. You could tell someone that's halfway doing okay or somebody that's struggling."

Danny's thoughts on oyster pie draw on a deep sense of terroir, that taste of place resonant in Kenny Marshall's description of oyster pies prepared and eaten by watermen on their workboats "down the bay" when "men went down and laid in boats for a week at a time before everybody had outboards." He locates the oyster pie in a culinary ecology centered on the vast marshes and open water between Virginia's barrier islands and Seaside communities on the mainland of the Eastern Shore. "The term 'down the bay' wasn't really talking about a place, it was talking more of a situation or a condition." Kenny's distinction is key: "You'd say, 'Where's old Uncle Joe?' 'Well, he's down the bay.' It wasn't really saying where he was, it was saying he's down there working on low water at catching clams and oysters. High water, he was fishing or hunting—whatever the season. It was a situation he was in rather than a place. And the old term 'down the bay,' of course, included a lot of food: down the bay bread, chowders."

Kenny speaks of the oyster pie he learned from his father when they went out on the water to work the clam and oyster grounds. "I grew up with them down on the boat," he starts, noting that every boat was outfitted with a small woodstove "not much bigger than a large bowl." Despite their tiny scale, he explained, "If you could get a pan of biscuits in there, you could get an oyster pie in there." Those were the pies he learned to bake. "Mom cooked the same kind of things, but she was in charge of the kitchen," he laughs. "She really didn't want me underfoot too much, you know, or Dad either."

The challenge embedded in pursuit of the resurrection of oyster pie is in negotiating the balance between those that were "ordinary" and those that were "precious." With the archaeology of oyster pie sorted and recipes collected, I turned to contemporary chefs. Its apotheosis, certainly one that would find its place in the revered canon of gumbo or shrimp and grits, demands felicity and creativity in a single culinary gesture. Chef David Speegle of Spike Gjerde's Baltimore's Artifact Coffee and Woodberry Kitchen was up to the task, and so we undertook the project of making individual oyster pies for fifty or so guests on a rain-soaked late April evening.

Working in a bustling restaurant kitchen while sous-chefs processed baskets of freshly harvested ramps that infused the atmosphere with the rich, sweet scent of garlic and earth, our enterprise begins with shucking two hundred Seaside of Virginia oysters provided by our friend and proprietor of Shooting Point Oyster Company, Tom Gallivan. Oysters opened and their liquor strained into a second container, we accomplished the task of boiling, skinning, and fine-dicing two dozen potatoes. David turns to making roux amid the background clatter of mixers, fans, and chopping. He beats one cup of flour into a roux, drizzling in the oyster liquor until it stiffens in a large saucepan. He adds a half gallon of milk, stirring continuously, bringing the heat up slowly so the roux will neither burn nor stick. In went a "heavy dose" of black pepper and chopped parsley, with David and me taking turns to stir. "This is a lot of roux," I reflect.

David turns the heat to low, stirring all the while, and then lets the mixture rest a minute. More fresh herbs: a cup each of dill and bronze fennel and the leaves stripped from seven stalks of tarragon. David notes, "You got to try it once to make it right," and then offers a tasting spoon: "There are eight ingredients, and you can taste them all." He is right. Meanwhile, David quickly browns some butter and sautés the whole oysters until their edges curl. "Just enough," he says, "to evaporate their liquor." No soggy pies for us!

Assembly time. David rolls out his premade buckwheat pie dough, fits the bottom crust into metal rings, adds four oysters, diced potato, and the roux. Contents arranged, David completes the construction process with the top crust, fluting the edges for a tight seal and cutting a steam vent in the top. My original plan was to have a tiny oyster crab peeking out of the

Amy Brandt's oyster pie, Cheriton area, Virginia.

vent, but none of the pink crustaceans were to be found for our endeavor. The pies slide into the 400 degree oven for ten minutes, and then they are done.

David Speegle's oyster pies are enjoyed by all present that stormy, sodden evening. Those pies also pose questions about what defines tradition and its relationship to invention. The addition of fresh herbs was not in the pies described by Danny, Buck, and Kenny. Neither were the buckwheat crusts nor the individual serving size. The roux poured over the oysters, however, reflects the idea of a thickened oyster stew. The addition of potatoes is certainly within the bounds of remembered practice. In essence, the oyster pies crafted that evening "remembered" their antecedents within a familiar culinary idiom. If we understand tradition as the everyday work of making sense, then our oyster pies came to the table grounded within the customs and conventions of long-standing culinary practice.

Still, the apotheosis of oyster pie sparks a lingering doubt about the renaissance and elaboration of "ordinary" and "utilitarian" cuisine. Buck, relating his mother's and aunt's recollections, repeats, "Well, the older people ate it. It was one of those things. Aunt Darlene didn't like it. Uncle Cary, he ate a little bit. He really liked the crust more than anything. He didn't like the oysters, but he'd eat the crust because it sucked up all that flavor. But, Mom-Mom and Pop-Pop [Buck's maternal grandparents] loved it to death. 'Old people's food,' that's what she said."

The people savoring David Speegle's oyster pies in Baltimore that evening hail from a world far removed from life "down the bay" or the experience of "a nice dish for a bad time." Yet as guests sample and then devour their oyster pies, they consume a terroir mapped not just by culinary habit but also by imagined sensibility. There is, as Danny suggests, the paradox of placing one's self in a society they can never know, of dining on somebody else's lived past to summon forth an imagined one of their own. Still, the revival of oyster pie is tasty—and I'd eat it again without hesitation, guilt, or regret. I'd politely ask for seconds.

A CHEF'S RECIPE FOR HOME

OYSTER PIE

Spike Gjerde, Woodberry Kitchen, Baltimore, Maryland
Spike Gjerde's oyster pie braids the deep history of this dish on the
Eastern Shore of Virginia with his curiosity and respect for regional
ingredients and recipes.

Makes 4 individual pies

Special equipment: 4 pastry rings, about 3½ inches in diameter and
¾ inch high

For the rye brisée
   300 grams (2 cups) rye flour
   5 grams (1 teaspoon) salt
   225 grams (8 ounces) cubed cold butter
   75 grams (⅓ cup) ice water
   5 grams (1 teaspoon) apple cider vinegar
For the oyster cream
   2¼ cups (600 grams) heavy cream
   1 dried fish pepper
   4 garlic cloves, crushed
   1 cup (250 grams) roughly chopped onion
   Herb sachet containing 1 bay leaf, several stems of lovage, and
   several sprigs of thyme
   1½ teaspoons (8 grams) salt
   6 egg yolks
For assembling the pies
   36 shucked oysters
   Egg wash made with 1 beaten egg and 1 tablespoon water
   Hot sauce (optional)

To prepare the rye brisée
   Combine the flour and salt in a large bowl and cut in the butter. Add
   the water and vinegar and mix well. Press the dough into a flat slab,
   wrap it in plastic wrap, and let it rest for 2 hours in the refrigerator.
To prepare the oyster cream
   Combine all the ingredients except the egg yolks in a pot and bring
   to a simmer over medium heat. Reduce the heat and keep the
   mixture at a very low simmer for 1 hour. Whisk the egg yolks in a

183

medium bowl and pass the cream through a strainer over the yolks, whisking to combine. Chill.

To make the pie

Preheat the oven to 400°F.

Roll out the pastry and cut out 4 circles large enough to line pastry rings with a half-inch overhang. Cut 4 more circles the size of the rings for the tops of the pies.

Working with 1 pie at a time, line the ring with the larger circle and fill it with about 9 oysters (more or less depending on the size of the oysters). Top with the chilled cream mixture, then brush the edge of the pastry with the egg wash. Top with a smaller pastry circle and crimp to seal. Brush the top crust with egg wash and decorate as desired, making at least a couple of small slashes in the top. Repeat with the remaining pies and space evenly on a perforated sheet pan before placing in the oven. Bake for 12–15 minutes, or until deeply colored.

Transfer the pies to warm plates and remove the rings. Serve hot, with hot sauce if desired.

Clam Fritters and the
Quest for Perfection

"You can make a fritter out of anything," says John Marshall, Hog Island descendant and former waterman turned tree surgeon, choking with laughter. "I remember talking to somebody—we were killing frogs, skinning out the frog legs and frying them up. 'Well,' he says, 'What do you do with the rest of the frog?' I said, you put them in the blender and make frog fritters out of them. They believed me!" John catches his breath and reflects, "I guess you could, though." As unappetizing as the thought of a frog fritter may be, it summons up a fundamental truth about fritters—clam, oyster, corn, sweet potato, apple—and their prominence in Eastern Shore of Virginia cooks' arsenals of recipes. Fritters are, as John asserts straight-faced, "simple." That is their challenge. When it comes to the simplicity and perfection of clam fritters, everybody has an opinion. A lot of mischief lurks in simple things.

Griddle- and pan-fried across generations in the crucible of the everyday cuisine of the Eastern Shore of Virginia, the fritter's origins, whether clam, conch, pumpkin, corn, or frog, emerge from a coming together of African and European cooking traditions. Fritter (or "flitter," in local parlance) variations are legion, but what unites them all is a skillet, oil, and frying. Eunice Crumb Glaxner, raised in the fishing village of Oyster, preserved her mother's recipe for pumpkin fritters: "1 egg, 3 tablespoonful of sugar or more, ½ cup flour or enough to stick together good, pinch Baking Powder, a little cinnamon, about 2 Cups Pumpkin." Belle Haven cook Carrie Polk Kellam compiled a list of fritter recipes on a piece of church stationery in the 1930s, listing plain, banana, apple, and corn: "Corn Fritters. 1 cup corn, 1 cup flour, 2 teasp salt, pepper, 1 egg, ½ cup milk, 1 tablesp. olive oil. Beat egg—add remaining ingredients by spoonful in deep fat—fry 6 to 8 minutes." Sweet or savory, leavened or not, a fritter is always fried. They appear on the plate in the form of pancakes, hoecakes, some-

185

times as dumplings, or even a croquette. The Maryland crab cake, all frills and fancifications set aside, is a fritter.

When it comes to clam fritters, also known in Eastern Shore parlance as fried clams and clam cakes, four qualities unite them. First, they are in the core repertoire of nearly every Eastern Shore of Virginia home cook—and nearly everyone, unsurprisingly, argues that their fritters are the best. As Larry "Big Mo" Young of Willis Wharf put it, "My mom, she cooked a lot of clam cakes, a lot of oyster cakes, fish, you know what I'm saying."

Second, recipes descended for generations through family trees, as noted by Kelli Gaskill of Big's Place family restaurant, "Grandmom and I sat down one day. We were trying to trace back how many generations the clam fritter recipe goes back. And I think we've got it back to about 100, 150 years for the same recipe passed down from one generation to another."

Third, a good clam fritter is not an occasional thing but a staple dish. Kenny Marshall, John Marshall's father, gets to the point: "My recipe is keep it as simple as possible. Very few ingredients. I never measure any-thing." As my friend and culinarian Pooh Johnston says, "It's not about the end product. It's about the process." Maybe.

Fourth, clam fritters flourish as a favorite local dish associated with the fishery and life on the water. Billy Bowen, an experienced local clammer, for example, links clam fritters to quick meals prepared on boats working the clam and oyster grounds in the vast Atlantic marshes. "Oyster stew, fried single clams, clam fritters, clam chowder, oh yeah. Yeah, you did all that. You even catch fish sometimes, you would even fillet some of them and cut them up into little pieces and stew them with taters and stuff."

Clam fritters begin with clams, specifically the hard clam (*Mercenaria mercenaria*), or quahog. Eastern Shore aquafarms such as H. M. Terry, Walker Brothers, Shooting Point, and Cherrystone cultivate hard clams in the tens of millions on thousands of acres of flats from the tip of the penin-sula at Fisherman's Island all the way to the Maryland line above Chinco-teague. Surveyed and staked, the clam grounds thrive in protected waters designated by the United Nations as a biosphere reserve. These are really tasty clams cultured on a scale beyond ordinary reckoning and through a dynamic fusion of laboratory science, homegrown technology, and hard physical work.

Tom Gallivan, of Shooting Point Oyster Company in Bayford, outlines a process that begins with seed clams hatched in laboratories and then grown through a succession of fine-meshed seawater filters until they reach a size of three to four millimeters. The tiny clams are then put out in fine-mesh bags to begin growing to size on the clam beds. As Tom explains, there's a lot of handling involved: "At that point, they're in some sediment so there's some sand and some sediment around them. They're kept clean because they're small, and they can't be kept buried too deep. Then they are transported and sieved on progressively larger and larger sieves and mesh sizes. And then they are placed under sort of a final grow out, starting anywhere from a third of an inch up to about a half of an inch mesh size."

As the clams mature, they are moved from place to place for optimal growth and protection until "they're about a year old, maybe a year and change. Then they're planted. They're dug or they're pulled up out of their overwintering area. And they are placed in their final grow out." Covered with enormous nets designed to prevent predators, for instance cownose rays, from devastating the beds, the clams grow to market size as little necks, middle necks, and top necks. The numbers in the tens of millions are staggering.

Chowders are the biggest clams, and in the context of aquafarming their status has largely evolved into bycatch. Even after the rise of aquafarming, Tom observes, watermen would still work the public grounds, "scratching" for wild clams. He says, "The thing that really is striking is that we go out every day of the week, maybe not on the weekends, but in the wintertime and in the fall and the spring. When I first started seventeen or eighteen years ago, there was always three, four, five gentlemen that would come down from Chincoteague that were wild harvesters. That would come and scratch clams."

The clams they caught were largely chowders, some five or six inches end to end. Tom continues, "I can't tell you the last time I saw a guy, it's been at least three or four years that I've not seen a wild harvester out there. Occasionally, you'll see a younger kid, maybe they go out for a day or two, but no one consistently. These guys would go out in a little skiff every single day, they'd be out there working the tide. Which was cool. Those guys were good guys, and they kind of kept an eye on your stuff, and you kind of kept an eye on them and made sure if they had a breakdown or whatever, that they got brought in. They were good guys." Chowders are the clams for clam fritters, and clam fritters have slowly morphed into associations with bygone work on the marshes and flats of the Atlantic wetlands.

Marketed globally as chowders, top necks, middle necks, little necks, cherrystones, and pastas, farmed clams from the Eastern Shore possess a distinctive briny flavor—but they are not the clams of clam fritter lore on the Eastern Shore. That distinction belongs to the wild-caught chowders found on tidal flats or sunk into the soft mud of marshland guts, drains, and ditches. Sure, you can make a first-rate fritter from cultured clams, but the clams that local fritter makers remember are, more often than not, the wild ones.

Clam workers' gear drying on a packinghouse wall, Willis Wharf, Virginia.

Those clams resonate with stories about working the water in ways that speak more to the art of local knowledge than the science of aquafarming. Long after the advent and success of aquaculture clams, families on weekend outings still take their boats out onto the old clam grounds and scratch for wild clams. This is a different kind of work that celebrates memory and a sense of place and serves up the clam fritter as its communion. Looking back on his work on the water, clammer and oysterman Bobby Bridges muses, "It was an enjoyable way of life. It was hard at times. At times, it was a lot of bugs, in the wintertime it was cold. I liked it. I thought it was the greatest thing in the world." Bobby makes a great clam fritter, following a recipe passed down through his wife Debbie's family, a fritter that holds connections that reach back to her great-grandmother's Smith

Island lighthouse kitchen. Clam fritters begin with clams, and the clams in question evoke recitations on work, skill, community, and natural history.

Late on a mid-October morning, blue-sky bright and warm, Billy Bowen and Pete Terry sit in the sunlit living room of Billy's Willis Wharf home speaking of gunning for marsh hens—and then the conversation turns to clamming in Hog Island Bay. Pete's daughter Heather and I lean forward to catch the details. Billy Bowen talks of days not so long ago when watermen would go out on the clam grounds for days at a time. "And then the fall of the year," he goes on. "That's when we come signing clams. You lived aboard of a boat. Say, a thirty-eight-foot boat. That's what you lived in, that's what you done. . . . You'd stay for a week at a time, sometimes you'd stay for a week and a half, sometimes two weeks."

"There would be other boats around down there, too," he recollects. "But nobody tied up alongside of one another. You always anchored off to your own, did your own thing. I've seen in the summertime down there, I've seen as high as twenty-seven boats laying out there. It looked like a small city. Wading clams day and night." Billy explains that putting in and out of the Willis Wharf docks, "Most people would go out by themselves or bring someone else, maybe two in a boat. Went in and out with the tides and come into the dock, and back then there was at least four or five clam buyers down there and pick out which one you wanted to sell it to."

"A lot of Chincoteaguers would come, the clams had pretty much been caught out up in Chincoteague," Kenny Marshall recalls, leaning back in his chair in his decoy carving shed. "There were probably 100, 150 boats, layboats anchored up in High Shore Sink, we called it. Between High Shore Marsh and Hog Island, find a sink in there with some rocks you could work on." "It would be like a small town at night with all these lights from these layboats in there," he smiles. "And they'd shuffle from boat to boat visiting, playing cards, and having a bag of fudge, and listening on the big old battery-operated radios to boxing matches."

Kenny Marshall's clamming partner Bobby Bridges smiles, remembering some of the folks camped out on the clam grounds. He adds, "There was probably a hundred people a day that did it, most of them had a small 16- or 18-feet Chincoteague scow, a small 35-horse Johnson. Probably the most interesting aspect of the whole thing is just the characters you'd meet. There was quite an array of characters, a lot of riffraff, scallywag-type people."

"Before outboards were available to everybody, the men would work in crews on what they called a layboat, larger boat with an inboard motor," Kenny Marshall reminisces, "Four to five guys would get together on this one boat and have their own individual skiff that they worked out of. You go down to Hog Island and anchor up for the week. You just pulled off to do your clamming or oysters or whatever you had to do seasonally. Oystered in the winter because clams you had to get in the water. It was too cold in the wintertime, so you went oystering. You'd stay down for a week at a time. You'd come in on the weekends, and that's the way it was. And there was always one guy, he never got paid extra as a cook, but he liked to do it and everybody liked his food. One guy usually did all the cooking, and we would unload his boat for him and maybe kick in a dollar or two at the end of the week, too, but it was really simple fare." The arrival of outboard motors for boats spelled the end to the weeklong stays on the marshes. Now that watermen could easily motor in and out of Willis Wharf, Red Bank, Quinby, and the other settlements on the Eastern Shore mainland, there was no sense in overnighting "down the bay." As Kenny Marshall concludes, "When I got out of high school, I went and got an outboard rig."

Extended stays harvesting the wetlands of great Atlantic marshes required provisions, often purchased on credit from shoreside merchants such as E. L. Willis in Willis Wharf: "You didn't take a lot of groceries with you, you didn't have no refrigerator to keep things cool, you know, to preserve hamburger or pork chops and stuff like that. So what you caught and what you killed, if you caught fish or whatever, that's what you eat down in the bay. That was it. You took lard and flour with you, that was the main two ingredients, and molasses. That was it. And salt and pepper."

There's a great deal of local knowledge fried into a clam fritter, measuring the turn of the seasons, charting the tides, and the discerning the habits of shellfish. Folks working the water before the advent of aquafarming harvested clams one of three ways: signing, wading or treading, and raking.

"Signing" is the art perfected by professional clammers whereby they locate their quarry by the signs left in exposed sand or mud. Signs range from keyhole-shaped "breathing" holes to slight dimples on the surface. Billy Bowen places clamming in the natural history of the waterman's year: "Here we come into March, bay warming up, clams started signing then, and you go clamming."

"If clams stop signing in the middle of summer when it got so hot they quit, you'd go wading for clams," he says. A waterman's work knows no clock less than the celestial dance of moon and planet, the uncertain measure between tempest and calm. "Sometimes you put ten, twelve, fourteen hours a day in working. I mean, that's a watermen's life if you're going to try to get by." Billy Bowen summarizes: "Nobody worked eight hours a day and then goes home, because you've got to work according to the tide, you've got to work. . . . If the wind's blowing one way, you have to go some-

Bobby Bridges's clam fritters in the pan, Willis Wharf, Virginia.

where else to get lower to the marsh if you're signing clams, because you can't sign in ruffles of water. All this stuff made a difference."

Few things are ever as simple as they might seem on first blush, and signing for clams is one of those things. With the skill of a naturalist's eye, Kenny Marshall, Billy Bowen, and Pete Terry detail the range of signs they recognize on the clamming grounds. Kenny Marshall enumerates the core vocabulary: "There's basically five. Of course, the old keyhole, everyone knows about the keyhole," he begins, describing how a buried clam cycles seawater for oxygen and nutrients through its siphons: "Take the nutrients out of it and back out of this little tube that they stick up to the surface. One hole is bigger than the other, makes it look like a little keyhole." "In the spring of the year they mainly were keyholes," Billy Bowen amplifies. "Just like a skeleton key that fit into that door, that's just the way they looked. Because a clam has two spikes, it has a big one and a small

Bobby Bridges with a clam fritter sandwich, Willis Wharf, Virginia.

one. You would find this in the fall of the year, too. Dad taught me how to sign. Mom taught me how to tread."

Claudia Ballard sketches the distinction between treading or wading for clams and signing or finding clams by their breathing holes, "It's a keyhole. You walk along the beach, and you'll see two little holes in the sand, and it resembles a keyhole, an old keyhole, and normally, you just take your clam pick—it's a long wooden handle with a claw on the end of it, and just stick it down a few inches, and most of the time you'll hit a clam." "That's the keyhole," she expands, "and when you get in the middle of them, it is so much fun. Because it kind of spurts the water out a little bit when they're under there. You just run around and dig them up. I used to love to do that. Dig them up, drop them, and then come back with a basket and collect them."

The signs quickly get subtly complicated, as Billy Bowen recalls. "Late spring and early fall, you would find the litter signs and sink signs and the squirt sign. There's a *litter* sign, which once they got through feeding," Billy explains, striving for delicacy in his choice of words, "the stuff they would siphon out would sprinkle around where this clam was. Usually down tide, a little streak down tide." Pete Terry adds: "Now the rice sign or a litter sign like Billy first said is a clam's feces, and it looked like a little piece of rice, don't eat it. But you'd see, what, maybe ten or fifteen of them? And it doesn't, the clam's not always under them, but it's kind of in that area." "They got another name we had, too," Billy Bowen laughs.

Buried in the darker mud and sand below the sun-bleached surface of the flats, clams produced the blue sign. "It's where the clam's pushing mud out of the bottom," Pete Terry declares. "It's a blue, a real light shade of blue." "And it's about as big as a quarter," observes Billy Bowen. "Sometimes it ain't no bigger than a dime. But it's a blue sign, it's a little bit bluish. The bottom would be brownish, and that would be a real light blue, sometimes it would be grayish. There would be little bit different colors there." Only a practiced eye, I think, could spot a blue sign in the blinding glare of sun on water and wet sand.

Kenny Marshall places the blue sign in the ebb and flow of the tide: "And then later on, some day that would wash away, and of course, the surface of the sand flats or mudflats, it had to be fairly stiff. You couldn't work if it was really muddy out. Or bleached out or whatever from the sunlight. Beneath that it was a darker-looking, almost a bluish look. And they would spit that out, and they would call that a blue sign."

Rounding out his lexicon of signs, Kenny Marshall introduced the sink sign: "If there was no color, no nothing, it was little slight little sink. We call that a sink sign." Billy Bowen speaks to the deceptive nature of the sink sign, which was little more than the slightest depression on the flat where the clams repeatedly cycled seawater. "It's a little sink," he says. "That's all it is." The problem is that all the various shellfish that reside down in the bottom make these dimples, a fact that Billy acknowledges. "There's so many of them, but you know which one is and which one ain't. Every now and then you'll say, 'Huh, somebody left the sign and got the clam.'" He laughs in the telling, "It fooled you. There could be several of them there, but you know which one's got a clam in it and which one ain't. It's just something you know, something you learn."

Billy Bowen and Pete Terry posit additional signs, for example, the opposite of a sink sign is the sandbow, where the clam creates a little mound of filtered sand. Finally, there was the spit sign, as Kenny Marshall observes, "Of course, you could walk around, bang your clam pick on the bottom like that, and that caused them the spit. The spit sign, we called it. It wasn't really a sign, but you could find out where he was."

That's a first step in a clam fritter recipe—a deep knowledge of how to read the gestures of the natural world. "Once you start seeing one, you start digging, you never looked at him no more, you were just looking off for another clam or so," Billy Bowen avers. "Sometimes when you were really signing, you would see three or four signs, man, you were solid going! It was hard on your back, you walking around with half a basket, a basket of clams, and you're bent over for a solid stretch. You have to have a strong wrist and a strong back and a weak mind. That's what it took to be a good clam signer."

Signing wasn't an ability mastered by all. Buck Doughty, sitting in the shade at the Riggin family clam house in Red Bank, confesses to his own inability in comparison to his grandfather's superior skills. "He was a clammer," Buck says. "He had a reputation for being a really, really high-end waterman." "Anyway," Buck plunges into his recollection, "he'd carry us out, and he was out there. He caught his five or six hundred that he wanted that day, which wasn't nothing for him. He got that in about an hour or two. He was probably in his early seventies." "Me and Aunt Darlene went out there," Buck talks over the din of the folks on the neck dock who had just hooked a large cownose ray and were struggling to reel it in. "We were on that rock. He put us on this old 'chaffey'" rock, just old rusted shell. I couldn't see no signs out! I mean I might of caught one every once in a while." "And she hollered up there," Buck's voice rises. "'Daddy, where are these signs? They stopped signing, didn't they?' 'No, they ain't,' he grabbed his old pipe out of his mouth, he started pointing, 'There's one. There's one. There's one. There's one.'" "He could see them like that," Buck looks back with wonder and admiration. "As old as he was, he could just sit right there and clam his tail off. He had out-clammed us to death! I never could sign worth a darn," Buck spits. "I mean I would sit there and literally chew the whole area up. I mean I just plowed!"

In deeper water, clammers would "wade" or "tread" their quarry. "Treading is just a matter of walking along the bottom and just feeling for the clams," Claudia Ballard explains. "It's almost like crushing grapes, that kind of thing you would do if you were mashing grapes. You'd just kind of go along the bottom, kind of scoot along with your feet. . . . Oh, you can feel it. You can feel the roundness of the shell when you put your foot on it, you can feel the difference. The bottom really has to be sandy. If it's a mud bottom, it's kind of dangerous business because you don't know what you're going to hit in that, but if it's a good sandy bottom, you can feel them down there." Not every waded shell is a clam, though, "I've dug other things up, too, before. What they call boxes. That's just the clamshells with the mud in the middle, and they're no good."

Buck Doughty offers a detailed picture of wading for clams, a skill, unlike signing, he mastered with ease. "You get a real, real thin little boot like these little boat shoes that you get now. They're nice. We used to get these little plastic booties, and we'd go out there and catch it on an outgoing tide. You'd go out, work it from the high point out and then back in. You just go out there on a nice spot to get some clams and you can feel them with your feet. You just kind of smear your feet and you just kind of wipe along with the edge of your foot and you'll feel the edge of those clams. You'll feel the bill roll underneath your foot. Now, a lot of the stuff under there feels like a clam, but if it catches your foot, it's probably an old oyster shell that will cut the shit out of your fingers, so you got to have gloves on."

He laughs, remembering a recent oyster shell gash on his hand. "You listen and you feel. I always liked wading because I'm tall. I don't like bending over and working bent over all day long. When you're wading, you kind of feel them with your feet and kick them out. Slide your two fingers down, get and slide the clam, and shake him off while you're feeling with your feet. Get another one. When you're in them it's fun. You can feel like two or three when you're wiping your foot. You can feel the bills and you'll roll right over them and you'll sit there and kind of just pull them on out."

I ask about the depth of the water, and he answers: "Just about waist level. Enough so that you can reach down and not get your head in it. I like to be in it because it's buoyant. Kind of keeps you up. If you're too deep, you start falling off your feet when you go in. Your feet will come up. You'll float. If you're too shallow, then you're working to death! It's nice to have it just to the top of your legs," Buck describes. "It's a good level to feel them. You know where they're at. You get in the water. So you'll just go out with the tide a little bit and work that spot and back in. I try to do that, but when you're in them you just chase whatever you feel. . . . You always follow the tide out and back in."

Following the tide up a narrow gut was not without its dangers. Buck recounts how his grandfather always told him, "Don't clam up a creek on an outgoing tide." Buck shifts into story mode: "He told me a story about a man—he was warning him, 'Don't do that! You don't clam up the creek on an outgoing tide like that. You're going to trap a shark up in there!' Sure enough, he did, and one day he saw the wake out of the corner of his eye, and the shark was coming out. You know, you'll push that shark up that creek, up that gut, and after that tide gets low enough, he's coming out! When he realizes he's got to get out, he's going to come full force at you! He caught that shark out of the corner of his eye. He leaped in that boat, and about that time he got underneath of it—I mean, it threw him up on the marsh as it got out! Threw the boat up. It was a huge shark that they had penned up that creek."

If that wasn't enough, there are the recollections of swamped and grounded boats filled with clams, sheltering under overturned scows during fierce lightning storms, and accidental maroonings when workboats drifted away on rapidly rising tides. As Buck puts it, "It'll humble you out there. It's not enough time to even think about whether you wanted to be in that situation or not. It takes you over like that." As for the unfortunate waterman who penned a shark while wading clams, "He didn't go no more!" Buck looks east toward Hog Island Bay, "'That was enough for me!' he said. He didn't know that could happen. He didn't know that kind of animal was up in them areas."

"Wading clams," Billy Bowen explains, "you wore a pair of moccasins. You bought a cloth and you would make you a pair of moccasins and you'd sew them up so that they fit your feet, nobody else's. Then you'd go on the flats, the edge of rocks, and wade clams. Even on a rock, when you feel a clam, you knew it was a clam. Wasn't no doubt in your mind what it was." He nods to Pete Terry, "It's just something you learn. Pete and myself, we've gone out there and worked with nets and stuff. We stopped by these rocks here, and times were tight then, too, and wade a couple baskets of clams apiece. Then come on in."

Robert Bridges recollects how his father, Bobby, and Kenny Marshall made their moccasins: "We would go to Pinky James's store in Nassawadox, which is closed now and gone, and they would buy yards of canvas and they made moccasins to wear on their feet so their feet didn't get cut up.

Walker Brothers cultured clams, Willis Wharf, Virginia.

When Pinky's closed and it was harder to get canvas, they started going to Gladden Tire in Exmore, buying old inner tubes, and they sewed up moccasins out of inner tubes. So they would always have a couple of pairs with them and wear those on their feet until they wore through one. Then they'd grab another pair and put them on. They made them themselves."

Others raked for clams. Evoking a foraging practice documented back to the 1700s, Kenny Marshall says, "My dad and them did a lot of raking clams, and same thing, get in the water this deep, just drag the rake."

Robert Bridges recalls the clam rakes wielded by his father, Bobby, and his partner Kenny Marshall: "I just remember they had teeth and they were a little rounded on the backside for baskets — and they always added more wire because they never really liked how they were made. They were real particular about the teeth. Long-handled rakes." Trying to avoid back strain, they used their left arms as braces. "They raked with their right hand down on the rake, and then their left hand, they wrapped around their back and held the handle like this — something my dad had learned from some guy on Chincoteague that he worked with a long time ago. It didn't work your body as much." Robert adds, "Now everybody has those harnesses and they're using bigger rakes."

Buck Doughty employs a hybrid combination of raking and wading. "Don't ever dig. Just work it out with the rake. It's good to have a rake, because a rake has got some points on it. You can sit there and really get them out. If you're raking clams and wading, you just kind of feel them with your feet. You'll take the rake and as soon as you feel one," Buck makes a sharp, scratching sound in the back of his throat. "You'll hear that," he repeats the scraping sound. "You'll hear it go over top of the edge of the shell. You'll feel it kind of slip over it, and then you just get up on him and pull him out and let him fall in the basket and keep working back until you get him back to you. You listen and you feel."

Still, it's signing ability that distinguishes experienced clammers. "I was a good signer," Billy Bowen states. "I ain't saying I ain't, I was. You do it enough, you become good at something. I did it a lot, and I was good at it. I'm no brag, just facts. There were a lot of good signers down there. There were some that they weren't very good, but they thought they were." Kenny Marshall, too, claims with pride, "I was good at it. I was one of the best around. I've had guys come up to me and I'm signing, with sink signs especially, it's just a slight little sink in the bottom and it's irregular looking, too. You get used to it. 'What in the world are you digging? How do you . . . I don't see no signs!' I say, 'There's one right there!' 'Where? I don't see it! Where?' 'Right there! Don't you see that?' They come on out and say, 'I didn't see nothing.' It kind of gave me a kick showing those fellas up. But I signed three thousand a tide, three different times, but I never went over that. . . . One time I picked up a hundred bushels of oysters and signed one thousand clams on the same tide."

Tales of ability and monumental hauls live in family stories. Buck Doughty recounts his grandfather's abilities, exclaiming, "He was a clammer! He had caught like forty-five hundred clams in a tide. He had a reputation for being a really, really high-end waterman. . . . He'd catch two thousand, three thousand a day." That's a lot of clam fritters by my count.

Johnson's United Methodist Church clam fritter supper, Johnsontown area, Virginia.

Claudia Ballard invokes her mother's clam fritters: "I could never ever make the clam fritters like my mother did. I tried, and I have tried, and I have tried, and I cannot do it! She could make those fritters like lace. Do you understand what I'm saying? That she could spread them out and thin and very, very crispy. Where most people, they puff up and they're very thick. She made the best clam fritters to this day that I've ever had and I cannot duplicate it. I have tried and I cannot do it. I don't know what I do wrong. If I cannot stretch it out, maybe my oil's not hot enough when I put it in there or whatever. I finally gave up on it. I just can't do it."

"A lot of people use pancake flour," Claudia continues. "She did not. And I probably—I just can't do it how she did it. They were just as thin and crispy as they could be, and they were delicious. . . . She'd have an egg, and little enough flour in there to hold it together, and she would drop them in that hot, just a little bit of oil in that pan, and she could spread that out and get that just right and flip it. And they were awesome."

Emory D. Ross of Onancock compiled a recipe collection in the early 1960s. Her preparations included dumplings, pies, cakes, and, importantly, instructions for clam fritters.

CLAM FRITTERS
1½ cups flour
2 teaspoons baking powder
½ teaspoon salt
⅛ teaspoon pepper
⅛ teaspoon paprika
½ cup milk or clam juice
2 eggs
1½ teaspoon grated onion
1 teaspoon melted shortening
10 clams, minced

Two characteristics define Emory Ross's clam fritter recipe. First, she offers a list of ingredients and the vaguest of instructions—minced clams, grated onion, melted shortening. Her assumption is that anyone reading her directions already knew the process. Things are never quite that straightforward, as Kenny Marshall remarked, "It seems that every batch I make turns out a little bit different. . . . Sometimes I just can't do much with them. I'll still eat them no matter how they come out."

Second, her list of ingredients verges on the fancy with the inclusion of paprika, a spice generally absent from most local pantries of the day. Compare her recipe to Fairy Mapp White's 1958 version, which adheres to a much plainer culinary tradition:

FRIED CLAMS

18 large or 25 small clams

2 tbs clabber (sour milk)—if none, use milk

2 level tsp baking powder

⅔ c. flour

pinch bread soda

Process:

1. Wash clams and open. Drain free of all liquor.

2. Cut clams on an old china plate, or put through meat chopper.

3. Pepper and salt to taste, add to the clams the flour, clabber, and soda.

4. Fry at once in hot fat, by dropping tsp. into the fat.

Note: If you want crisp clam cakes, have fat hot and shallow.

This is the clam fritter Claudia Ballard remembers.

Clam fritters start with clams. "A clam fritter is basically a minced clam," Buck says. "You just take a clam and cut him up. You get a Seaside, big old chowder clam." Already there's room for debate. "You want nice big chowders, of course," Kenny Marshall states, and "the thing to do is stick them in the freezer overnight, and when they freeze, set them out, and when they thaw, they'll open right up, and you can shuck them real easy. You don't have to beat the bill off." The shucked clams in a bowl, the cooking process begins with preparing the clams—and this is where prior knowledge is key. Cooks are invariably specific about how the clams should be minced. "Grind your clams," Kenny instructs without equivocation. "I grind up, say for twenty-five clams." Bobby Bridges, too, grinds his clams with a venerable hand-cranked meat grinder, as does the cook at Capt. E's on Saxis Island: "We hand grind our clams. Actually, we went through a lot of blades before we found the blade we wanted. We didn't just throw them in there. Because some of them, they make it too fine. So we took the biggest blade, so you can feel the clam in there."

Barbara Gaskill, of Big's Place family restaurant, however, admonishes, "We chop ours. You got to have fresh clams." Violet Trower affirms the chopping method. "I used to chop mine up with a knife," she says. "You had that piece of whole clam instead of putting them in a grinder. You don't have no taste to it. Chopping them up with a knife, big old meat-cleaver." Dee Spady got her husband to help: "I don't want my clams in the freezer, so we open the clams and Peewee takes scissors and cuts them up with scissors."

Shirley Griffin, a retired cook from the glory days of the old Wachapreague Hotel, parses grinding versus chopping. "I don't grind them anymore. They're alright grinding, but when you chop your own, you get more clams. I have a chopping board." She pauses, "I can mix them either way, I don't care." Whether they grind or chop their clams, whether they mince them fine or prefer them coarse, all experienced clam fritter cooks agree that the worst thing you could do is to run the clams through a food processor.

Minced (hand-chopped, ground, or scissored), the clams need to be drained. Bobby Bridges placed them in a colander and pressed down. Others just let them drip. The goal is to get the clams as dry as possible. Kenny Marshall directs, "Drain the clams as well as you possibly can to get them as dry as possible, because you have to have enough flour to make them batter-y, so you spoon them on a skillet or a griddle. But you got to be really careful because you can get too much flour and it tastes doughy. So, when you get them so there's not such a doughy flavor." He is not alone in this concern, as Barbara Gaskill reveals, "It has some moisture in it, but it's not much. Just enough probably to put it together."

Dee Spady's instructions vary somewhat: "You drain them because you've got to drain all that grit and stuff off of them. You don't want to get all the liquid out because you don't want them real dry. I put them in the colander and let them drain. We wash our clams first. You still sometimes have sand in them, then drain, and let that settle. Let the juice settle." It is at this juncture that the simple gets complicated in two major categories: ingredients and frying.

Emory Ross and Janice Weatherly Walters, an accomplished home cook whose family hails from Willis Wharf, stipulate flour with baking powder added. Bobby Bridges, Kenny Marshall, and others use Bisquick or pancake mix. Kenny Marshall explains, "I said flour, but you've got to have some baking powder in there with them. Here lately what I've done is just use old prepared pancake mix. Same thing basically. Aunt Jemima's. Thicken it up with that." Although printed recipes, such as Emory Ross's, list measured ingredients, the reality in Eastern Shore kitchens defaults to an ingrained understanding of texture and consistency.

The marshaling of clams, flour, and baking powder maps a crossroads of ingredients. Bessie Gunter offered a stripped-down version in her 1889 *Housekeeper's Companion*. Like her successor Fairy Mapp White, Gunter identified her dish, not as a fritter, but rather as fried clams:

TO FRY CLAMS.
Take one dozen raw clams. Open them and chop them very fine on
a hard board, Mix them with one egg, well beaten, a little flour and
pepper. Then fry in lard.
    —G.

Kenny Marshall in his decoy-carving shed, Willis Wharf, Virginia.

Before the widespread introduction of baking powder in the mid-1800s, clam fritters were likely to be thinner and denser. Buck Doughty's mother, Jean, similarly takes a slightly more complicated approach that echoes more contemporary clam fritter recipes across the Eastern Shore of Virginia: "I think she puts egg in it. She says this is what helps bind it. She usually puts just enough breading in there to bind it together. Salt and pepper it up really heavy and cut a lot of onion into it. She likes to dice a lot of onion in it."

Kenny Marshall uses less: "I usually use a dash of Worcestershire sauce in them. And salt and pepper. And that's it." Charlotte Ann Weeks draws on a more elaborate constellation of ingredients, beginning with chopped onion and including "egg, a little pinch of pepper, pinch of Old Bay seasoning, and the seafood breading. You don't want to put a lot of Old Bay seasoning in it because the seafood breader is already seasoned." Simplicity is the idea, Richie Gaskill observes, "Flour, onion, Old Bay. Couple of eggs." Paprika is a flourish—and so, too, is Old Bay, some would argue. The embellishment of clam fritters can trend to the exotic, for example, clam *fritos* concocted with chopped green chilies, red pepper flakes, minced fresh parsley, and paprika. Delicious, I'm sure, but not the fritter of legend and lore.

All the ingredients beaten together, the fritter batter is ready for frying. Charlotte Ann Weeks says simply, "Fry it and that's it. Fry it on both sides." A diversity of opinion lives within those few words. "Get the batter tight," instructs Janice Weatherly Walters, "and I'll drop them on down. Flip it once, flip it twice on each side, and take it out." Kenny Marshall speaks to technique and his efforts to get the fritter the right thickness and diameter: "If you try to get them too lean with flour, you can't turn them over, they'll crumble all up when you cook them on the skillet. But it takes a little practice really. The key thing is to not get them too doughy because they taste like flour. And that's not good. You don't want them thick. Because to stand up and cook, they're going to be doughy. You don't want them to spread out too much, because you won't hold them together, but I use, maybe pile up some on a spoon, you know. Plop them down, and then pat them down a little bit. Thin them up while I can. And hope for the best."

Doughiness can be a problem, as Barbara Gaskill notes. "If you got to put too much flour in it, it's like eating flour. They don't get nice and crispy and light and fluffy like they're supposed to be. They get kind of soggy. They don't crisp."

Buck Doughty attests to the aesthetics of clam fritters frying: "They've got to be slow fried until they get a really thick rind on them, like a real golden rind on them." He continues, "Just fry them about on a medium heat in Crisco or something like that. Get them golden brown. That's a clam fritter!" He concludes, "I want them big! I want them hanging halfway over the bread! If you like the taste of clam, you'll eat the big one."

Dee Spady adds her perspective on grease and heat: "Get your frying pan nice and hot, drop them in there. You add a little bit of baking powder. Baking powder will make it crispy. . . . Bacon grease is the best kind of grease you ever want to use. It's good for clam cakes. That's a good recipe. You can fry a clam cake say in Crisco oil and you can fry one in bacon grease. The one in bacon grease is going to taste the best." Of course!

Kay and Ron Crumb capture the essence of the modern clam fritter with a seriousness and specificity that would make a Le Cordon Bleu–schooled chef reconsider the complexities of everyday cuisines. "Fresh clams, especially off of a sandbar, they're usually a little bit bigger, a little bit tender," Ron starts and then recommends, "If you had time, you can gut them, you know, take out the gut. They come out really good then." "The recipe is really easy," he reports, and so it seems: "It's like two cups of chopped clam, a cup of milk, a cup of flour, and the seasoning, little bit of Old Bay, little bit of Worcestershire sauce. Get the batter the texture you want. My key to cooking them is to cook them kind of slow in just a little tiny bit of oil. Not deep fried, just enough to get them." At this point his sister breaks in: "To keep them from sticking."

Ron proceeds, "I just let them take their time. But the middle, they come out lighter and tenderer. But it takes like a few extra minutes because you get that moisture cooked out of them. They're pretty damn tasty!" Like all the other clam fritter makers of reputation, he makes a point of hand chopping or crank grinding the clams and draining them of excess liquid. "They're usually three-eighths to no more than half an inch. Not even that, three-eighths of an inch probably." "You want two on a bun," Kay adds. "Two on a bun, with mustard. Good old yellow mustard." He describes the clam fritters he crafted at his restaurant: "I didn't put a lot of spice in it. I didn't add onions and peppers and all kinds of stuff to it. I just wanted to keep it middle of the road, so you got the flavor of the clam. A lot of stuff overpowers it. We'd go through two or three gallons a day of them." "Keep it simple," Kay admonishes with conviction.

Out of the pan, clam fritters come to the table sometimes plated with sides but more often than not served as a sandwich with yellow mustard. Watermen carried cold clam fritter sandwiches for their lunches, and the kitchen staff of the Wachapreague Hotel packed them into picnic hampers—a taste of authenticity—for sporting vacationers on fishing excursions.

The clam fritter satisfies an appetite for traditional things and the comfort of community. Churches fry clam fritters for fund-raisers, firefighters place them on the menu for carnival fare, restaurants highlight them as local cuisine—all moments celebrating the taste of place and liberally seasoned with a heavy dose of authenticity. When the signboards of churches, usually reserved for inspirational maxims, advertise clam fritter suppers, people take note. Newspaper ads appear headlining clam fritters on the promised bill of fare.

Ron Crumb, former proprietor of Paul's Restaurant in Cheriton, and his sister Kay Crumb Downing recount their local clam fritter church supper. "Our church, Cheriton United Methodist, has clam fritter sales twice a year," he begins. She adds, "They are in the spring and fall. And people will stop what they're doing to come and get one of Granny Crumb's clam fritters. Because that's the recipe they used. He has it." They confide, "Secret recipe that everybody knows now!" "I'll call up people," Kay explains, "and say, 'Okay the fritters are coming off today.' They'll stop what they're doing, and if you don't get there early enough—they start around nine-thirty, ten o'clock—if you don't get there by eleven-thirty, twelve, they're gone."

Buck Doughty stakes out similar status for the clam fritters made by his mother, Jean. "Mom, she lays claim to fame on them. She goes up there to the church with Bobby Heath. He was my Boy Scout leader back in the day. But he runs a church up in Pungoteague now, and they get her to sell clam fritters up there. They sell them for five dollars apiece, and they're sold out as soon as she puts them out on the table."

Hot oil, medium heat, golden rind, lacy edges, thick, thin, silver-dollar size, sandwich size, on a plate with sides, served up on white bread with yellow mustard—simple things invite legions of possibilities—and yet, in all that variety, cooks and diners come together on common ground. When Buck proclaims, "That's a clam fritter," he speaks not to an ideal but rather to a universe of possibility. Obviously, there's a lot more to clam fritters and the search for perfection than hot oil, batter, and frying. A diversity of clam fritters inspires an array of opinion. A diversity of opinion leads to conversation and debate. Conversation with a mouth full of clam fritter is where terroir and cuisine are cultivated and remembered—in the complexity of simple pleasures.

As for Violet Trower, she recalls an encounter with a fritter while dining out: "I went to a restaurant and tried a clam cake. I told the lady, I said, 'Honey, you sure don't make clam cakes like I do. Just don't have that taste to them.'" Ouch!

A CHEF'S RECIPE FOR HOME

SEAFOOD FRITTERS

Amy Brandt, Amy B Catering, Cheriton, Virginia

Adapted from an Eastern Shore clam fritter recipe. Amy reminds me that cooks on the Eastern Shore use only clams. The blend of clams, shrimp, and rockfish are for folks "from away" who might think of an all-clam fritter as bit too clammy. On a different note, if you are going to chop fresh clams, buy chowder clams, freeze them, then shuck and chop them frozen.

Makes 6 servings of 3 fritters apiece
1 cup chopped clams (see Note)
1 cup finely diced rockfish
1 cup finely diced shrimp
⅛ teaspoon nutmeg
⅛ teaspoon cayenne pepper
⅛ teaspoon finely chopped fennel seed
½ teaspoon finely chopped lemon zest
½ teaspoon kosher salt
¼ teaspoon black pepper
2 large eggs
¼ cup rice flour
¼ cup chopped fresh parsley
Canola oil
Horseradish, yellow mustard, or super spicy cocktail sauce, for serving

In a large bowl, combine all of the ingredients except the oil and condiments. Cover and place in the refrigerator for 1 hour.

Heat a heavy-gauge sauté pan over medium-high heat. Add enough oil to cover the bottom by ¼ inch. When the oil shimmers carefully drop the fritter mixture by tablespoonful into the pan. Cook for a couple of minutes until well browned on the first side. Tipping the pan away from you so the oil is in the curve of the pan flip the fritters. Cook until the second side is well browned. Serve immediately with horseradish, yellow mustard, or super spicy cocktail sauce. If not serving immediately, transfer to a cooling rack set on top of a sheet pan and keep warm in a 200-degree oven for up to 1 hour.

Note: If you're using fresh clams be sure to check each clam for any bits of shell left from shucking, then chop the clams fine and drain well.

A Taste for Toads

 Nobody speaks more rhapsodically to the swelling toad than artist and former restaurateur Danny Doughty, who grew up in the fishing village of Willis Wharf. "My parents had a fish market from 1964 (I was only four years old) and I grew up with toads as being a big deal. They were the chicken of the sea." Toads in this corner of the world designate blowfish, known by a range of aliases: blow toads, swelling toads, puff toads, puffers, sugar toads, sea squab, chicken of the sea, green eyes, or simply toads.

I soon discover that when Danny talks about toads, he does so with marvelous passion and a gourmand's lust in his eye. "They processed them," he says, describing the fish house business founded by his father, Kenny. "At one time they were so prevalent that they were just a big commodity." Things change. "Over a cycle of time, they almost disappeared. Then they cycled back and came back. We used to buy them from the fish trappers and people that went toading with crab pots, using crab scraps for bait."

"I remember just having truckloads of them piled up, just over the top of the cabs of the trucks, and we had to skin every one of them suckers." Danny shifts into high gear: "There would be thousands and thousands of pounds of them, and you could hear them puffing up. You'd get so mad because they expand. They get full of water. We'd skin them until you had literally no fingerprints left if you didn't have gloves on. It would just eat right through the gloves because they were so coarse and prickly, and you didn't realize it until you'd done it a couple times, 'Oh, my god, what happened?' It was an awful pain, as you can imagine."

I am mindful of Theodore Peed's incisive summary of a process that, in its way, dresses a fish by undressing it. Peed, an Eastern Shore of Virginia home cook renowned for his annual game dinner featuring snapping turtle and "50 weight gravy," emphasizes the abrasive skin and hand strength at the cen-

W. T. Nottingham, Pickett's Harbor Farm, Townsend area, Virginia.

ter of converting a toad into an ingredient: "It takes a man to skin a toad!" Meat in one hand; dross in the other.

Danny's flood of memories is overwhelming—and he is far from done. "The other side was the great side—eating them," Danny mixes personal biography with culinary fervor. "From a small child, I definitely got my share. My dad in the fish market, usually on a Friday afternoon, whatever was left over from the week, we'd clean up and have a fish fry and the neighbors would come out there. Toads were usually one of the spotlights." He notes, "They were usually one of the cheapest things at the time. Now that's not the case."

Danny summons forth a picture of a Friday fish fry as if he's imagining a composition for one of his paintings. He speaks in paragraphs. "We had an old hot-water heater and burner, because our neighbor worked on the LP gas stuff, and we had an LP tank. He'd put an old cast-iron frying pan on this old big burner, and just take a couple blocks of lard off the shelf in the store, flip it in the frying pan, let that get really hot. We'd have the toads all piled up, skinned." Working through a mountain of toads, Danny's father "cut them right off of the bone so it'd be like a toad finger, almost. Just a little sliver of pure meat. He'd roll them in cornmeal and drop them down in the lard. Oh, my god! Until they were a nice golden brown. We would just eat them suckers! We used to have fried potatoes with it, or just some white bread, but it was very simple." He adds, "Not the healthiest thing for us, the lard and the other part, but oh, my god, they were best things! I might have some right now!" I'm wondering if Danny has a cache of toads secreted somewhere on the premises and where we might reconnoiter a broken-down burner ring for a fryer. All kitchens are not created equal.

Danny takes a breath and plunges on, introducing the rise and fall of toad populations and the Eastern Shore fishery. "They just disappeared for years," he says. "My dad always said that it was always running in cycles. He lived on the water all his life. And they did come back. But now, they're still around some, but nothing like it was in the day back in the sixties and seventies. They finally resurfaced in the latter mid-eighties, and now they're still around, but not as plentiful as they were at one time. It was a big, big deal." Danny sighs with remembered delight, but he's not yet done, linking his recollections to the art around us, large canvases in colors, bright and muted, depicting a gentle past with grace and affection.

"A lot of the local people that I depict in my work, the paintings—honey, they'd kill you over a toad," he starts a new thought, quoting an imagined conversation: "'Baby, I'm having toads tonight. We're going to have toads and biscuits.'"

"It was just like the caviar of Eastern Shore living," Danny proclaims. "That was the Cadillac, baby! I mean, you had them, you were in high cotton! You were the stuff! You say you're having them, you'd have a lot of people over looking at you. If the light went out and everybody went for them at one time, you'd probably get stabbed with a fork!"

Danny's not finished! "It's so funny and quirky—you see this blown-up fish with this puffy face, and it was so unbelievably good. It was such a mainstay for so many people. In the day, when they were so prevalent, they were so cheap. It was cheap eating that was so wonderful. In the later years when they came back—before, they were like forty cent a pound, thirty cent a pound—now, they're like six, seven, eight dollars a pound," he winces.

Danny jumps to the larger history of seasonal menus. "Back in the day, when the season came in for them—that, and whatever was coming off the fields at the same time was like the best of the best. It was a part of our little history that is going to be forgotten if somebody doesn't get it down to carry it on," he looks at me taking notes, reinforcing his view that the history of Eastern Shore place and palate is important. "I tell my son, he's had them already; he's seven, and he thinks they're chicken. I said, that's what they called the 'chicken of the sea,' because it was such a mild meat. If you really know how to cook them, and know how to cut them, so you don't even have the bone in the middle, they're sweet." Danny expands the idea of terroir beyond the taste of place to embrace the taste of time.

He careens back to his own past. "I was a very healthy young boy. I had quite an appetite, and my food of choice would be toads. My dad and his friends, they weren't the bluebloods of the area, but it was quickly noted that as my middle name was Todd—Daniel Todd Doughty—they started to embellish that." He laughs with a blush of embarrassment. "When we would have toads, I would be eating quite a bit more than my share. They'd look at me and say, 'That ain't Daniel Todd, that's Daniel Toad Doughty.' It still goes on. People still go, 'Danny, I remember the toads.' I'm like, 'You can stop right there,' because they're going to call me Daniel 'Toad' Doughty. They'll probably put that on my gravestone when I go, because some of the older ones will never let it go. They'll say, 'Those toads—I'll never forget they gave you that name.' I'm thinking, 'Yeah, neither will I, because I didn't think it was that funny at the time.' I loved to eat them, but I didn't want to hear anybody say, 'Daniel "Toad" Doughty.'"

Still, there's more! "I would be out there—because I'd probably eat god only knows how many. My father would be cutting them, and breading them, and throwing them in the hot lard, and he'd say, 'Dammit, Danny, you've had enough now!' I'd get all mad and I'd storm out the front and sit on the step of the fish market on that old cement step."

"Some of the women that I paint today," he refers to the figures of African American women who populate his art, "bless their hearts, would see my chunky little self sitting out there just leaned over. They'd make a joke, too, because it'd looked like I was blown up like a swollen toad. I'd be pouting mad because my father cut me off from having the toads, and those women would just scoop me up and just give me a big old kiss and say, 'Baby, it's alright.' It made me feel good for a while, but that aroma would get me every time. He'd go, 'Danny, come on, you can have some more.' He'd finally give in, and I'd take myself in there. I was just as happy as I could be then."

Danny looks at a painting of women in long red skirts, hands raised, encircling the fish truck his father drove between African American hamlets. "They're like, 'Danny, I remember you laying up on them steps blowed up like a swollen toad because you couldn't get no toads when your daddy was cooking.' Oh, my god, I'd be mortified! I'd be worrying, 'Somebody's going to remember that all my life.' And they have! But it comes full circle. Now I just love it when somebody says that, because it brings back that flood of feel-good comfort of the food and the people and the time."

"The puffers," Alan Davidson explains in *North Atlantic Seafood*, "are essentially warm-water species, but this one is found as far north as New York and even the south of Newfoundland. It has no counterpart in European waters." "Puffers," he expands, "have two unusual protective devices. They can inflate their abdomens to a remarkable extent, thus making themselves too much of a mouthful for predators. Moreover, their scales have been modified into small prickles which stand out when the abdomen is inflated, so that the prospective mouthful is not only too big but also too prickly." Those prickles, as Danny noted, shred through the toughest work gloves.

Swelling toads (toads for short) are awkward-looking fish that range up to a foot or so in length. Taxonomic descriptions by marine ichthyologists paint a dreary portrait of the toad's pigmentation. Robert L. Shipp and Ralph W. Yerger observe in "Status, Characters, and Distribution of the Northern and Southern Puffers of the Genus *Sphoeroides*" that "the ground color is light grey or brown, with an area of slight intensification forming an indistinct saddle between the dorsal fin insertion and the caudal base. A similar saddle, usually slightly more intense, is present at the dorsal fin base. An interorbital bar is present and more distinct than the saddles. A few dark blotches are present on the dorsal surface. The most striking character of the species is the presence of small jet-black spots, about 1–2 mm in diameter over most of the pigmented surface."

The toad I know, however, is a far more colorful creature with a sandpapery hide mottled tan, gray, and brown with yellow highlights on top and a brilliant bright white abdomen. A marine scientist views the toad within a palette that categorizes. A different perspective assays the same skin hues in aesthetic terms. A diner with a taste for toads sees the mottled hide only as an impediment to dinner.

Toads possess an abrasive skin, eyes that move independently, and beetled horn–like brows. Their skeletal system is composed of little more than skull and vertebra. The arrangement and musculature of their fins makes them slow and wallowing swimmers. At rest, a toad displays a paunchy physique; threatened, they inflate themselves into taut spheres. Toads of the Eastern Seaboard possess hard, beaklike mouths that enable them to crunch through hard-shell blue crabs. Attacking crabs, toads have been observed to work in concert, with one or more toads distracting their quarry while another attacks from the rear.

Warm-water fish, toads migrate with the seasons, moving into near-

Toads, Nassawadox Creek, Virginia.

shore and estuarine waters in late spring and returning offshore in late autumn. They appear in the Chesapeake Bay in May (the females laden with eggs) and depart in early November. The warm months offer an extended period during which toads spawn their young, depositing their sticky eggs in shallow depressions on the bay floor. Unlike some of their distant cousins whose parent (usually the male) tend the eggs until they hatch, the infant toads of the Chesapeake Bay are left to their own devices.

A toad is a complicated creature. They test the boundaries of Leviticus and chart the dangers of gastronomy. My friend Peter Miller, dean at the Bard Graduate Center in New York and knowledgeable in the field of most things kosher, gently offered the judgment "treif"—not kosher. "*Treif*," Giora Shimoni explains at *The Spruce Eats*, comes from "the Hebrew word *teref* which means torn," adding, "In Exodus 22:30 it is written 'Do not eat meat from an animal torn in the field.' Thus Jews were forbidden to eat meat from an animal that was torn or mortally wounded." Knowing that toads were cleaned aboard boats and on docks—in the field—would seem sufficient cause to knock them off the kosher menu, but there is more. Rabbi Aryeh Citron, delineating the mysteries of kosher fish at Chabad .org, notes that two features determine the worthiness of a fish for a kosher table—the visible presence of fins and scales. "As with the other laws of kosher," Citron adds, "the Torah doesn't give a reason as to why only a fish with these signs is considered kosher. These laws are considered a *chok* (a decree beyond comprehension)." I read the impressive list of non-kosher fish, now aware that toads (variously labeled puffers, blowfish, swellfish, and sea squab) occupy a place between sharks, rays, and sturgeon. At least they keep good company.

Naturalist chefs describe toads in contexts that range from their migratory habits to cuisine, noting the existence of well over one hundred species and remarking on the legendary lethal toxicity of Pacific blowfish, or fugu. Toxicity, a protective mechanism discouraging would-be predators, is limited to the skin, viscera, and reproductive organs. Careless handling during cleaning can taint the meat. The fact that fugu prepared improperly can kill the diner led marine biologists Paul F. Robinson and Frank J. Schwartz to investigate the toxicity of Chesapeake Bay and North Carolina toads in the 1960s. Trapping toads in a variety of locations, the scientists dissected the animals, liquefied isolated elements of skin, flesh, and viscera, and injected traces into laboratory mice. Two test mice died. Their conclusion stated: "The most pressing question, that of whether or not the northern puffer is a safe food, seems to be answered in the affirmative. . . . The evidence of toxicity found in certain of the viscera by us and other investigators would hardly lessen the safety factor, since the puffer is eviscerated and skinned before marketing." Tell that to the two mice.

Still, hesitation tempers gustatory abandon when it comes to toads. "The only puffer I would ever recommend eating," James Peterson recommends in *Fish and Shellfish*, "is the blowfish—sometimes called sea squab—fished off the Atlantic coast, because most of the other species are poisonous. . . . East Coast blowfish are another story and may be eaten safely. . . . Blowfish fillets look like miniature chicken drumsticks and have a single bone running between two tasty little morsels of chicken-like flesh. They are easy to pick up with your fingers and gnaw, but if you want to be more refined it's also easy to slice the pieces of flesh off each side of the backbone before cooking. While good in themselves, blowfish are also a great substitute in recipes for sautéed shellfish such as scallops or shrimp, or for frogs' legs."

In quest of toad histories, I am directed to Jeff Wynne, a descendant of the Ballard family of fish and shellfish wholesalers in Willis Wharf. He speaks softly and with humor about genealogy and the fishery before inviting me to screen a home movie shot in the 1940s or early 1950s. The film I watch is brief and extraordinary. The silent footage opens with a title shot of a "Ballard Brothers Saltwater Oysters" can perched in front of the family's Willis Wharf fish house, then cuts to the vivid pinks, yellows, and oranges of sunrise breaking over the marshes and a distant tree line black in shadow. A compact fleet of boats motors out of the fishing hamlet, cutting through leaden, choppy water, heading eastward across Hog Island Bay to the open Atlantic to fish the ocean pound nets or fish traps. The film transitions abruptly to a crew of watermen, black and white, balancing side by side in a bouncing boat with its gunwale low to the sea. They scoop thousands of glittering fish out of the net they have hoisted into the bilge of a second boat opposite.

The film segues to the crews arriving at a second pound. Clad in black and yellow oilskins, they position their flat-bottomed workboat between the upright poles, some forty feet and more in length, that hold the stationary nets. The pound fishermen, nine in all, untether the nets and haul. The mesh trough that forms between the two boats spills with thousands of perch and bycatch. One of the crew in the catch boat unceremoniously forks what appears to be a huge monkfish over the side and back into the sea, then another. They put their backs into raising a third net. The mesh trough filled with thrashing fish takes shape—and then my attention diverts to the squirming fish, where I see the spherical forms of toads in the silvered shimmering mass. Fully inflated toads, scores of them, bounce and roll, their bright white bellies taut in self-defense. They are an unwanted nuisance.

The loaded boats return to the Ballard fish house. A crowd of men gathers at the wharf to view the catch. The camera pans to the fish lying still in the bilge and then shifts to dockhands offloading the fish in open, heavy wire baskets and into wheelbarrows. I see no toads. They were culled and pitched away at sea.

The Seaside ocean pound nets are gone, but a few remain in play in the Chesapeake Bay at the lower end of the peninsula. H. M. Arnold, who used to work his own pound nets along the bayside of the Eastern Shore of Virginia, sketched the plan of a fish trap one afternoon and explained its intricacies. A pound net consists of a row of heavy poles, some twenty to forty feet or more, set in an evenly spaced line perpendicular to the shore. Some pound nets begin just off the shoreline; others stand well out in the bay. They are situated perpendicular to the flow of the tidal currents back and forth along the shoreline. A second set of poles form a square enclosure at the end of the line. The poles are hung with nets stretching from the shore out to the enclosure, where more nets are hung in a pattern around a "heart," or funnel-like pen at the trap's center. The principle is simple. Fish schooling in the currents parallel to the shoreline encounter the net and turn toward deeper water, attempting to swim around the barrier. The glitch in their instinctual plan is the enclosure at the end, where they swim into the pound and then the heart. Trap fishermen ride out to the pound and haul the nets, shaking their catch into the bottom of the boat. Too many toads defensively disgorging seawater, I am told, can swamp the boat.

Eddie Watts, a waterman working out of his family boathouse on Hungars Creek, knows this from experience: "You have to pop them when you bring them in. When they're coming up, I use a pot hauler, and it comes up so fast you can see them, they're swimming. They're swimming in the pot. The pot's behind them, and they're swimming for their life. They fill up with water. I guess they go on defense. When the pot stops, before you can get that pot out of the water and over the side of the boat, they swell up. They fill up with water. I've had pots with so many fish in it, so full of water, that I've had to stand up on the side of the boat—and literally stand up with the pot and jump back in the boat with it because it was so heavy when I was out by myself."

When it came to hauling a surfeit of toads on board, pound netting offered its own challenges. W. T. Nottingham shared his experiences working the pounds along the Chesapeake Bay shore in the 1980s and early 1990s: "When we fish trapped, you'd web them up all one side of the fish trap, and all at once they'd all start expanding at the same time." His friend Marshall Cox looks up from the kitchen table, "Puff themselves up. Pop them with an ice pick." W. T. explains, "You bail them into the boat, you got a thousand little balls"—he makes a spherical shape with his hands somewhere between the size of a baseball and a softball—"all full of water and they'd all start spitting. You'd take an ice pick and pop them, put them in a box, carry them home, and skin them."

A thousand toads disgorging seawater into the bottom of a boat could spell trouble. If a boat lacked provision for self-bailing, the volume of water and weight could cause it to swamp. W. T. Wilkins elaborated on the danger: "I mean you've just got to keep bailing it out. Where they were bailing them out of the pound nets, they'd be full of water. I'm sure they'd have to pop them and bail the water out. Just have a knife and stick him. Like in those pots, as soon as you started moving that pot, he'd start pumping himself up, so when they come to the top, they're all swelled up and solid full of water. Now out of the water, they'll blow themselves up with air, but when they're in the water like that, they can't get any air, so they pump themselves full of water. I mean that's just a defensive mechanism to make them look big so another fish won't eat them."

Pound nets offer one strategy for catching toads, but the more common practice involves trapping them in peeler pots, wire-mesh cubes designed to catch blue crabs in the early stages of molting on the path to becoming the delicacy of soft-shell crabs. Edward Smith of Tangier Island connects the toad and crab fisheries: "They used to use the hard crab pot with the bigger mesh for the bigger toads. Now they've gone to peeler pots. Bait them up with crab scrap." "October," he observes, "is usually the best month for them up in the shallows up off of Onancock. Down this way," he says, referring to the waters around Bayford, "I'm not sure. Follow the seasons—work their way right on out the Chesapeake Bay."

The precision of knowledge about the clockwork mysteries of the natural world enable watermen like Eddie Watts to refine their fishing strategies. "It seems as though you catch the majority of what you're going to catch in the first two or three hours," Eddie explains. "You can fish your whole rig of pots, say if you've got fifty, you can fish those fifty and go back two hours later and you'll have the same amount. You can leave that pot, say it's got twenty fish in it, you can count them and put that pot back overboard and go back to it the next morning and it's still got twenty. Maybe twenty-one or -two, but whatever it catches within the first two or three hours." W. T. Nottingham notes there is a rhythm to potting toads, "They would bait the pot, fish the pot, skin the fish, and go back and start all over again. When they potted them, of course, they'd skin them on the boat." He draws a distinction with pound netting around the pace and volume of the fishery: "I don't think we ever did skin any on the boat coming in, because it's just too much to take care of."

Potting toads requires bait. Toad potters know that their quarry's favorite food is steamed crab or conch. "We'd go to the crab picking houses and get the scrap and use that," W. T. Wilkins explains. "When you put that overboard in the pot, you'd just see the oil floating out of it from the fat of the crab when it was steamed. It would cause a slick on the water, and they would just smell that drifting and come to it."

"I've done it for years and years and years. You use a pot, like a crab pot, only it's got a smaller mesh—a peeler pot," Marshall Cox explains. "You use crab scrap for bait. Crabs that have been picked. You crush it up with your feet and put it in the bait box. That's what you use." Then he and W. T. link new challenges around fishing for toads to another fading seafood industry. "That's what got me out of the business," Marshall sighs. "I couldn't get no bait. We used to have a lot of crab picking houses where you'd get your scrap." W. T. adds, "Now, it's nowhere to go to get your crab scrap." "You've got to catch the crabs yourself," Marshall inserts. "Steam them. That's a pain." The picking houses are almost all shuttered W. T. explains: "What two or three little crab picking houses is left, I don't even think they have a steady enough supply probably to keep one person going, let alone five or six."

Amy Brandt's apotheosis of the toad, Cape Charles, Virginia.

Because picking houses are in decline on the lower Eastern Shore of Virginia, the bait supply has dwindled, compelling fishermen to catch and steam crabs for their pots. Eddie Watts of Sparrow Point describes toad fishing in detail. He begins with the bait, "They definitely like their food cooked." He elaborates on his technique: "There's two baits that I use. Conch guts that come from Bernie's Conchs in Cheriton, and they're cooked. The other is steamed crabs. They don't seem to have a preference for the male or female crab. It's just crab. But it has to be steamed. You can bait a pot with a raw crab, stomp it, and put it in your row, and put a pot with steamed crab on either side of it, and the pot with steamed crab will have thirty or forty fish and the pot with raw crab will have three or four. Don't ask me why."

Although toads are not considered a fish that schools, they often exhibit group behavior—a fact remarked upon by fishermen but not elaborated in scientific and natural history literature. W. T. Wilkins remembers, "I had a guy tell me he got ashore one time laying beached there, so he just threw a pot over the side of the boat and watched them. He said they just came there around it, like minnows will do around a minnow pot, and he said one of them went in there, and when they did, every one of them followed, just like a minnow would do. Every one of them just followed him in there. . . . I don't know what triggers them, but all of a sudden they'll all try to get in there at the same time."

Eddie Watts remarks on this behavior, observed while toad potting along the Bayshore: "My brother and I did it down off the Sand Hills one time in real shallow water, and we ran fifteen pots out in water you could see the bottom in. We came back to the first one, got close to the first one, shut the engine off, and poled. Shoved up close enough to the pot to see the bottom and see the pot. You could see the toads." "The pot's got four funnels in it," he explains, "and you could see the fish all around the pot. Just like this. All of a sudden one fish went in. When he went in, it was like a vacuum cleaner sucked. Thump! Just like that, and they were all in there." Toads, once trapped, cannot find their way out again. Eddie Watts continues, describing how he sets and fishes his pots. "Depending on the time of the year, the depth of the water, you can catch them on the flats, you catch them up quick in shallow water." He fills in the details, "You have to keep moving your pots just like anything else." Eddie knows his toads.

The reality of cleaning a toad, as Danny Doughty testifies, is rough business—a violent act that translates the animal into ingredient. W. T. Wilkins, who fished for toads out of Hungars Creek near Eddie Watts, outlines the cleaning process: "Cleaning toads can be hard on your hands without gloves, because they have very rough skin. You just make a cut across the back of his head, and bend his head back, and the end of the meat will flip out. Take a knife blade and hold it down and pull the skin right off of it." "I did it on the boat," he says. "We'd fish pots. Forty or fifty pots or whatever we had out, and then we'd sit down and skin off what we'd caught and then go back and fish the pots again. Do it two or three times a day. Just depended on how many we were catching."

As for skinning toads, "Sometimes you'd wear out a couple of pairs of gloves a day. The hand you were holding them with, not your knife hand. It's just like you've got real sharp sandpaper that you're handling all the time is what it amounts to." The remembered quantities are staggering: "You take on ten bushels of them and set there and cut them for two or three hours and it's a lot of handling and lot of abrasion."

The skill and speed involved in cleaning a large catch, as Eddie Watts remarks, was a point of pride among watermen. He nods toward a stack of heavy plastic baskets, each with roughly a bushel and a half capacity. "See those fish baskets over there. I can clean two of those in an hour. That's popped fish," he explains, referring to deflated toads. "A lot of people will—

because us watermen like to brag—say, 'Well, I had ten baskets.'" "Well, okay, you had ten baskets," Eddie has no patience for human puffery, "but if you didn't pop them and keep topping them off as you're working and letting them settle, so that when you get done you've got ten full baskets." The implication is clear, if you intend to boast, there had better be some substance to your words. Toads out of water settle. "A basket of toads," he resumes, "even if you pop them and you're catching a lot of fish and you fill that thing right up, an hour later, you've got a half a basket." Providing a sense of scale, he notes, "A full bushel of popped toads if you top it off will basically yield you twenty-five to thirty pounds of meat."

It's the violence of cleaning a toad for cooking that captures my attention. A flap of skin connecting the severed head to the body provides sufficient purchase to turn the fish inside out, leaving head, skin, and entrails in one hand and the meat of the fish in the other: "You skin him," H. M. Arnold says. "The guts come with it, and the roe." "In the fall, of course," he adds parenthetically, "he doesn't have any roe—so you're just skinning fish."

Responding to questions from his friend W. T. Nottingham, Cox estimated that he would harvest a hundred pounds of dressed fish in the course of a day of working his pound and drift nets, "Three hundred to four hundred toads. All depends on the size of them. There's no other fish that's any easier to clean than that, though. It's just a one swipe deal. There's no scaling. Once you cut it one time and bend it over, it's out. It's an easy fish to clean, but you have to know how to do it because your hand is right there by the knife. I've cut my knuckles many a time." Cox's matter-of-fact description of the deft gesture that turns the swelling toad inside out is vivid. The toad is rendered a culinary delight through a wrenching translation. Torn apart, the toad is divided into flesh and waste, delicacy and poison, creature and commodity. Skinning a toad is a muscular editing that separates everything that defined the toad as a living creature into the morsel that we consume.

Out on Nassawadox Creek early one blue-sky morning, H. M. is pulling up his peeler pots for the season. We grapple and lift one pot after another into the boat, empty the contents. H. M. deftly sorts through the snapping, retreating crabs, reserving the peelers for his shedding tanks back at the Bayford oyster house. I stack the pots in the bow of the boat. Periodically, H. M. lifts a pot with two, three, or four toads in the bottom. No crabs. The toads have eaten every one. H. M. sets them aside. "What goes around comes around," I reflect to myself, eyeing the fish, looking forward to toads for supper.

Visiting the New Fulton Fish Market in New York City at 4:00 a.m.

one rainy November morning with a group of companions from the Bard Graduate Center, I unexpectedly find myself in search of toads. They are conspicuous in their absence. Just as a reluctant acceptance of a toadless reality takes hold, the proprietors of the Blue Ribbon Fish company remember a few "in the back" and bring them out for our inspection. As our fishmonger hosts are quick to point out, the toad is noteworthy for its capacity to inflate itself into a coarsely textured sphere intended to gag its predators. One purveyor picks up a toad, pushes a ballpoint pen barrel into its abdomen, inflates the fish, and tosses the softball-sized sphere to a surprised and appalled student. Toad humor is what it is.

For fishermen the swelling toad's defense mechanism out of water is a source of amusement and occasionally ribald humor. Marshall Cox, sitting at W. T. and Tammy Nottingham's kitchen table, gestures to an apple, laughingly pretending that it is a toad inflated with air, "Now pick that toad up. Look it over. Now hold it up next to your ear. Shake it. Shake it! Shake it hard. You hear anything? No? Then it must be a female, because if it was a male you'd hear its balls rattling."

W. T. grins, "You're about the hundredth person that's been caught on that one!"

Humor aside, the toad, once considered a trash fish consumed largely by the poor, eventually garnered the gustatory devotion of a certain class of connoisseurs. In southern fishing communities, discernment takes on an enthusiastic cast that is as much about identity couched in terms of terroir and nostalgia as it is about gastronomy. A November 2009 Facebook entry trumpeted: "Exmore Diner. Today we have Swelling Toads $10.95 . . . served with 2 vegetables and rolls," to which a local patron joyously exalted, "Swelling toads for $10.95! This is why I love the Eastern Shore!"

Evonia Hogan, who grew up in nearby Cheriton just behind the old Webster tomato cannery, recalled her first encounter with toads, touching on themes of delicacy, danger, souvenir, pleasure, and the local: "Toadfish! The first time someone brought me a toadfish, they said, 'We've got some toads.' 'A toad?' I said, 'I'm not eating no frogs.' And, they're like, 'Taste it. Taste it.' We ate it, and I say, 'Oh, my god, this tastes like shrimp. This is not a frog.'" Evonia continues, "She said, 'No, it's a toad.' And I said, 'What's a toad?' She showed it to us. It's a blowfish—spiny blowfish. She actually brought us one that was blown up with the spikes and everything. I said, 'That's a poisonous fish!' And she says, 'No. If you know how to fix it right and you get the poison sac out of it.' You skin it, and cook it. Of course, when they showed it to us it was already ready. The head was removed and everything. All of the bad parts were gone, and it was absolutely delicious."

"It's a small fish," Evonia brings her story to its close, "but it's the best fish you can eat. We had the toads—and that was a rarity because they didn't catch them too often. Most people who got them wanted to keep them for themselves. In the summer of probably 1972, when we first returned to Virginia, that was something people liked to serve in their houses. I have not been able to find them any place where you can buy them publicly—or get them in any restaurants. I haven't heard of any on the shore, but I do know that's something the locals like to eat among many other seafoods—lots of fish."

Evonia's narrative touches on several themes, including the physical oddity of the fish. She was shown a preserved souvenir specimen of a spiny blowfish that had been inflated, dried, and likely varnished as a collectible curiosity. Related to the sandpapery toad and also found in the Chesapeake, the spiny blowfish was not the one she ate. In her recollection, she also links the Chesapeake toads to the Pacific fugu and its reputation as a potentially lethal food. Her reference to the perils of fugu is not unique on the Eastern Shore.

Kelli Gaskill, who ran the now shuttered Big's Place restaurant near the little town of Painter, looked back on the reaction of a Japanese customer who pulled off the highway for lunch. "A few weeks ago, I had some customers in for lunch," Kelli begins, "and the wife was trying to explain to her daughter why she could not eat swelling toads. She was prohibited from eating swelling toads. Her daughter, who was about eight or ten years old, didn't understand. So the mother was explaining to both her daughter and sharing this story with me that she is a descendant of the Japanese royal family, and in that region of the world, the puffer fish or swelling toads are poisonous. Anyone, a servant or anyone, who serves a royal swelling toads was put to death. Any of the royals who ate swelling toads, there was also a punishment for them for eating that. She grew up avoiding any type of puffer fish at all cost because she was a descendant of that line of the royal family. Swelling toads, puffer fish, blowfish were strictly prohibited. She said even to this day in that region of the world, in Japan, it is highly taboo to eat anything in that family, in that species of puffer fish." Kelli finishes, "She was sort of taken aback to see it on the menu, and her daughter was fascinated by it, 'Hey, can we try it? They're offering us a free sample.' 'Absolutely not,' her mother said, 'No!'"

Evonia Hogan places her encounter with toads in a history of scarcity. The appearance of toads on the family table was a rare treat. Other local recollections of the toad, though, speak of its abundance as a bycatch that plagued crab potters and pound fishermen. Cecil Watts, who grew up in the Hare Valley community near the village of Franktown recalls the toad as a perceived nuisance: "A toad was a fish—and the fishermen would catch

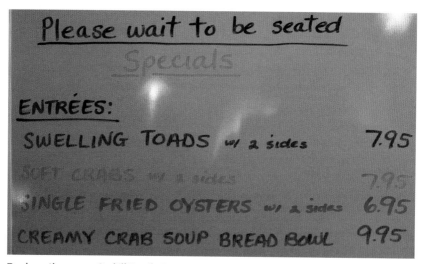

Please wait to be seated

Specials

ENTRÉES:

SWELLING TOADS w/ 2 sides   7.95

SOFT CRABS w/ 2 sides   7.95

SINGLE FRIED OYSTERS w/ 2 sides   6.95

CREAMY CRAB SOUP BREAD BOWL   9.95

Toads on the menu, Gaskill Family Restaurant, Painter area, Virginia.

them, and you could go to a dump near home and see bushels or baskets of them thrown out into the dump because they hadn't gotten used to eating them. They would throw them back because the fishermen would think that they were ripping their nets. The skin has a rough texture to it. They would tear their nets up." He emphasizes, nodding, "They would take them to the dump so they wouldn't tear their nets up and throw them away."

The toad's capacity to inspire culinary rapture is a comparatively recent phenomenon and one that increasingly anchors local identity. When the Gaskill family first served toads at Big's Place, their restaurant, they labeled the entrée "chicken of the sea." Later, they changed their marketing strategy to advertising the availability of "toads." Eastern Shore people knew exactly what the word entailed and came to dine on their local history. A display at the door, complete with photographs, instilled adventurous diners from "away" with a taste for the exotic and whetted the appetites of those "from here" with the taste of home. In either instance, the toad entered the privileged sphere of Eastern Shore of Virginia terroir.

Toads, once reviled as bycatch, are now the focus of a small but dedicated fishery. A swelling toad fished from the sea, made the butt of jokes, skinned and gutted, cooked and consumed, remembered and narrated speaks to the artifice of cooking and dining. The toad reminds us at every turn of how we cook, eat, and know the world. Where a waterman describes how toads approach the baited pot in the fashion of minnows, food writers note that the edible bit of the toad yields an alternative to shellfish and frogs' legs. A recipe for Toad Provençal states: "I love frog's legs, but they're hard to find, and often very expensive. The blowfish fillets are every bit as satisfying, but inexpensive." Simply and sadly, as most culinarians opine, it is "like chicken"—a quality that elevates the toad's status on the basis of a lack of distinction. When all else fails, things taste like chicken. For folks who grew up with toads on the seasonal table, they taste like home; for diners unfamiliar with the fish, it tastes like authenticity—especially when well seasoned with stories. The toad is a creature that is haunted by all its histories. "Grandpop," Edward Smith reminisces, "used to eat quite a few of them. That was the sixties then—the early seventies. Been around for a while eating them."

Marshall Cox outlines how he prepares swelling toads: "I fry all mine just like a piece of chicken. You cut them and put them in pancake mix. Roll them up, put them in a frying pan with a lot of oil. Just like southern fried chicken. That's how I do mine. I don't know of anyone who cooks them any different. That's why they call them 'chicken of the sea'."

"I throw mine in a fryer out here," W. T. seconds, tilting his head toward the kitchen dooryard, "in a cast-iron Dutch oven that's got some oil in it, and deep-fry them just like he talked about. Dust them. That's the only way to cook them."

Evonia Hogan echoes Cox, "We used to bread them up with cornmeal, sometimes we would use Old Bay Seasoning, and then we would fry them. We would deep-fry them. They were absolutely delicious!"

Toad roe, fine grained and subtle in its flavor, found its own privileged place on the plate. "The roe?" W. T. Nottingham asks rhetorically. "We fry them, too.' Marshall Cox, agrees, "That's good with scrambled eggs. With the roe."

W. T. Wilkins observes that while fried toads were the way most diners enjoyed them, new concerns about healthful diets were exerting an impact: "We'd fry them. We'd put them in a microwave and cook them, you know, with some butter or olive oil or whatever in a dish, and two or three minutes they'll start peeling right off the bone. I was brought up eating fried fish, so that's the way I like them most of the time. Either that or broil them. I got so I eat a lot of it broiled now." Personally, I like to broil my toads with a little garlic and white wine in the pan.

Eastern Shore cooks fry their toads, but they do so with noteworthy variety. Some roll the toads in flour while others use cornmeal or Bisquick. They season their fish variously with salt, pepper, Old Bay, cayenne, and other ingredients. Repetition creates a space for invention, offering a constant opportunity for culinary discovery. Each iteration of fried toads offers fresh possibilities, sometimes leading to truly innovative outcomes. One local household cooks double the number of toads required for a meal. The surplus are deboned and set aside for toad tacos enfolded in homemade tortillas purchased from local Guatemalan and Mexican cooks. Kelli and Richie Gaskill created fried toads stuffed with crabmeat—a menu favorite that regularly sold out.

Eddie Watts draws on his mother's recipe for stuffed flounder and invented a layered baked toad casserole: "I like them fried. You know everybody loves fried fish. But I tried something one time. I love stuffed flounder, and my mom had a real, real good recipe for flounder with crabmeat stuffing. What I did, I took a bunch of big toads. They don't have any bones in them. They just have that cartilage down the middle, and I would slice the meat off the cartilage. Just have a little strip of meat like that. I'd take a baking dish, put a layer of swelling toad meat in the bottom, then my crabmeat stuffing, and then a layer of the swelling toads on top, and then strips of bacon on top of that, and then baked it in the oven. I'm telling you, it's hard to beat. Hard to beat. It's her stuffed flounder. I just substituted the toads for the flounder. It's awesome! You bake it for thirty or forty-five minutes covered, and then the last fifteen minutes you take the cover off. Let that bacon get crisp and that grease run down in there. It's hard to beat."

No argument on that score. Cuisine flourishes in the delight of invention.

A CHEF'S RECIPE FOR HOME

SUGAR TOADS

Jeremiah Langhorne, The Dabney, Washington, D.C.

Makes 5 dinner-size servings

For the dressing

1¼ cups plus 3 tablespoons (360 grams) Duke's mayonnaise

1¼ cups plus 2 tablespoons (350 grams) sour cream

1 cup (250 grams) buttermilk

1 tablespoon (15 grams) minced garlic

4 teaspoons (20 grams) minced shallots

2 tablespoons (30 grams) hot sauce (use your favorite but not a super-spicy one)

3¾ teaspoons (18 grams) bourbon barrel Worcestershire sauce

2 tablespoons (30 grams) grated local Pecorino-style cheese

¼ cup (50 grams) apple cider vinegar

2 teaspoons (10 grams) fresh lemon juice

1 bunch chives, chopped

1 bunch tarragon, chopped

1 bunch parsley, chopped

Salt and pepper to taste

For the salad

2 heads heirloom lettuce or other greens, torn into bite-size pieces

10 small radishes, thinly sliced

2 tablespoons extra-virgin olive oil

Juice from half a lemon

Salt and pepper to taste

For the hot honey

2 cups honey (use your favorite)

⅔ cup hot sauce

¼ cup toasted benne seeds (not sesame seeds)

For the sugar toads

20 sugar toads

½ gallon buttermilk

2 cups (500 grams) all-purpose flour

¾ cup (200 grams) cornstarch

2 tablespoons (30 grams) garlic powder

¼ cup (50 grams) onion powder

6 teaspoons (20 grams) kosher salt

1 teaspoon (5 grams) celery seed
1 teaspoon (5 grams) cayenne pepper
1 gallon canola oil

To make the dressing

Combine the mayonnaise, sour cream, buttermilk, garlic, shallots, hot sauce, Worcestershire, cheese, vinegar, and lemon juice. Add the herbs and mix well. Season with salt and pepper. Set aside for serving.

To make the salad

Toss the lettuce in a bowl with the radishes, dress the salad with the olive oil and lemon juice, and season with salt and pepper.

To make the hot honey

In a medium bowl, combine the honey, hot sauce, and benne seeds; set aside.

To prepare the sugar toads

Clean the sugar toads and remove any fins or excess skin on the tails. Set aside. In an 8-quart pot, heat the oil to 350°F.

Place the buttermilk in a nonreactive bowl. Combine the flour, cornstarch, garlic powder, onion powder, salt, celery seed, and cayenne pepper in a shallow baking dish for dredging.

Bread the toads by dipping them lightly in the buttermilk and then in the flour, shaking off the excess, and then repeat that process to double coat them. Set them aside on a tray.

Carefully add the toads, one at a time to the pot of oil and fry for 5–7 minutes or until golden brown or the largest one is warm in the center and cooked through. Don't hesitate to cut one open to check for doneness—an undercooked toad is not delicious. Remove the toads from the fryer and place them on a plate lined with paper towels or a cooling rack to drain.

To serve

Cover one-third of the bottom of a large serving bowl with the buttermilk dressing. Toss the toads with the hot honey and place them in the center of the bowl next to the dressing. Transfer the salad to the other third of the bowl and serve immediately.

The Wachapreague Fireman's Carnival Cake Wheel

The Wachapreague Volunteer Fireman's Carnival runs for four weeks, Wednesday through Saturday, from mid-June to mid-July. The fairgrounds in the middle of town resemble an old southern camp meeting. In the fishing village that is home to just over two hundred residents, the carnival offers one of the greatest pleasures of summer. One of the last two town carnivals (the other, Chincoteague) on the Eastern Shore of Virginia, the Wachapreague fair offers rides, an open-air bingo parlor, game booths, food concessions, and an entertainment stage. Families attend, enjoying clam fritters and fried soft-shell crabs, along with more generic carnival fare. Restless teens cruise the grounds, "coolness" factors turned up high. The salt scent of the great Atlantic marshes across the street on the far side of the old ice plant flavors the evening air. The sun dips livid against the underbelly of rising clouds, rides whirl, the shouts of children on the loose punctuate the white noise of grownup conversations on the midway. Crowded with other good-natured bettors on a warm evening, Rebecca plunks fifty cents on the painted game board and then stands back as others jostle for their numbers. She wins a lemon crunch pound cake at the Wachapreague Carnival cake stand with her lucky number 4.

Where we eat speaks to the idea of terroir grounded in the places where folks share meals and conversation. More than the taste of place, the terroir, the taste of place, of where we eat goes beyond experiences of breaking bread and maps how we know our place in the world, not just through what we eat, but also how we remember and speak of locale. The literal consumption of place nourishes our understandings of who we are. The power of taste is immersive, a deep plunge into a river of memory and flavor. Where we take our meals reminds us of our place in the world. Where we eat combines place and

Delivering the first cake, Wachapreague Volunteer
Fireman's Carnival, Wachapreague, Virginia.

event. It bridges the everyday and the exceptional occasion. It speaks to a fundamental truth: events take place, therefore place matters.

The Wachapreague Fireman's Carnival is unique only in its details in a place where homecomings of all varieties are occasions for long-standing celebrations on the Eastern Shore and where favorite foods afford communions of remembrance and reminiscence. Each bite brings forth recollections and stories.

Historian Henry Howe, author of *Historical Collections of Virginia*, in the 1840s summed up the annual roundup and "penning" of wild horses on Assateague Island as "a frantic carnival, without its debauchery." Apparently finding the idea of a rural bacchanal suspect, Howe described first how the annual June roundup attracted people from near and far: "These occasions of festal mirth were astonishing. The adjoining islands were literally emptied of their simple and frolic-loving inhabitants, and the peninsula itself contributed to swell the crowd."

The penning concluded, a hungry multitude descended on the concessions. "The booths," Howe reported, "were soon filled, and loads of substantial provision were opened, and fish and water-fowl, secured for the occasion, were fried and barbecued by hundreds, for appetites whetted to marvellous keenness by early rising, a scanty breakfast, exercise, and sea air. The runlets of water, and the jugs of more exhilarating liquor, were lightened of their burdens."

Howe evokes a poetic reprise of the event, "music and dance, and love and courtship, held their undisputed empire until deep in the night, when all sought shelter and repose on board of their boats, moored by the shore, or among their island friends, who gladly entertained them with characteristic hospitality." Howe immerses us in the romance and nostalgia of his recollection, "Many a winter's evening tale did the incidents of those merry-making occasions supply . . . and from one anniversary of this half-savage festivity to another, all was talk of the joy and transports of the past, and anticipations of the future." That's how it is with the Wachapreague Fireman's Carnival—with the nurturing exclusion of spirits.

Food appears without fail in tales of celebration—sometimes in a supporting role and at others on center stage. Author of the *Foolproof Cook Book*, Fairy Mapp White described the annual Methodist conclave at Turlington Camp Meeting as it was in her childhood. Like the Assateague Island horse-penning, Turlington Camp Meeting (1871–1900) was a much-anticipated event that drew folks together for a week of preaching, praying, singing, socializing, and eating. Even as she speaks to the spiritual substance of the meeting, White lavishes her attention on the details of the Methodists' week in the woods—especially the meals: "The date chosen for the meeting was in early August. . . . Most of the crops were laid by or not ready to harvest, there were plenty of goslings and frying chickens, and an abundance of vegetables and fresh fruits, figs, grapes, pears and apples, for nearly every farmer had a good orchard, and of course there were plenty of cantaloupes and watermelons." "The tent holders," she reported, "provided food lavishly, and friends, kin and the preachers and their families were made welcome to eat."

Provisioning the meeting required advance planning. Animals were slaughtered, butchered, salted, and preserved in brine. "The women before the meeting," White writes, "canned peaches, fried apples and pears, and made large quantities of pickles and preserves." Well-to-do faithful brought their African American family cooks as well as wood-fired stoves that they installed in rickety kitchens covered with shed roofs and slatted sides. While some of the cooking was undertaken by the cooks laboring in the small kitchens erected behind family tents, a "boarding-tent" provided daily repasts for all. White remembered the bill of fare in mouthwatering detail. When it came to breakfast, she enthused, "I do know there was an abundance of it, fried apples, fried ham, eggs, hot biscuits, and coffee in big white cups, all served by colored men." At dinner, the big midday meal, she recollected, "we always had fried chicken, most days pork, mutton or beef, corn, butter beans, two kinds of potatoes, stewed tomatoes, quick biscuits, yellow firkin butter (usually soft), coffee, iced tea, served from pitchers with a big piece of ice in each." "The suppers," she added, "were like dinners, but fewer vegetables." White then turned to two dishes favored by the worshippers in their annually constructed wilderness retreat: "pork hash was highly seasoned with pepper and home grown sage," and "biscuits were thick, rich and good, as cooked in woodstoves."

Many of the same characteristics that marked Turlington Camp Meeting defined the Fourth of July on Hog Island. Born and raised in the long-vanished Broadwater community on the island, sisters-in-law Gertrude and Viola Bell saw the Fourth of July as the most celebrated holiday of the year, surpassing Christmas and Thanksgiving. Much more than a patriotic holiday, the annual gathering was an occasion that marked a homecoming for Hog Island families. Their combined recollection, each sister-in-law interrupting the other as they piled on detail after detail, epitomizes terroir as a homecoming to which all were invited.

VIOLA: The Fourth of July, well, they would prepare from one year to the next, and then when the Fourth of July would come, they would move big tables. Evidently, I think the tables they built— it would be like on these horses, you know.

GERTRUDE: You know, like these big picnic tables that you buy.

VIOLA: That you buy today.

GERTRUDE: Well, they were tall tables.

VIOLA: And you know they built them! And they would just have long benches. They wouldn't have chairs.

GERTRUDE: They would just be as long as—near about as long as this porch. Yes. They would. The table and the benches.

VIOLA: Yes!

GERTRUDE: They would have several set up. White tablecloths on them.

VIOLA: Probably sheets, half of them were—but that's neither here nor there. And they didn't have paper plates.

GERTRUDE: No! They didn't have paper plates then.

VIOLA: They had regular china dishes. People would—like, say if your mother lived there, she would probably bring out a set of dishes, and my mother, and this one. You know, they would bring their dishes.

GERTRUDE: And their cooking utensils.

VIOLA: And then they would take their range, wood range, out of the house. And they would take them down there . . .

GERTRUDE: There was five or six wood ranges.

VIOLA: and they would set them up and then they would do all the cooking.

GERTRUDE: They'd roast all the . . . they had roasted . . .

VIOLA: . . . lamb.

GERTRUDE: They had roasted beef and all the fried chicken. Everybody had fried chicken.

VIOLA: Hams.

GERTRUDE: And ham sliced. But when they got ready to fix their oyster flitters . . .

VIOLA: Clams.

GERTRUDE: That's the reason they had to have the woodstove. They'd have to fry their oyster flitters hot and their clam flitters hot.

VIOLA: And bake their bread.

GERTRUDE: And bake their bread hot. And have the potatoes hot. And they'd cook all that on the stove outside. You could go near about from one end of that island to the other and smell all that stuff a-cooking. And people would make all these great big bowls of salad, you know. And all this made, don't you understand?

VIOLA: And years ago when you got lard, you know, lard, it would come in fifty-pound lard tins. And they would save them from the

The cake wheel bettors convene, Wachapreague Volunteer
Fireman's Carnival, Wachapreague, Virginia.

stores and clean them out, you know, and keep them nice and clean,
and that's what they would keep their lemonade in.

GERTRUDE: Make their fresh lemonade.

VIOLA: And put their ice in it. And sell the lemonade. And then they
had big ice cream freezers, because I remember Grandmom . . .

GERTRUDE: They were tall.

VIOLA: . . . and they would start that ice cream the day before to get it
all frozen cold. And then they would sell homemade ice cream. And
they'd have cake, some pies, you know, whatever you wanted.

GERTRUDE: Plenty of hot coffee.

VIOLA: And where they had it was all these big, big, big pine trees!

GERTRUDE: Everything was shaded.

VIOLA: And it was like this opening here. Big clearing. And they had everything set up here. Everything was in the shade. It was really nice if you could've seen it.

VIOLA: And then all these people would come. Some would come in their own boats and a lot of people would come on the mail boat . . .

GERTRUDE: Or hire boats to bring them.

VIOLA: Like say the day before, and if they didn't have no friends or anybody, they would pay to spend the night there. And then they could go to the beach if they wanted to go in swimming, they could walk over, whatever they wanted to do, just walk on the beach. And then in the afternoon, they would leave. Get on the boats, whoever brought them, and then they would go back. And people would come from every place—we had company all week. People from Hog Island actually is scattered all over, from California to Maine to Florida. All over. And they would wait until that time to have their vacation to come back there. You know, it was like a homecoming to them.

GERTRUDE: The Fourth of July morning, where we lived, you could look across that bay and it was just like it is out here on this highway today. You'd see nothing but boats coming. That's the truth. And all you could see was nothing but boats. Just boats coming to the island.

Where we eat is about the substance of the occasion as well as the bill of fare. So it is with the Bayford oyster house annual potluck dinner party thrown by H. M. and Mary Lou Arnold. The party transforms the old work building into a one-night palace of culinary delights. Some diners come for the "atmosphere of the old building," but, H. M. adds, "a lot of them that come through, they grew up here." Slow-roasted venison hams rendered as barbecue are the centerpiece of the menu, along with homemade sides including crab dip, macaroni and cheese, collards, string beans, and coleslaw. "People just go out of their way to make good stuff," he continues. "My gosh! Food keeps coming until ten o'clock!"

As guests arrive, they arrange their dishes on the old concrete-topped shucking tables. Diners file by, filling their plates as they go. Overhead strings of lights illuminate the proceedings. Talking and drinking, small groups of friends and acquaintances cluster together, politely standing back from the serving line. Outside, the crowd grows, and conversations multiply. New arrivals walk down the hill, enter the oyster house, and pay their respects to the "old heads" at ease in plastic armchairs arranged in something of a receiving line. "They're pretty much gone now," H. M. says with a sigh. "I had a lot of old friends, and they'd sit in here and people would pass by and they'd say, 'Now, who is that? Oh yeah, I knew their granddad. I knew their dad.'" The dishes shared at the Bayford party are memorable, but it is the being there that matters most. When H. M. Arnold says that people come for the atmosphere, he speaks to a larger truth. The setting in and around the old Bayford oyster house is wrapped in memory, familiarity, and renewal. The Bayford party, like the Assateague horse-penning or Turlington Camp Meeting or Hog Island Fourth of July homecoming, reminds us that in the worlds of everyday life and all the richness of its associations, place and memory are on the menu. Where we eat is what we eat—and what we remember and share in stories through the rest of the year.

Playing the cake wheel at the Wachapreague Fireman's Carnival is that place.

A little history seasons the taste of place. Wachapreague, proclaiming itself "Little City by the Sea," owes its late nineteenth-century origins to a long-vanished railroad spur, the fortunes of the oyster and fishing industries, and, in later years, the recreational fishery. Victorian houses and tidy bungalows from the opening decades of the 1900s document an era when oyster shucking houses ran full tilt and captains guided their charter boats through the snaking channels that led to Virginia's barrier islands and the open Atlantic beyond. Today the village is home to the laboratories of the Virginia Institute for Marine Science, a Coast Guard station, and a modest but vital fishery.

The fire company, formed in the early 1950s, hosts the annual carnival as a fund-raiser. Sean Fate, one of the volunteers, summarizes the event, "It's a great thing in the summer. This is where people get together. If you haven't seen somebody in eleven months, families come out here, and you see their kids growing up another year. What's nice about our carnival is we really push to make it family-oriented for kids and grandkids and grandparents and mothers and strollers." His colleague Kerry Wallace adds, "This is not just a carnival, I mean, people plan for years in advance. That's their vacation, people all over everywhere: Florida, Texas, New Jersey, everywhere. They come here every year. This is a family. A family. People come here, they turn their kids loose, little teeny kids, they turn them loose because they know everybody here's watching everybody's kids." Sean underscores the freedom of childhood, "You don't even have to watch your kids. They're just running around the carnival grounds or riding the rides." He then neatly summarizes the importance of the event in a larger community, "The town has always been a fishing village, but during the summer, up and down the shore, it's 'Let's go to the carnival.'"

Kerry Paul, the fire company chief and overall "systems engineer," elaborates on the early fairground buildings: "The original buildings were built in '51. The buildings that are here now were built in 1958. The original buildings—the lumber was purchased, or was donated, from a mill down in Quinby. What they donated was, the outsides of the trees, where they still had the bark and stuff on them. That's what they built the first building."

"The only thing that's here that's original to the 1951 carnival," Kerry gestures, "is the pole where the flag's at, and the bingo stand that was built around that in a circle. They used to use corn to put on the cards for your bingo. But, like I said, in '58, they built these buildings with the regular, what they call roofers, which is tongue and groove." Things change.

The buildings, Sean Fate says, "have been out here long enough, probably forty-five, fifty years, but as the carnival grew they added on. That telephone pole right there used to be the center post of the bingo stand. 'Course, we got a newer building there. I say 'new building.' It's probably forty years old. All these buildings were all built by fire company members back in the inception and the expansion of the carnival as it grew up. Some of them are showing their age."

The layout of the fairgrounds radiates outward from the bingo stand and the food concessions. Rides, including a venerable Ferris wheel, are arrayed at the front, and a concrete bandstand rises at the back. The cake stand anchors a line of brilliantly whitewashed booths near the bandstand. Capped with a hipped roof, each booth possesses a large hinged drop shutter that is raised with crab pot line threaded through pulleys.

Kerry Paul traces the cake wheel back to the carnival's founding. "The cake wheel was originally started when the carnival started in 1951, and it was the solo fund-raiser for the ladies' auxiliary. That's basically how it got started, and it's been going ever since. 'Course, years ago, we only got cakes from town. There was a lot more people living in town, permanent people then, than it is now. It wasn't difficult at all to get a lot of cakes. They had people that would go around and pick them up, and that's basically how it's been done ever since. Except now, we go to communities in Quinby and Keller in the surrounding areas and we collect cakes. Accomac, places like that. That's how it got its start, was from the ladies' auxiliary in 1951."

For me, it's all about the cakes and the cake wheel.

Every evening brings a diversity of cakes. Some home bakers contribute contemporary confections drawn from the pages of glossy food magazines; others offer long-standing favorites, some with local pedigrees stretching back to the late 1800s and earlier. Sean Fate enumerates some of the cake wheel favorites: "Caramel cakes and a lot of Bundt cakes and pound cakes, pineapple upside-down cakes, sometimes they're just in a little tin-

The cake stand opens, Wachapreague Volunteer
Fireman's Carnival, Wachapreague, Virginia.

foil tray. Sometimes they've actually showed up in someone's personal
Bundt pan with a note on the bottom, 'Please call me when you're done
with the cake and return my pan.'" The most sought-after cakes—caramel
and coconut layer cakes—go quickly. What makes them desirable is a combination of a baker's reputation, a cake's appearance, and the memory of
texture and flavor. Caramel, coconut, and pound cakes are objects of peren-
nial lust. All three appear with variations in Bessie Gunter's 1889 Eastern
Shore of Virginia cookbook in recipes that often presume the reader's expertise. A recipe for "cocoanut cake," for example, offers only a list of ingredients, "1 cupful butter, 3 cupfuls sugar, 5 cupfuls flour, 1 cupful sweet
milk, 1 grated cocoanut, 3 teaspoonfuls baking-powder, whites of 6 eggs."
That's it. After that you're on your own—no mixing instructions, no baking
times, no directions for construction and frosting.

A different contributor to Gunter's collection provides instructions but
almost no itemized ingredients, "Make cake as for cup cake, then bake in
layers. Make an icing of three eggs, two cupfuls of sugar. Spread icing between layers and sprinkle with grated cocoanut. Dress top in same way."

The possession of common knowledge essential to the taste of place appear in family recipe collections again and again. Carrie P. Kellam, residing in Belle Haven, recorded her recipes in a composition notebook through the 1930s, 1940s, and 1950s. Neatly penciled on the last page is her recipe for "coconut": "1 qt. milk, 1 scant cup of sugar, 2 tablespoons cornstarch mixed well, 4 egg whites."

Gunter devoted nearly forty pages to recipes for cakes, cookies, jumbles, and macaroons. The detail and complexity of some offerings underscore origins from beyond the art of baking within frameworks of local knowledge. Cake wheel favorites, caramel cake for example, bear the hallmarks of concision and familiarity: "One pound of brown sugar, half cupful of cream, a piece of butter the size of an egg. Boil twenty minutes. Spread this between any kind of cake preferred, baked in layers. Flavor with vanilla. Sponge cake is very nice."

Laura Dennis, who as a child in the Great Depression helped her mother by delivering weekend cakes and pies door-to-door in Cape Charles, preserved her mother's and her own recipes in a neatly typed family cookbook. Careful to cite the origins of many of her recipes, she included instructions for both a sponge cake and caramel icing.

SPONGE CAKE

6 eggs
2 cups of sugar
1 cup of boiling water
3 cups of flour
2 teaspoonful of baking powder
Beat yolks light, add sugar, then water, then flour & baking powder, bake in 350 degree oven.

She adds the note, "This is Cathern Goffigan recipe." The caramel icing, however, was her own:

CARAMEL ICING

1 lb. of brown sugar
1 cup granulated sugar
1 cup carnation cream
Cook until forms soft ball remove from fire add ½ stick of butter, and vanilla cool, then beat until right consistency to spread.

Revered as a baker by fellow members of her Methodist congregation, Laura Dennis regularly contributed caramel cakes to church bazaars—and her cakes sold in fevered bidding wars for eighty dollars and more.

Cake wheel logistics are a marvel of coordination. Every night of the

Wachapreague carnival requires a selection of cakes collected from a different community served by the fire company. Dave Fluhart, a village firefighter, explains, "Each town, like Pungoteague and Hacksneck, and Locustville, they're all kind of unique and they probably all have their own little story. There's one, like a caller, from town, or whoever handles the cakes, and then they'll call somebody in Locustville or somebody in Quinby, and then that person is responsible for calling for the cakes around the town. Depending on how big the town is and how many streets, and how many cakes you expect to get, they may divide the town up and only call a certain street tonight, another street the next time, and so everybody's not having to make a lot of cakes. Each town probably has its own way of doing things. Sometimes the people individually bring the cakes. Sometimes they'll come over from Hacksneck with a van loaded with cakes, where they've collected them all day from Hacksneck and bring those over. With some of those towns, like Hacksneck and Pungoteague, we usually have plenty of cakes, so it's really a good night. People come and look forward to the cakes coming in from Hacksneck, they're all going to be good cakes, so that's usually a real good, successful night."

Kerry Wallace describes the chain of command: "What Selena does is she has a person on each street that's like the contact person, and they call the people on the street." Kerry provides an example, "Tracy Waterfield is the person in Quinby, and she calls everybody in Quinby, and we leave the church door open all day with the air conditioner going, and all the cakes come there, and then George and Virginia load them up and bring them up here. I'm sure every town has their own system. Tracy is the one, she's a schoolteacher, she does all the calling for Quinby. You know, we use the church for everything." He laughs.

Reputation is everything in the cake wheel universe—and there are bakers whose confections are objects of fierce competition. Among the most revered of bakers was Nell Ward of Quinby, the Seaside hamlet that remains a primary landing point for the oysters and clams farmed in and around the waters of Hog Island Bay. "Some cakes," carnival stalwart Ben Byrd observes, "they'll know who baked them, they'll say, 'Oh, well, that's a Nell Ward cake.' She's known for her cakes. That's the first pick. That's the first cake going off the shelf."

Ward honed her baking skills over a lifetime, as her granddaughter Julie Ward remembers, "She would make cakes every Sunday, and we'd all get together as a family and eat her homemade caramel cakes." Julie pauses and then resumes, "Hers were just the good, down home, made with lard, and nothing healthy about them. We'd all sit around and eat the cakes." "She never had a recipe." Julie concludes, "Everything was in her head, and

The Bayford bash begins, Bayford, Virginia.

a pinch of this, a little bit of that, and just threw it all together, and the cake always turned out perfect. My grandmother never knew what it was to buy icing from the store. If it didn't get made in her kitchen, it didn't go on her cakes."

Kerry Paul recalls Nell Ward as a prolific baker. "Mrs. Ward in Quinby, she used to bake a lot of cakes, and they were—I mean homemade cakes, weren't no box mix from the store, I mean, they were all homemade! Then she'd make a whole gang of them every night, seemed like." Kerry Wallace

241

added to the praise for Quinby's preeminent home baker, reprising his favorites: "Coconut, that would melt right in your mouth, coconut and chocolate. Oh, they were the two—my favorites . . . , at least two layers. Some of them were even three layers. Once in a while, you'd get a good pound cake. Her pound cakes were delicious. I mean, they were nice and moist. They were good. But my favorite was coconut. That's always been my favorite."

Nell Ward also contributed cakes for less accomplished neighbors. "She baked a lot of cakes for the different ones who couldn't bake. She'd bake them for them, charge them like five or six dollars to bake them. Then they would buy them and they'd donate them to the fire company. And that's the way it was for years."

Dave Fluhart remembers the nights when the supply of cakes was not where it needed to be and the cake wheel organizers would turn to Nell Ward: "When we would have trouble getting eight or ten cakes a night, Ms. Ward—we'd actually buy cakes from her. She'd make eight or ten, or five. We'd get them and that would fill in when we were kind of short of cakes."

The best cakes, though, are defined by more than the fine points of icing and pastry. The bettors around the cake wheel advance their quarters with an appetite for the authentic flavor of place. The best cakes, like those of Nell Ward, come complete with stories. Julie Ward locates those cakes in a landscape of memory: "She was, she was somebody special. She was one of those grandmothers that always seemed to have an apron on in the kitchen. She was always cooking. There was always community stuff going on around in her house. My grandfather would go out on the water, get crabs, and then they would all sit around, my grandmother, my grandfather, and some other people, picking the crabmeat. Probably back then, probably weren't supposed to, but, you know, selling it to locals. She was just awesome. You couldn't do any wrong, in her eyes, when you were her grandchild." She concludes, "I like experimenting in the kitchen. My one sister actually can come pretty close; she can make my grandmother's cakes. And, my aunt, I believe, can." The implication being that no matter how good they might be, those cakes will never surpass those of the beloved master baker.

Nell Ward may hold a privileged position in cake wheel lore, but she is not alone.

Kerry Wallace diplomatically states, "I think everybody did a good job of baking cakes. I mean, back years ago, everybody made a cake. Years ago, every house in Wachapreague was occupied, and everybody baked cakes. We'd have anywhere from twenty-five to thirty cakes a night. They were homemade cakes. They weren't store-bought cakes. Everything was out and out." He continues, "People would bake them, bring them out to the carnival ground, or if they weren't able to do that, we'd go by and pick them up and bring them out. It'd be a real good, fresh, homemade cake. Everybody wanted one." Homemade cakes tempt all comers. As Kerry Wallace observes: "It's so many, so many good cakes because they're homemade. It's not store bought. It's not box made; it's homemade." "As soon as the cake wheel building opens," Kerry Paul notes, "they're picking out which ones they want. Or, they'll say, 'Who made that one?' Or, 'Who made this one?' You know, they can tell what they are."

There are fourteen cakes up for grabs on the warm late June evening we attend the carnival with a roll of quarters in hand. Some regulars who have attended the annual volunteer fireman's carnival for a lifetime will play for a particular baker's confection; others bet to win a favorite—a coconut layer cake or a caramel cake. Tonight a thunderstorm threatens to the west, so players advance their quarters with a measure of urgency.

The rules are simple. The cakes are arrayed on the rough wooden shelves that ascend the rear wall of the open-fronted booth built in 1958. A mat marked with forty numbered squares is spread out on a narrow wooden counter. A wheel mounted on a post displays forty numbered wedges. Bettors place their wagers on the mat—one bet per number. The barker spins the wheel, metal pins ratcheting against a flexible metal strip. The wheel chatters, slows, stops, and the cake booth workers call the winning number. The lucky winner shouts, waves a hand, and is ushered into the booth to choose the cake of their desires.

There is one winner per spin. The losers sigh, dig for more quarters, and place new bets. Wagering for cakes has worn the surface where bettors play their quarters. "You can see the boards kind of, the numbers aren't clear as they used to be," says Sean Fate. "It used to be a canvas laid down here. We made this up a few years ago. We didn't change the wheel, we just changed the—we call that a 'lay.' There used to be a canvas lay that the numbers were on the canvas, stretched over the top board. But the sun got to it."

The betting proceeds in a brisk rhythm. "When they open that window nights, people flood there," reports carnival volunteer Mitzi Paul. "Not everybody can get to play as soon as they open. They have to kind of wait their turn to wiggle up there to put their money on the board. Come early, because like I say, if you don't get up there in the very beginning to get your spot so that you can play your number, you're going to have to wait your turn." Her husband, Kerry, adds, "I mean, it's crowded. Everybody's trying to get their quarters in. They'll load that board up every time. Some people double up on numbers, but, yeah, they'll load that wheel up easy. And it goes fast. If you've got ten or fifteen cakes, they're gone! I mean, the stand doesn't stay open long. They really go for it big time." It's a rare evening when a cake lingers orphaned at the cake wheel.

Playing the cake wheel begins with discernment. Julie Ward relates how Quinby folks drive up the Bradford Neck road to attend the carnival and play for cakes on the night that their cakes are on offer: "They'll come up and play for cakes. The cakes—they normally drop them all off at the church, and we try to bring them all up in a group, or some individuals will bring them all up, but yeah, they'll come up and try to bid on the cakes. It's funny, people will watch. You can see. They'll watch to see who brings what cake, and what it looks like when they bring it up, so they know when they go to play which one they want to win." She adds with excitement in her voice, "But if you think, 'Ah, yeah! This is a good cake,' then you go." Mitzi speaks to the reconnoitering of cakes in advance, "Some will come early and sit either in their cars or to this table, and watch who brings cakes into the side door, so they kind of get an idea. Like if I'm coming with my cake and they've won that before, then they might try to win that three-layer coconut cake. . . . I've had somebody right here in the carnival say to me, 'I've got to have that cake.' And they would go over and try to play for it. Somebody probably beat them out. They might not have picked the winning number at that particular time."

Kerry Wallace describes the fever of the moment. "If you win, if your lucky number comes up, you got your pick of whatever cake you want." He imitates an imagined bettor's voice: "'I don't know if I want a coconut cake, or a chocolate cake, or a pound cake.' Someone will spend dollars after dollars, you know, just to get one. Someone could, actually, cover the whole board and buy one cheaper than what they would ordinarily spend on it." Covering the board, he cautions, runs counter to the spirit of fun. "The sport is picking one or two numbers, even four numbers. Most of them usually spend a dollar a turn. They'll pick four numbers, and then somebody'll pick four numbers, and somebody'll pick four. 'Hey, I want that number!' 'Nope, can't have that number 'cause that number's been picked.'" "Next time," he slaps his palm on the table for emphasis, "they put all the money down fast before somebody else gets it."

The competition gets as thick and heated as the evening air, Sean Fate laughs: "People fight over some of this stuff, especially if they know someone's cakes in here. Mary Lou's cake's in the cake stand tonight. She's made this beautiful lemon pound cake, and people will fight over it. You want to be one of the first ones to win because obviously you get to pick." He nods, "I've seen some big smiles when somebody walks away with a cake they really wanted. They walk around the carnival grounds proud, just like that little kid with that giant teddy bear." That's how it goes in the world of high-stakes gambling for cakes.

Kerry Wallace pulls it all together: "I think that everybody looks forward to the cake tent, whether they make a cake or not. If they don't make one, they'll come here and try to win one. We don't sell them. You put your money down, and it's just power of luck, if you get it, you get it." "A lot of people say," he imitates a voice for effect, "'Hey, can I buy this cake?' We don't do it that way. Put your money down, if you win it, you got it."

Rebecca gives me the cake she won, the purest gesture of true love where I come from. The first big raindrops crater the dust. The rich scent of dampening earth rises, mingling with the smells of clam fritters on the griddle and the tang of machine oil from the venerable Ferris wheel. The players shelter under the raised wooden shutters, wagering on one more spin of the Wachapreague Fireman's Carnival cake wheel. This is the taste of homecoming; this is terroir.

A CHEF'S RECIPE FOR HOME

REBECCA'S CORN BREAD

Rebecca Y. Herman, Westerhouse, Virginia

Rebecca Herman's cornbread recipe features a cornmeal ground from a nineteenth-century heirloom varietal that has been preserved by Bill and Laurel Savage on their farm near Quinby. Ground from a "dent" strain, the cornmeal is rich in flavor with a lovely speckled appearance.

Makes 8 servings
2 large eggs
2 cups buttermilk (full- or low-fat)
3 tablespoons melted butter
1½ teaspoons salt
1 cup yellow cornmeal
1½ cups Pungo Creek Mills Pure Indian Cornmeal (see Note)
1 teaspoon Clabber Girl baking soda
1½ teaspoons baking powder

Preheat the oven to 450°. Heavily grease a 12-inch cast-iron skillet and place it in the oven.

In a large bowl, beat the eggs together. Add the buttermilk, butter, and salt and stir well to combine. In a small bowl, combine the cornmeals and add them to the egg mixture; stir until smooth. Dissolve baking soda in 1 tablespoon cold water and add it to the cornmeal mixture. Add the baking powder and stir thoroughly. Pour the batter into the hot skillet and bake for 15–20 minutes, or until the bread is golden brown.

Note: For more information contact Pungo Creek Mills, P.O. Box 69, 19530 Pungo Creek Lane, Painter, VA 23420; pungocreekmills @verizon.net.

Barbacoa de Cordero de Hog Island

There are times when it's hard to discern where something begins and something ends. That's how it is with Hog Island mutton *barbacoa*. Still, every story has its start, for example, when David Garcia came over to paint the window frames our friend Robert Bridges had just crafted and set in the old brick walls of our house. The workmanship was beautiful, and the installation was in its closing stages. The draughty winter days when frigid winds hissed through crevices in the rotten sills were banished. A sweltering August afternoon, thunder groaning on the horizon, and I was thinking of glittering ice crystals drifting on the beach in January and how snug we would be. "Hola," David, sweat trailing on his temples, greeted me. He knows that other than food nouns and some necessary conjunctions, he's exhausted my Spanish vocabulary. I keep thinking to myself that I really need to learn Spanish. Still, I always try to make good use of those food nouns. Segueing to English, David asked, "How is your daughter? She is a hero in our family."

Our daughter Lania's heroic status arises from the fact that she located David incarcerated in the truly labyrinthine depths of the U.S. immigration system. It seems that David, who has lived on the Eastern Shore for a good many years and learned the building trades from Robert, was driving with an expired inspection sticker. A county deputy pulled him over, found his papers not in order, and hauled him in. Federal jurisdiction took over, and David was shipped to a detention facility somewhere in Pennsylvania. His wife, pregnant with twins, could not find him and turned to Robert, a soul defined by an extraordinary generosity of spirit, who reached out to our daughter, a law student at the time, to locate and help in securing David's release. She accomplished her tasks in short order, and David and his family now reside secure in our community. This makes our daughter, as Robert says, a "folk hero" in our corner of the world and in the hearts of David, his family, and his friends. "Hola," I replied. "She's doing great, working now as a public defender across the bay." "Remember us to her," he answered, "she is family." David paused, "You are family. We are having *barbacoa* on Sunday. You and your family must come."

Now, *barbacoa* happens to be in my Spanish lexicon: "What kind?" David hesitated, looking for the word. "Sheep!" "Sheep! You mean like a grown-up sheep, like mutton?" "Si, yes, sheep, *cordero.*" *Carne de cordero*, mutton, is something I don't come across too often, and here stood David inviting us for Guatemalan *barbacoa de cordero.* "Where?" I asked. "At my sister's house. You know, Maiana, I think." Oh yes, I do! Maiana Garcia looms large among my sources for homemade tamales and sweet potato empanadas. I've stood at her side in her kitchen and marveled as she wrapped the seasoned *pollo* or *puerco* in the masa harina (dough made from ground corn) laid on softened cornhusks and then stuffed the fifty or so I ordered for the night before Thanksgiving into a steamer the size of a Florida sinkhole. What we don't eat on arrival gets stockpiled in the freezer for culinary emergencies, to which I seem unusually prone. "I'll be there," abandoning any pretense to polite refusal, "but my family cannot come with me." "You come," David concluded, "you are family." And I went.

Barbacoa preparations apparently began the night before, when the cooks killed and butchered the sheep, dressing the meat behind the house. When I arrived, the only non-Spanish-speaker on the premises, David greeted me along with his niece Jessica and sister Maiana. I was, as David reminded me, "family," introduced as such, and quickly absorbed into the clattering chaos of overheated children racing around on a summer Sunday afternoon, the calm of older folks chatting in the shade of Maiana's chayote arbor, and the focused energy of women cooking in the kitchen, under the carport, and in the yard behind the house. A ten-gallon pot of mutton-based *sopa* filled with vegetables bubbled next to the picnic table that served for staging and serving. Out in the yard, another larger pot gurgled on a homemade grill of concrete block and repurposed scorched-metal plates set askew over a wood fire stoked with chunks of scrap and windfalls. Jessica came over, offered to let me take a peek, and lifted the lid. "A taste?" "Oh, yes, please." Wonderful! "Gracias." "De nada, it is nothing." Not where I come from.

Jessica then provided a tour of Maiana's garden. David and Maiana come from Guatemala, and Maiana takes great pains to keep her family's culinary identity alive and vibrant. The smallest children played on the grass between the feet of the adults seated under the chayote. Epazote flourished next to the henhouse. Fruit trees, including a fig, or *higo*, grew in an archipelago of scattered beds around the house. Jessica smiled, identifying the plants by name along with their origins. Maiana, it turned out, is a seed saver known in local Spanish-speaking circles as a memory-keeper for ingredients that evoke histories of distant origins and difficult passages.

The time for *barbacoa de cordero* arrived. I took a seat next to David at one of the half-dozen church hall tables set up in the shade of the carport. There is no serving line; rather the women organize and distribute the plates, bringing each diner a selection of *sopa*, *frijoles*, spiced *arroz*, and *barbacoa*. A sharp salsa and a stack of homemade tortillas grace every table—and we go for it. David demonstrates the art of using a tortilla as a utensil—and, more importantly, the transformative power of salsa. We eat with gusto. Across the table, the twins, not yet two, go at their portions with equal enthusiasm. No children's table here; no child-size helpings. Replete, David and I settle back and talk about family and friends. His pastor joins us and asks if I attend church. He's thoughtful and listens. We exchange perspectives and share slices of cold watermelon. And then it hits me. "David," I ask, "where did you get a full-grown sheep?" "Robert," he says. "Robert?" "Robert." "Is this a Hog Island sheep?" I respond. "It is a sheep from Robert," he repeats by way of clarification.

Now, I happen to know that Robert and his wife, Jen, up until that moment were the keepers of a handful of Hog Island sheep, a rare breed relocated in the 1970s from one of the Eastern Shore of Virginia's offshore barrier islands. The flock from which those sheep descended were left to wander and forage the island after the last of the human residents fled the aftermath of hugely destructive hurricanes in 1933 and 1936. The island refugees took their possessions and even their houses to the mainland, resettling in fishing villages: Willis Wharf, Oyster, Quinby, Red Bank, Wachapreague. Some, Randolph Higby for instance, dug up treasured figs and grapes, transplanting them to new gardens where they still flourish. The sheep, though, they left behind.

Following the acquisition of a significant portion of the island by the Nature Conservancy, the decision came down that the island should be conserved as a largely untouched natural habitat. Bad news for the sheep that had resided there for generation upon generation. Sheep roundups followed, and in time the Hog Island sheep were relocated to the mainland. Rare-breed keepers acquired ewes and rams with the intent of preserving the breed, and as a result substantial flocks gambol at Mount Vernon and Colonial Williamsburg. Robert and Jen, however, possessed among the very last flocks of Hog Island sheep on the Eastern Shore—and as far as I knew, these were all the sheep they husbanded.

"This sheep is from Robert?" I asked. "It is from Robert," David said. And he continued, "This is the second time Robert has given us a sheep,

Hog Island sheep, Bridgetown area, Virginia.

but the first time when we went to get it, he was sitting on the ground by the fence with water on his cheeks. He was looking at the sheep—maybe it was Bertha." I leaned closer, and David elaborated. "'Robert,' he said to me, 'I can't let the sheep go. I'll pay you to leave her here.'" David remembers his reply: "'Robert, she is already your sheep. You cannot pay me for a sheep that is yours.'" I imagine the scene: Robert having second thoughts, David arguing the illogic of the moment. In the end, reprieve was granted. In fact, I had seen the sheep grazing in their penned meadow just a day or so ago. But then things changed: Robert gifted David the sheep, and here we were eating Hog Island rare-breed sheep as Guatemalan *barbacoa de cordero*.

As I made my farewells and offered thanks to David and his family, I asked for a bit of leftover *barbacoa*. Two thoughts were on my mind. First, the source of the sheep needed to be verified with Robert; second, the *barbacoa* demanded sharing with my beloved friend David Shields, renowned author of *Southern Provisions* and *The Culinarians*, who was deeply immersed in the search for the heritage foods of the American South and overseeing their listing on the passenger manifest of the slow food movement's Ark of Taste. One of the questions the Ark of Taste nomination form poses, sensibly enough, is, how do things taste? When it comes to Hog Island rare-breed sheep, this had up until this moment posed something of an issue. But now I had the answer in the cooler in the back of the car. My first stop, though, was Robert's house. Verification was on the evidential menu.

Turning off of Church Neck Road into Robert and Jen's crape myrtle-lined drive that leads to the back door of their house and Robert's woodwright's shop, I came to a stop under the big tree that they festoon each Christmas with gigantic illuminated ornaments fashioned from mashed crab pots. Robert, accompanied by his rambunctious dogs, Bear and Blue—both rescues—stepped from the porch into the shade. Robert asks, "How's it going?" Aflame with curiosity, I skip the pleasantries and get to the point: "Robert, did you give David one of those Hog Island sheep?" "I did. I gave him three, two six-year-olds and an eight-year-old." "Did you know he was going to have a *barbacoa*?" "I did," Robert answered with a hint of sorrow in his voice, "but I forgot . . . and I don't think I would have gone." "The rest of sheep, the little ones, are all down at Capeville," Robert quickly added, assuring me that there were Hog Island sheep still living near their ancestral home. "Do you want a taste of *barbacoa de cordero*?" I offered in reply. "Sure," Robert took a pinch out of the freezer bag I held out. Chewing thoughtfully, "This is really good! I thought it would be stronger." "Do you want some for you and Jen?" "No, thanks, I think I've had enough." Later I learned that when Robert told Jen that he had sampled the *barbacoa* that had been their former sheep, she looked into his eyes, gave him that gaze of heart-heavy sadness trimmed with a soft sigh of disgust, and asked simply, "How could you?"

I called David Shields, my epicurean comrade in arms, that evening. "Dave, guess what? I've just come back from a *barbacoa* up the road where we dined on Hog Island sheep Guatemalan style!" There are not too many folks I can cold call with this sort of news and get an informed response, "What?" "I ate Hog Island *barbacoa de cordero*—and I have some for you to sample and an answer to that taste question on the Ark of Taste nomination." "That's a rare-breed sheep," there was a moment of hesitation, followed by, "Well, what did it taste like?" "It was very tender and not at all strong in the way that I associate with mutton—and the salsa added to the shredded meat gave it some zing." "Bernie," Dave responded, "when the fellow who ate the last passenger pigeon was asked about its flavor, he responded, 'Fatty and herbaceous.'" Dave can't sucker me with that kind of leading comment. "Neither," I said, "more like delicate and rich—not at all like chicken." I paused, "Do you want me to save some for you?" "Absolutely! How will it get here?" "You have to come to it." "What can I bring to complement the *barbacoa*?" This was the question I'd been angling for, knowing that Dave was deeply committed to the restoration of Carolina Gold rice that grew in fields favored by rice birds, or bobolinks. Small birds, they once swarmed the fields, ravaging the crop. Now they're protected. I hesitated for dramatic effect before answering, then said, "How about a lovely rice-fed bobolink pie?" Silence at the other end of the line. "Could be a problem," he answered at last, "but it's possible." "How possible?" "It won't be a big pie."

Every entrée has its backstory. Sheep, estimated to number in the hundreds at the turn of the twentieth century, roamed the barrier islands of Virginia from Assateague to the southernmost tip of the Eastern Shore of Virginia. Resourceful foragers, they ran free until the end of the twentieth century, when the last animals were corralled and removed to the mainland. The Livestock Conservancy, which has as its mission the protection of endangered livestock and poultry breeds from extinction, identifies key characteristics of the Hog Island sheep. "The sheep of Hog Island," they note, "evolved in response to the island's natural selection for hardiness, foraging ability, and reproductive efficiency." "Most of the sheep are white wooled," they explain, "though about twenty percent are black. Newborn lambs are frequently spotted over the body, but the spots usually disappear as the lambs mature. The face and legs of these sheep can be speckled brown, white, and black, or have black faces and legs." Their summary concludes, "Mature animals weigh between 90–150 pounds. The ewes make excellent mothers and most often give birth to twins. Hog Island sheep are excellent foragers and prefer to browse rather than graze, if given the opportunity to do so. They stay in very tight flocks and are extremely alert in nature." Given their long sojourn in the saltwater environments of the offshore islands, the sheep have also evolved a trait for thirst tolerance.

The last roundup concluded a distinctive sheep husbandry that had flourished on the Eastern Shore since at least the mid-1600s and was the object of curiosity from the late 1800s on. From the outset, the Hog Island sheep and their neighbors were kept for wool that could be shipped to urban markets, as recorded in a speculative proposition in 1830: "As the price of wool has advanced very much, I hope you have still my wool on hand. It is worth from 25 to 30 c. here & in great demand. . . . I am sure by a little exertion on Hog Island & else where, we might make a pretty speculation." Wool was kept as well for local use, as recorded in early twentieth-

Maiana Garcia in her garden, Accomac, Virginia.

century photographs of island homes. One of those uses likely involved the making of wool or felt moccasins worn by local watermen for wading clams in the salt marshes.

Hog Island, one of the largest in the barrier chain, was described in 1911. The correspondent for the *Eastern Shore Herald* wrote, "The island is about 10 miles long and the inhabited portion about a mile wide. It has a long and wide stretch of sand dunes and beach. Its pine woods, though reduced in extent by the encroachments of the sand, are still beautiful, and these, together with its myrtle groves and cedar thickets form its distinctive features." "In the early years of the settlement," the writer also noted, "the big landed proprietors took up these coast islands. . . . Proutt's and Cobb's Islands were owned by the Floyd family and formerly pastured hundreds of sheep and cattle, but are now a waste of sand dunes." The observations of 1911 echo an 1836 account shared with the readers of the *Farmers' Register*, "We passed near to a large island, called Prouts', which is uninhabited, except by flocks of sheep. We had not time to call. This bears almost no trees; and wherever visible from the water, seemed to be but little else than sand hills very scantly covered with weeds or grass. It was said, however, that in the interior there is much of good grazing land. The north-western part of the island, which we approached, is losing greatly by the encroachments of the sea."

The islands held several advantages for tending sheep. Surrounded by extensive marshes, guts, and creeks, they effectively isolated the animals from the depredations of dogs and other threats found on the mainland. A contributor to the *Peninsula Enterprise* outlined the extent of the problem in 1882, "We find from the United States census report of 1880 that Accomac county produced 5,379 fleeces from the sheep raised in 1880. . . . This is sheep country. . . . The grazing and climate are all that could be desired. One thing, and one thing only is in the way of sheep raising—the everlasting 'yaller dog' is now, has been, and will be an obstacle, until they are thinned out."

The situation remained sufficiently out of control twelve years later when in 1894 ordinances were introduced into public debate. One of the most heartfelt and pointed pleas in favor of a dog law appeared in the local paper: "The sheep industry here is decayed. Few farmers dare attempt sheep raising because Tray, Blanche, Sweetheart, Brindle, Pug and Little Fancy spread themselves over every acre of land fit to graze, and roaming at will with a taste for racing and mutton forbid the attempt. The hundreds and hundreds of worthless dogs, worth nothing to their owners, an annoyance to neighbors, a foe to sheep, all over the Peninsula, destroy all hope, of raising sheep. . . . We are overrun with [dogs], and seem to have the same superstitious awe of them as the Turks in Constantinople—for they increase fabulously with none to make them afraid or kill them. . . . Sheep-raising can be made profitable here without the mousing pointers and crossfield hounds, that run at will over everybody's field, but not with them. . . . The case is, Dogs vs. Sheep. We give our verdict, duly considered, in favor of mutton. Tax the dogs out—let the sheep in." In addition to the predations of "yaller dogs," flocks endured the torments of wool pulling and sheep riding inflicted by small boys larking about the fields and grazing grounds.

The islands, however, were not entirely safe havens. In addition to the summer torments of heat and biting flies and winter's aching cold, extreme tides associated with hurricanes and northeasters overwashed the low-lying islands with deadly results. "We were visited on Tuesday night last with one of the severest wind storms ever experienced in this section, and unquestionably the highest tide within the knowledge of any one now living, the water reached a point at least 3 feet higher than the great September blow of 1822," a witness reported in 1878. "On Cedar Island nearly all the stock perished, Capt. O. A. Browne being a heavy loser. His loss there will be fully seventy-five cattle, and as many sheep . . . ," the writer continued, "No report has reached us from Revel's or Hog Island, but on the former, it is feared that Charles M. Dunton, Esq., has lost heavily in stock." A decade later a telegram to Richmond reported: "Intelligence has just reached here from the seaside that seven horses, two hundred sheep, and some cattle, belonging to Powell & Garrison, John A. Brittingham, and others, of Wachapreague, Va., were swept off Parramore's beach [the island to the immediate north of Hog] during the storm last Saturday night and were drowned."

Still, barrier island sheep weathered a passive husbandry that isolated them on islands where they foraged in the native scrub, sometimes tended by the occasional resident shepherd. As for the shepherds and their households, reported Howard Pyle, an artist and occasional local-color writer hailing from the Philadelphia area, they lived in small dwellings, for example "a little log-built hut, containing but two small rooms. The lower one, half filled by a gigantic bedstead, is used for kitchen, sitting-room, bedroom, and dining-room all in one; the upper, for some mysterious purpose."

Sheep simply wandered. An observer noted in 1907 the sheep on Parramore's Island between the south end of Cedar Island and the northern tip of Hog: "These animals run wild, and make their own living from the grass, seeds and young shrubs growing on the island, and drink from small pools of land water scattered here and there among the sand hills. . . .

The sheep are not used for mutton, but are kept on account of their wool, which is of a superior grade." Casual experiments in improving the island sheep, notable for their durability in a challenging environment, involved the introduction of other desirable strains into the wild with the expectation that crossbreeding would occur in the natural course of events.

Hog Island sheep were rounded up annually for shearing. The most elaborate description of this event appeared in an account penned by artist Howard Pyle. In 1879, he trekked the length of the Delmarva Peninsula for a three-part travel account that appeared in *Harper's*. Pyle's exploration landed him on Hog Island, where he was hosted by an unreconstructed Confederate veteran: "It was sheep-shearing time, and as we were curious to see not only these island sheep, but the manner of shearing them, we had an excellent opportunity of examining both the one and the other under the pilotage of the owner of one of these islands." On the day before the shearing, Pyle boarded a "large flatboat, with a leg-of-mutton sail," along with his host, four sheep wranglers, and "a small negro boy." They provisioned themselves with "the freight of two baskets of 'grub,' sheep-shears, and a demijohn of water, for rarely any thing but rain-water can be obtained at these islands." The following morning, joined by the shepherd, the crew began their work: "The men started to scour the island over and collect the stray sheep in a flock. They were scattered in all directions, some along the Atlantic surf, some across the marsh, some in the thickets in the southern part of the island. At length the sound of distant bleating was heard, and soon the drove—constantly augmented by the stragglers that joined it from all directions—slowly and reluctantly moved toward the sheep-pen; a moment more and they rushed tumultuously into it."

Pyle elaborated, writing in the idiom of Jim Crow humor: "The shearing was done on a long table, a carpenter's work-bench, the small negro being sent into the pen to catch the sheep for the shearers. It was amusing to watch him—the cautious way in which he would approach the frightened drove huddled in a corner, he scarcely less frightened himself. Suddenly he makes a dive, misses his sheep, stumbles, and the whole flock gallops over his prostrate body. Another rush is more fortunate, and he fastens his black little hands in the shaggy wool on the back of some old ram, which drags him, grinning, yelling, and with gleaming eyeballs, half around the pen before the animal acknowledges itself conquered. In the afternoon the wind blew up from the northeast and rain set in; the poor denuded sheep, shivering in the cold wind, looked so miserable that B— in very pity stopped the shearing."

The sheep-shearing scene reprised by Pyle achieved a celebratory status for other island communities in an annual cycle of Eastern Shore of Vir-

Maiana Garcia constructing tamales, Accomac, Virginia.

ginia events. The yearly sheep penning on Assateague Island, for example, occurred in the first week of June when young men from neighboring Chincoteague would gather, drive the sheep to Sheep Penning Hill, shear the flock, cull out a few for lamb and mutton, and return the rest to graze at large for another year. By the 1880s, the event had evolved into a holiday and a tourist draw. A journalist for the *Peninsula Enterprise* documented the 1883 proceedings, "The sheep penning on Assateague, Wednesday, was attended by a large concourse of people, and everything passed off pleasantly. The great feature of the occasion was the attendance of the 'Led Astray Club' of Chincoteague. Early in the morning the organization assembled in front of the Capitol Hotel, elegantly attired in their glittering uniforms, said to have been made expressly for the occasion by Worth of New York."

"The stirring rhapsodies of the Chincoteague string band, led by Prof. Paddock, rung out on the morning air, and at 9 o'clock a.m. sharp, Brig. Gen. Oliver Logan Wimbrough gave the battalion marching orders," the reporter continued. "The line of route was as follows: Up Broadway to Chestnut street, up Chestnut to Duncan's Hotel, where the battalion performed some very remarkable feats of drilling, and a copious supply [of] refreshments were furnished the club. The order forward, march, was again given, and the battalion moved down Chestnut street to Broadway and up Broadway to the post office, where three cheers were given for Boss Mahone." The marchers then departed for Assateague, where they conducted the roundup and shearing. For all the pomp and revel of the event, the object was clear—wool. Hog Island mutton surely graced more than one table, but roasted or stewed, culinary outcomes were purely a secondary consideration.

Hog Island mutton, however, is a rare treat, not unlike the *agneau de pré-salé*, or salt meadow lamb, associated with the vast marshes of northwestern France. Discerned from the escarpments of Mont-Saint-Michel overlooking tidal marshes stretching to the horizon, sheep are readily seen nibbling their way through native salt grasses oblivious to the culinary lust of distant, hungry would-be diners. Waverley Root, author of *The Food of France*, offers, "The greatest culinary asset of the sea is here produced on land—the sheep pastured on meadows whose grasses are saturated with salt from the ocean winds which provide the salty mutton known as *prés-salés*." Speaking to the cuisine of Brittany, Root embellishes, "The fine salt-meadow mutton . . . requires little more than expert seasoning and careful roasting to make a fine dish." Roasted constitutes the premier French preparation. He concludes, "In Brittany the standard combination is shoulder of mutton with white beans."

Julia Child devotes considerable space to lamb and mutton dishes in *Mastering the Art of French Cooking*, where she records her opinion that "the best French *agneaux* are considered to be those fed on the salty grasses of the northern coastal regions, *les prés salés*," and adds that the "most famous French mutton," meat from animals more than a year old, hails from the same locales. Child observes that the *prés salés* mutton may be roasted, braised, boiled, or fricasseed but, like other cooks and gourmands, places the roasting option at the head of her list of preparations. Although French roast mutton could be sauced, stuffed, or larded with garlic, the art of the dish resides in a technique with seasonings more often than not limited to fat, salt, and pepper.

The consumption of Hog Island sheep and their island kin as part of the Eastern Shore diet was limited. Bessie Gunter recorded only two recipes in her 1889 *Housekeeper's Companion*—both for lamb:

ROAST LAMB.
Choose a hind quarter of lamb, stuff it with fine bread-crumbs, pepper, salt, butter and a little sage. Sew the flap firmly to keep it in place, rub the outside with salt, pepper, butter, a little of the stuffing, and roast two hours.
—Mrs. A. T. G.

and

ROAST LAMB.
Take a nice tender quarter of lamb, either hind or fore quarter. Salt and pepper it. Put it in a pan with a little water and cook in a quick oven, basting well while cooking. All meats and fowl should be well basted while cooking.
—Mrs. J. G. F.

The mutton from Hog Island Sheep consumed well over a century later stands out for its sweetness and lack of gaminess.

Maiana Garcia sits at her dining room with her daughter Jessica, who has volunteered to speak as our interpreter. I've come in quest of instructions for making the *barbacoa de cordero* as well as the *sopa de cordero* that she shared with her family, congregation, and me two years earlier. The splendor of that meal lingers in my memory.

Maiana and Jessica devise a recipe for a five-pound piece of mutton. I discover that much is lost and gained in the process of translation, not just across languages and generations but also across a universe of experience. They offer specificity when asked, but they also assume a level of common knowledge—a generous assumption, but one that, in my case, is unfounded. As we talk, I am increasingly aware that the distinctions among recipe, narrative, and autobiography blur. The difference between recipes written and spoken is significant. Where the written recipe codifies the process of making a dish, one spoken builds community through conversation. Maiana's *barbacoa* contains all the flavors of her life and the worlds she inhabits—and shares.

As far as recipes go, her instructions for *barbacoa* are epic, beginning with the animal freshly butchered: "The men cleaned it, they took off all the hair and skin, all of it. Then it is put whole in a big pot of water overnight with a little white vinegar." Maiana adds a bit of salt to taste, stressing the importance of the vinegar. "Then the next day," she instructs, "you wash it off again."

Even as the mutton soaks, she begins to prepare the rub for the meat. "By that time, I had already ground up the cloves, peppercorns, onion, garlic, *guajillo* chili. I ground that up and I also ground two big ancho chilies." "For five pounds of meat," Maiana says, maybe a half bag of this chili." She counts out *guajillo* chilies on the table. "There's more than six. Ten chilies." The chilies pile up until there are fifteen. The number of ancho chilies doubles from two to four. Smiling, she directs that I should remove the seeds from the chilies but cautions, "You'd have to wear a glove with that."

Jessica adds tomatoes to the list and notes, "You can use two onions. It takes a lot of garlic. A head of garlic, with the cloves peeled, because that kills the strong smell of the meat."

Maiana and Jessica continue their tutorial with extraordinary patience, "It cooks together, the garlic, the onion. All of that cooks together, you boil it together. The onions, *chiles guajillo*, all that. The cloves. At medium heat . . . maybe five minutes. I touch them, and if they're soft I take them out. . . . You have to preboil the chili with the onions and all the spices, the cloves. After that, you add bay leaves, and blend them, so that the food has aroma."

"You blend it well," mother and daughter explain, "so it's fairly thick. It's like a salsa but it's not to be used for salsa. It is to be spread over the meat. You put it over the meat with its seasoning, salt, and bouillon." Here they note either beef or chicken. I seek clarification around the volume of water and the consistency of the rub, "A cup. Very little, it has to be thick." Maiana emphasizes, "This salsa has to be thick so it can be rubbed on the meat." Jessica glosses, "It's better for it to be dry and add in water little by little than to have it too watery." "It's by taste," they agree.

"When you have everything blended together, your meat is cleaned, you put this and this in the salsa, well mixed in," they tell me. "Then you take the meat, dry, with no water, nothing on it, and you bathe it in this, like,"

Maiana makes a caressing gesture over the imagined haunch of mutton in front of us, "with the hand, with a brush. . . . It is easier for me with the hand. And when you're mixing it up, you taste it to see if it has enough salt. If not, you add another bit to your taste."

Next, "When the salsa is ready, you're going to rub it all over the meat and wrap it up like a tamale in aluminum foil. When you have wrapped it up so well that you're sure no water will get to it to change the flavor, you put it in a steamer pot. It could be a big pot, it could be a small pot." Maiana looks at me and says to Jessica, "If he is thinking of making five pounds, he would wrap it like two big tamales. He could cut it in two, three, four pieces so it will cook faster."

Jessica explains the next step, elaborating on her mother's instructions: "You have all your stuff in there. You put water on it to make sure the water level is up high or where it can cover it all." "You can either use the fire— you can either do it yourself with wood," I recall the homemade concrete block and metal stove in the backyard, "or you can use one of those stoves, the outside stoves."

Experience and knowledge of ingredients determines cooking time. "It depends on the animal," Maiana says. "If the animal is young, like one year old, maybe eleven months, in two hours, it's ready. If the animal is older, and the heat is going pretty high, then from three to four hours." The pot remains covered throughout the process: "If it happens that the meat is still tough, you can keep checking it, like a tamale, check the water to make sure it doesn't burn." Jessica adds that the volume of water will reduce as the *barbacoa* cooks but that vigilance is imperative to prevent burning.

At last, the *barbacoa de cordero* is done! "You take it out, you put it on a table or wherever you want, open it up, and let it get cool. It can be cold or just warm enough so you can stand to shred it, because now it has to be shredded like *barbacoa*," Maiana holds the end in sight. "The flavors from the salsa are already cooked in, you don't put anything else on it. The meat has consumed all the seasoning." For serving, she says, "you have to make your own spicy salsa or whatever you want, in another bowl, separately, to put on the *barbacoa* afterwards. With rice and tortillas."

I think I can manage this, but I am secretly relieved by the reality that I do not have Hog Island mutton on hand. Some things are for the best.

Maiana is not done. She reprises the *sopa de cordero*, a simpler recipe and one that makes use of every bit of the *barbacoa*: "Where the meat was boiled, the flavor gets distilled. It's the juice that is left in the pot when you take the meat out, the juices come out of the tamales, and the juices are in the water, in the pot. That's why you need to keep it from burning up. That juice, I move it to another pot, a smaller pot. I add another bit of water. You put in onions, chopped, garbanzo, . . . diced carrots. Little potatoes, if you want, diced potatoes. And that is it. That is your soup that you're going to make. And the diced onion, chopped cilantro, and if you want a green chili, diced, you add them after the soup has been served in the cup or bowl, you put it on top. And lime."

Our conversation began with Maiana and Jessica walking me through the instructions for *barbacoa* and the *sopa*. I ask, "How did she learn to cook the *barbacoa*?" Maiana speaks; Jessica translates that she worked in a restaurant in Mexico City. This is not what I expected. Jessica continues, "She wasn't the cook, but she usually helped around in the kitchen." "In the restaurant," Jessica elaborates, "she learned how to . . . ," and pivots mid-thought, "like where they live, they didn't eat meat often. They ate it, but it was once in a while." Maiana's impoverished family lacked even the resources to purchase or grow ingredients we assume are part of every-day Latin American cuisine; for example, chilies. As Jessica says, Maiana "couldn't cook food with them because they couldn't afford it." In the restaurant, "she learned how to cook all of the different meats and how to cook different food with the meat. Where she's from, they usually just cook beans, rice, vegetables." The family's everyday diet in the absence of chilies and other seasonings was strikingly plain.

Our conversation veers in an unanticipated direction. I ask not only, "How did she learn to cook?" but also, "How did she learn to invent?" After all, the Hog Island sheep from Robert was an unanticipated gift. Jessica poses the question. Maiana's answer is succinct, "Hunger is tough!"

I ask Maiana to explain, and she responds through Jessica: "She says, because hunger is hard, that she learns how to, or tries to invent new food, either for her to eat, to consume, or to make money from it. She usually makes different foods and sells it."

I ask if Maiana and her family ever enjoyed *barbacoa* in Guatemala. "No," Maina says, "not there. We didn't have money to make this type of food. We made it here. Those with money cooked it for parties, like weddings and birthdays." Then she offers a parting observation. "I would recommend that everyone would learn to cook, because your flavors and the well-being of the family depend on that. The spirit of the family, yes. Because the flavors of the food, they keep the family together, because everyone likes it. The only thing that was memorable to me was a *barbacoa* of the little creatures. It was a birthday, it wasn't just a regular dinner. But all my family was at peace, happy, and they said, 'Mmm! This is delicious food!'"

A CHEF'S RECIPE FOR HOME

EASTERN SHORE OF VIRGINIA LAMB (OR MUTTON) BARBACOA

Amy Brandt and Gricelda Torres Segura, Amy B Catering, Cheriton, Virginia

Makes 15 servings

For the sauce
- ½ cup canola oil
- 12 guajilla peppers, seeds and stem removed
- 2 ancho peppers, seeds and stem removed
- 1 garlic head, peeled
- ½ medium onion, peeled and quartered
- 8 allspice berries, divided
- 6 tablespoons cider vinegar
- 2 tablespoons brown sugar
- 1 teaspoon salt
- ¼ teaspoon whole cumin seed, toasted and ground
- ¼ teaspoon ground cinnamon
- 1 teaspoon oregano

For the lamb (or mutton)
- 1 package banana leaves
- 6 fig leaves, divided
- 4 mandarin oranges, cut across the middle into ½-inch-thick slices, divided
- 6 bay leaves, divided
- 5 pounds boneless leg of lamb
- Salt to taste

For serving
- Homemade corn tortillas
- Diced onion
- Chopped fresh cilantro
- Roasted salsa verde

To prepare the sauce

Heat the oil in a heavy-gauge sauté pan over medium heat. Fry the peppers until they turn a bit brighter in color, about 10 or so seconds per side. Place them in a blender along with the remaining sauce ingredients. Purée until smooth and then strain. Discard the solids.

To prepare the lamb (or mutton)

Preheat the oven to 325°.

Place about 1 inch of water in the bottom of a large pot. Place a rack in the bottom of the pot to elevate the lamb above the water. Line the pot with the banana leaves, overlapping them in a crisscross pattern to completely cover the rack and sides of the pot, letting the leaves extend at least 8 inches above the pot. Place 3 of the fig leaves in the bottom of the pot, then half of the sliced mandarin oranges, and then 3 of the bay leaves.

Remove the lamb from its packaging and rinse. Pat it dry and place it in a large bowl. Add about 2 cups of the sauce to the bowl and rub the sauce on the inside and outside of the lamb. Season with salt.

Pour ½ cup of the sauce on top of the leaves in the pot. Add the lamb and place the remaining oranges and bay leaves on top, along with another ½ cup of the sauce. Place the remaining fig leaves over the meat. Fold the banana leaves over the lamb and tuck the ends under it.

Cover and cook the lamb for 2–2½ hours. The meat is done when it can be easily shred. The sauce from the cooking will get mixed in with the meat.

To serve

Serve warm with the corn tortillas, diced onion, cilantro, and roasted salsa verde.

Drum Head Soup

Over dinner one evening, our neighbor Jon Moore spins stories of his fishing adventures on the Eastern Shore of Virginia. Jon describes a youthful trek with friends from his home in Princess Anne, Maryland, to Cape Charles in quest of drum and, at day's end, his discovery of drum head soup. He is laughing with remembered delight even before he begins: "There were four of us going fishing down in Cape Charles. About four in the afternoon, the drum started biting. We got the drum onboard, and we decided to hang onto the smaller of the two, and I let the one I had go." The fishing party left Cape Charles and headed north to Princess Anne, where Jon was living. "We put the fish on ice and let it sit on ice overnight, and then the next morning Jim and I got up and went out and proceeded to clean that black drum. Now, black drum is not that easy to clean. It's got scales the size of a silver dollar, and you have to get those off to actually fillet the fish." Folks on the lower Eastern Shore of Virginia refer to filleting drum as siding.

"So," Jon continues, gesturing the action in his story, "we went and got a garden hoe and scaled that fish in the road, right by that drainage ditch for the rainwater." Then Jon turns to the heart of the action: "While we were doing that, this black man came rolling in named Leroy. He gets out of the car and starts talking to me, and he's real concerned about what I'm doing with this fish. I said, 'It seems like maybe you would like some of this. We'd be happy to give it to you.' He goes, 'All I want is the drum head.' I go, 'Okay, that will be fine.' I went ahead and filleted the fish, and we put the drum head in the trunk of his car, and he went off happy as a clam. But before he did, I asked him . . . , 'If we get one, do you want me to bring you a whole drum?' He went, 'Oh, man, you'd do that?' I said, 'I'd do that.'"

Jon, laughing, pauses to catch his breath and resumes, "We went back fishing the next night, and when we were fishing, 265 we caught a drum and decided to take that back over to his house. When I drove up and asked if Leroy was there, the biggest black man I'd ever seen in my life came to the front door. I said, 'Is Leroy here?' That guy said, 'What do you want with him?' I got that cold feeling down my back. This might not be the right place to be. However, he goes, 'What do you want with him?' 'I have a drum for him.' 'Oh! You're drum man!' 'Yes, I am.' So he came out, got the drum, and he proceeded to clean the drum in his backyard. So I said, 'Well, this is kind of interesting that you're that excited about these drum. What do you do with them?' He goes, 'We make drum head soup.'" I said, 'No kidding?' He says, 'So we've got two heads now and fish for the rest of the family.'"

Jon's encounter with drum head soup sent me on a quest for recollections of the dish and ultimately to a rich and enduring cuisine of one-pot meals. Cuisine is experience and emotion, embodiment and immediacy, custom and invention, destiny and storytelling. When people talk about cuisine, they speak about themselves and the pleasures of the table and the company they keep. Cuisine is as much about where and how stories are told as it is about the stories themselves. Jon's tale of drum head soup reminds me that an awareness of cuisine resides in the pleasures of tasting—tasting and experiencing food from its cultivation to consummation, what gets marketed as "farm to table." The idea of cuisine captures how we choose to locate and consume the essence of place through food and story. What I learn is that drum head soup entails powerful histories of white and black, rich and poor, want and renewal.

The black drum (*Pogonias cromis*), Alan Davidson writes in *North Atlantic Seafood*, is "a silvery fish with brassy lustre, turning grey after death." From April through June, drum spawn in the waters off Cape Charles and as adults are found on both the Bayside and the Seaside of our narrow peninsula. Vertically striped black and silver, juvenile drum sneak into my oyster cages every summer. The lucky ones will live forty to fifty years. A member of the Sciaenidae family, drum is related to croakers, weakfish, kingfish, and the iconic spot; all share a general ability to make a variety of drumming or croaking sounds. Although black drum and red drum (the fish of blackened redfish) swim through the same waters and are members of the same family, they are different species—perhaps best thought of as tasty cousins.

As one chef's guide notes, "The common name 'Drum fish' comes from their ability to make a drumming sound during courtship or when pulled from the water. They do this by rubbing special muscles against an air bladder thus producing the drum-like sound." When artist Howard Pyle introduced drum to his *Harper's* readers in 1879, he emphasized their percussive presence: "The drum somewhat resembles a large black-fish, and receives its name from a peculiar drumming noise it makes under the water, probably caused by the sudden expulsion of air from the air-sac or bladder. On a calm day their smothered thum! thum! can be distinctly heard in all directions." Cookbook author Davidson adds, "Its scales are also remarkable. They are large and silvery and very firmly attached, so that a really heavy blade (or even an axe) is needed to get them off." I've seen those scales, the size of a twenty-five-cent piece, recovered from local archaeological sites dating to the 1600s. The drum's heavily scaled skin and booming sonic attributes may not translate into recipes, but they fascinate culinarians. Me, too. The black drum—the variety destined for Jon's evocation of drum head soup—is one of the larger fish in the Chesapeake Bay, occasionally ranging up to a hundred pounds. Compared to larger sixty-five- to seventy-pound fish, though, H. M. Arnold, proprietor of the Bayford oyster house, notes his preference for smaller fish, "twenty-five to thirty pounders, they're better eating."

Drum are a seasonal fishery. "If you were really lucky, you could catch one the end of March, but it's usually the first or the middle of April when they first show up," offers Ron Crumb, the former owner of Paul's Restaurant in the village of Cheriton, once known as Sunnyside. "It depends on the water temperature." "There used to be a little competition in the town of Oyster," he adds, "it was two hundred, two hundred fifty people that lived there. It was another two or three hundred that worked the shucking houses, but the local watermen, end of March, first of April, they used to have bragging rights who could catch the first drum." For Danny Doughty, whose family operated a succession of fish houses in Willis Wharf, Exmore, and on the highway near Painter, the arrival of the drum carried huge significance. "It was the cornucopia of food! It was anticipated like an event from God to run up the coast here." Danny charts the drum migration: "They would hit some in Mississippi, they'd hit some in Louisiana, they'd hit some down in North Carolina, they'd hit some all down in the South coming up—and then, when they got here, they'd hit their zenith because we had all our local fishermen. Then we would get them out of Delaware Bay, and then we would get them out of New Jersey."

The coming of the drum signaled the arrival of the new year, and folks, black and white alike, looked forward to their arrival. "It was almost a sacredness about it," Danny remembers. "They understood this passing of this fish coming through here in early spring that it was like they couldn't miss out on it. It was a big part of their social interaction with each other and the surrounding areas." Still, the appetite for black drum remained an Eastern Shore preference. "Drum fish in this area," Ron Crumb observes, "is really popular," qualifying that popularity with the caveat, "It's more of a regional favorite fish." H. M. Arnold, talking with friends one early December evening in the warmth of the Bayford oyster house, maps the geography of a taste for drum with precision. "Everything was local. Nobody eats drum north of the Maryland line and south of Virginia Beach, hardly. Even in Carolina they don't eat black drum."

Folks fished for drum using a variety of techniques that evolved over time. Howard Pyle reported on fishing for drum along Virginia's barrier islands in 1879: "They are taken with a harpoon, which the fishermen throw with the greatest accuracy, striking the fish at a considerable distance below the water. When the fish is struck, the pole comes loose from the gaff of the harpoon, to which it is attached by a cord some six or eight feet long; this then serves as a float, constantly drawing the fish to the surface until it is exhausted. The drum, strong and lusty, sometimes runs for a mile or more, dragging the pole through the water with surprising velocity. Away goes fish, and fisherman in pursuit, up and down the channel, until at length, fairly tired out, the victim is captured and hauled into the boat. We were told that these fish are sometimes taken weighing over a hundred pounds."

Watermen on both the Bayside and the Seaside used hand lines, a wooden spool wound with line. Pete West, with his granddaughter Hannah listening attentively, remembers, "It used to be that there was a lot of hand-lining. It's just a ball of twine with hooks on it; you throw it over and just use your hands. I like two hooks. One fish chases another fish. That's the way I look at it. Right down here after the war, we were hand-lining off there, and there was a mussel bed in the bay. My daddy hooked a big cobia down there. It came out of the water, it was at least six-foot long, if not more! He had a hand line, and he grabbed it and he cut his hand. I can hear him to this day, 'Run, you son of a bitch! Go!' He had to let him go. He cut his finger right to the bone. I fished for drum with them. You'd get your hand cut up good. I know how we used to hook drum—go to the Coca-Cola plant and get a box of ice picks. Stick that in the deck and tie a line around it with the big bait, and when he grabbed it, he'd flip it—he'd flip himself. It was up to you to get him in. You'd just push it into the wood and tie it onto the top, and he'd flip. You always had extra line."

Luther Moore recalls how in the days before outboard motors, watermen in quest of drum and other fish would sail out of the creeks and landings along the Seaside. "We used to enjoy those bateaux, because I'll tell you where we were fishing like that, we'd have to go in the middle of the night sometimes on the tide. Go out with the tide. Go down to Cedar Creek, we'd call it. Cedar Creek is near to where we would fish down near the inlet.

We were a long ways from there, because we would stop up in the marsh where it would be protection if the wind blowed or anything. Then we'd throw our anchor along the windward shore. Throw the anchor out. Take those sails and wrap up in them and go to sleep until the next morning when it come light. Light good so you could see. Went on down the spit and fished. Hand lines. Only used one hook. That's all we ever knowed to use. One hook. We caught trout, spot, hogfish. Plenty of fish, every kind then. We had a certain season for every fish, every kind of fish." Drum included.

Many gillnetted. "One of the funnest ways to catch drum is using gill nets," waterman Andrew Bunce explains. "What we call drifting for them. We'll take about two fifty-pound shots of net. We'll run them out on the seaside in the inlets right before dark. You'll run them out. Sit there and drift in your boat. Stop and have a little cocktail while we're waiting. If it's real still and the drum are there, you can hear them. Drumming on the bottom, what they call it. You can hear them, 'Bhoomm, bhoomm, bhoomm.'

You can sit there and listen to them. It's pretty neat. You'll sit there for about an hour, you'll drift on out of the inlet with the ebb tide. Sometimes you'll catch the flood tide. Sometimes you catch some, sometimes you don't." Commercially, Ron remembers, "They usually had ten-inch gill nets, and the smaller ones would go through. Years later the guys found out they could go down to an eight-inch gill net and catch smaller ones and catch more, but Dad was always conservative. He said, 'Leave a little bit for next year.' He never got greedy. He just wanted to make a living, where some people will take the last crab if they thought they could sell it."

The drum emerged as a sporting fish beginning in the Victorian era when chartered boats would sail out of seaside hamlets in pursuit of the large fish: "Drum-fishing is coming on at the north end of Hog Island, between the locations of Revel's Island and Broadwater Club, the latter in Northampton county. Drum fish weighing from 25lbs. to 75lbs. are caught in great abundance in the latter part of May and first few days of June. Last year one boat would often bring up forty to sixty, the result of one day's fishing. It is a common thing for two or three men to be hung to different drums on the same boat at the same time, cutting and sheering the boat in all directions. As a food fish for immediate eating the drum is fine." Other visitors to the islands would surf cast from shore: "We had a taste of drum fishing, casting a line baited with half a crab, weighted down at the end with a lead sinker into the surf. Alas, the big fellows were not biting and most of the time the line twisted and kicked until we had to admit that casting a drum line is not for the uninitiated. Perhaps it is just as well, for had we caught a drum . . . we would never have stopped telling the world about it. In ten years that fish would have graduated to the school of whales."

Catching drum was only the first step. Processing the massive, heavily armored fish came next. When Jon spoke of scaling the fish in the road with a hoe, he didn't exaggerate. "You knock the scales off, but you got to use a spade or a hoe, and then you just hang him up on a pole by his tail. And you just cut around it like you would a fillet," Andrew Bunce notes. "You just cut down a little bit. You cut a hole right in the little tail part and then you rip the whole side right off, and it comes off just like you cut it with a knife." Theodore Peed agrees, "The hardest thing is the scaling. That's the hardest thing to do, is scaling them. As far as cutting them up, it's nothing. All you need is a nice sharp knife. Zip, zap, zoom—it's gone!"

Danny Doughty walks through the cleaning process in detail. He starts with the arrival of the drum at the fish house. "As they brought it in, we'd weigh it," he began, outlining how the fish were sorted for shipping to other nearby markets in Maryland and Delaware or tagged and frozen or cleaned on the spot for immediate sale: "It was let over to me and some of the other ones. Just start cutting them as fast as you could, dressing them. We would have someone on the floor with a V-shape you'd put right to the wall so the head would go in. You'd take a flat shovel, just hit them, get that, flip them over, do the same thing. Then they had a piece of crab pot rope . . . and make a loop out of it. You put that loop and swing it around the tail of the drum and pulled the other side up, which made it, when you pulled it, tight around the tail, and then you pick it up and put it on a hook, and that's hanging in front of you. I've done this ten million times."

He takes a breath, "You first cut a little hole up by the tail about an inch to two inches so you can get your finger in. But you start cutting at the top of the tail, follow the sides of the drum all the way to the stomach to the back of the head and the gills, then come back up around the other side where the fins and all are, back up to the tail, and then you would make a cut inside, sliding it right down the edge of the backbone as tight as you could get it so that you don't miss no meat that you have to. Then you get 75 percent of it with the fillet knives, and then you take your finger and go snatch it off." Danny makes the ripping motion as he relives the action in his story, "and then it would rip right off, and then you'd throw it in a box."

As H. M. remembers, "We used to sell at the family fish market. He would clean them there. We'd clean them, and he'd give us a dollar a pound cleaned. Of course, that market would just be saturated. So then he'd buy them from you for thirty cents a pound, and he'd clean them."

Not everyone possessed the means to catch fish. Their needs were met by fish trucks that drove through the communities, in particular the African American communities, as described by Big Mo Young, who worked in the Terry family's Willis Wharf shellfish business. "Back in the days," he says, "you had guys that rode around, and that was their business. They sold fish. Whatever kind of fish they could get, they would sell to you. We never caught those kinds of fish, but a lot of people back in those days just rode around with trucks and boxes on the back of them, and ice on top of them." "The guy was blowing his horn," Big Mo laughs gigantically. "He'd ride down the road slow, blowing his horn. That's what he did. That was his living, his way of making a living. He sold fish. They would only do it on Friday and Saturday because that's when they knew that everybody would get paid. On Fridays and Saturdays. Most of the time by the end of the day he done sold every piece of fish that he had on that truck."

Jon Moore, driving home at the end of a day recreational fishing, sold fish in the African American neighborhood near his home: "We would go out and fish in Tangier Sound, and I would catch all sorts of sea trout, croaker, etc. And not too far down from where I lived was a black neighborhood. They loved the croaker, they called it a hardhead. I would go in there, and I would have a cooler full of hardhead or croaker, and I would basically charge them twenty-five cents a fish. The ladies would come out. They had pans. And they were squabbling over who would be first, 'Get out of the way! That's my fish!' I would usually have anywhere from ten to twenty fish in there. There's be four or five women out there wanting those fish, and they'd take them in the house and clean them, and away they went with them."

Youngsters sold fish to neighbors as well—sometimes with unfortunate outcomes, as related by Pete West: "When I was little, we used to go hand-lining and I had a little red wagon; that's the first fish I ever sold." Elnora Giddens and Tom Collins, who lived near him in Jamesville, he recollects, "were my two best customers. I could take the wagon to them and sell six or eight big hardheads for a quarter. Six for a quarter. Great big—all you wanted. We'd go catch them. Everybody ate them; first fish I ever sold." Then Pete pauses and announces, "I'll tell you a story you can write in your book: We went hand-line fishing. We caught so many hardheads, we had to make two poles, and we strung them up—we had them on our shoulders. We were way down on Nassawadox Creek. A thunderstorm broke out when we were coming back; we had these fish, and we took our clothes off. We were stark naked. We were coming back and a lady looked out the window and saw us and yelled at us. We dropped the damn fish and took off. We dropped them right in her driveway, about two hundred yards from James-ville. We were a mile from the water and we were tired—we just dropped them. We took off." Upon their return, fully clothed, the fish were gone.

Theodore Peed was in his garage kitchen cleaning up some cast-iron pots and frying pans, smoking a thin cigar, and relaxing with his dog, Russell. "When I was coming up," he starts, "black people didn't catch no drum. The whites, they would give us drum. They didn't want the carcass—just give us the backbone and the head. They'd give us some nice meat, too." "What my grandmother would do," he reflects, "was she'd make stew with it. She would put it in a big roasting pan—the head and the backbone. Season it down. That time the only seasoning we had was salt and pepper. Got me? We'd do that, cut up onions in it and dice up potatoes like in quarters. Put that in the oven for about an hour and a half. You'd take it out. What we'd do is put water in the pan with it. Then what we'd do is take a little flour and make a little thickener. We didn't want it watery, but just a little thick. Season it down, thicken it just right. Sometimes we would use instead of potatoes, we would boil a pan of rice. It's real simple."

H. M. Arnold, Mr. Peed's friend, captures the basics of drum head stew. "You get a recipe for fish chowder. You can find that pretty well anywhere. The drum, behind his head and gills, behind in the back there, it's an awful lot of meat. When we sided it off, we just didn't mess with it. And the back-bone, of course, when you sided it off, in between the backbone, it's meat. They would chop that up and boil it, and that gave you your seasoning. It was like marrow out of a cow. They would do the same thing with fish back-bone, and that would boil the meat out of it, take the bone out, and then they would chop up the meat also and boil that in there with it. And you had almost like a stew or chowder, and you'd add your potatoes. Just like clam chowder—not a whole lot of difference."

Danny closely associates drum head soup with the African American community and poorer white families: "It was not that big of a jump from poor whites to the black community. They were entangled in it, but the black communities took it to another level. I think white people were thankful for it, but black people felt it was almost a spiritual thing to help them have food to sustain them through time." Danny emphasizes how cooks translated the throwaway pieces of the drum: "The greatest pieces of it were the pieces most people would throw away—the white people would throw away. They really did. Every piece of it! The tail fins, the underneath fins, the side fins, all up in the head—the meat all up in there—they would take it down until there was nothing left." He expounds, "The head would be cleaned and chopped. The cheek meat cut out. The fins cut off. That would make the most awesome base for a stew or chowder or whatever. Of course, you would throw some chopped-up bacon or bacon ends and pieces (it's usually the seconds) in there to give it a little more flavor and all. The little bit of meat that was left on the bone and all that would have come off into the water, in the base of what they were doing. That would go on in those pots. Onion was the seasoning, and potato was a filler. That flavor would go through them, especially as it sits for a while. You could literally eat off that for as long as until it ran out. You could stretch it a long way. I remember going in people's houses. They would run them pots for days and days and days. Keep adding a little more to it, a little more to it. It would just keep getting better with time, especially in the winter months."

I ask Danny Doughty to walk me through the process of making drum head soup. He begins with the fish and carefully recounts each step: "We're going to start off and say we've got a forty-pound drum fish. That's kind of not too big, but fairly decent. First thing, of course, you clean it." The fillets sorted into boxes, Danny turns his attention to breaking down the "scrap" that forms the base for drum head soup: "The drum has such a heavy body bone structure that it was pretty substantial, so they would take a hatchet and chop the head off and then in about four- to five-inch increments cut blocks of the backbone until they got all the way to the tail. Then they took that and put it in a basin of water, and then they'd start on the head, cut-

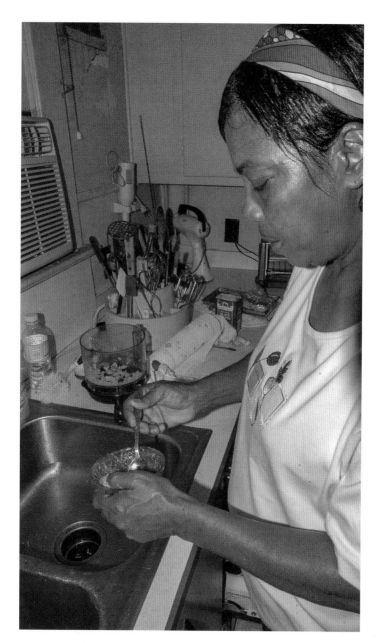

Violet
Trower,
Belle
Haven,
Virginia.

ting all the fleshy parts out of the inside of the head on the top of the crest of the head, all in the cheekbones, and anywhere there was any flesh or any bone structure that would give flavor. They'd get it right down to where there was not much left at all. That was for stew or like a soup, chowder, depending how thick you made it."

At last, he gets to the soup: "Some people would intentionally use enough

Irish potato in it to give it a more thicker consistency. Let the potato break down enough so that it starts to granulate a little bit. It would do it with time after you reheated it anyway. A lot of times they would add a little more water to it, a little more salt, a little pepper, or whatever. Taking a big pot, probably like a couple-gallon pot, they would put so many pieces of the backbone, maybe the tail, a couple of the fins, and maybe some of the meat out of the head—and a little bit of salt in the water. They would start to boil that, and they would add most of the time some chopped-up bacon ends and pieces and put in there. Then they would use one or two onions they would cut up and put in it. They would take white potatoes, peel them, cut them up like cubed up, and put them in there. Let that sit on the stove and stir it every so often, because a lot of them would use enamel pans and they would stick really bad if a potato would sit down on the bottom. They would kind of stir it and add a little salt to tweak it a little bit. That was the main course. Actually, people would come to love that as much as they would the best part. They would prefer the scraps in the soup or the chowder, depending on the consistency, or a stew. The less water you had in it, it was more of a stew, but most people used it more—it was almost between a stew and a soup." "And biscuits," Danny turns to thoughts of dinner, "just regular lard tin biscuits, little hard, worked biscuits. Oh, my god! Even if after an amount of time you might get tired of it, it was awesome. It was just good, so good." Danny concludes his recitation, sharing the voice of experience, "I have had it every conceivable way!"

Violet Trower grew up eating drum head stew. "Oh, my god, that is the best eating! A lot of people go to the store or fish market. We black people go to the fish market and ask simply for big fish heads and fish bones, the backbones. That's where the sweetness is, next to the bone of a fish. That's why a lot of times we don't like to fillet fish, we want to have fish with the bone on it, because it tastes so much better . . . but a lot of people don't like to pick bones. I like taking fish, bake it in the oven with onion and surround that fish, bones and stuff, with white potato and sweet potato. That is so delicious. When you cook it, it's going to fall apart. It's going to cook enough, where you are going to pick it out. The fish head, believe me, has a lot of meat. Especially the big fish, like drum heads. Oh, my goodness, there's enough meat there for four or five people to eat off one head. You take the gills out. The eyes. A lot of people like fish eyeballs. My daddy used to love fish eyeballs. Oh, my goodness! My little niece, she was raised up around my daddy so much, and he used to love fish eyeballs, and she said, 'Oh, Violet, keep the head on the fish because I want my eyeballs.' Oh, my god, it's good eating. You'd be surprised the seasoning things have that you wouldn't eat."

Drum on the menu at the Exmore Diner, Exmore, Virginia.

Soup is not the only drum option.

Drum ribs, Theodore Peed inhales, "My friend got me hooked on them. I don't skin them. That skin will pull right off after you cook. Got me some grease, deep-fry him. Them ribs, hah, those ribs! But you want them fresh, though." Amplifying a gourmand's perspective for the uninitiated, he claims, "A black drum got the best ribs than a red drum. You get a big black drum, his ribs are thick; a red drum's ribs is thin." It's good to know these things.

"The ribs were taken off of the fillets, and then the ribs were prepared." Danny describes the local delicacy that originated in the African American communities but has gained broader favor in recent years: "Some people baked those. We always fried them. I loved them crisp, fried, a little light dusting of breading on them, and then some really hot oil, like 375 degrees."

"I'll say that up until the last ten years we never ate them," says H. M. "Black folks ate them. We used to clean drum down here. We'd have fifty, seventy-five drum a day, and we'd clean them right here on the dock." He describes the scene on the Bayford dock: "Folks would come down and get the backbone, the head, and they'd get all kinds of meat off that and make soup and stews. And ribs, of course, when we'd sell it by the side, we always left the ribs on. Well, most people that I knew who bought it, they'd always cut the ribs off. Never ate them. In the last ten years, everybody's fighting for them now. I never knew they were that good. My dad would eat them sometimes, but he never told me how good they were." When drum ribs appear on the menu at the Exmore Diner, customers come.

"I cook drum." Vera Williams has a hungry look in her eye as she recites a preparation nearly identical to Theodore Peed's: "Bake it in the oven with onions (cut-up onions) and potatoes in it. Put it in the oven and bake it for a while. Then take it out, mix up a little cornstarch, and pour it in the juice and make it a little thick. And that's baked drum." For drum head stew, "They do that same way. Put it on the stove, put water in it, put the head in it. Let it boil a while until it gets kind of soft. Add onions and potatoes in that—and that's it. Put a little salt and pepper in it, a little bacon grease in it—that's it. I learned to cook from my grandmother and all them way back then. Or you can stew the drum ribs, put it in some Reynolds wrap, some butter in it, put the ribs in there, put a little salt and pepper on it, wrap it in the Reynolds wrap, put it on the grill, stew it there, let it cook down. It's real good, too, that way. Or you can fry the ribs, too. A lot of people eat them fried."

Tim and Dorothy Bailey, assembling drum sandwiches for the Juneteenth celebration at the county airfield near Weirwood, shared their recipe for baked drum as Black Elvis played to the crowd in the background.

BAKED DRUM
A slab of drum cut in sections
Butter and water in a pan
Cook 20 minutes
Onions, celery, potatoes to your taste, just mix it up
Flour mixed in water

Remove the fish and leave the vegetables

Stir until thick, you know when it's done because the fish is flaky

Ron Crumb and Kay Crumb Downing remembered drum cooked in a roasting pan on top of the parlor stove: "He would take a drum and he would side it, and if he was frying it, they would steak it up. If they were baking it, a lot of times they would just take that whole side and put it in the big roasting pan and just slow-baked it. Most of the time they would bake it in like an inch or so of water to keep it moist. Drum doesn't have a lot of fat, so you don't want to overcook it. It's kind of like a tuna if you overcook it. It's really a delicious fish unless it's overcooked. Drums are kind of the same way. They would put them in big roasting pans. Sometimes she would actually bake it in the oven, but most of the time for convenience, it was—because you know she was going to have dumplings or something with it—you did the roasting pans. She would do it on the stove. The family oil stove in the living room. She would start it first thing in the morning and just put it on there, and it was kind of like a slow cooker. It would just cook for three, four, five, six hours. It was a big oil-burning stove, and it basically heated the house. It stood up there, and it had a control. You could jack it up or turn it down. She just put it there, and it was, by the end of the day, it was just bubbling." Ron makes bubble noises, "But it was cooking."

Arlen Church baked fish stews made with hardheads or croakers. "The croakers, they call them, you baked them with onions, then she'd slice some." Arlen claps her hands, "Fat meat, they call it, cut it in little, small pieces, and put it in the oven. She would bake them with onions and this fat meat I'm telling you about, and then she'd take some flour and beat that up real good, and then pour that in there and run them back into the oven and let them brown." Stewing, frying, and roasting drum and other large fish often overlapped, a blurring of culinary borders that Sean Hart, owner of the Exmore Diner, acknowledged: "Typically, most folks that's how they cook larger rockfish. They bake it with potatoes and onions, salt and pepper, and that type of stuff."

Big Mo Young recalls a variation that combines frying and stewing: "I'll eat basically any kind of fish. But the best fish that I like is drum fish. And the way my mom used to cook drum fish, man, she used to fry it and smother it down in gravy. A brown gravy. After you cook the fish, you steam it there, you put it in a frying pan, you make your little gravy up, and you let that fish simmer in it. Let it simmer, turn it a few times. And by the time that the gravy gets done, you know that fish is already done because you already done steamed it. Any kind of grease you can get. Lard, meat, any kind of grease. You know how it was back in those days. It's very rarely that you'd use bacon. The only time you used bacon was in the morning. It's very rarely that you cooked with bacon in your supper meals. Usually you used fat meat."

He turns to the particulars of drum head stew. "Sometimes you have people cooking their fish with their heads still on them because people used to love eating the back of the head of the fish, which is a lot of good meat, it's just like making a soup. What you do, you just drop the drum head in the water and add whatever you want to it. And just let it cook."

FISH STEW
Two slices salt pork diced—fry golden brown
1 large or 2 small onions chopped
About 1 pound fish
Put all in a frying pan and cook slow about thirty minutes in just enough water to cover fish. Remove fish and make flour thickening and put white sauce on fish. Thin sliced onions may be added to onions and fish.

"I'm partial to drum, sand mullet, and spot," H. M. says, but "drum is just a good meat. A good thick pork chop. I usually fry it. I'll usually bread it. I'll cut it in good inch pieces, and I'll skin it. I'll take the skin off of it, and we'll bread it and sit it on wax paper and let it absorb the bread. We drop it in a deep fryer, and when it's brown we take it out. And it's good on the grill."

Janice Weatherly Walters, whose family frequented Danny Doughty's family's fish store and who still brings Danny the occasional gift of yeast rolls, describes a dish of drum and dumplings: "Fish and dumplings is what my grandmother used to do. Grandmother would take that fish and take that bone." Janice pauses, "We being so many people, she would take that bone and make, and boil that fish, and the broth from that fish, she would put it aside, and she would make up her dough for dumplings, and she would use that base of the fish for her dumplings. Those fish bones, we ate those fish bones, we worked on those fish bones, they were just bones, but it was good."

Janice introduces the possibility of drum cracklings. "We saved the rest of the fish for another meal. You save the actual meat for another meal. You also take that skin. There are several ways you can eat out of that piece of drum. You take that skin off, pull that skin off, Grandfather did. You take that skin, and you put it in a pot with some lard. And deep-fry it. That's how we had our crackling. Or we had our meat skins off of that drum. Take that drum, clean that drum real good, put it on this big board. Nail it down. Let it dry, and after it dries, then he would take and cut it with a knife in little blocks, and that was our little treat that we had. Cut it in squares and fry it. If we were good, we got a treat."

Then there were side dishes. Janice itemizes familiar options: "The fish and dumplings, I'm telling you, with the juice of the dumplings you put a little bit of that flour—remember that ten-pound bag of flour—you use some of that for your thickening. You put that in the pot, and that's how you're going to get that broth. She'd take white potatoes, boil them, make them up as cream potatoes. Then she'd take some string beans. You got a meal, there's our meal. On the side we got biscuits. If we don't have biscuits, we have corn bread or sweet potato biscuits."

For Theodore Peed, the season for drum fish coincided with the strawberry harvest. "Drum fish and strawberries. You know drum and strawberries run about the same time. In May. You'd get some fried drum and probably another side, like we used to eat a lot of white potatoes. White potatoes and onions. I don't want no white potatoes that don't have onions in them!" He grins with remembered pleasure, "That's right! Bowl of strawberries on the side. It was a real good dessert anyhow, but all of them went right together."

In its day, drum was a menu mainstay, and it's still out there. Arthur Webb advertised drum on the menu of his Exmore sub shop, which opened onto the old Cameo Room, a disco-era hotspot: "At the restaurant here, I used to sell drum. I'd have drum for lunch—I'd do a drum fish sandwich." A drum sandwich, I agree, is truly a wonderful experience! Arthur's cook Dorothy Baines, eulogized for chicken and dumplings that would "smack your momma," made a drum fish dinner that he exclaimed was "good eating!"

"They could get like five or six variations from that fish, from a soupy soup to a kind of a stew to the drum ribs to the drum either being baked with sliced steaks or fried steaks," Danny Doughty summarizes an array of drum possibilities. "I mean after that drum was processed and cooked and if you put it out on a table, it would fill a table by the different ways they would approach and use every bit of it." With strawberries and biscuits, the nuance of cuisine.

Fish stews connect with a larger tradition of one-pot meals on the Eastern Shore of Virginia, mapping a coming together of traditions including American Indian, African, and European. Fish, freshwater and salt, were foraged by enslaved people and provisioned by white masters. Variations recorded throughout the South describe a mainstay that made use of every edible bit of the fish along with the additions of onions, potatoes, and other ingredients, including tomatoes. Farther up the Eastern Shore peninsula, African American cooks seasoned the dish with fish peppers, a cultivar imported into the Chesapeake Bay country from the Caribbean in the 1800s and used in a variety of seafood dishes. West African fish stews and soups remain standard fare in a global kitchen. And then there are all those European one-pot fish stews, bouillabaisse not the least among them. James Peterson in *Fish and Shellfish* introduces a New England fish chowder made with cod, instructing his readers to ask the fishmonger for the head and bones. Reading his directions, I think of customers at the Doughtys' fish store and folks on the Bayford dock requesting drum heads, fins, and backbones. "It's mostly a black tradition," Theodore Peed declares. "Like I said, we couldn't catch them. We had to get mostly what was called scraps."

Charlie and Fred "Picky" Weatherly sit in office chairs at H. M. Terry's premises in Willis Wharf overlooking the great marshes stretching out to the barrier islands. They connect those early soups and stews to a necessity for one-pot meals that fed large African American families such as their own. Charlie describes these dishes as "pots," linking them to the larger family of chicken or black duck and dumplings: "They knew how to make pots. We grew up on pots—they put whatever they had in the pot to feed the family. That's what I mean by pot. We didn't have all this single stuff here—just this and that. The pot, if they had chicken—might not have but one—what they would do with it is they would boil that chicken, cut them up in little pieces and make chicken and dumplings for the whole family." Exactly like drum head soup. "That's where we grew up on dried beans, rice, all stuff like that. Like people take for granted. We had to eat." The Weatherly household was not alone. Violet Trower, an accomplished home cook, remembers her family's meals: "With so many of us, there was twelve of us, so when we was coming up, this is the way it was. It was always, when we got off the school bus, always was a big pot of something. There was no three-course meal or no big desserts. We always cooked a big pot. How else can you support a family—a big family?"

The Weatherly brothers talk about how their mother, working in a white family's kitchen, would prepare her employers a chicken dinner, reserving the backs, necks, and other parts that would be discarded. Those scraps she carried home for her family to be cooked as chicken and dumplings or chicken and rice. "They're going to have chicken on that Saturday or Sunday," Charlie remembers. "So she'd go down on that Saturday, by working for them, and clean this chicken for them, and they gave her all the other stuff. They call it waste. They would give away the best parts. The rest of the stuff, the gizzards, the necks, and all that stuff, they had all that in the pot, too."

The connections to drum head soup are obvious—and so is the link to other animals such as pigs that could be raised on scraps and forage.

The truism "we ate everything but the oink" carries real weight. I imagine drum as pigs of the sea and reflect on the deep histories of the rural poor, black and white, making do. When it came to drum, Charlie Weatherly and Danny Doughty make that point. "We wouldn't waste," Charlie leans forward in his chair. "We didn't have great things. But we know how to survive. That's what they was—pots. Everything cooked in a pot. It wasn't no frying pan. There wasn't a whole lot of that."

Theodore Peed expands on the Weatherlys' commentary of creating cuisine out of necessity and what wealthier neighbors considered scrap: "Around here, nobody did it but mostly black people. It's like at the store you could buy neck bones. Neck bones was cheap as hell at one time, because black people was the only ones that would eat them. Like a gizzard soup or something, you know what I mean? Yes, sir! Boil them with onions, maybe cut-up piece of celery and diced-up potatoes—put them in the last, you know old gizzards, it takes them a long time to cook. It takes them about an hour and a half to cook." He shifts his thoughts to his mother's technique: "You know, you boil them. She always put just a little pinch of thickening, because she didn't want it watery. Not thick, thick, thick! Not like a gravy, but just a little body to it. Something like a chowder." Listening to Mr. Peed, I have learned that the main ingredients in drum head soup include necessity, invention, and renewal.

By the time the drum migrated up the coast in spring, Danny says, "Everybody's resources had run to an end, and they were desperate to get anything." The arrival of the drum—he reaches for the right phrase, then speaks—"was like the rejuvenation of life for this new year. It was the first sign of prosperity and life." The early days of spring, the arrival of the big fish booming through the inlets, the salvation and pleasure of drum head soup, an Eastern Shore of Virginia cuisine, a South you never ate.

A CHEF'S RECIPE FOR HOME

DRUM HEAD SOUP

Harper Bradshaw, Harper's Table, Suffolk, Virginia

Harper Bradshaw has a long association with the Eastern Shore (including Maryland). He prefaces his recipe for Drum Head Soup with this recollection:

About ten years ago I had an amazing day of fishing with a very close friend a bit further up the Delmarva in Deal, Maryland. It is near the top of the Bay where you can stand on the eastern shore of the Chesapeake Bay and see the western shore in detail. We ran thirteen rods that day from a 20 something foot center console and had the boat in the water before the sun had even broken the horizon. My buddy's dad, the captain, wouldn't even put a line into the water until we all had an open Budweiser in our hand. Needless to say, it was a memorable day.

We caught our limit of two huge rockfish each and took them home at the end of the day to clean. It is a tight knit and small fishing community with many families that have been there for generations. When I asked what they did with the heads (they were probably four to five pounds each) and they said they just discard them. I thought that may have been the answer before I even made the voyage up, so I had conveniently brought some eggs and salt with me to prepare for my hosts.

I salt roasted all of the heads for about an hour and removed them from the oven covered in the egg white hardened salt crust. When I cracked the crust open and showed them the joys of finding all of the pockets of meat that were normally discarded they were ecstatic. We had such a fun memorable day and thought you might appreciate a little back story for my experience with fish heads . . . and the recipe for drum head soup below.

There are three parts to this recipe. None are overly complex, however, it is a fun and slightly more refined approach to drum head soup. This soup is prepared using the leftovers from a black drum that has been scaled and the fillets removed.

Makes 6–8 servings
For the fish
    2 black drum heads
    1 (3-pound) box kosher salt, plus more as needed

8 large egg whites

For the broth

Bones of one large black drum

2 leeks, sliced in half lengthwise, rinsed, and cut into half moons

3 celery ribs

2 onions, peeled and halved

Small bunch fresh thyme

1 fresh bay leaf

2 tablespoons black peppercorns

2 cups Chardonnay

For the soup

1 cup diced country bacon (see Notes)

2 onions, diced small

1 leek, diced small

1 bulb spring garlic

4 celery ribs, diced small

½ cup all-purpose flour (for a thicker soup, optional)

4 cups diced small Eastern Shore potatoes

1 cup Chardonnay

2 tablespoons chopped fresh thyme

Salt and ground black pepper to taste

Fresh lemon juice

Hot sauce (such as Tabasco) (optional)

Handful of young arugula and/or watercress leaves

Fresh herbs such as chives, tarragon, parsley, or dill (don't use dried herbs)

To prepare the fish

Rinse the drum heads well in cold water. Preheat the oven to 375° and line a sheet pan with parchment paper.

In a large bowl, using your hands, mix the egg whites with the salt until well combined. The mixture should feel like wet sand. You may need to add a bit more salt to get this consistency, depending on the humidity.

Spread a ½-inch-thick layer of the salt mixture on the prepared sheet pan, covering an area large enough to accommodate both fish heads. Place the heads on the salt bed and pack them down with the remaining salt mixture. Bake for 1 hour. (It seems crazy, but the egg white will harden the salt into a rock-solid dome that will gently steam the fish inside.)

Remove the pan and place it on a flat surface. Use the back of a knife, a hammer, or a crab mallet to break open the salt crust and reveal the steamed heads within. Cool slightly. Remove all of the meat and place it in a bowl. (The best pockets will be found at the cheeks and the top and back of the head where the fillets were connected. To keep the broth flavor clean, resist the temptation to use the tongue, eyes, or other odds and ends for the soup.) Set the meat aside.

To make the broth

Rinse the bones well and make sure that there are no guts or skin remaining. Place the bones in a pot, fill the pot with cold water, and bring it to a boil. Bring the broth to a boil and immediately remove the pot from the heat. Drain the bones and rinse them carefully with fresh water to remove any scum. (This will help make the broth cleaner and clearer.) Wash the pot.

Return the bones to the pot and add the remaining broth ingredients and enough cold water to cover the bones by 1 inch. Slowly bring the liquid to a simmer over medium heat, being careful not to let it boil. Simmer for 1 hour, skimming any foam or scum that floats to the top and discard. Set the broth aside. Roast the drum heads while the broth simmers.

To prepare the soup

Slowly render the bacon in a large, thick-bottomed pot until just crispy. Remove with a slotted spoon to a paper towel. Add the onions, leeks, garlic, and celery to the bacon fat and cook gently for a couple of minutes. Add the flour, if using. (Omitting the flour will yield a clear broth and a lighter soup.)

Add the potatoes and wine. Cook for a couple of minutes over medium heat and then add the broth to just cover the vegetables. Simmer until the potatoes are cooked through and have a creamy texture. Add the thyme and season with salt and pepper.

Just before serving, add the fish head meat. If there is more meat than you want to put in the soup, reserve that for a nice fish salad, fish cakes, or something else.

Taste the soup and add a few drops of freshly squeezed lemon to brighten it up (but see Notes). Add a dash of Tabasco, too, if you'd like a little heat.

To serve

Taste one final time and adjust the salt and pepper as needed. Just before serving, put a scattering of tender arugula and/or watercress leaves and the chopped fresh herbs on top to garnish. Just-steamed middleneck clams are a wonderful addition to the soup, too.

Notes: Country bacon can be found at many of the stores along Route 13, the north-south highway that runs up the spine of the peninsula. I suggest buying a slab there for a true nod to the Eastern Shore of Virginia. I like getting it either at Stingrays when I stop in for sweet potato ham biscuits or from one of the fireworks shops when we're there in the summer.

If you decided to thicken the soup with flour, a splash of heavy cream makes for an even more delicious and richer version of the same recipe. *But omit the lemon as it can cause the cream to curdle.*

Mengue de Cangrejo de Guisante

Working with his crew on the Hog Island Bay clam grounds one day, Tom Gallivan noted their lunch. "One of the things that showed up were these things I almost thought were cookies at first, but in fact they were a little shrimp fritter that they had taken our local small shrimp and large shrimp and incorporated it into this little kind of fritter." Tom recounts how he posed his questions to Jesus Enriquez, whose wife, Adriana, provided her husband's lunch: "The story behind it, when I asked and ate a few of them, I asked were they something they ate back home. They said it was because it's so hot down there, and there is such a lack of ice that they needed something they could carry to work and go work on the beaches and in the bays. So they made these little shrimp cakes [*mengue de camarones*] that were a little fried shrimp thing." "It was interesting to see," Tom draws connections between older local foods and recent Latin American influences, "because we certainly have clam fritters and fried shrimp, but I've never seen a fritter made in this method. It was cool! They were salty, but they definitely had a little bit of spice to them—not incredibly spicy. I think it was something they definitely had a lot of down in Mexico. Now they're making them up here using local ingredients and, most importantly, sharing them."

Tom asks his crew if they will share the recipe—and a day later they do. Penned in a neat hand on two sheets of lined exercise paper, the recipe records making *mengue de camarones* the previous evening. A colleague at the Center for Documentary Studies at Duke University, Xaris A. Martínez, translates the text from Spanish into English for me. She prefaces her rendition with the following: "Here's my best stab at translating the recipe you showed me; I would advise asking someone who works in the cooking/restaurant world who is bilingual to translate, since many of the terms (including "mengue," which I think may just refer to the shape given to this mix-

Food truck, Cheriton, Virginia.

ture) are not ones that I am familiar with. And I think watching someone make it would definitely help in determining what the ingredients are and what order things should happen in." Acknowledging how elusive language can be, she then offers her annotated translation:

Ingredients to make shrimp "*mengue*" ("*mengue*" in my usage is used to refer to a diminishing or decreasing—it is also slang for devil in certain parts of South America—not sure how the writer of the recipe is using this word OR whether they meant to spell it like this *mengüé* OR *mengüe*)

1. Shrimp

2. Corn with lime to whiten the corn (the lime here may be referring to slaked lime or calcium hydroxide)

3. *Apazote* (I believe this is referring to some kind of paste, but can't tell from the context)

4. Butter or oil

5. Achiote or colorant/coloring (*achiote* is a type of fruit—not sure if this is liquid or dried coloring)

6. Green chili, to taste / to your liking

7. Salt, to taste / to your liking

HOW TO PREPARE SHRIMP *"MENGUE"*

1. Boil 6 pounds of corn with a little bit of cal (see note above in #2). Afterwards, wash the corn and then grind until you have the dough.

2. Grind the corn with the *apazote* and with the green chili.

3. Separately, add a little salt to the top of the fresh shrimp and let it sit for 30 or 45 minutes.

4. Peel all the shrimp until they are just the flesh. The water that drips/drains from the shrimp is not thrown away, you mix it into the dough (as if it were the juice of the shrimp, so to speak OR in a manner of speaking).

5. Once you have the dough, and you've mixed the shrimp into the dough, then add butter or oil (do this in a large bowl).

(dough, peeled shrimp, butter, salt to taste, all mixed together)

(a little colorant/coloring)

6. After all those steps, you start to prepare the balls, which is also known as *mengue*. Make sure each *mengue* has enough shrimp.

7. Finally, the prepared *mengues* are placed in the oven, which should be at 350 or 400 degrees.

Finally, we wait for one hour or one hour and a half, depending. You have to be checking.

I note that, although the *mengue* appear to be fried, they are in fact, slow-baked.

Xaris's translation captures the slipperiness of words not just in language but also in terms of practice. Some things are better witnessed than read. In the translation from actions to words, from Spanish into English, Adriana's recipe retains the liveliness and flexibility of cooking in the moment, of what is witnessed and consumed as common knowledge in her kitchen. Her recipe is an emblem of an evolving Eastern Shore terroir.

Adriana delivers the recipe with two aluminum pans heaped with crispy, salty, slightly spicy baked fritters. The fritters are a rich reddish brown and crunchy from the coarsely ground cornmeal and extended baking time. One pan contains *mengue de camarones*; the other is filled with *mengue de ostra cangrejo* (oyster crab *mengue* by any other name)—an innovation that arose from the gift of three pints of oyster crabs from Steve Bunce's shucking house. The *mengue de ostra cangrejo* reveals the essence of tradition as

Shrimp (left) and oyster crab *mengue*, Bayford, Virginia.

a process of opportunity and invention through terroir and cuisine. Tradition is about making sense in the moment and moving forward in creative, sometimes unexpected ways.

I think back to Maiana Garcia's *barbacoa de cordero* and her reconciliation of two culinary worlds. "In the United States she has more opportunity of buying all the ingredients she wants or she has to use or she needs to use to make different foods," her daughter Jessica translates as we sit at the dining room table, "to make different sauces or different foods." Yet Maiana's efforts to re-create the tastes of home are hampered by what is available in the supermarkets and roadside *tiendas* (shops): "Here she says she cannot find all the ingredients that they used to have over in Guatemala." The results, Maiana explains through Jessica, "it's part in Guatemala but is also part of the Eastern Shore, because basically you use some products from here from the United States, so it's basically half and half." I sense a new cuisine in the making.

"She would recommend for everybody to learn how to cook." Jessica stresses the connection between family and food: "If you learn how to cook, the spiritual family stays together—the flavor of the family always stay together." Maiana's favorite memory centers on the *barbacoa*. "When she did the barbecue," Jessica reminds me, "the whole family was here. There were no problems, no arguments or nothing, and they all said the food was delicious." Maiana Garcia's lesson resonates in other conversations with immediacy and complexity and nuance.

Mother and daughter Irma Ramirez and Laura Gonzalez attend to the griddle and counter of their food truck parked in the shade behind the Tru Blu gas station and convenience store on the old Route 13 leading into the town of Exmore. The truck has moved around over the past several years, leaving its old stand next to a *tienda* out on the main road between a barber shop and a tax preparation operation notable for advertising its presence with very large replica of the Statue of Liberty. I am unsure as to the connection between filing my taxes and Lady Liberty, but then some things are destined to remain mysteries. Irma leans over the take-out window of her truck in its new location while Laura peers over her shoulder ready to translate. Typed lists of gordita, taco, and *torta* (hearty sandwich) options are Scotch-taped to the faded blue truck on either side of Irma.

At the outset, Laura frames her mother's work in the food truck: "The only reason she is doing this is because she was interested in the flavors of the food." Irma has devoted years to re-creating the flavors of her Veracruz childhood here on the Eastern Shore. The arc of her efforts is mapped by the reconciliation of remembered tastes with the opportunities and limitations offered by local ingredients. Her menu is map and logbook combined. Irma elaborates, "Because I didn't know how to make tamales, but one time I thought, 'I want to eat the tamales that my mother would make for me.' I went through flavor after flavor until I hit on the flavor that my mother made with her tamales." Laura amplifies Irma's history: "She was a seven-year-old girl when her mom passed, but she still remembered the flavor of her tamales, and she said that she had somebody to teach her how to make tamales, and then she started cooking until finally, she found the flavor that she was looking for that flavor." It is exactly the search for "that flavor" that stands at the heart of Maiana's Hog Island *barbacoa de cordero*.

Irma's efforts embrace every dish she makes, but her *barbacoa* holds pride of place, served in the gorditas, tacos, and tamales she provides her customers, the majority of them Latino watermen employed on the clam and oyster grounds of Hog Island Bay. Gorditas, a flat bread made with cornmeal and packed with meat and other fillings, including cheese and vegetables, sell especially well. Irma and Laura continue, describing the connection between family, a distant home, and re-created flavors. "My family," Irma says, is in everything she cooks. She tells of visiting her uncle

Irma Ramirez in her food truck, Exmore, Virginia.

in Veracruz: "I visited him when I was around forty years old. I visited him and asked him the recipe for *barbacoa*, and he gave it to me. From there, I was trying, trying, until I found the flavor that was his *barbacoa*." Again, Laura expands on her mother's words, "Most of the recipes, it was her mom." But some of them came from other family members, "like an uncle that used to cook the Mexican barbecue. She stopped seeing him when she was little after her mom died." "After forty years," Laura says, "she finally met him again, and so she asked him about the recipe of the barbecue, and he wrote it for her, but at the beginning, it wasn't like the flavor that she was looking for, but she kept trying and trying until finally that was the flavor. The barbecue that she cooks right now is one of her uncle's recipes."

Avelina Torres serves gorditas, tacos, *tortas*, and more from her bright orange food truck parked beside the *tienda* on the highway on the south side of Nassawadox. "It's a pleasure for me to cook, and I'll do it until I can't anymore," she says through our interpreter, Erika Peterson. "The joy in it is inventing new things that are going to please the people who eat them, because I didn't study cooking." Like Maiana, Avelina learned much of her art working in a restaurant in Mexico City: "In Mexico, in the restaurants where I worked, I would cook. I would make posole. Then they would let me choose a dish that I wanted to make that I thought people would like. I would try it and keep going along those lines. I even modeled the posoles in a restaurant. I would hold different bowls and show the people the different types of posole." I admire her fashion sense.

Avelina's path to her food truck at the Nassawadox *tienda* speaks not just to the invention of cuisine but also subtly to an invention of self. She serves her story in reluctant portions, beginning in Mexico and ending on the Eastern Shore, where members of the Spanish- and English-speaking communities consume her gorditas, tacos, *tortas*, and *barbacoa*. "Mostly I was washing dishes," she begins. "Well, I had a problem with the manager because I was still learning how everything worked, and he left me this huge pile of dishes and told me that I had to wash every dish and pot, and I mean, they were really deep pots that were full, and everything had to be ready and clean before the next shift came on. I told him that I couldn't, it was too many dishes and pots to wash that fast just by myself, and he said that he was going to report me to the owners of the restaurant, and I told him, 'You do what you want, because there's just no way I can do all this.'" Avelina did not wait to be reported to the restaurant owner: "I asked him, the manager, 'Do you want me to wash dishes or do you want me to fix you something to eat?' He said, 'No, I want you to wash dishes.' So I went straight up to the office, and I talked to the owner, and I told him, 'Hey, this manager just wants me to wash dishes.' He said, 'Yeah, that's right.' I said, 'Well, I don't want to wash dishes because we're having too many problems.'" Most folks would have been fired at this point, but Avelina was having none of it.

"I couldn't be a waitress," she digresses, "because I didn't have enough education to be able to write down the orders fast enough because there were so many people in there and you had to write your orders down very quickly." "I didn't want to wash dishes anymore"—I envision the scene— "The cooks even cried because it's so much pressure. They would cry." "Actually," she confesses, "I kept washing dishes in Mexico." Not entirely, as it turns out. "When I had that time when I had the problem with the manager, I did prepare a meal for the clients, for the customers." Avelina persisted: "They [the owner and manager] asked me, 'What do you know how to cook?' I told them some things, and they said, 'Okay, cook something for us.' I don't remember what I made that day, I think it was chicken and *salsa verde*, and I made it for them, and they liked it, so I did that some, but

Avelina Torres in her food truck, Nassawadox, Virginia.

I didn't want to be a full-time cook because it was too much pressure." She had suffered too many laments from the weeping chefs around her.

Avelina charts her career path—as an assembly-line worker, a laundress, and a dishwasher—from Mexico to the Eastern Shore, where she went back to washing dishes at a roadside restaurant and gas station. "I was happy washing dishes," Avelina tells her story, "but there were a lot of problems, so I wasn't content there anymore." Chance and circumstance intervened.

"I went into the store one day to buy something, and I saw that they had a lunch truck outside. I said, 'So what are you guys going to do with that lunch truck? Are you going to sell food, or are you looking for someone to work there?' They said, 'Yeah, we're looking for somebody.' I said, 'Well, I want you to hire me to work here. But I want you to give me full-time.'" Avelina smiles, "They just said, 'There's your lunch truck, señora!'"

"I know that God put them in my path, because I went to the store on my day off, and I was supposed to go back to the restaurant the next day, but they were waiting for me the next day to start working for them, and I told the restaurant, 'No more!' I left, and I came here and asked the guys to give me work, and I've been here for three years." "I love the kitchen and I like working here because the guys, they leave me alone, they don't bother me," she laughs lightly. "They know what I'm going to do, and they'll tell me if they want me to make something special or different."

Avelina's culinary journey is unique only in its details. Like Maiana, she learned to cook out of hard times. "I just learned to cook out of necessity because I was orphaned at the age of seven, and our family would just make us cook whatever. We just had these little thin noodles called *fideo*, would make like a soup with that, beans, rice, tortilla, and salsa. We didn't make anything fancy."

On the Eastern Shore, two things have shaped her cooking: plenty and absence. Plenty is found not just through access to more and better ingredients but also through the ready availability of prepared foods. Her cooking, she observes, "It's changed a lot, because now everything that I use comes in a can or a bottle. Before, I would make everything from scratch." Her words speak to a new absence, time. "Both tamales and *chiles rellenos* are problematic foods," she says. "It takes a lot of time and a lot of work to put them together. I like the process of preparing it, and people are like, 'What are you doing? That takes a long time.'" Avelina links the gift of time to sharing: "Sharing what I make is very important. I feel like everyone should share more. A lot of people ask me, 'What do you put in your food, señora?' And I say, 'A lot of love. A lot of love, so that you can eat well.' And they say, 'That's good!'"

Time, it seems, is part of tradition—and feeling. Heladio Hernandez Ochoa, who owns the *tienda* where Avelina cooks in her food truck, speaks to the gift of time and care. Customers come and go as I listen. Erika translates, "My grandmother, she would make *manjar con arroz* [rice delight or rice delicacy]. It's a dessert with rice that's like a gelatin. It's just milk and rice flour, sugar, and cinnamon, nothing else. The rice, she would wash it and put it out to dry in the sun, like for four days. Every day. Then at night she would bring it back in. She would grind it in the metate until it was fine enough for the dust to sift through a cloth napkin. All of it she would have to sift through, that is how she made rice flour. Nowadays, no one does that. Now they buy rice flour in a box of Maizena, that little yellow box over there. It tastes good, but never the same. It won't taste the same because that is processed rice flour. That was natural, ground by hand until it was fine enough." The *manjar con arroz*, Heladio concludes, is about "the art—and the time—the pleasure of being in the kitchen, preparing, cooking."

Avelina, Heladio, and Maiana link tradition to memory. "I would like people to know the importance of not forgetting the traditions and the foods that go into those traditional foods in Mexico." "I keep those memories. I share them here with the people, and I'll nag them, too, you know, when I'm serving them and they'll say, 'Oh, ma'am, you forgot to give me napkins,' and I'll say, 'Hey, remember when you were growing up poor and there were no napkins. You had to clean your face on your sleeve!' Just playing around. They'll try the food and say, 'Oh, I don't think I've ever tried anything like this before.' I'll say, 'Well, didn't you eat anything like this at home? Didn't your mother prepare this for you?' And they'll say, 'Well, I left home so young, I don't know,' or you know, they never learned in the first place. Then they go back to Mexico, and their mother is stirring the pot with the *atole* cooking on it." *Atole* is a sweetened warm beverage made with cornmeal and other ingredients that vary from region to region, family to family. "They're going to say, 'Mom, what is this cooking?' And they're going to say, 'Oh, Mejito, you've even forgotten about *atole*.'"

Heladio echoes and amplifies Avelina's thoughts in his own words: "I think we are trying to rescue and continue our traditions and our typical dishes from the places we are from. There are those of us here from different places, from Veracruz, Guatemala, Chiapas, Puebla, and we all bring different foods, different recipes, different flavors. I believe it is our youth. Our youth, those who will come after us, our descendants. They have to learn to value Mexican food. Because many people go to a Mexican restaurant, but from my point of view, it is not Mexican food, it is Americanized food."

Heladio addresses a larger sense of loss. "Every day it is less and less. People know how to cook less, they don't like spicy food. In fact, in my own

Heladio Hernandez Ochoa in his *tienda*, Nassawadox, Virginia.

homeland in Mexico, there are many traditions being lost." "Everything is becoming modernized," he shrugs. "Everyone goes for what is easiest, people are buying more processed foods. It is something that is ending." Maybe so, but tradition looks forward.

Tom Gallivan, oyster and clam grower, recognizes this as we happily eat our lunch of gorditas and tamales from Avelina's food truck in his Bayford kitchen. "It's small entrepreneurs making food with care and with love that isn't coming out of a frozen Sysco box," he says. "It's coming out of a recipe that is part of their family and part of them. You might scoff at a taco truck, but typically the woman that is working in there is putting some care into that food—and it's usually damn good!" I look up from my gordita *al pastor* and nod agreement.

José Macias arrived on the Eastern Shore in the 1990s. Over time he has worked in the tomato, squash, and cucumber fields, on the clam and oyster grounds, and in the Chatham Vineyards owned and operated by Jon and Mills Wehner. He acknowledges that when he arrived there was no Mexican or Central American culinary infrastructure, "Nothing! We made everything homemade. We made the tortillas by hand. The ladies, the wives, they make the flour tortillas and the corn tortillas in the house. We cook rice, chicken. We cook the beans, we cook everything out of the house. Everything is homemade." Mexican or Central American ingredients were scarce, requiring families to make monthly trips north to Delaware, Pennsylvania, and Maryland to secure pantry staples. Now, he remarks, there are *tiendas* everywhere, and Food Lion and Walmart maintain reasonably well-stocked Mexican shelves.

José describes how Spanish-speaking households fill in the gaps, cultivating gardens planted with Latin American chayote, chili varietals, and herbs such as cilantro and epazote, as well as more familiar tomatoes, squash, and fruits. He remarks on how he and others have acquired a taste for seafood and learned to forage oysters, cast nets for fish and shrimp, and mudlark for crabs. Hailing from the inland reaches of Guadalajara, José emphasizes the regional diversity of his Spanish-speaking friends and coworkers and how they learn from each other as well as their more deeply established Eastern Shore neighbors.

Bundled against the chill of a winter afternoon, he provides the example of how he learned to concoct *ceviche*, or what he calls "cocktail." José explains that he learned the dish from "a Mexican guy who used to work on the waterfront. He makes a big pot of it." José sketches the recipe: "Oyster, shrimp, and fish—everything together. Everything chopped, limón, cilantro, onion." José's coworker Esgar Astudillo interjects, "Lime." Ingredients combined, "you let it sit one hour—just one hour." "Ahh," José sighs, "That is so good!"

For José, every encounter with an ingredient affords a universe of culinary possibilities. "You know the drums?" he asks. "The big one? We buy one of those. About twenty-five pounds, right? We make *chicharrones*. *Carnitas*. We did drums. They tasted like pork. You know *carnitas*, right? Instead of the pork, fish. The drum is big. Take all the scales off of the skin, you have to use a shovel." Drum fish *chicharrones*, riffing off the familiar snack staple of pork skins, is a possibility new to me! Fascinated and thinking of Janice Weatherly Walters' description of drum cracklings, I ask for an explanation. "You fry it in a big pot like pork," José obliges. "We make it like, we call it, pork skins, but the fish. Oh, that tastes so good!" There is rapture in his voice. "We get a whole drum," he resumes, "we make it into little pieces and put it in a big pot. Cook it like pork. Everything together. Mix it with the skin." I ask how he makes the drum *carnitas* crispy, and he answers, "Put the oil on it—you just fry them. Make sure everything is done." "Make a salsa like a *pico de gallo*," the imagined drum *carnitas* are on the plate, "with *taquitos*." And where did the idea for drum *carnitas* originate? "The guys, they come from Matamoros. They cook a lot of those because they are fishing on the ocean. They catch a lot of those drum. They know how to cook very well!" José talks about food with a good deal of enthusiasm.

Like José, Tom Gallivan's crew takes advantage of the opportunity for collateral entrées. "Whenever we encounter, and we do on occasion, octopus or any small fish that ends up stuck in our gear," Gallivan says, "my crew will fry those fish whole and eat them that way. Sort of fried almost crispy hard on the outside. Put a few slices down the side of the fish. They're wonderful! Those will show up from time to time." In the same way that ducks, geese, and venison taken on Jon Wehner's farm and vineyard, where Esgar and José tend the grapes, make their way into José's kitchen.

Moles and tamales are dishes for special occasions including birthdays, festivals, and marriages. They manifest skill, art, and celebration. "They will make mole for special occasions and bring that in," Tom says, "and that's always incredible. Recently, we just had some mole tamales, which I had never had before, which were also great." Tom sounds wishful in this moment of reverie. "The same homemade mole that they put a little chicken and put in a tamale. The other thing that they did, that I haven't in the past encountered, was my crew and some other local people are starting to use banana leaves more and more. I don't know if it's a regional thing or what. I don't know if it's the smell of the banana leaf or if it's imparting a little of the flavor. That unique flavor that a banana leaf brings out but that a corn husk does not. A corn husk seems like it's a pretty neutral thing. That's a whole other level of flavor that the folks that work with me use. It's cool!" Eat and learn.

Cultural exchange is a two-way street—one with a lot intersections, crossovers, and feeder lanes. Even as the Mexican and Central American cooks on the Eastern Shore of Virginia create new recipes and adapt familiar ones, they exert a powerful influence on their new neighbors, employers, and even people simply passing through.

Gricelda Torres Segura works with chef Amy Brandt in her catering kitchen located off the main road near Cheriton. The two colleagues and friends take a break from cleaning up after an event the previous evening and sit side by side on a bench at the long dining table near the doorway. The sun filters through the trees outside. It's early August, and fig season is kicking into high gear. In quest of Eastern Shore flavors, they recently created Hog Island *carne de tamales de cordero*. They describe mixing the salsa, braising the mutton, making the masa from scratch, and steaming the finished tamales. Gricelda, the architect of the salsa used for seasoning the braised meat, speaks to the heart of culinary invention as a collaboration between family and friends, over generations, and across culinary worlds of experience and imagination. That process is clearly evident in the back and forth between Gricelda and Amy as they talk through the recipe for making the *salsa roja* for the *tamales de cordero*.

"It's a super dark red," Amy starts. "It's just this rusty red, beautiful color, and it's deep, and the flavor is kind of bitter but kind of not. It's really delicious." Gricelda picks up the thread: "I use dried *chile ancho, chile negro*, and *guajillo*. I just take off the seeds, open it, and fry it." "After the frying," she cautions, "not really frying, because if you toast it too much or you fry it too much, it turns really black. Your salsa will be too strong. We call it *amargo* [bitter]. It's not like good flavor in your mouth." Amy agrees, "It's very important." Gricelda moves forward, "Light frying and take it off and pour in some water, hot water, and sit it in there for maybe one hour." "I use the same oil for frying all the ingredients," she offers an aside, "like garlic, onions, and cumin." The cumin, she clarifies, is ground with a mortar and pestle. "Whole seed," Amy keeps track of the details. Gricelda nods to Amy, "She teach me. It's better flavor if you roast the cumin. It tastes much better. Also, I put some *chile de arbol*—a little bit spicy. Not a lot, because this kind of pepper is just really spicy."

Gricelda moves to the next stage: "I put it in the blender with a little bit of stock, like chicken or pork or beef. Put the stock in, and put the cumin, the garlic, the onions, and everything. I put a little onions, chives, salt, and pepper. We just mix it up in the blender. It's got little pieces, so we drain it. Drain it in the colander. After that, we are frying again with the same oil. Just waiting on your boiling. I put it on medium temperature. If it's really hot, it burns so fast. It's very important to make the pan not too hot, not too cold. Just medium." As the mixture cooks, Gricelda explains, "you can start trying the flavor, and if it needs more salt, if it needs some more pepper or more stock, you can add more stock until you got the flavor you want."

Amy looks on as Gricelda addresses texture and consistency. "It's supposed to be a little bit thick. If you put a lot of water, you can't put lots of stock, and the flavor is not going in the salsa. So it's just a little bit of water. Sometimes when you take out the peppers from the water, it's still wet, so you don't need to add much water. Put the stock in until you can blend it enough. It's supposed to be thick, not really juicy. When you cook it in the pan, you're going to add some more stock. You say, 'Okay, is it good enough, thick enough?' Or like soft or wet enough for the tamales. You're going to add the meat and the salsa and mix it up, all of those together. It's not supposed to be too wet, because if it is too wet, when you make the tamales,

Gricelda Torres Segura, Cape Charles area, Virginia.

Gricelda Torres Segura's blue crab tamales, Cape Charles, Virginia.

the juice is going to leak out of the tamales. A lot of people, they like it, they like it wet because the juice can go in the masa." Amy is not one of those people: "I like it to stay inside."

With the salsa made and the mutton braised, the final steps proceed. "We take the meat and we shred it. We got a bowl with the salsa and put the meat in the bowl and mix it up, all of those together. When I put the masa on the corn husk, I put in the filling. It's already the meat with the salsa together. I just put one spoon in and close and put it in the steam pot. After that, when the tamales are ready, we save some salsa so you can put it on top."

Gricelda's tutorial with Amy's refinements offer much more than a set of instructions. "When we make tamales," Gricelda says, "a lot of memories come on my mind. Always I'm talking right here with Amy, and I'm talking and talking. I told her about my old traditions in Mexico. Everything. Something new all the time. 'Ooh, I remember when we cooked tamales like this or we used this kind of stuff for this.'" Gricelda tells a story, "When I make tamales, too, I remember when my mom told me her story about when she started doing tamales the first time. I think she put a lot of baking powder. A lot! It made the tamales really hard. They can't bite because it was really hard. My mom throw them outside and the dogs, they can't eat it. The cars go on top. They stay the same shape! And I'm scared sometimes to do tamales, and I say, 'I don't want to have tamales like that.' So I'm really scared. This kind of memories I got in my mind when I make this kind of food. Like *chiles rellenos*. Like *barbacoa*."

"I told Amy many times," Gricelda confides, "nobody taught me how to cook. I just look how they do it. Nobody teach me how to do the salsa. I just learned it myself. My grandma tell me some, and my mother tell me something else, so I just put them together and figured it out, played with the flavors. I like this, I don't like this way. So I'm trying to make it to myself. Everybody got different kinds of recipes, but some, for me, I say, that's too much flavor [in] it, or that one is too simple. I just play with the flavors, and I say, 'Okay, I want to do it like this.' Amy teach me a lot of stuff, too, to cook. Put more flavor on it, like she'll say, 'Okay, a tiny more salt, a tiny more this, a tiny more spicy.' Both together, joined together. They're good flavor for everything." "I love to cook," Gricelda exclaims, "I love to learn something different all the time. You know, like make people happy. When they eat it and say, 'Oh, my god, this is the best.' I don't know, I don't have exactly the words to say that, but I love to cook." I imagine Maiana, Avelina, and Heladio whispering in the background, nodding their agreement.

"I look all the time and ask all the time," Gricelda muses, "'How can I make this? How can I make that? Or what can I put on it?' Trying to find something for my brothers and sisters. I think that's why I started to cook, and I really love to cook. I think I'm learning a lot." Then, she adds a somber note, tears in her eyes, "It's really hard because, like right now, a lot of people they say all Mexicans or Hispanic, we are criminals. Sometimes we've got only one reason to come to the United States—survive. Get something to eat. Teach other people how they can survive and get better life. To survive in this life, in this world."

I ask Gricelda and Amy what they have learned from each other through their culinary interactions. "Good question," Gricelda responds. "You know what, she's an amazing person. Amazing! When I started working with her, my English was like zero, and she teach me a lot of English. A lot. She's a very lovely person. I never find a person like that before in my life. So I believe it began in God. Sometimes I feel like he's right here with me. When I met with her, I say, 'He's real. He's right here.'" "I'm learning," Gricelda looks at Amy, "how can I be better person in my life? And about cooking. She teach me how to play with the flavors. A lot. Amy, she put love in the food always. She put love in the food, and she teach me how to do them better all the time. Like, 'Okay, that one. Mmmm, it needs something. Um, that one, no, it's too much.' Or, 'How can we fix it?' Or, like, 'Play with the flavors. That's very good. That's very good.' She teach me a lot of stuff."

Amy takes her turn. "My biggest lesson that I have learned from Gricelda is a life lesson. And it has to do with the story that she told about her mom and dad coming to America, and that she took care of the family, and that they scraped for what they had to eat and doing clothes and getting to school and protecting each other. She comes to the Eastern Shore of Virginia to be with her mother. She holds no resentment towards her mother at all. She loves her mother and lifts her mother up. To me, I think that is a gift to see how someone can open their heart and not exclude somebody for a painful choice that they made. I think it's an easy reaction to do that. To say, 'You hurt me and so I'm going to hurt you.' It was a big lesson for me to watch her with her mother and to take care of her mother, and how they care for each other. And that she teaches her mother." "I think Gricelda," Amy reflects, "is probably more mature than her mom and has been the nurturer for her mom. I think it's a big life lesson for me to watch that. It has flowed over into my life for sure."

"As far as cooking lessons," Amy returns to the work they do together in the kitchen, "for me it is to see the technique, and watch it and see that this was something born of necessity, born of tradition. How she prepares the chilies for the *salsa roja*. The dry chilies, they're fried first and then . . ." Gricelda interjects, "We take off the seeds." Amy resumes, "You take the seeds out and then fry them, and everything has a method. Like, making the tortillas on the *comal* [griddle], how they should puff first. They're just things that I didn't know—and how it makes such a big difference."

All of these thoughts in mind, Gricelda reflects with hope and optimism on her intersecting Eastern Shore of Virginia communities. "Last Sunday, they doing Mass in Indian Town Park. Everybody made a dish and take, like whatever you can cook for your country. We got a big table. Different kinds of food—a lot! We got tamales, posole, tostadas, flautas, rice, beans, different kind of food. The kids dance with the big dresses and big hats, sombrero. There's traditional Mexican music. It was really, really beautiful."

She evokes an extraordinary communion. "They celebrate Mass in Spanish and English—two priests, two fathers. Spanish, English." I conjure the image of the two congregations in one under a warm summer sky. "We got American people on one side and Mexican people on the other side." The English-speaking congregants, she smiles, "They really love why we're doing it. Our traditional countries—Salvador, sometimes Mexico. It's very nice. We can connect the two countries. It's very good, and it was very interesting. American people, they really love why we're doing it, and they love us for it." At that juncture, Gricelda describes the call to table. "The lady in charge says, 'Okay, we want to serve the food, and we can tell you guys which one is the spicy or which one is not.' They say, 'I like the spicy food!' They're eating the spicy food, too. It was a really, really good day. I can see how we still got very nice people around to us." That, to me, is the joyous, hopeful essence of the southern "welcome table."

It's not just the invention of *barbacoa de cordero* or spicy *cordero* tamales in *salsa roja* or savory *mengue de camarones* or any of the many dishes that have emerged on the Eastern Shore of Virginia over the brief span of a generation. It's about tradition as the cultural and artistic process of making sense. That process may be most apparent in the excitement of changing tastes and new preparations—but it is powerfully present in the most ordinary things, and it cuts both ways. Take tortillas, the mainstay of nearly every meal.

Jon Wehner, sitting in the office of his vineyard and winery, Chatham Vineyards, on a warming winter morning, shares a story that reveals the overlays of an evolving culinary infrastructure. Furnishing context, he sets the stage: "One of the things that we did about ten years ago is we fixed up the 'pick house.' The pick house is that dormitory-style building at the front of the farm—and that was the name, the 'pick house,' from the 1920s, where farm labor would stay. It's a cinderblock building. But we invested to get central air and heat and to put a nice kitchen in it and a nice bathroom. It's three bedrooms."

"But the tortilla story you're referring to," Jon begins, "started with a phone call. José [Macias] called me one day, and he said, 'The stove no good.' I said, 'José, what do you mean the "stove no good"?' He said, 'The burners are no good.' I was a typical landlord, so I went down there and looked. Sure enough, the burners—all of them—were toast. They were burned up. This was a stove that was maybe three months old." Jon laughs, "I thought, 'Well, gosh, that's interesting. The burners have all burned out. It must not be a very good stove.' I ordered four new burners. Two large and two medium size that go on the stove. I put them back in, and I thought, 'That should take care of that.'" Wrong.

"About three months later," Jon settles into his story, and I can tell this is going to be epic, "I get another call from José, saying, 'The stove is no good. It's not working!'" Jon shakes his head and laughs again. "I thought, 'Gosh, maybe I need to get somebody in here to take a look at this stove.' So I called the nice folks over at Tyson appliance repair [a family-owned business up in Accomack County], and I explain the problem."

Jon leans forward in his chair. "The serviceman, Steve, sort of laughed, and he goes, 'I know what's wrong with the stove.' He said, 'Do you have Hispanics living in the house?' I said, 'Yes, they're the vineyard workers that are helping me.' He said, 'I'll bet the whole top of that stove is burned out.' He says, 'I see it often when I go to repair the labor camps. They go through stoves every six months.' I go, 'Well, could you take a look at this stove? It's six months old, and it's a three-hundred-dollar stove, and I want to make sure it works fine.'"

Arrangements made, Jon continues, "He comes and takes a look at it, and he says, 'Wow! I've never seen a stove this burnt out! Even the insulators and the burners are cooked!' I said, 'I don't understand how this happened.'" Jon is laughing harder with remembered disbelief. "José is standing right next to me. Steve says, 'Well, you see what they do is take a piece of steel, right.' He looked over, 'Actually that piece of steel that's leaning against the wall, they take that and they set it on top of the burners.' I said, 'Oh, really?' Steve says, 'Oh, yeah, and then they turn the burners way up on high.' José's nodding in agreement. Steve says, 'They get this steel, not orange, not red—they get it white hot. At that temperature it does a really beautiful job of cooking tortillas.' José at this point is smiling and agreeing with the guy about how great a job it does with tortillas. José says, 'We do tortillas every day. We have them in the breakfast, with our beans. We have them at lunch. Ah, we have fresh tortillas every day.'"

Jon closes in on the lesson he learned: "José started talking about the ingredients and how wonderful it was." "I immediately realize," Jon's words slow to underscore his point, "this was a very important cultural must. We just had to figure out a better way of doing tortillas." "We ended up getting a new stove for three hundred dollars *and*," Jon says with emphasis, "we ended up getting one of those outdoor burners. Those bayou burners on a separate propane tank. We set up a work station outside, so they could get very high heat on this piece of steel and do tortillas." Then he adds, "Those are some of the tortillas you had last week with our lunch." I remember those tortillas with real affection and appreciation. "It did reinforce to me," Jon observes, "the importance of food with that culture. That was a nonnegotiable deal. Tortillas were a must, and we had to figure out a way to do it. Like anything in business, if it's not working, you find a better way to do it. In the end, we were able to continue to have tortillas, and I benefit from fresh tortillas from time to time."

When I shared this story with my colleague Xaris A. Martínez, she responded: "Thanks for the email—and for sharing the interview with Jon Wehner. How fortunate that his response was 'We had to figure out a way to do it.' Not only because this endears him to the folks who work for him, but because it is in finding ways to keep these cultural traditions and foodways central to our community alive that we come up with fusions that can be passed on to the next generation. I've seen that same dynamic play out in making Mexican tamales when I was growing up in Guatemala. What do you do when the pans and ingredients (and geographic elevation!) are not the same as the ones used by your grandmother? Well, you find ways to make the pans and ingredients that you have work and you find out that the Mexican-Guatemala fusion *tamal* that has both rice and corn *masa* (dough) is actually delicious. And also, that adding olives and roasted chilies to traditional Guatemalan *chuchitos* works. Yes, there will always be the 'purists' who say you have to do it a certain way for it to be 'authentic' and truly representational of a culture—which I completely understand. But sometimes you do what you have to do to make sure the tortilla saga continues for years to come." I imagine Avelina, Heladio, and Gricelda chorusing, "We told you so!"

Tradition is constantly at work in the creative instant of drum *carnitas* and stovetop tortillas. When it comes to Hog Island *barbacoa de cordero*, my thoughts turn to the inventiveness of our Spanish-speaking neighbors and how the cuisines of Mexico and Central America have entered into our own. Maiana's mutton *barbacoa* occupies a privileged position on my perfect Eastern Shore menu—so, too, do Gricelda's Hog Island mutton tamales, Irma's Veracruz *barbacoa* gorditas, José's drum *carnitas*, and Jesus and Adriana's fried *mengue de cangrejo de ostra*. Tradition forges forward.

A CHEF'S RECIPE FOR HOME

BLUE CRAB TAMALES

Amy Brandt and Gricelda Seguro Torres, Amy B Catering, Cheriton, Virginia

Makes 20 tamales

Special equipment: A steam pot or a large pot fitted with a steamer basket

> 20 dried corn husks, soaked for 24 hours
> 1 cup Crisco shortening
> 1 cup manteca (rendered pork lard, available in the refrigerator section at Mexican grocery stores; be sure to mix before measuring)
> ½ of a 4.4 pound bag masa harina
> 2 tablespoons salt
> ½ teaspoon baking powder
> About 6 cups warm shrimp stock
> 1 pound crabmeat
> 2 poblano peppers, blistered, peeled, seeded, and cut into
> 1- × 2-inch strips
> ½ pound queso fresco, cut into 1-inch cubes
> 1 bunch cilantro, washed, dried, and leaves separated
> Salsa Verde (recipe follows)

Drain the corn husks in a colander for 30 minutes.

In the bowl of a stand mixer fitted with a paddle attachment beat the Crisco and manteca on medium high until light and fluffy. Add the masa harina all at once and beat the mixture until completely combined. Add the salt and baking powder and combine thoroughly. Add the stock a little bit at a time until the dough is soft and passes the float test (drop a pinch of the dough into a small bowl of cold water; if the dough floats, it's the right consistency).

Working with 1 corn husk at a time, place it on a flat surface with the pointy end facing away from you. Place 3 tablespoons of the tamale dough onto the husk and spread it evenly over the bottom two-thirds of the husk. Place 4 cilantro leaves in the middle of the dough, then top with a tablespoon of crabmeat, one strip of poblano, and one or two cubes of cheese. Fold the sides of the husk in and then fold the pointy end up to seal. Repeat until all the dough is used.

Fill a steamer pot with water to just below (and not touching) the steamer bottom. (Alternatively, place a steamer basket in the bottom of a stockpot and add water to just below the steamer basket.) Place the tamales side by side, open end up, in the pot. Cover the tamales with a dish towel folded and tucked around the tamales, then wrap the top of the pot with plastic wrap to create a tight seal. Bring the water to a boil, cover the pot, lower the heat, and bring to a simmer. Steam the tamales for 45 minutes. Turn off the heat, remove the top and towel, and let the tamales sit for 20 minutes before removing. Serve immediately with the Salsa Verde.

SALSA VERDE

Makes 4 cups

6 jalapeños, stemmed
10 tomatillos, husks removed
1 garlic clove, peeled
½ onion, peeled and rough chopped
1 bunch cilantro, washed, and shaken dry, and rough chopped
Juice of ½ lime
Salt and pepper to taste

Heat a cast-iron pan over medium heat. Place the jalapeño, tomatillos, and garlic in the dry pan and toast the vegetables until lightly blackened (they should be just slightly cooked). Transfer the vegetables to a blender and blend just until chunky. Place the onions and cilantro in medium bowl, add the contents of the blender and the lime juice, season with salt and pepper, and stir to combine. Serve cold. (For best flavor, refrigerate the salsa overnight or up to 1 week.)

Missing Ingredients

Sara Ross was born into a space between two worlds, her mother African American, her father white. She lived in the tight-knit town of Accomac, the county seat, for nearly a century until her death in 1992. She belonged to two churches, the Episcopal church in Accomac and the Presbyterian church in nearby Onancock. In her eighties, Sara Ross described herself as adopted, but apparently no record of an adoption exists in the county clerk's office. Still, "Cook" Ross, as she was known throughout her long life, and others in her community believed her to have been legally adopted by a branch of her father's family. The official adoption of an African American child by a prominent white family would have been extraordinary in the racial mores of early twentieth-century Virginia and the American South. A century later, I'm reading through the index cards, clippings, and notes in her recipe tin, wondering about her identity and reputation as a local cook. Some stories, I discover, prove hard to relate. Still, they require telling. This one begins with a recipe collection.

As far as tins go, Sara Ross's recipe tin is not much to look at. Roughly eleven inches across and four inches deep, the dark blue tin likely began as a container for cookies or fruitcake. Neither lid nor label identifies its origins. Packed inside, though, are two metal recipe file boxes as well as several hand-sized bundles of paper that include handwritten recipes, clippings, letters, photocopies of an *Eastern Shore News* profile, and the typescript of her obituary.

The obituary was a thoughtful addition inserted after the fact of Sara Ross's departure from this world. The recipes that fill the file boxes and lie loose in the tin consist largely of columns cut from newspapers published in Baltimore, in Norfolk, and on the Eastern Shore of Virginia from the early 1950s through the 1980s. Index cards, many bearing the preprinted legend "from the kitchen of . . . ," and scraps of paper bear the names and instructions for a variety of favorite foods, with a heavy emphasis on baked desserts and gelatin salads. Instructions for Sara Ross's remembered specialties—yeast rolls, chicken salad, cookies, and cakes—are either absent or represented by contributions gleaned from publications or sent by friends and acquaintances.

Recipes for local dishes are notably missing. Other than clippings for a few crabmeat dishes and directions for a fish stew published in the local paper, seafood goes unmentioned. No recipes for oysters, spot, drum, swelling toads, and other Eastern Shore of Virginia favorites. Aside from a sampling of sweet potato concoctions largely generated by promoters in the course of sweet potato marketing efforts, local produce is conspicuously absent. No recipes for greens, beans, wild asparagus, figs, or blackberries. Not a single mention of fried tomatoes or clam fritters or dumpling dishes. The expected bone and sinew of Eastern Shore of Virginia cuisine that sustained Sara Ross's reputation as "Cook" is simply not preserved on paper—and yet the tin and its contents are the material legacy of a woman known throughout her community as a cook of extraordinary skill and generosity. What is present is the palpable substance of absence, an awareness of missing ingredients.

When friends and acquaintances recall Cook Ross, they almost always work around to the topic of yeast rolls and a universe of sensation: the way the aroma of Cook's rising dough and baking bread infused her kitchen's atmosphere with warmth and desire, the sound of Cook's voice, high, squeaky, and slightly rough, as she conversed while yeast rolls baked, the taste and texture of rolls plucked from favored locations—the lightest ones in the center of the pan or the slightly crispy ones lodged in the corners. Those were Sara Ross's yeast rolls, and as her friend Captain Bill West remembers, "Cook was famous for her cakes and her rolls, but her rolls, everybody would want some."

Amory Hartnett Bunce recollects how as a child she and a friend would pedal their bicycles to the Ross house, where Cook would invite them into her kitchen. Amory remembers her visits to Cook Ross and the delight of freshly baked yeast rolls in exceptional detail. "She was a little old lady, always wore a white pressed blouse," I lean forward listening as a dog barks in the background, "a little skirt that was long. Black shoes that laced up with the old heels. She walked a little hump-backed. She always smelled good, and her hair was always pulled back in a bun and she had little glasses on. She had a little raspy voice. I can remember hugging her neck and she smelled good. I just loved being around her." Amory's portrait is vivid.

"She always invited us in. We'd knock on her door and she'd say, 'Come on in, come on.'" Amory mimics a voice from long ago, "'Come on in, come on children.'" "We would always go to Cook's house, especially when she was cooking her yeast rolls, because they were the best in town, or even all around, and we'd say, 'Cookery, did you make any rolls today?' Cook would respond, 'Oh, yeah, come on, let's go back in the kitchen.'" Amory reprises the sound and cadence of Cook's voice. "The kitchen," she continues, "was the warmest place, and we all would go in there. It was wintertime, and she pulled the hot rolls out of the oven that also heated the little kitchen." Amory recalls Cook's kitchen with precision: "It was a small kitchen. It wasn't very big at all, and the floor slanted a little bit. It was always warm. Summertime, wintertime—it was always warm." The furnishings included "a little kitchen table with that white enamel top. She'd put her rolls on there. The stove was really little. It was kind of narrow, always running. Seemed like it was always cooking something." Amory adds, "She represented the way good old Eastern Shore cooking was."

Amory's not done with the yeast rolls yet. "She'd let us look at them and she'd pull them out of the oven and they smelled so good." "We'd go in there and sit with her, and she'd give us a Coca-Cola and a couple of rolls each." "We got them right when they came out, and they were just sweet and buttery." Cook's visitors were particular about their yeast rolls: "We'd always have to get the rolls in the middle, because they were the softest. The ones on the outside, they were crusty." Amory expands on her connoisseurship of Cook's yeast rolls; the ones in the middle, "they were the softest, but when Cook made yeast rolls, the outer ones were even soft! If you've ever seen a round stack of yeast rolls, most of the time they're not crusty but a little bit hard. Hers were always soft, even on the outside. But it's that center roll that had the best, sweet taste to it." "I don't think anybody," Amory concludes, "has ever been able to make them since she stopped."

"That yeast roll smell," Amory smiles. "You can't describe it. It was kind of sweet, it was yummy. It was a scent that you could see in the air and you just followed it. It just smelled so inviting. You felt welcome. You smelled the home and you knew you were going to be welcomed because cooking is love."

Amory sets me to thinking about the poetry and emotion of yeast rolls. They occupy a privileged place in the collective culinary memory of Eastern Shore folk. I reflect on Sara Ross and the currents of family and community she navigated over the long arc of her life. I imagine her yeast rolls and other delights, recollected by Amory and others, as a form of currency used to book passage. First, though, a little biography is in order.

Sara Hatton debuted in the Accomack County census in 1900, listed

Sara "Cook" Ross's recipe collection, Accomac, Virginia.

with her mother, Cora, who worked as the resident cook in Sara's father's parents' household preparing meals and laboring as a domestic. Ten years later Sara Hatton appears as eleven-year-old Sara Ross, employed in housework for Louis J. Ross, the brother of her paternal grandmother, Sara Ayers. The census taker identified Sara as a black servant unable to read and write and not attending school. The 1920 census enumerated Sara Ross as a servant still residing in the Ross household now headed by Louis's son William. Sara Ross, by her own account late in life, taught herself to read and write. The census also listed her race as white.

In 1930, the census found Sara E. Ross, unmarried and designated "Negro," still residing in the Ross household and employed as a servant for a "private family." Significantly, the census recognized her as the head of her own household within the white Rosses' house, which stood on the south side of Accomac where the town ended and the surrounding farms began. Even after the last Ross moved away, Sara Ross remained in the family home until the late 1980s, when Louis Ross's grandson William sold the house. Compelled to leave the only home she had ever known, Sara Ross moved into new quarters provided by another Accomac family who, as her funeral service noted, "looked after her so diligently, so thoughtfully, and so properly."

At her memorial services, the minister eulogized Sara Ross as "Cook," the name with which she was remembered with heartfelt affection by generations of white Accomac families. The minister spoke for many when he praised Cook Ross for her generosity and faith.

We give thanks to You, O Lord, for Cook's life here on earth:
—for the love and devotion she showed to countless numbers of people in Accomac and on the whole Eastern Shore. We remember so many things she did for so many of us in her modest, genuine way:
—her compassion for, and dedication to, the Ross family with whom she lived for 62 years.
—the birthdays and other special days she remembered, and the hundreds of cakes she made throughout the years to honor her friends.
—the hams she cooked and sliced, and the rolls she baked each month for the luncheons at the St. James Episcopal Church where she was baptized.
—the homemade strawberry ice cream she served each June to the women of the Makemie Presbyterian Church—and the monthly meetings she so faithfully attended.

The celebrants prayed, remembering

—how she taught herself to read and write
—about the butter she churned, and the cows she milked, and the chickens she raised, and the milk and eggs she delivered to regular customers
—the wood stove on which she cooked, the kettles of soap she made, and the Model T she learned to drive.
Everyone around here knew and loved "Cook" Ross—and she knew and loved everyone in return.

Twenty years later, many in Accomac's white community continue to celebrate Cook Ross with deep affection.

The white community with which she identified remembers her best as a "lady," formal and genteel in her manners, with a particular love for the children who lived in or visited her neighborhood. "Oh, yes, I remember Cook," Betty Edmonds Dunn wrote to her friend Anne Nock. "In fact, she took care of me first when I was just a few weeks old. She was an asset to the whole town. She was like part of everybody's family. She would go to see anybody who was sick or had a death in the family—and she always took the person a cake or homemade rolls or something," she marveled, "I don't know how she did as much as she did, there taking care of the

Rosses and always helping everybody else in town." "I loved to go over to the Rosses' house," Betty Dunn reminisced. "Whenever I had a few minutes, I'd go right over there, sit down, and talk to Cook and Mrs. Ross."

Cook's visitors sought her in the Ross kitchen, where she produced her seemingly endless cavalcade of cookies and cakes as well as the savory dishes she carried to church and the homes of acquaintances shut in by illness or circumstances that ranged from a new baby to a death in the family. The society she kept centered on the Ross household, white women in the town, and, importantly, the parishioners of the two churches, Episcopalian and Presbyterian, that she attended and served throughout her adult life.

Rummaging through Sara Ross's recipe tin, I am drawn to two recipes for yeast rolls written in her own hand.

MRS. SMITH'S ROOLS

¼ cup butter
½ cup sugar
2 teaspoon salt
1 cup Milk
3 eggs well beaten
1 yeast cake dissolved in warm water
Melt butter, sugar and salt in milk then work in 5 or 6 cups flour along with yeast. Let rise then make in rools.

MRS. LILLISTON'S ROOLS

8 cups sifted flour
1½ Package yeast [dissolved] in water
Boil Potato & 1 cup mashed (2) in liquid
¾ Crisco in potato
2 eggs beaten
1 cup of milk cold
1 full tsp salt
¾ cup sugar
Add to flour and yeast. Work in well, cover, let rise. Cook 325 for 15 Min.

Both are fragments. Neither contains all the information required to confect yeast rolls from scratch—for example, proofing times, number of risings, and type of flour. What the two recipes contain are the bits of information Cook deemed important in the continuing development and perfection of her art: proportions and directions for mixing. She omitted instructions that were common knowledge and in that unselfconscious gesture underscored her place in the worlds she inhabited and made her own. Knowledge is capital, and the memory of Cook's yeast rolls is its measure.

Mary "Mama Girl" Onley with her oyster shuckers tableau, Fearrington, North Carolina.

There is variety in yeast roll recipes. Bessie Gunter, in her 1889 *House-keeper's Companion*, shared a recipe contributed by Mrs. Montcalm Oldham of Accomac:

YEAST ROLLS.
1 quart of flour.
5 eggs.
1 tablespoonful of lard.
1 tablespoonful of sugar.
1 teacupful of yeast—a pinch of salt.
Mix all together and if too stiff add a little warm milk or water. Knead until smooth. Set to rise and when light knead a second time. Make into rolls and set to rise again.
—Mrs. M. O.

No times, no temperatures. The presumption of working knowledge offers ample room for disaster for even a practiced baker.

Fairy Mapp White addressed the full complexity of yeast rolls sixty years later in her *Foolproof Cook Book*. Communicated to White by Mrs. Marietta M. Eichelberger living in the railroad village of Keller just above the county line, the recipe begins with an introduction, "I asked a Northampton County woman for this recipe, because I knew that the housekeepers of our sister county make exceptionally good rolls." That may be so, but she added the caveat, "The process is mine." The versatility of her recipe allowed for the dough to be fashioned into loaves, buns, and turnovers as well as what she termed "plain rolls."

MARIETTA'S YEAST BREAD RECIPE
2 good size white potatoes
7 to 8 c. flour
2 ye[a]st cakes
3 level tsp. salt
1 c. sugar
¾ c. lard (to 1 c.)
1 c. milk
2 or 3 eggs
½ c. potato water

Process
Sponge
   1. Boil potatoes, peeled and cut thin, in as little water as can. Drain well and mash. Use only 1 c., no more, too much will make dough sticky.

2. Put sugar in a big bowl (preferably crockery), add mashed potatoes while hot, eggs well beaten, salt, yeast cakes dissolved in a little *lukewarm* water.

3. Melt lard (cut in thin pieces) in milk and potato water, over low heat to keep lukewarm.

Add this liquid to mixture in bowl with 1½ c. of the flour.

Note: If the sponge is lumpy, put through a potato ricer. Cover sponge and put in a warm place, until bubbles come on top, about 1 hr. or more.

The Dough

1. Work into the sponge, at first with a big spoon, enough flour to make pliable, firm dough. The amount of flour varies, but do not use less than 7 cups, and if dough too dry, add a little lukewarm water.

2. Work hard 5 min. or longer. Wash the same big bowl and grease well, and put the dough in it, cover, and let rise until double in bulk, 2 to 2½ hrs.

Baking

1. Make dough off into loaves, turnovers (a flat piece of round dough, folded over with a thin slice of butter on lower side), plain rolls, muffin rings (1–2–3 pieces dough in a ring), large buns for hamburgers, sandwiches, or cut in half to toast.

2. Let loaves and rolls rise in warm place (not hot) until about double in bulk. Bake in 350°–400° oven. Yield about 60 medium size rolls—or 30 rolls and 2 loaves.

Note: We put half of the dough in ice box in a pan with tight lid to use later. It keeps well for a week. Use half of the recipe if you prefer.

White helpfully adds instructions titled "How To Avoid Failures":

1. Never chill or overheat the yeast germ in the yeast cakes—liquid lukewarm, put sponge, dough, bread to rise in warm place never in hot, cold or drafty place.

2. If Rolls have not quite doubled in bulk, put in oven when lighted. If bread has doubled in bulk, put in oven after preheating.

3. Follow all directions carefully. I used this recipe in 1958 about 30 times (1800 rolls) without a failure. If you fail, do not be discouraged, try again and soon you will be treating your family to delicious rolls, at half the cost of store rolls, and better too.

The two recipes Cook preserved in her collection reflect the skill and knowledge of Eastern Shore home cooks. For example, Arlen Church of Treherneville, an African American settlement just off the main highway that bisects the two counties, reflects, "East [yeast] cakes, they called them." Her mother, she clarifies, "I do know she used to sift her flour, put just a little pinch of salt in there, and then she'd whip her east cake up—east cakes was in blocks then—and whip that up good, and let that rise. Then she'd pour that in there, take her flour and all that up there together and set it back—in the wintertime, she'd set it on the back of the cook stove, and it would rise fast. That's the way she made that. Then, after it rise as far as she thought it would go, she'd take it over, work it over again, and then pat them up and put them in the pan. That's the way she made them." Her recited recipe aligns with the two in Cook's collection and Gunter's Victorian-era instructions. They are recipes learned hand in hand, perfected in practice, and savored in near ecstasy. White's painstakingly precise directions from the 1950s echoes a different sensibility and a certain uneasiness.

When it comes to yeast rolls, people have a lot to say, and they say it rhapsodically and with deep feeling. Mary Onley, whose papier-mâché tableaux frequently feature Eastern Shore of Virginia themes, including oyster shuckers and crab pickers, sets the yeast roll on the family menu. "That was a family food on Sunday," she says. "That was the family day for everybody to get together. It was more when I was growing up, like the day after church, everybody sat down to a good old dinner." "Through the week," she smiles, "nobody had time to wait for nothing to rise. It was just plain like bread through the week."

Given the investment in time and care required for making yeast rolls, Mary Onley would prepare ahead. "I had made mine Saturday night," she says. "Set them in the refrigerator. I'd make a great big batch. I'd put one batch in the freezer and then I'd put the other batch in the refrigerator, and then take them out Sunday morning before I go to church. Now I had another batch for the next coming Sunday. If I had something through the week, I can pull it right from the freezer, and it's already in the pan. Pull it out of the freezer and let it rise and shove it in the oven and there it goes." "I made yeast rolls until up about sixteen years ago. After my husband died, I forgot about that cooking and I didn't want to make no more yeast rolls. And a matter of fact, I forgot how to make them." She laughs, evoking the sensations of rolls in the oven, "Oh, boy, it smelled like bread everywhere!" She laughs softly and shakes her head. "If your door is not tight in your bedroom, you got some bread smelling good in your bedroom. You going to sleep with that scent." The link Mary draws between scent and comfort reminds me that the remembered aroma of yeast rolls rising and baking speaks to feeling through desire.

Brother and sister Ron Crumb and Kay Crumb Downing from the fishing village of Oyster grew up in a constellation of women who were accomplished family bakers. "Every single one of them could make the best yeast rolls you've ever put in your mouth," Kay enthuses. Ron adds, "They were all different." And, Kay elaborates, "Gosh. Sunday mornings especially, Saturday or Sunday mornings, you could go to Aunt Faye's, Aunt Booth's, Aunt Edith's, you know, Johnny Crumb's mother, they'd just . . . I mean you can't describe them, they were so good. It was just like heaven, eating a piece of heaven. It was wonderful. Their yeast rolls. Like it was nothing. Homemade rolls. Homemade rolls were absolutely fantastic. We usually had those every Sunday."

Janice Weatherly Walters, whose family worked on the water and in the houses of the more well-to-do, talks of how she learned to make yeast rolls and links them not just to Sundays and special days but also to changing ingredients. "My own yeast rolls is the main thing that I know how to cook. My mother showed me how to do it, but I took it upon myself to do it my way. I learned her way, but it's better my way." She shifts to process, "That is how you knead in the dough. She didn't have to knead it much because the dough back then, the yeast was stronger. Today, the yeast, it's not as strong as it was back then. I have to use more yeast now because they had it in the jar and you could scoop it out. It's on the market now, but it's not strong like it used to be when my grandmother and mother used to do it, because back then when they were doing yeast rolls, everybody around knew their bread was being cooked. Today, you can hardly smell it."

Dee Spady, who learned to cook in the public schools and still bakes on request, linked the luxury of yeast rolls to the challenges of hard times: "When you grow up poor, you could take leftovers, and you could stretch it. You do things from scratch. Corn bread from scratch. Rolls from scratch." "Eastern Shore people are not used to having a lot," she notes, "and we had to make things stretch, so to make things stretch we had to make it taste good. It's homemade." "I remember when I was living with my grand-mother when I was young," she continues. "Every Sunday morning home-made yeast rolls. Every Sunday morning, and they wasn't no little teeny rolls. They were the great big rolls. She would make them up on Saturday night in the dish pan, and they were the best rolls." "But," she qualifies, "a lot of people is getting out of making homemade rolls because so many rolls you get are just like homemade rolls." "The Sister somebody," she refers to Sister Schubert's frozen dinner rolls, "that you can get at Sam's Club, they are very, very good. You heat them in the oven, they are good. Very good." Still, "The best rolls," she states, were special and memorable, "because it's homemade and it's cooked with care."

Mary Onley, whose art often teaches themes of food and faith, intro-duces a yeast roll variation that incorporated sweet potatoes—and is not to be confused with sweet potato biscuits. "My kids love yeast rolls," she says, "They still do, but they like the sweet potato yeast rolls." She connects her children's favorite to the seasons. "That was sweet potato time. When sweet potato season was over, we might not have no more sweet potato rolls until the next coming year for sweet potatoes again." Mary credits her grandmother: "I learned from her how to make sweet potato yeast rolls by watching." She sketches the recipe. "You've had sweet potato bread?" she asks me, attempting to gauge the depth of my ignorance and how much she'll have to explain. "You make them the same way. The only difference is with them, you don't use as much water with your yeast because they already have water in them. You just mix that with your flour and make sure you don't have too many sweet potatoes and not enough flour."

"You boil the sweet potato first," she walks me through the steps, "then after you boil it, you peel it. You let it cool off, and then you put that in first. I put that in first. Then I put my eggs and my sugar. I put eggs in mine, not everybody know that. Then my sugar. After I put that in it, I mix my flour up in it. I get my flour and my yeast in at just about the same time. I mix it with my hand. You mix it enough to get it kind of a little stiff, like you would do so you can batter out your little rolls, you know, but you have it just stiff enough. Not too loose. Not too loose. You put your margarine. Your sweet potatoes. You stir that up first. Then you put your eggs, your flour, then you mix that in with your yeast cake. And that's it." Right.

Mary Onley cautions that proofing yeast rolls, sweet potato or otherwise, is a delicate process. "Most people put it on top of their stoves, because you know where the stove has that pilot light. And that's when it rises, from that." "They'll fall, especially if you got a shaky stove. Don't let your floor squeak, your rolls go flat," she laughs. "Don't put too much sugar in it," she cautions as an aside. "You got heavy bread, and what I mean by heavy bread, you eat two rolls, it feel like you done swoll up inside, because it's heavy." Avoid the temptation, she admonishes, to hurry things along. "Then you peeping at it, you peeping at it." She describes the rising dough, "Oh, it's coming up, it's coming up, it's coming!" She's acting out the process of bearing witness to the yeast rolls' progress. "Oh, please, please, please, please, please don't shake it, don't shake it. When you go to put it in the oven, you scared to death."

Drummond Ayres, retired *New York Times* journalist and Accomac native, recalls the admonishments he received as a boy when it came to the delicacy required for yeast rolls to rise. "Everybody had yeast rolls then. When I walked in the house from school in the afternoon, the call would come, 'DON'T STOMP ON THE FLOOR. YOU'LL CAUSE MY ROLLS TO COLLAPSE!'"

Yeast rolls are the stuff of reputation and esteem, a fact that Cook Ross fully grasped. Nobody speaks to this point with greater passion than artist Danny Doughty. We sit in his gallery on a midwinter afternoon. Sunlight streams through the windows, illuminating auras around the little dust motes floating in the air.

Danny rolls his eyes with pleasure. "Like so many things, you were a master once you were known to have the yeast roll to beat all yeast rolls — and it grew all over the place. There was a woman that could cook amazing things, but that yeast roll would trump anything. I can see them now, just getting that mixture of yeast and everything just right, and proofing the bread and all in places and ways that most people would never ever, because they'd have a proofer, or they'd have somewhere they could put it where it was really needed to do that. They knew, if they had been using the oven and they weren't using it anymore, that they could slide a pan in the broiler underneath of it because there's just enough heat inside it, and the stillness of it. A lot of them would put like a cup of water in there to create humidity. They really didn't know what it did, most of them, but they were taught it from their mothers and grandmothers. That was like the Holy Grail. It's funny, you say yeast roll today because when you mastered that, it went like wildfire. People knew it. I mean there was no meat, there was no vegetable that rated any higher than an awesome yeast roll. I attest to that, because I could eat a pound myself when they come out of the oven!"

He recollects the talent of a baker who worked in his Willis Wharf restaurant years ago. "Bessie Edwards, she used her recipe for me and my place. She didn't spoil you. You weren't getting yeast rolls every day. It was a special thing. When they did it, they'd do a lot of them, and then they'd skip two or three days, and by the time they made them, people were to the point of, they need like a fix. She had a recipe that was so good. One of the things they rated them by is how much they could get them to rise. Not only to proof them to rise them, but to get them even taller. Some of her rolls were like, four plus inches tall! It was because of the way she did hers."

Danny takes a breath: "Some people never put sugar. Some people would take warm water, yeast, and mix it, and let it sit, and then add it to the flour later. On the Eastern Shore, almost everything got a little sugar in it, and a yeast roll was one of them. Myself, I love a little sugar in a yeast roll. Some of them would swear, swear on their life that putting sugar in that yeast, in that warm water, would make them not do as well, when others could do it and they were perfect."

He evokes the sensorium that captured the recollections of Amory and Mary. "I mean, the texture, the smell of them. I think they took on a life of their own because they were associated with something special going on." Yeast rolls were not everyday fare. They were special. On occasion, it worked out that a few survived as leftovers. "The next day," Danny says, if you were lucky enough, there was a few left over that you could have. When they made them, they didn't sit around. They went!"

Danny returns to the attainment of reputation. "It's funny in a sense that if one of the ladies that were known for doing a really good yeast roll," he elaborates, that "if something bad had happened, a death or sickness, or something good had happened, or whatever, and them to make and bring you yeast rolls was huge. It was big. It was sweet. It was so endearing to know what they were doing was showing their best thing. That was the ultimate statement of their love, for them to bring their yeast rolls. It truly was, it was. There was a lot of integrity about it. It was like they wanted to show the world part of their little magic thing. That something they could make with their hands, that was theirs and they were known for it—and to be able to honor other people that they cared for with them. It was a real tradition."

Danny's opinion is shared by others. Ellen Clevenger-Finley, who grew up in Baltimore, visited her maternal grandmother every summer, staying in the family home in Cheriton, the railroad town first laid out by her great-uncle William Stratton Stoakley in 1897. "When I was there as a kid, there was always a housekeeper and a cook in my grandmother's house," Ellen starts. "My mother was doing whatever with my grandmother, and I hung out with the cook in the kitchen." Of the three cooks she encountered through her childhood, Ellen remembers Thelma Thomas with particular affection. "She'd make homemade cheese. She'd take a quart of milk and a little bit of cream and buttermilk, bring it up to a heat, separate it out, and make, probably what I would call farmer's cheese or ricotta. Little bit of salt. Little bit of whatever. She made that because it was high protein and my grandmother was ill." Then came the yeast rolls. "She'd take the whey, the warm liquid, and we'd make bread with it," Ellen explains. "This warm, perfectly temperature liquid to make homemade yeast bread. She'd do that, that cycle once a week. Everything would be used. On Fridays, we'd make it into rolls for the weekend. It smelled incredible. Wonderful! And then we'd have fresh fig jam for the rolls."

Ellen turns to the link between yeast rolls and reputation. "Thelma Thomas, who was the cook in my grandmother's house for at least six years if not a little longer, described someone else's—the best yeast roll maker in her church, which she felt was not her even though I thought hers were wonderful—she described the rolls as 'heaven's pillows.' That was her words, 'She makes rolls like heaven's pillows.' They were light enough to float away—heaven's pillows. They had to be that light, that delicate, that lightly browned, perfect." Summoning the image of a pan of fresh rolls, Ellen adds, "I liked the edge. She liked the center. The edge has a little crispier, browner around the outside. The center, because there's rolls all around it, there was no crispy at all, because they're soft on all sides. Those were the pillow rolls."

"Thelma took me at one point to the African American Methodist church in Cape Charles," Ellen recalls. "She took me there and they had a Sunday afternoon picnic. I remember her talking about the different rolls, 'This is the lady who makes heaven's pillows,' or this. . . . I was with her for this picnic and everyone brought food." Ellen describes an apprentice's walking tour of yeast rolls, "She was whispering. She wasn't going to say it out loud, 'Those aren't as good. You don't have to eat those.' I was twelve or thirteen, and she would introduce me, saying, 'She's learning how to make rolls.' I kept trying to do it, and it was something we would do every summer. Food made visiting down there a good time." Ellen continues to follow Thelma Thomas's recipe preserved on a folded sheet of aging paper:

ROLLS

Take one yeast cake, dissolve in a little water, then add a little lukewarm water to make a cup full. Try it with your finger. Add this water to your yeast cake.

Sift one good quart of flour to that, add a little salt about two (2) tablespoonful to lard. Beat two (2) eggs separately. Two tablespoonful of sugar. If you find this to[o] sweet don't put as much sugar [in] the mixture.

Put everything in your flour in your cup of water with yeast cake last. Now fix [mix] everything. Don't have it soft, make it a little hard, and work it a few minutes, that will make it soft enough.

Try this one Saturday.

Make it up at 2:00 P.M. Set aside to rise for two (2) hours. End of two hours, work it over to form, turn overs. Roll the batter on board like biscuits. Cut with biscuit cutter, then *fold* the dough *over*, put a little butter between each one. Give them plenty room in pan. Let them rise one hour. Have your stove at 425°, or near that, and bake for 15 minute.

You can make this up over night, put it in the Rfg [refrigerator], when you take it out give it one hour, before baking.

There is no mention of whey. Some secrets are shared only in whispers.

In Ellen's and Danny's words, I catch a glimpse of the territory that Cook Ross claimed as her own. Her memorial is her recipe tin. Not all memorials are made of stone. Her eulogy is written in the memory of the scent of yeast rolls baking. Not all eulogies are spoken. Cook's recipe tin remembers her in a specific way. It is a book of sorts: part scrapbook, part album, part journal, part memoir, part history. As a collection it says much about how Cook Ross saw her place in Accomac society but little about the things she made that sustained her reputation in the hearts and appetites of her neighbors.

Cook Ross witnessed a century of change. She lived through four wars and the Great Depression. She was born into a southern society in which many black women supported their families cooking for their white employers. She lived a century that began with deeply entrenched conventions of racial roles and expectations that demanded faithfulness, deference, and respect on one hand and expected little beyond employment on the other. Local cookbook author Fairy Mapp White nostalgically celebrated the complexity of these relationships in her memoir of the Turlington Camp Meeting written in the 1940s.

White's rapturous description of cooking at the annual religious retreat in southern Accomack County turned to the cooks who labored in the hottest days of high summer: "Back of the tents most of the tent holders had dining tables, where they ate, and not to[o] far away kitchens, with slatted sides and shingle roofs, and chimneys for wood cook stoves. . . . The cooking was done in the little kitchens located back of the tents, by faithful colored men and women. Mrs. George Stockley had Mary Snead, Mrs. May Stockley had Rachel Tigg, Mrs. L. J. Hyslup had Manie Harmon and Grace Stevens, and Mag Hatney to wait on the two cooks. I wish I knew more of the names of those faithful cooks, most of whom have gone to their reward probably with the words of some of our good old Methodist hymns steadying them for the last great event in one's life. They made possible an old fashioned hospitality that would not have been possible without their faithful services."

When the work was done, the cooks stood at the edge of the gathering and listened to exhortations on conversion, repentance, redemption, and salvation: "At night it was not an unusual sight to see the colored people both men and women (who faithfully served the tent holders) standing back of the pulpit listening to the sermon and reverently bowing their heads in prayer. I have been given to understand that some nights around the kitchens a group of colored people down one line of tents would get together to pray and sing, and even shout, which goes to show that religion is contagious, if warm enough."

Mapp's repeated use of "faithful" to describe the service of the African American cooks recognizes the centrality of their work to the conduct of the Christian gathering. At the same time her narrative conveys an un-stated sense and tacit embrace of particular forms of domestic order. The honest affection and genuine warmth that flow through Mapp's reminis-cences should not be denied, but it is a wistfully nostalgic sentiment sup-ported on deep foundations set in the habits of privilege and power. The repeated invocation of that faithfulness betrays a hint of anxiety in White's nostalgic narrative. As in Cook's recipe collection, at least two histories are in play.

Sara Ross saw her mother marry and leave the South as part of the Great Migration northward in search of work and independence. She lived through Jim Crow, the civil rights movement, and the continuing struggles for equality in the United States. Whatever thoughts she held on these matters were her own. By her own account, her life was truly re-warding and her greatest pleasure found in cooking for others in the white community that supported her even after the last of the Ross family had moved on and she found herself dispossessed of the home she had known since childhood and believed her life right.

Cook's recipe tin reveals an etiquette of memory, a process shaped not by the content of what we recall but rather by unstated rules of memory and how we remember. Remembering, like yeast rolls, is an art form. As an object of memory and remembering, Cook's recipe collection archives a body of correspondence between friends and intimates. It is part of a larger culture of commonplace books, handwritten compendia of poetry, philosophical reflections, and other writings circulated among women, in a practice that stretches back over three centuries on the Eastern Shore of Virginia. As a collection, her recipes provide a scaffolding around reminis-cences of Cook Ross and how she created and occupied her place within the Accomac community. Those stories follow their own recipes. Together they cohere as biography crafted from anecdote and convention and evoke re-membered worlds of warmth, sweetness, and flavor.

Billie Mason, a distant relation to Sara Ross, fills in some of the blanks. "My grandmother didn't say much, they lived together. One was Annie and one was Anne. Anne Hope Mason was my great-grandmother, and she was the one who was Cook Ross's aunt. Cora Hope, which was Cook's mother, was my great-grandmother's sister . . . and she moved to Philadelphia and she had four daughters after she moved to Philadelphia. Now I don't know where those girls are, but they were real pretty girls. Anne Hope Mason. I guess I'm getting you confused, my mother taught us to call her grandma, and our grandmother we called her 'mama,' because we called Mother 'mother.' And my grandmother was 'mama,' and my great-grandmother was 'grandma.' So you hear me say grandma, that's my great-grandmother.

All Mama did, my grandmother, all she did was sit and rock and hold her leg. I can see her now with her leg, rocking. She was sixty-six when she died, and her hair was black, there wasn't a white strand nowhere."

Billie Mason builds more context: "Macedonia African Episcopal Church. Cook Ross's family was from there, too. My grandmother, my great-grandmother was a member of that church. And my grandmother, which we called mama, was a member of that church. The whole family." Except Cook Ross, who attended the white St. James Episcopal Church in town. "She never came to our church. She never even went to church school—she knew the white Accomac more than she did the black Accomac." To amplify the point, she explained, "Now she would visit Aunt Daisy Widgeon. Aunt Daisy was a cousin. My mother did not allow us to call anybody cousin so-and-so, so if they were older she taught us to call them aunt or miss. Aunt Daisy was my cousin, like a third cousin. And she used to go visit her, and I recall they always said that she would come and blow the horn. And Aunt Daisy would go out to her."

Billie Mason's commentary is to the point. Other of Cook's friends and acquaintances from the white community, for example Anne West, expressed an awkwardness in their attempts to locate their friend in the space between two worlds. "I think that Cook really was never," Anne pauses and reaches for the right words, "I don't know how to say it, but she wasn't comfortable with Negroes, and she wasn't comfortable with Caucasians. For instance, I could never get her to call me Anne. Year after year she came here to dinner. She didn't sit in the kitchen by herself, she ate with us, she was one of us. For Christmas, Thanksgiving, Easter. She would say Mrs. West, and I'd say 'Cook, I'm just Anne,' but she could never do that." "She ate here with us," Anne continues, "and had her place at the table. It's funny, like Elizabeth Simms [a mutual friend] been coming for so long that she knows where she sits and somehow they just get comfortable in that spot. Cook was like that. But she never felt . . . ," Anne grows silent. Her husband, Bill, completes the thought, ". . . totally at ease."

Virginia "Pete" Smith, a friend who lived outside Onancock, also touched on Cook's sense of her conflicted place within her community. As a member of her Presbyterian "Women of the Church" group, Pete hosted gatherings in her home and Cook would attend. The meetings always included refreshments that Pete made and served from the kitchen. "She did love to come to Women of the Church here," Pete begins, "but she wanted to be in the kitchen, so that was her place, in the kitchen." This, Pete states, was Cook's choice. "She didn't belong in the living room," Pete explains. "She came as a friend and a Woman of the Church. We always had a little refreshment afterwards, and she would volunteer to make something for it. I said, 'No, I'll make this myself. You'll have to eat what I make.' We had the meeting in the living room. I wouldn't let her come to the kitchen until I went into the kitchen. She had to stay put in there." When the time for refreshments arrived, Cook would join Pete in the kitchen, and "she would come help me pass it."

Pete speaks with candor. "I have not known one soul that was a black person that was her friend," she says. Her son Rick, who has joined the conversation, adds, "The one thing I remember, that quote of hers was that when she died, she wanted to come back anything white, even if it was a goose." He continues, "She was neither white or black in the early part of the twentieth century. Especially in the town."

Pete speaks of Cook's character with affection and respect. "She hardly ever charged anything. She did it out of the kindness of her heart. If you asked her to cook a ham, she'd cook it. But she didn't want you to pay for it. 'You can do something else some other time for me.'" "She was very independent," Pete pauses, "or at least I thought she was." "She was a good person," Pete concludes. "That's the most important thing I can say to you. She was a genuine friend, and good gosh, what would the Episcopal church have done without her? She came to all of the Women of the Church. And the Presbyterian church. She was as good a Christian as you ever wanted to know." Gifts of food and kindness were the currency that booked her passage. As Anne West summarizes, Cook's was "really almost a lonely life if she hadn't made it otherwise by her giving of herself."

I wonder at Cook's nickname. Billie Mason suspected that Cook got her name because "she probably started cooking when she was very young. Because some, I recall, I have heard—I know one lady, one of my son's grandmothers, said they hired her out when she was like twelve years old. She was standing on a stool and washing dishes and cooking. A lot of young black women started that way, cooking." Rick Smith surmised, "I know Cook Ross's mother was a cook, right? And that's how she got the name Cook, because her mother was the cook?" Anne West shared this view. "Now you know why she was called Cook? Well, it's because her mother was a cook and so she was called Little Cook, and that just stuck." The link to her mother's domestic service and her own upbringing in the Ross family household where, at the age of eleven, she did housework resonate.

Cook embraced her nickname as both an endearment and a lifelong marker of her place in Accomac society. She may have been beloved as Cook in her community, but the persona she created for herself was not about domestic service. Rather, she constructed and enhanced her status through the confection and gifting of birthday cakes, meals for shut-ins, chicken salad, and yeast rolls. Ann Hartnett, Amory's mother, confirms the particularity of Cook's position within her community. "Cook was above that sort of thing," she says, referring to domestic work. "I don't think anybody would have ever asked Cook to do it. She was too much like themselves." Indeed, the territory she inhabited lay between the two worlds charted by her birth and the singular story of her upbringing.

Drummond Ayres remembered Sara Ross in St. James Episcopal Church. "She would come and sit in the back pew. Their pews are boxes. She would sit in the back pew. In those days, the Episcopal church only did communion once a month, and she would sit back there and the rector would have the communion service, and then after everybody else had gone back to kneeling in their pews, saying their prayers, whatever, she would rise, walk up the aisle, turn, go to the front of the rail, the rector would be there, she would kneel, he would give her a wafer and he'd give her the cup, and she would turn and she would walk all the way back. Even when I was a child, I knew something was wrong." As I listened, I caught the hint of the performance of a subtle rebuke and public reminder of her complicated standing within her chosen community.

Billie Mason remembers Cook Ross from the perspective of the African American community. "When I learned she was driving that little tin car, she was a lady driving a car, and my father, which was Willie Mason, told me that that was my grandmother's niece, I said, 'Well, Daddy, she's always at this house.' He said, 'They raised her. Her mother went to Philadelphia.' I said, 'Daddy, well, whereabouts in Philly?' I recall him saying they were in Philly on some street and that they left Cook Ross here because the Rosses wanted her. She was a little girl. So my aunt left to go up there with another aunt, which was my grandmama's sister. I recall my father said, 'She looked like she was never white.'"

"Because they adopted her," Billie explains. "Daddy said she was adopted by them. When her mother left them, they adopted her as [their] daughter." I ask Billie how usual it was for a white family to adopt a black child, even when that child was a blood relation. "I really don't think it happened before." She paused and replied, "No. That was the only one on the Shore. She was blessed, because they adopted her, because it was an unusual thing to do. I recall my father saying that you would see her with the little eggs at the store and trading them for different items at the store in the Accomac."

Billie's story shifts: "When I got to know her, you know, because she was raised with white people, she was different, and we were different so she didn't bother with us much." "She got to know me," Billie speaks to being judged by her friend, "and she told me I had very good grammar, and I told her—at that time I was thirty-two or thirty-three, she thought I was a little young girl—and I said, 'No, ma'am.'" Billie's formality pleased Cook. "She was very impressed with me because I could speak very well, and I said that's one thing my mother had taught us to speak good grammar. That's how I got to know her. One or two times I worked with her at Mr. Hartnett's and they were having dinners. She was there to help me. That's how I got to know her." Cook's role in these events, when she chose to be involved, tended to be supervisory, monitoring the flow of food, keeping an eye on the work of others in the kitchen.

Still, Cook Ross is remembered most of all for her cakes, yeast rolls, and finely carved ham slices. She kept track of birthdays, baking the gift of cakes for children. Billie Mason recalls, "She used to make them a lot for different people for birthdays. Everybody that she knew in Accomac, she would make birthday cakes for, and I used to get a piece. She knew what each person wanted and when their birthday was. She must have kept a record." The cakes she baked were intended for "just the white" children in the community. Margaret Young adds, "My sister Carol, when I asked her about Cook Ross and growing up here in town, she remembers cookies. She loved to go to Cook Ross's house because Cook Ross always had good cookies. If Dad was going to take her fish—he would take fish to various ones in town—Carol made sure she was with Dad when he would go to Cook Ross's house, because she would get some cookies. We didn't have many sweets at our house."

The nature of missing ingredients lies not in the fact of absence but of what absence compels us to remember. Cook Ross's recipe tin presents a different kind of book not unlike a family album composed of a collection of photographs kept in a box. When Kellam Doughty, who lived near Weirwood in neighboring Northampton County, spoke of his family history on Virginia's barrier islands, he would take out his cardboard box that held snapshots, studio portraits, and other images. As he spoke, Kellam dealt the photographs on the kitchen table in a sequence that followed his recollections. The sequence of the deal changed with every telling, the order of pictures as richly inflected, animated, resonant, nuanced as Kellam's voice. I imagine the work of Cook's recipe collection in much the same way. I see her reading the index cards bearing the names of friends; I picture her unfolding the letters received, "Dear Cook—Mother said you asked for my recipe for . . ."

All of this brings me back to a blue tin crammed with recipes—what they remember and what they forget—the silence and seduction of rising dough, the warmth of yeast rolls remembered, the ethereal pleasure of heaven's pillows.

A CHEF'S RECIPE FOR HOME

OYSTERS VIRGINIA
Walter Bundy, Shagbark, Richmond, Virginia
Walter Bundy notes, "This recipe was designed to utilize local products throughout Virginia to enhance the flavor of oysters grown on the Eastern Shore. In this recipe, we use shooting Point Oysters, which are absolutely delicious. The oysters are raised in the bay and finished in the ocean. This creates an oyster that is fruity and delicate with a nice salty finish. Additional local ingredients provide a unique flavor profile that creates a dish that is truly Eastern Shore of Virginia."

Makes 12 roasted oysters
12 Shooting Point oysters or other seaside salty oysters
3 (¼-inch-thick) slices Edwards hickory-smoked bacon or any smoky slab bacon from a butcher shop, cut into small cubes
2 tablespoons unsalted butter, cubed
1 medium shallot, sliced very thin
1 teaspoon red chili flakes
2 garlic cloves, minced
2 big handfuls baby spinach, washed and dried
¼ cup dry white wine
Salt to taste
½ cup finely grated Parmesan cheese
½ cup toasted bread crumbs (homemade or panko-style)
Lemon wedges and your favorite hot sauce (optional)

Clean the oyster shells by scrubbing them under cold water. Shuck the oysters one at a time with care, being sure to remove pieces of chipped shell, sand, or dirt from inside of the oyster. Cut the muscle, freeing the oyster from its shell. Gently flip the oyster over in its shell so the smooth side is facing up and place in a casserole dish.

Preheat the oven to 450°.

Place the bacon in a large sauté pan, and cook it over medium heat. When the bacon is crispy, drain the rendered fat from the pan and discard. This lets the bacon flavors come through and avoids any greasiness in the dish. Add the butter, shallots, and chili flakes to the bacon and continue to cook until the shallots are translucent. Add the garlic and cook until lightly golden. Toss the spinach into the pan, add the wine, and allow the spinach to wilt slightly. Season with salt if desired—remember oysters from the ocean are pretty salty! Transfer the bacon and spinach mixture to a plate lined with paper towels.

Top each oyster with a heaping tablespoon of the bacon and spinach mixture and a generous sprinkle of the cheese.

Roast the oysters for 7–10 minutes or until the cheese is melted and browned.

Sprinkle each oyster with the bread crumbs and serve with lemon wedges and/or hot sauce, if desired. Eat immediately or the magic will be lost!

Theodore Peed's Turtle Party

Two events mark the fall social season on the lower Eastern Shore of Virginia—H. M. Arnold's Bayford oyster house bash and Theodore Peed's turtle party. Venison barbecue anchors the late September menu at Bayford; an array of snapping turtle dishes, including fried turtle with "50 weight gravy," tempt the attendees at Peed's. Potluck dishes, savory and sweet, supplement the spread. For several years the two events occurred on succeeding weekends, but the stamina required for attending both, much less hosting them, exceeded the energies and dedication of all but the passionately committed. Eventually Arnold and Peed, longtime friends, agreed to a longer recuperative interval. On a bright, warm, windy morning in the changing days of mid-October 2010, and three weeks after the Bayford Bash, Peed and his family were deep into turtle party preparations.

Theodore Peed is a generous and impressive man with an operatic laugh. Lean, muscular, and energetic, he moves easily through cooking tasks. His salt-and-pepper hair and beard lend him a patriarchal air, and he speaks with a voice to match—a richly deep and rumbly voice that resonates part growl, part oratory. "Everything I do is simple," he says. "You don't need to be fancy just to cook good." Peed savors big flavors, too. Recalling the longed-for taste of bitter greens, he declares, "That first bite will knock your socks off, man! It'll make you cry! It'll shock you! Like a shot of liquor!" In the bustle of preparations, he greets friends and strangers alike with genuine enthusiasm. The legendary hospitality and humor of his garage kitchen stands as an open invitation. On the day of the turtle party, he muses, "I don't know if I'll do this again. It's a lot of work and expense. This could be the last one." Everyone who knows him understands, hopefully, that this is just Peed talking. The consensus among those helping with the preparations is that, of course, there will be a turtle party next year.

Theodore Peed in his garage kitchen, Hare Valley area, Virginia.

Theodore Peed's garage serves as kitchen, staging center, and working-men's community gathering spot. Located a few steps from his two-story house, the garage faces the road that runs from the crossing of Bayside and Rogers Roads toward a "T" at the fields where William Harmon and the Nottingham brothers grow their Hayman sweet potatoes. On the day of the turtle party Peed opens the garage doors. A table, newly made, with a varnished oval top trimmed with twisted polyrope, occupies the far corner, facing the television perched on a set of storage cabinets. An impressive collection of imperial purple Crown Royal sacks accented with bright gold thread hangs on the wall. Peed observes that there used to be many more in the grapelike cluster. A brother adds that Peed gave the bags to a family member for a quilt that is yet to be made. Family and visitors occupy chairs placed around the table, watch college football games, and chat. Peed's chair claims a proprietorial position at the head of the table.

The business part of Peed's kitchen commands a corner near the open garage bay. Lit by a window and overhead fluorescent lights, the cooking area is furnished only with his two-burner range and a folding card table for last-minute preparations. A row of cupboards to the side doubles as counter space and bar. Antlers and skulls on the wall surround a clock crafted from a snapping turtle shell and gifted to Peed by friends. The clock stopped long ago, marking the time at 7:38. H. M. says, "Somebody should set that clock to 5:00, then it'll be right most of the time."

More folding tables stand next to the refrigerators. When the dining hour approaches, the women in the house will come out and organize a serving line. The back wall is fitted with shelving and storage bins, all neatly screened with colored plastic sheeting. Pens for Peed's yelping hunting dogs range behind the garage; big black cast-iron cauldrons are stacked like helmets to one side; picnic tables used both for butchering and dining flank the gravel drive that leads to the street. Peed notes, "I use them black kettles. A lot of people call them old African kettles. That's what our ancestors used to wash clothes in and then, during hog killing time, cook the lard in."

The family's pets, Peed's Jack Russell named Russell (Russ for short) and his wife Kathy's sweet-tempered pit bull, Hazel, wander in and out, pursuing curiosity and the possibility of handouts. As more folks drift by, the deer feet presented to Russ and Hazel as chews increasingly lose their ability to hold the dogs' attention. The alluring scent of the turtle party's early preparations, the bustle of cooks and bystanders, and the occasional scratch behind the ears offer greater appeal.

Just after 10:00 a.m., Peed pulls a cooler up to his work area and begins unpacking dressed venison, layering it in his welded steel roasting pan.

The meat brined overnight is pale pink. A generous shake of Old Bay Seasoning spices each layer until the pan is full, the tenderloins being the last additions. With the venison prepped, Peed pulls out a knotted black plastic trash bag and heads toward the cooker in the yard. His brothers, Bill and Carl, follow carrying the venison. Peed bangs open the cooker's lid and with his brother shoves the venison into the smoke-filled black interior. He bends and unties the trash bag, extracts the pig carcass, and places it cut-side down on the grill with a soft thud. Satisfied with the arrangement, Peed closes and secures the lid. "The pig takes about four hours," he estimates.

Peed links the history of the turtle party to his reputation as a wild game man: "We started off maybe about fifteen years ago. We killed a lot of rabbits, and we just decided to have a little party with rabbit. Sometimes we would cook twenty-five or thirty rabbits. It would be in the wintertime, so there was collard greens, cabbage, turnip greens, all that stuff." The first rabbit dinners evolved from midwinter hunting suppers and football parties into the annual autumn turtle party. The turtle party also owes a debt to Peed's rainy-day hospitality when friends and acquaintances head to his garage for warmth, conversation, and a bite to eat. Peed's daughter Ebony and friend Chester Satchell join him in describing those occasions.

Peed begins, "You come here in the wintertime—"

Ebony interrupts, "In the wintertime when it rains, because everybody is mostly self-employed, and nobody works when it rains, so they just show up in here."

Chester laughingly interrupts her, "Yes, they do! They work right here!" His tone and humor bring into question the kind of work being done.

Ebony resumes, "They work right here . . ."

Chester presses forward with innuendo, "They work right here in this garage!"

Ebony, undaunted, perseveres, "Then they got to go home and get cussed off because they ate here and their wives . . ."

Chester breaks in, "And they can't eat when they get home!"

Ebony presses on, ". . . and they can't eat when they get home."

Chester concludes, "Remember that white boy stopped by here one day and said, 'I know I smelled some pork chops?'"

Chester's last point reveals a deeper history of the turtle party. Theodore Peed's garage kitchen hosts hunters, outdoor laborers, friends, neighbors, and drop-ins, black and white alike. Some stop by claiming they caught the smell of his pork chops and gravy out on the highway; others drive past Peed's house, sometimes three or four times, to see if he's in. No matter, they show up—and often with contributions in hand. Preparing a meal of

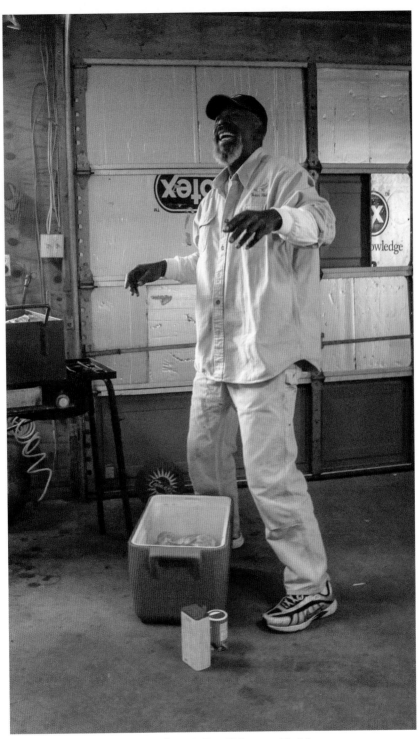

Theodore Peed cooking for the turtle party, Hare Valley area, Virginia.

stewed neck meat and potatoes for twenty or more friends sheltering from an icy winter rain is something Peed just does as a matter of course. The turtle party is "just my thing for my friends," Peed says. True enough, but it is also Peed's celebration of community and his recognized place in it.

Peed tells the story of how he learned to prepare turtle through layers of narrative that blend cooking and family history. Although he states that he taught himself the ins and outs of turtle cuisine, he also draws connections between different facets of the process in ways that highlight family history. Peed begins with his father. "The way I got hooked on them turtles was my daddy. He'd bring them home, but he never caught none, except crawling. But he knowed a few guys that used to 'sign' them. Don't ask me what the sign is. They'd go up in them guts in them creeks, and they'd see a little bubble or something. It had to be something. . . . We used to call it 'signing them,' like with clams. They'd take a hook, reach down there, feel them out around the shell, and pull them out of that mud. It'd be something. You start to get in that mud—it's rough!"

Bayford. H. M. Arnold regales his listeners with a turtle story remembered from his childhood. The refrigerator covered with decals hums; cubes clatter in the ice maker. His father, he recalls, skillfully signed mammoth snappers as they pushed through the muddy ditches and flooded drains of Nassawadox Creek. A thin exhalation of bubbles here; a faint ribbon of coffee-caramel-colored mud there. A small boy rapt in the stern of his father's bateau, H. M. closely monitored his father's moves as he scooped ten-, fifteen-, twenty-pound turtles from the bottom, landing them at his son's feet. The first turtle or two, H. M. remembers, were peaceable enough, drawing in their heads, peering out, justifiably suspicious, thinking as much as turtles think that their situation was not good. More turtles. H. M.'s father heaves the turtles one atop the other—and they begin to fight. We listen intently. I can almost hear the wet thud of turtles landing on the bateau bottom. H. M. details a scene out of an epic Japanese monster movie: Godzilla confronts Megalon! "They were climbing and clawing each other belly to belly! I couldn't get my feet up fast enough or high enough! They were chomping into each other's shells. It was like the sound of crunching Styrofoam egg cartons! I was crying!" H. M. casts a look around the shucking house room where we're gathered. "My dad turned to me as he threw another snapper into the bateau. 'Shut up, boy!' was all he said." We all let go a collective breath. Some sigh, some laugh. H. M. relights his cigar in a halo of smoke. I look out the door at the incoming tide. A pale translucent moon rises against a lurid setting sun. I imagine ghostly turtles trundling through flooded marshes. Snapping turtle soup will never taste the same—only richer and darker for the telling.

When it comes to processing the turtles for the pot, Peed shifts emphasis from his father's to his own abilities, stressing his efficiency and cleanliness: "They used to get them, bring them home, put them in a barrel, put stove ashes in the barrel with them to cleanse them out. I just put them in a barrel, let them stay for about four or five days, and then I kill them. My daddy never showed me what I know how to do with them. Take them, cut the heads off, wash them real good. They'd use lye soap! My grandma used to make that lye soap. Wash the shell real good, then cut him from the bottom there and tore his guts out. Then they used to boil him. Break the shell open and get that backbone out and everything. But to me that wasn't sanitary. You leave any shit in there and it'd be bad. Me, what I'd do, I'm killing two right now. I kill them now, I cut them out of the shell in the morning. Take my knife—my knives, they're sharp—I cut them right there at the edge of the shell and pull all their guts out. Cut him up and soak him out. Put him in the refrigerator for about two days and then put him in the freezer. . . . When I skin him, no meat touches the guts or nothing."

Peed's turtle party is also about the complex social networks that have evolved on the Eastern Shore of Virginia over the past four centuries. When Peed describes his cooking pots, he calls them African kettles and links them to deep histories of foraging, work, and race. The same references hold true for turtle, but with an inversion of social and racial roles. "If a hundred people was here," Peed says, "seventy-five of them is white. Black people will tell you, 'I don't want none of that turtle. Give us some ribs. . . .' Little kids [ask], 'Peed! Peed! Where the turtle at? Turtle soup?' I'm telling you. . . . And I've had a whole lot of rich Eastern Shore people come here who haven't come here before, and say they're coming back again for the turtle. That's a tradition that was popular with black people. They're the ones who really invented turtle. Now you look at TV down South, that's what the white people eat down there. Poor people had to eat. They had to survive, and they found this was something they could eat. It would fill them up and wouldn't make them walk slow. One year I cooked some for my white buddies. I cooked about two. Guys in the wintertime, we'd been hunting—I fried some turtle. I said, 'I'm going to cook some for them.' After they eat, they say, 'Oh, man, this is so good!' I said, 'Oh, I forgot to tell you one thing.' They said, 'What Peed? What, what, what!' 'You won't be walking slow tomorrow.'"

Satisfied with the progress of pig and venison under way, Peed turns his thoughts to breakfast and heads toward the porch and kitchen at the rear of the house. Fifteen minutes later, breakfast in hand, he is back in the garage that serves as the turtle party command center. Fried speckled trout, grits with butter, and fried potatoes with onion crowd his plate. Setting his cigar to the side, he turns to his brothers, Bill and Carl: "They got fish in the house for breakfast." Fish for breakfast is part of the life of this place, a long, narrow peninsula that frames the Chesapeake Bay on one side and provides a buffer to the Atlantic Ocean a few miles to the east. Some families serve their fish with pancakes and syrup, others used to fry salt fish with lard and top it with milk, a preparation that is largely a relic of the past. The Peed brothers recollect how their mother fried apples and pears as an accompaniment: "Fish, the fried apples, and the biscuits for breakfast. I like apples and pears cooked together. Fry a couple of slices of real good bacon. Use the bacon fat and put the apples and pears together. Real hard pears, you put them in about twenty minutes before you put the apples in. Stew them all the way down—got to scorch them a little bit." It was a high-calorie dish designed to sustain a day of manual labor. Peed calculates as he breaks apart his fish, estimating the number of expected guests at roughly a hundred.

There are no invitations to the turtle party, just a general awareness of the date and place and the understanding that family, neighbors, and friends inclined toward a game dinner are welcome. Peed works his way through the mental list of dinner items. The half of a young pig split lengthways and the roasting pan filled with seasoned venison were already cooking in the barbecue rig in the front yard. Bill, Peed's older brother from South Carolina, would stew up five gallons of turtle gumbo. "It's all in the roux and the imagination," Bill remarks. Gumbo is a recent arrival to this part of the South where another lesser-known regional cuisine prevails. Still, roux enjoys its local parallel as the base for "gravy." Peed outlines the preparation: "My ingredient is turtle. Then I make me a gravy. I can take a thirty-gallon pot, that cast-iron pot, and I can make gravy out of that sucker that make you want to smack your momma! My grandmother taught me the gravy. Them old folks—flour, they say, you got to scorch it a little. You got to burn it a little bit. I ain't talking about burning it up, but you just got to scorch it a little bit."

Peed continues checking his mental list. Five large heads of cabbage would be cooked with big chunks of ham rind, salt, and pepper in a cast-iron kettle perched on a homemade propane burner. He plans to fry eighty split marsh hens and the meat of eleven snapping turtles. Inside the house the women in Peed's family prepare potato and macaroni salads.

Peed follows a schedule as steady as the wind soughing through the pines that mark the border between his home and the adjacent cornfield. Parboiled turtle cleaned and picked the night before fills a big aluminum pot. Marsh hens brought plucked and halved by hunting friends occupy a cooler near the refrigerators. Aluminum serving trays, stacks of Styrofoam trencher-like plates, and plastic cups stand ready on folding tables. As the day progresses so, too, does the evening menu. Bill completes his turtle gumbo and sets it aside to season in the pot. Peed turns his talents to the cabbage. The coarsely chopped leaves go into another pot along with a seasoning of cured side meat, salt, and pepper. Ebony, Peed's daughter, scrutinizes the boiling cabbage, sniffs the peppery mix, and gives it a stir with a ladle. She turns to her father and asks pointedly, "Did you season it good?" Meanwhile, a steady stream of family and neighbors flows in and out of the garage, stopping by for a bit of chat and, more importantly, to monitor the proceedings. Men step to the garage; women head for the house. Peed gives the pot one last stir, "The cabbage is ready. I want it an itty bit crunchy." Bill approves, "That's a wonderful aroma coming out of there. It's nice when things come together." "Right on schedule," Peed notes. And the cabbage is done.

Midafternoon arrives, and an early cocktail hour gets under way. The television in the corner continues to broadcast college football. Michigan plays Iowa; Arkansas takes on Auburn; Western Michigan meets Notre Dame—all at 3:30, resulting in a ballet of channel hopping. Conversation touches on sports and local news. Now and again, two speakers bend their heads close together for an exchange of a more private nature. The wind begins to ease and more drop-ins arrive. "Wait until 5:00," Peed states, "and they'll really start pouring in here."

Peed starts the marsh hens, a local favorite shot from shallow draft boats poled through high marsh grass. Arnold helps him hoist and position a ten-gallon iron kettle—a real "double, double toil and trouble" affair— onto the two-burner skeletal steel stove. Peed pours frying oil into the pot, lights the burner with a flaming paper twist, and suspends a thermometer from the rim. Twenty minutes later the temperature hits the requisite 300 degrees. Peed empties two bags of House-Autry mix into a large, clear plastic bag, scoops up a handful of dressed marsh hens, gives the bag a shake, and starts dropping the birds into the oil. The thick, comforting aroma of railbirds frying swirls through the room.

Peed is not alone in his choice of the seasoned breader from House-Autry, a two-hundred-year-old milling concern located in Newton Grove, North Carolina. Like Old Bay, House-Autry debuted comparatively recently in Eastern Shore larders where salt, black pepper, lard, and sweet (sugar, syrup, or molasses) flavored most dishes. The sizzle, hiss, spit of the frying birds drowns out the television. "You know when they're done," Peed says, "just when they start to float." The first batch complete, Peed dips the crusty brown birds out of the kettle with a wire mesh strainer, places them in a paper-towel-lined aluminum pan, and taps the strainer three times

Theodore Peed's turtle party, Hare Valley area, Virginia.

on the pot rim. "That's the secret," a bystander reveals. "Three taps or they don't come out right!" Everyone laughs. "Try this," Peed commands. The fried railbirds are excellent—a dark meat like Canada goose, but with a richer flavor. Five batches later, all the marsh hens are fried and stored in a foil-wrapped serving pan. Peed opens the pot of parboiled turtle meat.

Snapping turtles are the big draw at Peed's annual dinner, and collecting enough turtles for the event without going to too much effort is a community project. There is no shortage of snapping turtles on the Eastern Shore. They live in boggy roadside ditches, farm ponds, and salt creeks bearing names like Nassawadox, Hungars, Mattawoman, Westerhouse, and Occhanock that define the succession of necks along the bay. In spring and early summer, the turtles are on the move, busily following the imperative of making more turtles. Pamela Barefoot, who lives on a branch of Nassawadox Creek, looked out her door one warm and humid morning and discovered a twenty-pound turtle on her doorstep. Driving down the length of Church Neck, it is not unusual to see three or four snappers in the road lurching along, dragging their thick dragon tails, primeval heads extended, intent on their destination. If the turtle is big enough, and the discoverer bold enough, the snapper is snagged and bagged. Occasionally tactical errors occur. Dropping a large and angry turtle in the trunk of a late-model sedan is ill-advised. The problem is not with turtle dirt but with close quarters, especially if the trunk is cluttered with the kind of items that you tend to find in this corner of the world. Things like crab pot floats, spare tractor parts, mesh bags for clams and oysters, and fishing gear offer real obstructions that complicate negotiations with a thoroughly irritated turtle. It takes an experienced eye and a quick hand to grab a cornered snapping turtle by the tail and lift it into a bushel basket. Peed's turtle providers possess that know-how—and share the scars and stories to prove it. The faint of heart or those in a hurry simply phone in their turtle sightings, and Peed or one of his friends hurries to the location to make the capture. The turtles are collected and dropped off at Peed's garage and the various locations he frequents. Arnold stores snapping turtles in transit in a bushel basket in the Bayford oyster house. A visitor might see the basket wiggle a bit on the concrete floor next to the old shucking tables or hear clawing inside and ask, "Peed?" It's a rhetorical question on the Eastern Shore.

Peed's ability to handle and process a snapping turtle is legend. Cigar in one hand, he reaches into the bushel without hesitation and expertly hoists the turtle, evaluating its culinary potential by heft and appearance. He kills the turtles at sunset, cutting off their heads and letting them drain overnight. The next day he carves the meat from the carcass with the grace of a surgeon. With an array of two or three scarily sharp knives and a hatchet, he separates the upper and lower shells, removes the entrails, and neatly extracts six large pieces of turtle meat. Peed is fast and neat: "Now a snapping turtle don't have but six pieces of meat in it. There's the neck, the tail, the two front legs, the two hind legs. There's only one piece of white meat in him, and that's his neck. The rest of the meat is dark meat. If you fry it, it's still like a white piece of meat, like a chicken breast. The rest of it looks like a chicken leg. It's dark." Snapping turtles are not the easiest animals to clean for cooking, but Peed, drawing on expertise developed over years of practice, can process a large one in less than ten minutes. He stores the dressed cuts of meat in a large metal pot before skinning, washing, and freezing. The rest of the turtle, shell and guts, disappears into the woods behind the beagle pens at the back of Peed's land. Peed saves especially large turtle shells as trophies that will be cleaned, varnished, and displayed on the walls of his garage kitchen along with the antlers of the deer he has shot over the years. The turtle supply grows through the summer.

For the turtle party Peed fries the meat harvested from snapping turtles that range in weight from twelve to twenty-five pounds. Prepping the turtles for cooking after butchering and freezing is labor intensive: "If you don't boil him, you cannot eat him. You can skin him, cut the skin off him, and fry him, and he's still tough. What I do [Peed motions toward the door of the garage], I got my pots out there. I have boiled twenty turtles at one time. They're all cut up. I got six pieces—like I said, it don't matter how big he is, there ain't but six pieces in there. You can take a turtle that weighs ten pounds and take one that weighs thirty pounds and you boil them, it will come out almost nearly the same. I boil mine. I look at the bones in it and when the meat starts leaving the bones. And that's the only bone a dog will not eat. He will not eat a turtle bone. It's so damn hard! After I boil them, I take them out, let them cool, and then I skin [them]. I take all that skin off right down to the lean meat. There's nothing on the neck. When you pull it, that's a piece you can cook right then and there if you want to. You still got to boil it, though. Boil that bad boy. Take my fork and hit him. If the fork goes through him like it's supposed to, cut the fire off, take the pot off the burner, let it cool off. Then we get here and start skinning him. Skin will roll right off, you know what I mean, we don't want no slime on him. Then I start frying."

The turtle chunks receive the House-Autry treatment and go into the pot. "I'm not bragging, but the only people that can beat me cooking turtle is somebody that's eighty or ninety years old. Ain't nobody my age around fifty-nine years old. I started cooking [turtle] when I was in my forties. And I've learned a little bit, too, you know what I mean, the more you cook you can kind of ease a little bit in it." The dinner hour is closing in, and more and more turtle-hungry guests fill the yard. Peed relinquishes the turtle-cooking duties to Dora Hyslop, a family friend, and turns his attention to organizing the setup for the serving line. Meanwhile Peed's brothers and H. M. Arnold extract the venison and roast pig from the big cooker and carry the cooked meat into the garage. On one foil-topped table, Peed's brother Carl pulls apart the pork and places the coarsely shredded chunks in a serving pan. A few of the hungry gather around and pick through the cracklings. H. M., long a family friend and turtle party supporter, gets the treat of the head and cheek meat. The venison, too, is pulled from the bone, chopped, shredded, and prepared for serving. Kathy Peed brings the finished turtle to the serving tables.

At some moment in the closing preparations, Kathy, her sisters, sisters-in-law, daughters, and friends take charge. They rearrange the tables into an ell with standing room behind. The sun gone down, guests collect in the pool of light flooding from the open garage doors. Peed circulates through the crowd, cigar in one hand and drink in the other. The noise level continues to rise. Folks foray into the garage to reconnoiter the lineup. Cakes

Theodore Peed's turtle party diners, Hare Valley area, Virginia.

and other desserts collect on the card table near the fryer. Mary Peed directs the placement of dishes in a logical succession: potato salad, macaroni salad, cabbage seasoned with ham, roast pork, venison, fried railbirds, snapping turtle, smoked bluefish, and turtle gumbo. The line continues to grow, snaking into the twilit darkness outside. More and more voices join the conversation, and with each new voice the volume rises. Eagerness and desire fill the air. Then Mary Peed's strong, dignified voice rings out: "There will be no dinner without blessing." The swiftness with which silence falls is startling. The boisterous crowd knows the rules and respects the event. Only the postgame commentary in the background breaks the reverent moment. Heads bow. "Father, we thank the Lord for this food we are about to receive. Lord, we ask that You will bless this food and sanctify it that it might be nourishment for our bodies. God, we thank the Lord for how You bless us time and time again. We thank You, God, for yet one more year that You have allowed this crowd to be together. And God, we give You thanks for this food. In Jesus's name. Amen."

A hungry, heartfelt *Amen* resounds through the early evening. In that instant the distinction between party and ministry dissolves. Conversation roars back to life. Jericho's walls fallen, the righteous victorious, turtle is served. Diners crowd their plates with some of everything, relishing the occasion and food in a moment of connoisseurship, friends and neighbors savoring the flavors that bind them together. The company's gustatory roar of approval is Peed's greatest thanks.

A CHEF'S RECIPE FOR HOME

GOMA-AE: EASTERN SHORE OF VIRGINIA JAPANESE-STYLE BENNE-SEED-DRESSED GREENS

Ross Riddle, HASHi, Virginia Beach, Virginia

Ross Riddle thinks a lot about Eastern Shore of Virginia foodways and ways of utilizing greens. In this recipe he experiments with *goma-ae*, a ubiquitous Japanese side dish composed of blanched spinach that has been squeezed of excess moisture and then dressed with a sesame vinaigrette. This dish requires a hearty leaf. In our conversations, Riddle mentioned that folks are growing benne seeds (an heirloom variety of sesame seed) on the Eastern Shore, and that artisans are producing miso and sake in the great states of Virginia and Maryland. The result is a new-regional riff on a classic from the East, by way of the Eastern Shore of Virginia—and a dish I think would nicely complement fried marsh hens. (See Note for sources for benne seeds, local vinegar, miso, and tamari.)

Serves 4

For the dressing

¼ cup benne seeds (or sesame seeds in a pinch)

2 tablespoons miso paste (chickpea miso or similar mild variety)

1 teaspoon tamari

1 teaspoon honey

½ teaspoon sake

1 tablespoon plus 1 teaspoon rice vinegar or similar

For the greens

1 bunch (½ pound) mustard greens, turnip greens, kale, or leaf spinach, stems removed, and roughly chopped.

To make the dressing

Toast the benne seeds in a frying pan over medium-low heat until a seed or two pop and release toasted fragrance. Set aside to cool. Once cool, place in a mortar and pestle and pulverize to a coarse texture leaving some benne seeds whole. Add the miso, tamari, honey, sake, and vinegar and mix until creamy in consistency. Alternatively, pulse the benne seeds in a food processor until coarsely ground, add the remaining ingredients, and process to incorporate.

To prepare the greens

Prepare an ice bath in a large bowl. Bring a large pot of water to a boil, add the greens, quickly stir, and cook for 30–45 seconds. Strain the greens and transfer them to the prepared ice bath to stop the cooking; cool completely. Remove the greens from the ice bath, strain off the excess water, and squeeze them by the handful to remove the remaining water.

Place prepared greens in a mixing bowl, add one-quarter cup of the dressing, and using your hands, stir the greens around and break them up as necessary to evenly dress. Taste, and add more dressing as desired. Serve chilled or at room temperature, garnish with whole toasted benne seeds. Can be made a few hours in advance and keeps well for a day, so long as moisture has been fully drained from the greens prior to dressing.

Note: Sources for benne seeds, local vinegar, miso, and tamari: Anson Mills (ansonmills.com), benne seeds; Keepwell vinegar (keepwellvinegar.com), vinegars and bitter lemon; Great Eastern Sun (great-eastern-sun.com), Miso Master miso, tamari; South River Miso Company (southrivermiso.com), miso, tamari

On Menus

Pooh Johnston, Cordon Bleu–educated chef, musician, oyster farmer, and bon vivant, and I stand in line in the crowded vestibule of the Glorious Church of Jesus Christ in the Bayside town of Onancock. Just a few blocks from the main road that leads to the highway, the church is an anchor in the African American community on the western edge of town. It's July and it's sweat-wringing hot. Outside, the temperature hits the nineties, and the light reflected off the shell parking lot is enough to shrink your retinas to pinprick diameter. An old fan rattles in the entryway. Where there's prayer, there's hope. It's Friday and the day the Glorious Church sells takeaway lunches in Styrofoam clamshell boxes. The line forms early in the tight confines of the sanctuary corridor, and folks wait patiently. The phone jangles madly with call-in orders, but the spirit of the moment is being there, agonizing over the menu options, absorbing the flow of banter and desire. Swelling toads and a crab cake for me; Pooh is all in for toads. Our choices collected with anticipation and joy, we head to Pooh's home at Only Farm for what folks around here would call dinner—complemented by an excellent rosé. You can't beat fine dining in the rural South.

Reading the Glorious Church menu is a revelation in what defines terroir. The single fuchsia-colored sheet leads with the headline "Friday ONLY—July 22, 2016 Dinners for Sale," followed by some logistical information and the note "Sponsored: Sis. Catherine Edmonds." Looking back, I am mindful of Sister Edmonds's connections to Sara "Cook" Ross, Billie Mason, and the Mapp family in Accomack just a few miles to the north. I read the menu, and it's a catechism of Eastern Shore of Virginia foodways: "baked chicken and dumplings, baked pork chops and dressing, baked turkey wings and dressing." Someone has penned in the addition of meat loaf. The next ten items are fried, beginning with chicken, sea trout, steak fish (or shark), drum, toad fish, and crab cakes. Then come the combinations: steak fish and crab cake, drum ribs and soft-shell crab, toad fish and shrimp. Pigs' feet and chitterlings, the priciest item on the menu, brings down the curtain on this tableau of delights. There are side dishes, too: rolls, butter beans, yams, and potato salad. Two homemade desserts are on offer: lemon pound cake and chocolate almond cake. A note at the bottom of the page requires "CASH Payment ONLY" with the italicized courtesy of "*Sorry for any inconvenience*" appended.

Pooh and I, wilting dollar bills in hand, are fully prepared—and hungry. An elderly customer gone limp, wearied from work and weather, straw hat pulled low, slumps against the wall near the old refrigerator, patiently anticipating his order. Menus from Fridays past lie atop the refrigerator. There are dishes that appear on a weekly basis, and there are those that chart the flow of seasons. I ask Sister Edmonds if I can collect a few. Busy at the stove, she nods. My midday dinner in one hand and a sheaf of Glorious Church menus in the other, I rejoin Pooh in the parking lot. Lunchtime has arrived.

Reading the Glorious Church bill of fare with Pooh, I am reminded of a newspaper clipping from the *Eastern Shore News* that Brooks Miles Barnes, the retired steward of the Eastern Shore of Virginia collections in the public library, sent my way. The subject was the 1925 account of a grand celebratory dinner held in Onancock thirty years earlier and well over a century before Pooh and I debated the pros and cons of our takeaway dining selections in the overheated foyer of the Glorious Church.

Those Were the Happy Days When the Banquet Table Groaned but the Guests Cheered and Made Speeches

One of our friends has unearthed a menu of a banquet held at the Onancock Hotel some twenty-six and a half years ago. The affair was given as an expression of the esteem in which Prof. F. P. Brent was held by his fellow townsmen, but we, being of a later day, the list of distinguished guests did not startle us as much as the menu.

Maybe we can, today, set out a bill of fare like the one Mrs. William West prepared almost three decades ago, but physicians and health guides tell us we're eating too much as it is (when we can get it) and besides it took real men and women to stand a meal like the one sixty guests had spread before them at the Brent Banquet.

Any housewife is at liberty to match it whenever the notion appeals to her and if the weather is nice and cool she may be assured that some old timers will be on hand to do justice to the cooking. The younger generation is too busy to spend the time in eating—even if it had the appetite.

Here's the menu:

Oranges, Apples, Grapes.
Oysters—Raw, Stewed, Fried, Half Shell.
Terrapin a la Accomack.
Meats—Roast Turkey, Roast Beef, Roast Chicken, Smithfield Ham,
    Cold Tongue, Omlet [sic] and Salad.
Relishes—Pickles, Olives, Cranberry Sauce.
Breads—Hot Rolls, Light Bread, Biscuit, Crackers.
Cakes—Pound Cake, Jelly Cake, Fruit Cake, Minnehaha Cake,
    Rochester Cake, Ice Cream Cake, Chocolate Cake.
Ice Cream—Vanilla, Lemon, Strawberry and Chocolate.
Salted Almonds.
Coffee, Milk, Tea, Chocolate.
Mr. Thomas W. Taylor was Toastmaster and the report of the banquet states that thus "the responses to the toast were full of wit and good humor." A dinner of that magnitude and variety would either make or break a man when it came to a question of after dinner speechmaking."

Notable in their absence are the staples of everyday fare mapped by baked fish stews, clam fritters, oyster pies, or Hayman sweet potatoes. This was a grand fete where a respected local cook's mastery of fancy delicacies was on full display for her discerning audience. The distinctively local—oysters served four ways and terrapin soup—cavorted with more generic roast turkey, chicken, and beef. The newspaper editor, looking back in amazement on the feast, marveled, "The banquet closed by singing *Auld Lang Syne*. Think of it! They sang after that meal!" I wonder if the toastmaster saluted the terrapin and oysters, who gave their all for the satisfaction of the assembled gourmands, even as the assembled diners raised their glasses to honor the distinguished professor.

The remembrance of the great feast for Professor Brent, like the Glorious Church weekly bill of fare, reveals the work menus perform around the promise of plenty, the cultivation of wonder, and the satisfaction (or on occasion frustration) of desire. I wonder about how the menu for a Gilded Age gala connects with Sister Edmonds's straightforward litany of offerings. Menus, I realize, are more than recitations of dishes for sale. They are collations of options and opportunities for pleasure and reflection. They map the crossroads of cuisine in each offering. A menu promises a destination that originates in shared understanding. No matter what fork in the

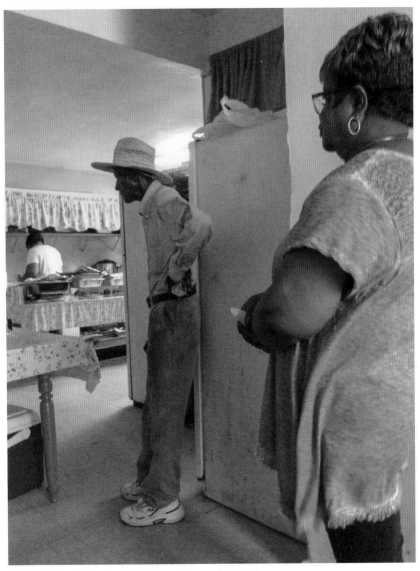

Glorious Church of Jesus Christ diners, Onancock, Virginia.

culinary road is taken at the Glorious Church, all paths converge on service to congregation and community made manifest in the taste of place. When it comes to the Eastern Shore of Virginia and other locales that celebrate the happy conjunction of place and plate, menus look to the past and promise the future.

I turn to chefs who know their way around a menu and what it takes to bring a memorable meal into the world. These chefs may be "from away" as folks "from here" are wont to say, but they know the Eastern Shore as

351

surely as they know a toad from an amphibian, a baked fish stew from a chowder, and a Hayman sweet potato from a Beauregard. They grasp the ingredients and cookery of the Eastern Shore of Virginia and respect the cuisine of place. In the universe of clam fritters and oyster pies they discern an infinity of possibility and the rewards of invention. Their observations cohere around some points and diverge markedly on others. What I discover in their diversity of thought are themes for "a South you never ate."

I read each chef the listing of Sister Catherine Edmonds's dinner entrées, side dishes, and desserts: "Meat loaf, Baked chicken and dumplings, $8. Baked pork chops and dressing, $10. I'll cut the prices now. Baked turkey wings and dressing, fried chicken, fried trout, fried steak fish, fried drum, fried toadfish, fried crab cakes, fried steak fish and crab cake, fried drum and soft-shell crab, fried drum ribs and soft-shell crab, fried toadfish and shrimp, pigs' feet and potato salad, pigs' feet and chitlings, rolls, mashed potatoes, string beans, butter beans, corn bread, macaroni and cheese, yams, potato salad, lemon pound cake, chocolate almond cake." I don't reveal who or where the menu comes from. I present it as a reading akin to a blind tasting.

"Can I go there right now?" Kevin Callaghan, chef and owner of Acme Food & Beverage Co. in Carrboro, North Carolina, asks, excitement and hunger in his voice. "Can I just have a late lunch? Can I just barrel into that stuff?" Kevin keeps Tom Gallivan's oysters on his menu, and when he visits the Eastern Shore, he leaves any hint of restraint on the far side of the Chesapeake Bay. He reflects on the list of dishes, "It feels like a place where people work. It feels like food for people who are sweating. It sounds very African American. Turkey wings—I know that that is something that's very southern. Potato salad, seeing that with pigs' feet, that reminds me of family that I knew growing up. It has a strong soul food component. It just reminds me so much of my growing-up food, like my grandparents' cooking. All that stuff sounds so," he hesitates, "—like the drum ribs, steak fish. Like what is that? It sounds so good to me!"

Kevin adds to his interpretation, "It lacks all pretense, which I really love. Steak fish, crab cakes, collard greens. Come get it. It seems to me like they're talking to you about something that everyone is in agreement about. Everyone knows it's delicious and it's sort of like the canon. Like, this is it! This is what we serve. Anything else makes no sense."

Kevin expands his remarks to make a second point that resonates with the Eastern Shore *mengue de camarones* we shared a week earlier: "I can go down to the street, to the taco truck, and get spectacularly handmade tortillas with delicious pork *carnitas* in them. He's using North Carolina pork, he's using North Carolina corn, he's doing all those things, but it's rooted

Glorious Church of Jesus Christ takeaway of fried drum, green beans, greens, and corn bread, Onancock, Virginia.

in his tradition, which is separate from mine." A menu, Kevin concludes, curates desire and speaks to histories, traditions, and inventions. "We're creating something, and we're involved with something that's important. Something that means a lot to us. We are saying that we value these things. We value these producers. We value these concepts, and we're going to express them through our menu. Again and again and again."

Chef Ricky Moore, who grew up in the Pamlico Sound country of North Carolina little more than a shout away from the Eastern Shore, echoes Kevin's menu commentary. "It's a document that is almost like a calling card for a place that serves food, or a calling card for the event," he begins. "It lets people know what's to come. It's the beginning and the future. The menu is ever living and breathing. That's the beautiful thing about it."

Ricky takes this to heart in the daily menu of Saltbox Seafood Joint, his down-home fish restaurant in Durham, North Carolina. "It continues. It is always continuing. You write a menu, you let the seasons dictate, but just like the season, it keeps coming back. It always continues. Always continues. I think that's another thing, too, the idea of a menu—it's always something to come." "I don't have a paper menu. I don't have anything to pass out," he describes his own bill of fare. "I've got it on a chalkboard." I recall the scattered photocopies atop the Glorious Church refrigerator.

"We wrote it on something, and we charged what we charged, and that was it," Ricky states. "It could be on a piece of paper, it could be on the back of a pickup truck. It just felt good to go to a place, man, where they didn't spend the time creating a piece of paper. They spent more time helping tell the story with what they had." Steak fish, drum ribs, pigs' feet, butter beans, yeast rolls, pound cake. "You've got to make sure whatever you're delivering, there's going to be people there who can appreciate what you're doing." Ricky underscores the importance of seasonality, lack of pretense, and the fact that a menu that says less subtly provides an index to an often unstated sense of place and sensibility.

"The art of the menu," chef Amy Brandt, who lives and cooks on the Eastern Shore of Virginia, begins, "is to make people feel happy and welcomed and also honored." She responds to the Glorious Church menu, "It's pretty black and white there. You know what you're getting. You know how it's going to be prepared, and you know what is coming. You choose the sides. So you have created your own, your own destiny with that menu. With that, you're creating your own destiny." A menu of destiny, I like that!

"There's definitely a trust factor there." Amy elaborates, "More words would be superfluous in that kind of place. That menu sits where it came from." That sounds like a convergence of tradition and terroir to me. "That menu, too," Amy notes, "encourages you to ask questions." I ask Amy what those questions might be. "That menu," she responds, "makes you ask, where is this from, how is it made, whose recipes are these?" Amy catches her breath, "Why are these dishes on this menu?" Helpfully, she provides an answer, "These items have deep connections to community!" The Glorious Church menu is about cuisine; it makes manifest the long and living arc of histories of everyday life in a distinctive corner of the world. It is testament and communion. It is midday dinner.

Chef Sydney Meers, owner of Stove in Portsmouth, Virginia, and a frequent forager for Eastern Shore seafood and produce, reminds me that a menu invites performance even as it relies on shared understanding. "The menu is like the playbill of the show," he says. "People come to the show. They may or may not have anything interesting written on that playbill, but they get keywords." For example, fried toad fish and drum. Common knowledge, he explains, means that "the audience, they all contributed to that menu collectively. It is a story people want to hear." Like his menus at Stove, where service staff often narrate and elaborate on the restaurant's offerings.

The menu from the Glorious Church is founded on the premise that diners know the terrain they eat: "That's an example of a menu that is about people who know exactly what it is, so you don't need to write a description or anything. You just list all this stuff and all these vegetables, and you pick what you want, take it, and go." "I look at a menu as a short, written book," Sydney explains. "In a way, when we write menus, they're like little small, quick-written books. I have all my menus, say, back to, from forever, because I reflect back on them to see what I was doing and thinking then and how I've progressed or if I went back to some of the old ways because I found them to be better. It's definitely a reference for me—and I'm sure it is for the other chefs. So it's kind of like a little book that you keep reading." Sister Edmonds's book is inspirational reading.

A menu is not just a book, it is a script, a history lesson, an archive, and an art form. Echoing Sydney's perspective, Ricky Moore notes: "I need to be my audience. You know what I mean? I need to think about the audience as I am also crafting or creating that menu." His menus are for the diners who frequent Saltbox and a living testament to his own art. A menu, he says, is a "crafted document that chronicles and speaks to what will be served." He builds an analogy to the scoring and performance of a musical work. "A musician and a chef, they share a lot of similarities, and those who have that talent to create something thoughtful and honest and pure and from a place of authenticity. The rhythm to the season. You define those ingredients, and you put them together in such a way so they're like harmonious, a natural fit or contrasting fit. For me, that's kind of how I look at it."

For Spike Gjerde, chef and founder of Woodberry Kitchen in Baltimore, a menu takes shape as a manifesto of place and season. "I believe that the menu of the future is abundantly populated with fish and shellfish from the Chesapeake and the nearby Atlantic. These traditions, they're dying away and they're dying out. They're dying with the people that have preserved them and kept them alive, as they pass away, and they are dying at the hands of our corporate food interests, and they're dying in the wake of trends and fads and our inability to appropriately value what we have, what has come before, and what is worth preserving."

I'm not quite so pessimistic, but I take Spike's point. Spike draws a connection between his menus at Woodberry Kitchen and the weekly listings at the Glorious Church: "I would say that my menu is closer to Sister

Kevin Callaghan cooking with Eastern Shore ingredients at
Acme Food & Beverage Co., Carrboro, North Carolina.

Catherine's menu than any restaurant menu that you could pick out for
me." He perceives "a unity of purpose with what she's doing around food"
and how the menu proclaims that purpose in words and explanations that
bring people together.

Spike periodically brings his culinary crew to the Eastern Shore of Virginia, where they sample oysters and clams and soft-shell crabs, forage
wild salt greens in the Atlantic marshes, taste fish peppers and strawberries, and debate the merits of fig varietals. Spike observes, "It's not a
place where a lot of things are from. There's a very specific roster of things
that are from there, but it's not lengthy. But if I'm there, that's what I want

on the menu. I want oysters. I want crabs. I'd love to have fluke [summer flounder]. I'd love to have figs, if they're in season—preserved or dried, if they're not. I'd love to have some clams from Tom Gallivan," Spike says, considering his options. "I'd love to have those stewed or in a soup if possible." He turns to the idea of a menu that could address all of the ingredients in his imagined larder: "I want a menu that follows the contours of the land and the sea. I'm interested in how the food that we eat relates to where we are." Then I hit Spike with Sister Edmonds's midday dinner listing from the Glorious Church in Onancock. "I would guess that's a menu that is geographically close to the region that you're writing about," he speculates, "and for that reason, I love it." "Is it close?" he asks. "I wish I could eat there tonight," Spike choruses Kevin and Amy. "I especially want to have . . . ," he catches himself midsentence. "Did you say drum ribs?" I detect desire in Spike's voice.

Like Kevin, Amy, Sydney, and Ricky, Spike situates Sister Edmonds's menu not just in a geographic locale but also within a constellation of shared understanding that is as much about community as it is about food. A sense of worry, however, tinges his reading. "I think there was a point in time where that menu, as an inventory, would've made perfect sense to someone and would be perfectly coherent. It says all that probably needed to be said about that food to someone that grew up there." "Because we've lost a lot of the commonality of our food experience," he collects his thoughts, "that's no longer the case. There might be differences in how our fried drum was prepared, but we basically knew what somebody meant—I mean, there are a lot of folks now that wouldn't necessarily know that drum was a fish."

"A menu like that without a lot of explanation or narrative," Spike explains, "was possible when traditions were stronger and still intact." "Steak fish and butter beans," he expands his observations on Sister Edmonds's menu, "It's so rare that anyone will kind of 'merely' cook what you know, what that place will provide." "It's just so rare that we get to taste that," he highlights the point, pausing for emphasis, "to get to taste something that's truly kind of connected—to a place—through its history—to experience what a place really tastes like. You and I are talking about, not only a way to feed ourselves, but also a way of living." Terroir and tradition are, in their humble way, still very much on the menu at the Glorious Church.

Sister Catherine Edmonds's bill of fare is unique only in its attachment to the Glorious Church of Jesus Christ in Onancock. Notices pinned to the community bulletin boards in local post offices, flyers taped to the doors and windows of Eastern Shore businesses, the daily specials enumerated on diner chalkboards, or the lists of gordita options displayed on taco

Spike Gjerde of Woodberry Kitchen, Baltimore,
preparing Seaside clams, Church Neck, Virginia.

trucks trumpet their declarations of the place. The Calvary United Methodist Church Supper in Parksley, an old Bayside railroad town, enticed diners (and likely a few hungry sinners) with the promise of "all you can eat" followed by "Menu Consists of: Clam Fritters, Crab Cakes, Fried Chicken, Baked Ham and much more." A century earlier the proprietor of the Wachapreague Hotel raised funds for his church: "Big dinner and supper 'Thanksgiving' at Hotel Wachapreague. Bill of fare—roast turkey and cranberry sauce, goose, oysters in every style, roast beef, chicken salad, venison pastry, mince, pumpkin and potato pies, cakes, chocolate, etc. Special dishes to order. Everybody invited, bring your girls, wives, brothers, sisters and friends. Music on Victor talking machine, piano, &c. Ice cream and oyster, &c., served every Saturday afternoon for benefit of the new church."

Visitors recounted local menu offerings with glowing narratives that paired terroir as the taste of place with the delectation of authenticity. Their accounts invariably rejoiced in the writers' gastronomic encounters with the rustic, the everyday, the homegrown exotic. Howard Pyle, in his 1879 narrative of his "grand tour" through Delaware and the Eastern Shore of Maryland and Virginia in *Harper's*, reprised a Hog Island repast with island residents: "These fishermen live in small cottages on the westward end of the island, standing back each in a little yard, some with a row of fig-trees in front, their outward appearance poorly indicating the sumptuousness of the bill of fare of the meal the visitor will receive within— ham and eggs, hot corn bread, drum-fish steaks, clam stew, coffee, and preserves. No matter how poor these people are, they always manage to live well, having for their every meal what people of the outside world consider dainties." His words resonate with the reactions of chefs Spike, Kevin, and Amy when I read them Sister Edmonds's Glorious Church menu.

A half century after Pyle, George Shiras III looked back on his sojourns on Revel's Island just to the north of Hog Island. In his reminiscence, Shiras, recognized as a pioneer in modern wildlife photography, lauded the culinary skills of "Aunt Caroline, a faithful and proficient colored cook, [who] had charge of the club kitchen for more than a generation." "Living in a State famous for its culinary art, she had few equals," he wrote, and then turned his attention to the menu she maintained for guests of the island hunting lodge. In addition to preparing oysters "in several ways," Shiras informed his readers that "the making of delicious clam chowder was one of her greatest accomplishments, and large clams were always available on a sandspit only about 100 yards away." "In the winter months, eels speared in their hibernating places in the mud at the heads of creeks were another delicacy on the bill of fare. In the hunting season Aunt Caroline produced the most appetizing dishes of perfectly cooked ducks and shore birds, besides stewed terrapin and snipe potpies. The memory of her pastries, including apple and pumpkin pies, puddings, doughnuts, and other tasty products of her skill, still remains with me."

Shiras enthused on the verge of swooning, "Even the little tin lunch pails that were sent out to the blinds with us were like little Christmas boxes with their varied assortment of good things to allay the hearty appetites we had sharpened by hours in the open air." The remembered bill of fare from Aunt Caroline and the unnamed Hog Islanders resonate with Ricky Moore's commitment to "plain" cooking as an index to the character of place and Spike Gjerde's celebration of terroir as a coming together of ingredients, technique, and local knowledge.

Every menu is much more than the itemized listing it provides. Menus are invitations to invention through pairings and juxtapositions. They are a literature where individual items speak to the expertise of the cook and the expectations of the diner. Menus are the most optimistic of all literary forms. They are about art and gratification. Eastern Shore menus like Sister Edmonds's are about the dynamic play of complement and juxtaposition that reaches far beyond the immediacy of meals and deep into the nuances and poetry of plate and place. When Howard Pyle wrote of a Hog Island fisherman's bill of fare and George Shiras recollected the perfection of Aunt Caroline's kitchen, they provided menus extracted from the worlds they encountered and how they consumed and enjoyed them on the most basic and intimate level. And, as they reported, there is always room for discovery, invention, and pleasure.

I drive north on a late spring morning, turning onto the highway from the sandy lane that leads to Amy Brandt's kitchen located just inside the entrance to Eyre Hall plantation just north of Cape Charles. Amy and I have just sampled a batch of Gricelda Torres Segura's crab tamales and exulted in their excellence. Gricelda smiled happily with pride and delight. I'm on an errand to H. W. Drummond's Belle Haven automotive (and just about everything else) supply store. I'm in immediate need of crab pot line, work gloves for culling oysters, and thirty feet of log chain to clear a fallen pine out of the fig orchard. There's work to be done before deepest summer sets in.

I drive past Cheriton and think of Ron Crumb and Kay Crumb Downing talking about the perfection of clam fritters. I catch the stoplight in Eastville and in that idle moment hear Jack Robbins describe his recipe for candied Hayman sweet potatoes. Closing in on Machipongo, I'm grateful for the abundance of Mr. Baines's strawberry patch in the season just past. At Nassawadox I cast a longing eye toward Doña Avelina's lunch truck and the promise of her *barbacoa* gorditas. By the time I reach Exmore, I'm thinking about early autumn and spot fried hard featured on the Exmore Diner bill of fare. I'm looking forward to Theodore Peed's turtle party and H. M. Arnold's Bayford bash. I recall the remembered affection for Cook Ross's yeast rolls and the Weatherly brothers' candid recollections of hard times and one-pot suppers. That bit of woolgathering puts me in mind of Seaside oysters and clams from Heather Terry Lusk and Tom Gallivan. My journey north is a recitation of places, people, terroir, and cuisine. Each mile marker along my route evokes an Eastern Shore of Virginia menu.

I turn off the highway at the Belle Haven light, knowing that up the road the promise enshrined in the Glorious Church bill of fare burns brightly. At Drummond's, I park and exit the car, inhaling the perfume of rain on warm asphalt. A photocopied bulletin posted in the window next to the entry catches my attention. The headline proclaims, "Country Cooking and Country Gospel!" The exclamation point strikes me as an unnecessary afterthought.

CHEFS' RECIPES FOR HOME

CAST-IRON SHELLFISH AND GRITS

Spike Gjerde, Woodberry Kitchen, Baltimore, Maryland
Spike Gjerde deftly synthesizes two great southern culinary traditions in his take on an Eastern Shore one-pot meal. You can substitute a very coarse grind of Pungo Creek speckled cornmeal for the white corn grits. The Pungo Creek cornmeal is milled from a nineteenth-century varietal grown and processed by Bill and Laurel Savage near the seaside village of Quinby.

Makes 2 servings
For the shellfish and grits
½ cup white corn grits
2½ cups water, divided
⅓ pound (150 grams) slab bacon, diced
2 dozen Eastern Shore black clams, shucked, and juices reserved for the gravy
1 dozen Nassawadox oysters, shucked
2 celery ribs, sliced widthwise ½ inch thick
¼ teaspoon (1 gram) fish pepper flakes
1¼ teaspoons (6 grams) salt
For the gravy
¼ cup (50 grams) bacon fat
1¼ cups (250 grams) chopped onions
½ teaspoon (2 grams) fish pepper flakes
¾ teaspoon (3 grams) minced fresh sage
3 tablespoons (35 grams) all-purpose flour
2 cups milk
1¼ teaspoons (5 grams) salt

To cook the fish and grits
Hydrate the grits in 1¼ cups of the water overnight.

Warm a 9-inch cast-iron pan over moderate heat. Add the bacon and cook, stirring occasionally, until the fat is rendered and the bacon begins to color, about 7 minutes. Remove the pan from the heat and cool the bacon and fat at room temperature until cool to the touch. Press the clams, oysters, and celery into the fat and move the pan to the refrigerator.

Bring the remaining water to a boil in a small pot. Whisk the soaked grits and soaking water into the water, along with the fish pepper and salt. Cook until thickened, whisking occasionally, for about 30 minutes.

Pour the hot grits into the chilled pan of seafood and return the pan to the refrigerator to cool completely, at least 2 hours.

Preheat the oven to 350°F.

Place the pan on the range over high heat. Cook for 4 minutes (the grits should be visibly frying around the edge). Place the pan in the oven to warm through, about 15 minutes. Meanwhile, make the gravy.

To make the gravy

In a skillet or frying pan, heat the bacon fat over medium-high heat, add the onions, and cook until well browned. Add the fish pepper and sage, then stir in the flour. Cook for 3 minutes (being careful not to scorch the flour), then whisk in the reserved clam juice and the milk. Add the salt, reduce the heat, and simmer for 5 minutes.

When the grits and shellfish mixture is done, invert it onto a warm plate and cut it with a sharp knife. Serve with the hot gravy.

WESTERHOUSE OYSTERS

Bernard L. Herman, Westerhouse, Virginia

This dish is a combination of several recipes from the turn of the twentieth century, along with white wine I've introduced into the mix. The idea, though, comes from the late Hooksie Walker of Bayford. When asked for the list of ingredients for his favorite oyster stew recipe, Hooksie famously replied, "Oysters." That was it. I take this dish a little further. It is also worth knowing that you can put this together in short order for a large group. The oysters are especially good served with sweet potato ham biscuits as a side.

Makes 4 servings
1 pint unwashed shucked oysters with their liquor
½ cup (1 stick) butter, divided
Dry white wine in equal volume to the oyster liquor
Cayenne pepper to taste
Paprika to taste
Flat-leaf parsley, chopped

Preheat the oven to 425–450°. Pour the oysters into a colander and let drain, reserving the liquor. Grease a 10 × 12-inch ceramic baking pan with ¼ cup of the butter. Place the oysters in the dish side by side—being careful not to overlap them.

Whisk the oyster liquor with the wine to thoroughly blend; set aside.

Place the pan of oysters on the middle rack of the oven and cook for 5–7 minutes or until the oysters start to puff and the gills curl. Remove the oysters from oven and carefully pour in the liquor and wine mixture, being sure not to completely submerge the oysters. Put a pat of the remaining butter on top of each oyster and season with a bit of cayenne. Return the dish to the oven for 5 minutes or until the liquid is hot.

To serve: Using a slotted spoon, divide the oysters among 4 bowls, then ladle the hot broth into each bowl. Dust with paprika and sprinkle with a bit of parsley and serve hot.

Thank-You Notes

This book began with the generous encouragement of Marcie Cohen Ferris and David S. Shields. Separately and together, they recognized the power of the Eastern Shore of Virginia's complex food histories and, more important, my deep and abiding affection for the place I think of as my home. Marcie invited me to speak to the Southern Foodways Alliance before the idea for a book was even set. Marcie subsequently introduced the possibility of a two-day Eastern Shore of Virginia foodways tour in 2009 for chefs, writers, and researchers. On our ride back from an early morning breakfast on Hog Island, she suggested, "You should write a book." So, I did—and I hope it meets her expectations.

David and I have shared more Eastern Shore of Virginia adventures and meals than I can count—and they are all memorable. My favorite occurred around 1973 when we were camping out in an early nineteenth-century plantation office overlooking the vast marshes stretching eastward to Virginia's barrier islands and the Atlantic. It was a winter night, bone-cracking cold, and we were trying to roast chowder clams balanced on bricks lined up on the hearth in front of an anemic fire. A third friend, Rick Belcher, huddled in the shadows wrapped in blankets, his shivering audible over the northeast wind rattling the door and windows. David was pounding away on a portable typewriter; I was encouraging the clams to get done. "What are you writing?" Rick asked, muffled in his wad of blankets. "A one-act play," Dave responded with good cheer, "about three characters who freeze to death in an unheated cabin." "Want a clam?" I asked. "Don't mind if I do," David looked up. Rick shuddered in frozen anguish and refused. Chowder clams are big and tough, so David and I chewed thoughtfully for a very long time. We are chewing, yet.

My greatest thanks go to the many, many people who shared their time and conversation over the years. Their collective recollections are the heart and soul of this book, and I hope they find that I have recorded their insights with respect, admiration, and affection. They are all mentioned by name throughout the preceding pages, but a few individuals require additional thanks. I turned to them on multiple occasions for clarifications and amplifications: H. M. Arnold, Theodore Peed, Danny Doughty, Mary "Mama Girl" Onley, Buck Doughty, Jon and Honey Moore, Kenny Marshall, John Marshall, Robert and Jen Bridges, Bobby and Deborah Bridges, Ron Crumb, Kay Crumb Downing, Caramine Kellam, Amine Kellam, Polk Kellam, Pete Terry, Brooks Miles Barnes, Dee Spady, Marilyn Sharp, Janice Weatherly Walters, Maiana and Jessica Garcia, Erika Peterson, Anne Nock, Pooh Johnston, Mills and Jon Wehner, Jack Robbins, Edward Owen, Bob Netherland, Deborah Krohn, Catherine Whalen, and William and Gloria Harmon.

Our region holds several dubious distinctions: declining population since 1930, longest history of persistent poverty in Virginia, and struggling schools. It is also a place of exceptional promise. My friend and museum historian Sandy Lloyd poses the question like this: "What song does this place sing best?" On the Eastern Shore of Virginia that song has always been about what people grew, what they fished, and how

Produce for sale, Cape Center, Virginia.

they cooked and feasted in times of abundance and made do in times of want. Around 2010 a small group of us came together and created Eastern Shore of Virginia Foodways, a small organization dedicated to the idea of "one job for one person so one family doesn't have to leave." Our principal goal remains the cultivation of an awareness of the extraordinary terroir and cuisine of this place. Group founders Tom Gallivan, Mills Wehner, Heather Terry Lusk, and Amy Brandt endorsed this project from the start. We have also had great help along the way. Thanks for forbearance and encouragement go to Ann Arsiniu, Jon Wehner, Paul Brandt, and Gus and Airlia Gustafson.

Hilary Hartnett-Wilson of the Eastern Shore of Virginia Historical Society hosted two *A South You Never Ate* dinners. Among the guests were high school students pursuing careers in the culinary arts with the goal of remaining on the Eastern Shore. Sally Dickinson and Laura Vaughan of the Barrier Islands Center generously provided opportunities for public presentations where audiences heard and commented on the project as it progressed. Robert Gustafson and Bill Neal readily experimented with the cultivation and preservation of historic cultivars, most notably Hayman sweet potatoes and Hog Island figs, both listed on the Slow Food International Ark of Taste.

I have been the happy recipient of encouragement and support from friends and colleagues at the University of North Carolina. In addition to Marcie, who has been there from start to finish, I offer particular thanks to my colleagues Elizabeth Engelhardt, Randall Kenan, Sharon Holland, Bland Simpson, Joy Kasson, John Kasson, Steve Weiss, Aaron Smithers, and Terry Rhodes. Ayse Erginer, Katherine Roberts, Emily Wallace, and Emma Calabrese, the editorial visionaries behind *Southern Cultures*, published by the Center for the Study of the American South, lifted this project more than they might imagine. Early versions of the chapters on Theodore Peed's turtle party, drum head soup, and spot appeared in those pages and were much improved through their thoughtful interventions. I thank as well the many students who assisted with the transcription of interviews and supplementary research. Katy Clune's efforts in the collection and editing of more than 750 oyster recipes created between 1885 and 1915 were heroic. A William R. Kenan Senior Faculty Research and Study Leave made it possible to complete the research and writing for this book.

I reserve special thanks for John Powell. His enthusiasm and support for researching, teaching, and sharing the diverse cultures of the American South is deeply inspirational. This book would not exist without his generosity of spirit.

Beyond the University of North Carolina, I am grateful for the enthusiasm shared by a community of growers, writers, home cooks, and chefs. Eating figs and ham washed down with prosecco with writer Lorraine Eaton as we listened to marsh hens clucking, chuckling, and rustling in the tall grass is an enduring moment. So, too, are conversations shared with Glenn Roberts, founder of Anson Mills, on the challenge of preserving the threatened cultivars that enrich the American table. Chefs welcomed the possibilities of an Eastern Shore of Virginia cuisine. In addition to those whose contributions are reflected in the book, I extend appreciation to Travis Milton, Bill Smith, Andrea Reusing, and Kevin Johnston. John T. Edge, Jessica Harris, Psyche Williams-Forson, Dana Bowen, and Molly O'Neill cheered this project forward at crucial moments. Sarah Camp Arnold Milam recruited an early essay on the Bayford party for the Southern Foodways Alliance journal *Gravy*.

I am thankful always for the support and enthusiasm of the University of North Carolina Press. Elaine Maisner shared crucial advice in the earliest formulation of the project. Mark Simpson-Vos guided the manuscript through the acquisition process, offering much needed guidance every step of the way. The comments of two anonymous external reviewers set the tone for revisions and amendments that surely improved the final work. Laura Jones Dooley and Mary Carley Caviness provided much-needed copyediting. Kim Bryant's patience in the design process was the epitome of collaboration.

Family was always there—at least in time for dinner. Fredrika Jacobs, my sister, and her husband, Paul, sampled everything and often asked for seconds as did their daughter, Jessica, her husband, Nikolai Roussanov, and their son, Peter. Peter, descended from a family of musicians, is a maestro with the goose call. My daughter,

Lania, helped forage for wild mushrooms, pick figs, and work our oyster ground. When it comes to more challenging possibilities of the table, she keeps an open mind. Lucy Spigel Herman, my mother, introduced us all to the Eastern Shore of Virginia—and we are forever thankful.

My greatest debt goes to Rebecca Herman. When we were first married and engaged in a formative dispute, she stepped back and said, "If you don't apologize, I'll never bake croissants for you again!" I was stunned—not because I might not ever have another of her croissants, but because I couldn't remember the first time and I couldn't admit to such an egregious sin of forgetfulness. My predicament was dire. I backpedaled as hard as I could. Later, much later, she confessed that she had never made croissants but figured she knew me well enough that the prospect of the idea of my having forgotten those first imaginary croissants would confuse me and carry her side of the argument. She was right. Subsequently, she baked croissants—twice—and I consumed them with pleasure and affection. She has always kept me honest, and I have always loved her. This book is for her—and the promise of croissants.

Crumbs A Note on Sources

Conversations are the heart and soul of this book. Over the course of a decade, Eastern Shore of Virginia farmers, watermen, cooks, gardeners, neighbors, and friends graciously and generously shared stories that touched on every aspect of the history and evolution of the taste of place that defines this distinctive American terroir. Folks told tales in their kitchens and living rooms, on the dock and in the fields, over the stove and at the table. Some conversations ran two hours long; some lasted mere minutes; no small number unfolded over months and years through planned and chance encounters. I always carried a notebook and small voice recorder in my pockets. Folks began to tease me in company, "Careful of what you say! He'll get it all down!" And still the stories came, told with laughter, wistfulness, seriousness, and a unifying desire to make their world of the table known to others. First and foremost, this book respects and honors the living voice of the Eastern Shore of Virginia. The quotations are direct and minimally edited to reduce repetition and conversational asides. The words spoken are rendered without abbreviation or any other gesture toward accent, intonation, or individuality of voice. They are true to words and phrases as uttered.

The Eastern Shore of Virginia is home to the oldest continuous court records in British North America. Unbroken from 1632, the legal proceedings of the two counties document everything from criminal acts to property transaction to litigation over personal estates. References to foods and foodways appear with exceptional frequency, but almost invariably in the context of some other legal proceeding. I'm mindful, for example, of testimony in an adultery case of the 1640s in which two witnesses discussed how they were "pounding a spell of hominy" while the accused cavorted in an adjoining room or the construction of a poisoned cake in the early 1800s that claimed the life of a mother and daughter. Inventories, the listings of a deceased person's personal property, are replete with manifestos of kitchen and dining gear—and on rarer occasions of foodstuffs. We learn the basics of what people ate from the enumeration of animals in field and farmyard, the contents of stores, crops in the ground, fishing gear, and the contents of dairies, smokehouses, and barns. It is a narrative recovered in the substance of thousands of incidental texts. Much of the first century of proceedings has been transcribed and published. All the records are open to the public in county clerks' offices in the county seats of Eastville and Accomac.

Historic sources abound. This book could never be what it is without the truly exceptional work of Brooks Miles Barnes at the Eastern Shore Public Library and his colleagues at the University of Virginia and University of Nebraska–Lincoln. Together they created "The Countryside Transformed: The Railroad and the Eastern Shore of Virginia, 1870–1935" (http://eshore.iath.virginia.edu), a keyword-searchable database of Eastern Shore print sources focused on the coming of the railroad in the 1880s and the impact of its arrival. Their compilation includes thousands of accounts of everyday life ranging from the infamous oyster wars of the Gilded Age to visitors' reminiscences. I returned again and again to this search engine as well as to the overview narrative written by Barnes, William G. Thomas III, and Tom Szuba: "The Countryside Transformed: The Eastern

H. M. Arnold
shucking oysters
for Christmas,
Bayford, Virginia.

Shore of Virginia, the Pennsylvania Railroad, and the Creation of a Modern Landscape"
in the online journal *Southern Spaces* (https://southernspaces.org/2007/countryside
-transformed-eastern-shore-virginia-pennsylvania-railroad-and-creation-modern).

    Cookbooks and recipe collections offer their own commentaries—and this book re-
lies on a good many of them. I regularly consulted Bessie E. Gunter's *Housekeeper's Companion* (1889), the first Eastern Shore of Virginia cookbook. This volume, along with a
host of other cookbooks and culinary treatises, is digitally available from Google Books.
Fairy Mapp White's *Foolproof Cook Book* (1958) was the first to follow Gunter's and owes
a heavy debt to the earlier volume. Both books are noteworthy as community compendia. Gunter and White solicited recipes from friends, acquaintances, family, and kin
from across their communities. White also added dishes collected from African American women in her employ. The number of Eastern Shore of Virginia cookbooks ex-
ploded in the ensuing decades. Many came into existence through the efforts of church
and community groups. Economic development organizations and independent businesses brought forth specialized collections focused on a single ingredient, such as
clams or oysters. Others appeared as individual compilations, for example, *Kitty Caters*,
by Catherine Kellam, or Yvonne Marshall Widgeon's gleaning of Hog Island memories.
To my knowledge, there is no centralized collection of these works.

    Manuscript recipe collections cited in these pages continue to descend through the
hands of families and friends. An assemblage of favorite recipes in a scrapbook, tin, or
box that survives more than a generation or two past the life of its maker appears to
be a rarity. I was fortunate enough to encounter several private collections through the
generosity of their stewards. As source material, the manuscript collections I worked

through were composed largely of clippings, exchanged recipe cards, and, only rarely, handwritten notes that indicated the descent of a particular dish through the family. Almost completely absent were instructions for everyday fish and shellfish, vegetable, and baked dishes. Yeast rolls for special occasions, yes; biscuits for daily consumption, no. Crab imperial, yes; drum head soup, forget it!

I tapped into a variety of secondary source materials ranging from scientific treatises on figs, strawberries, and sweet potatoes to natural histories of fish and shellfish to historic novels and memoirs to commodity histories. I introduce these in the text as they debut. Most can be found in online resources or libraries. The single best location, though, for a sustained immersion in the histories of the region's human ecologies remains the Eastern Shore of Virginia Heritage Center at the Eastern Shore Public Library in Parksley. The Barrier Islands Center in Machipongo and the Eastern Shore of Virginia Historical Society in Onancock hold additional primary source material, including manuscripts and audio and video interviews.

And then there's the land and water. I note that no citation guide provides conventions for the literal citation of place. That's a deficiency to be addressed beyond the scope of these pages! Any bibliography of resources for the study of the Eastern Shore of Virginia and its culinary histories is incomplete without acknowledging the poetry and power of the very landscape. I recollect an insight shared by H. M. Arnold that goes something like this: "If you want to learn about crabs or fish or oysters or anything, you have to get out there and study them. Book learning won't help you!" So it is with the sweep of tide and wind, the grit of soil and sand, the seasonal waxing and waning of daylight, drought of July and frost of January, moonrise at dusk and sunrise at dawn, and all the plants and creatures that render that world a text best read through all the senses, a text marked by infinite subtlety, variation, and grace.

Vegetable stand, Machipongo area, Virginia.

Index

Page numbers in italics refer to illustrations.

H. EUGENE AND LILLIAN YOUNGS LEHMAN SERIES

Lamar Cecil, *Wilhelm II: Prince and Emperor, 1859–1900* (1989).

Carolyn Merchant, *Ecological Revolutions: Nature, Gender, and Science in New England* (1989).

Gladys Engel Lang and Kurt Lang, *Etched in Memory: The Building and Survival of Artistic Reputation* (1990).

Howard Jones, *Union in Peril: The Crisis over British Intervention in the Civil War* (1992).

Robert L. Dorman, *Revolt of the Provinces: The Regionalist Movement in America* (1993).

Peter N. Stearns, *Meaning Over Memory: Recasting the Teaching of Culture and History* (1993).

Thomas Wolfe, *The Good Child's River*, edited with an introduction by Suzanne Stutman (1994).

Warren A. Nord, *Religion and American Education: Rethinking a National Dilemma* (1995).

David E. Whisnant, *Rascally Signs in Sacred Places: The Politics of Culture in Nicaragua* (1995).

Lamar Cecil, *Wilhelm II: Emperor and Exile, 1900–1941* (1996).

Jonathan Hartlyn, *The Struggle for Democratic Politics in the Dominican Republic* (1998).

Louis A. Pérez Jr., *On Becoming Cuban: Identity, Nationality, and Culture* (1999).

Yaakov Ariel, *Evangelizing the Chosen People: Missions to the Jews in America, 1880–2000* (2000).

Philip F. Gura, *C. F. Martin and His Guitars, 1796–1873* (2003).

Louis A. Pérez Jr., *To Die in Cuba: Suicide and Society* (2005).

Peter Filene, *The Joy of Teaching: A Practical Guide for New College Instructors* (2005).

John Charles Boger and Gary Orfield, eds., *School Resegregation: Must the South Turn Back?* (2005).

Jock Lauterer, *Community Journalism: Relentlessly Local* (2006).

Michael H. Hunt, *The American Ascendancy: How the United States Gained and Wielded Global Dominance* (2007).

Michael Lienesch, *In the Beginning: Fundamentalism, the Scopes Trial, and the Making of the Antievolution Movement* (2007).

Eric L. Muller, *American Inquisition: The Hunt for Japanese American Disloyalty in World War II* (2007).

John McGowan, *American Liberalism: An Interpretation for Our Time* (2007).

Nortin M. Hadler, M.D., *Worried Sick: A Prescription for Health in an Overtreated America* (2008).

William Ferris, *Give My Poor Heart Ease: Voices of the Mississippi Blues* (2009).

Colin A. Palmer, *Cheddi Jagan and the Politics of Power: British Guiana's Struggle for Independence* (2010).

W. Fitzhugh Brundage, *Beyond Blackface: African Americans and the Creation of American Mass Culture, 1890–1930* (2011).

Michael H. Hunt and Steven I. Levine, *Arc of Empire: America's Wars in Asia from the Philippines to Vietnam* (2012).

Nortin M. Hadler, M.D., *The Citizen Patient: Reforming Health Care for the Sake of the Patient, Not the System* (2013).

Louis A. Pérez Jr., *The Structure of Cuban History: Meanings and Purpose of the Past* (2013).

Jennifer Thigpen, *Island Queens and Mission Wives: How Gender and Empire Remade Hawai'i's Pacific World* (2014).

George W. Houston, *Inside Roman Libraries: Book Collections and Their Management in Antiquity* (2014).

Philip F. Gura, *The Life of William Apess, Pequot* (2015).

Daniel M. Cobb, ed., *Say We Are Nations: Documents of Politics and Protest in Indigenous America since 1887* (2015).

Daniel Maudlin and Bernard L. Herman, eds., *Building the British Atlantic World: Spaces, Places, and Material Culture, 1600–1850* (2016).

William Ferris, *The South in Color: A Visual Journal* (2016).

Lisa A. Lindsay, *Atlantic Bonds: A Nineteenth-Century Odyssey from America to Africa* (2017).

Mary Elizabeth Basile Chopas, *Searching for Subversives: The Story of Italian Internment in Wartime America* (2017).

John M. Coggeshall, *Liberia, South Carolina: An African American Appalachian Community* (2018).

Malinda Maynor Lowery, *The Lumbee Indians: An American Struggle* (2018).

Seth Kotch, *Lethal State: A History of the Death Penalty in North Carolina* (2019).

Bernard L. Herman, *A South You Never Ate: Savoring Flavors and Stories from the Eastern Shore of Virginia* (2019)